W9-CBD-104

Justice
Oliver Wendell Holmes

I

THE SHAPING YEARS

1841–1870

1. Holmes as an undergraduate, March 1861

Justice Oliver Wendell Holmes

THE SHAPING YEARS

1841–1870

By

Mark DeWolfe Howe

I

1957

THE BELKNAP PRESS OF

HARVARD UNIVERSITY PRESS

Cambridge, Massachusetts

Distributed in Great Britain by
OXFORD UNIVERSITY PRESS, LONDON

Library of Congress Catalog Card Number 57–6348
Printed in the United States of America

Foreword

This volume has been written in delayed and partial fulfillment of an obligation which I assumed before World War II. At that time Mr. John G. Palfrey, the executor of Mr. Justice Holmes, asked me to prepare a biography of the Justice and offered to make the Justice's personal papers available to me. Mr. Palfrey had already done much to facilitate a biographer's task, for he had secured and had made copies of many of the Justice's letters to European and American friends. When, after the War, I commenced my work as biographer Mr. Palfrey had died and I had to proceed without the benefit of his guidance and advice. Continuing the task which he had so industriously begun, I succeeded, through the coöperation of others, in procuring further letters of the Justice's. I also endeavored to bring some order into the scattering of personal papers which had come into Mr. Palfrey's hands when Holmes had died in 1935.

Had I attempted to write a foreword before I began to write the biography I believe that I would have described a volume of much larger dimensions than this. I did not then contemplate the possibility of publishing as a separate volume a portion of the whole work covering such a brief span of time in Holmes's life as does this volume. Innocence often has a wisdom that is lost with knowledge, and perhaps I have learned so much about my problem as biographer that I have lost the judgment essential in an author. Two elements, however, have combined to convince me that Holmes's earliest years deserve the close attention and separate treatment which I have here given them. His years of education were years in which his convictions and his doubts took their permanent shape. The task of understanding the influences which molded his mind and his temperament seems to me to be essentially different from that of interpreting his achievement. This portion of the contemplated biography thus deals with significantly different problems from those with which later volumes will be concerned. In addition, a well-nigh conclusive element in my decision to abbreviate the period covered in my first volume is the fact that the character of the materials available for consideration and interpretation greatly altered when Holmes's years of preparation had come to their close. During the Civil War, as on his first European trip and in his first two years of practice, Holmes kept diaries which have survived and in which daily events are recorded. Such sources of information thereafter cease, and his biographer, if he feels a responsibility to truth greater than to romance, must, in Holmes's middle and later years, treat his subject's career and achievements by installments of years and decades rather than by those of days and months. I have come to believe, accordingly, that the period of Holmes's life covered in this volume deserves the separate consideration which I have given it.

Many an author must have known the temptation to convert his foreword into an unfavorable review of the volume itself in the hope that by a display of humility he may disarm his critics. Rather than submit to that temptation I shall merely express the hope that readers who are charitably inclined will take this volume as an essay in intellectual history. For many reasons Holmes stands as an almost gigantic figure—certainly as an imposing symbol—in the tapestry of American life. It is my hope that this essay will contribute to an understanding not only of his personal qualities but of the story of the American mind. In Holmes's published works, whether they be his essays, his opinions, or his letters, he has told us very nearly all that we shall ever know with certainty of his convictions. He was careful to destroy all papers within his control which recorded those events and moods that he considered private. It is clear, I think, that he thought it none of our business to know more of his life than he chose to make public. Had my industry or good fortune uncovered information that my conscience told me he wanted to remain private, respect for his wishes might have controlled my pen. I have, however, never been faced with that problem of conscience, for his care has always outpaced my industry and my luck. As a consequence, my responsibility has been primarily that of interpreting his published writings. These, of course, include three collections which were published after his death—the *Holmes-Pollock Letters,* his Civil War Letters and Diary (*Touched With Fire*), and the *Holmes-Laski Letters.* I have seen the publication of each of these collections as the partial fulfillment of my responsibilities as biographer, for each has contributed important materials for our interpretation.

So many authors have expressed their gratitude to Mr. Justice Frankfurter that it is becoming almost a ritual of scholarship to acknowledge the indebtedness. He will know that in this case, at least, the expression of thanks, like continuity with the past as Holmes saw it, is not a duty; it is merely a necessity. Had it not been for his faith I should not have become secretary to Holmes in 1933; had it not been for his hope I should not have been chosen as Holmes's biographer. Were it not for his charity I should fear his response to the shortcomings of this volume.

My failure to name other persons who have helped me by varying acts of kindness is not owing to a lack of appreciation of their courtesy. It is owing to the fact that they are too many to be named and to the fear that if I list them in this volume they will believe that I have spent my thanks before I have performed my entire obligation. One special form of aid, and one person who made it possible, I must, however, mention. Financial grants from the Jacob Brenner Memorial Foundation and the Philadelphia Community Foundation, Inc. made possible the reduction of my other responsibilities in recent years and thus accelerated the completion of this volume. Had it not been for the energy and sympathetic imagination of Arthur W. A. Cowan of the Philadelphia bar, that aid would not have been available.

M. DeW. H.

Cambridge, Massachusetts
12 June 1956

CONTENTS

ILLUSTRATIONS

Justice
Oliver Wendell Holmes

I

THE SHAPING YEARS

1841–1870

I

Childhood and Inheritance

D*r. Oliver Wendell Holmes* was not the first father to wonder whether destiny had some special distinctions in store for his eldest child. The future was little on the Doctor's mind, perhaps, when he wrote to his mother on March 9, 1841 that "a nice little gentleman came to our house last evening between the hours of eight and nine," [1] but uncertain vistas of promise were suggested when he wrote to his sister on the same day describing the newborn son as "a little individual who may hereafter be addressed as —— Holmes, Esq. or The Hon —— Holmes, M.C. or His Excellency —— Holmes, President." [2] Even a sanguine parent at such a time, while the baby was "scratching his face and sucking his right forefinger," was forced to admit that few if any of the baby's traits were patrician, congressional, or presidential. On Sunday, April 25, the baby was baptized at King's Chapel, the citadel of Boston's Unitarianism, and was christened Oliver Wendell.

When the baby was twenty months old his mother in a penciled memorandum recorded a few facts of progress, perhaps as justification for maternal hope that little Wendell was to be out of the ordinary, but more probably as simple items in the annals of the family. From this memorandum we know that when one year and eight months old "o.w.h.," as Dr. Holmes described him,[3] called Grandma "Aah-ma," said "awk" for "walk," "Henny" for "Wendy," and "mik" for "milk." [4] At twenty-six months the child was "able to say almost anything," and had coined his own exclamation, "flug-ding." Other records of the infant's progress have not been preserved, but one can, perhaps, surmise from these conventional beginnings that the first years of his life were not unusual. When he was two and a half years old a sister, Amelia, was born, and when he was five a brother, Edward Jackson Holmes, completed the family circle. That circle, until the boy was sixteen, was centered at 8 Montgomery Place, just off Tremont Street opposite the Old Granary Burying Ground in Boston. From 1857 until 1870 the family lived on Charles Street but then, two years before Holmes's marriage, made the final move to 296 Beacon Street.[a]

Education in the outer world probably began for Holmes at a Dame's school in the neighborhood, at which of the many available we do not know. There is preserved among his papers a "Report of Recitations and Deportment" for the week ending June 19, 1847, in which the curriculum available to the pupils seems to have included a course in sewing.[5] It seems hardly likely that this "discipline" was offered at the boys' school at which Holmes is known to have been a pupil in October 1848. His accomplishments during the June week of 1847, though promising, do not seem to have been extraordinary; the record shows fifteen perfect and two imperfect recitations, no failures, no absences, no tardiness, and "good" writing. The record closes with one blunt and suggestive entry after the item "Conduct": "Talks too much." The child of six was evidently using, if not abusing, the capacity acquired at two of saying "almost anything."

It was in the fall of 1848 that education of a more serious sort began; Holmes then entered the boys' school conducted by Mr. T. Russell Sullivan in the basement of the Park Street Church. Sullivan had started his career as a Unitarian minister in Keene, New Hampshire, where in 1824 he had founded and until 1830 had

[a] Montgomery Place is now called Bosworth Street and runs from Tremont to Province Street. The house in which Holmes was born was demolished after the family moved to Charles Street. The Charles Street house, then numbered 21 and later 164, no longer stands. Evidently Dr. Holmes did not sell the house at Montgomery Place until 1868; see James W. Spring, *Boston and the Parker House* (Boston, 1927), p. 162.

edited a denominational periodical, *The Christian Preacher,* made up of Unitarian sermons designed to combat prejudice against the new faith of the liberals. In 1835 he renounced his ministry and came to Boston where later he established the school which Holmes was attending in the fall of 1848. In the same year Sullivan, still interested in theological matters, edited a volume of *Sermons on the Christian Communion.* One can obtain some impression of the curriculum in Mr. Sullivan's school by glancing at a copybook which Holmes preserved and in which are recorded his "compositions" from the fall of 1848 to the spring of 1851.[6] The third of the pieces, dated October 27, 1848, is characteristic:

Introduction of pure water into the city
This work was begun two years and two months ago and was introduced into the city the twent-fifth day of October 1848. The procession was two hours passing one point where 300,000 people assembled in the city. Thanks begiven unto him who visiteth the earth and wartereth it. Ps. 65, 9.

In December 1848, the following paper was submitted:

The gold country
Gold has lately been discovered in great quantities in California, And a party of people are just going from boston to California to seek gold. Some of it is found in clefts of rocks. Some on the stream; and some washed out in bowls, Some with a machine like a cradle. The precepts of the Lord are true and righteous altogether; more to be desired are they than gold, yea, than much fine gold Ps. 19.9.

A few months later the routine of the class was evidently somewhat altered, for the following item appears:

Boston, Mch 16th 1849

Dear Mr. Sullivan.

The exersise you have given is writing a letter instead of composition, and so I thougt I would write you one. But as we have got to write a short one I canot make this any longer.

Your affectiona friend
O. W. Holmes. Jr.

Mr. Sullivan's liking for the apt Biblical reference was, however, so persistent that it survived this entirely secular interlude and reappeared to sustain the boy's essays on "The Elephant," "The New Clock," and "The Spitting Snake." During the year 1850–51 the pupils evidently began to familiarize themselves with some of the dramatic incidents of ancient history, for the copybook contains numerous compositions on such classical topics as "Spartans," "Epaminondas and Pelopidas," "Xerxes," and "Pythagoras." The boy of ten even prepared a summary account of the different sects of philosophy from 550 to 200 B.C. and of the lives of their founders.

If Dr. Holmes toyed occasionally with the image of his eldest son as Congressman or President, Mr. Sullivan also seemed to take seriously his responsibility as custodian of the men of the future. On January 9, 1850, he took his pupils on a sleigh ride to the Fresh Pond Hotel in Cambridge, and for the occasion prepared a poem which Holmes entered in his copybook. The verses carried the title "A Feast of Reason" and opened with the promising lines:

> These children that seem of no note in your eyes,—
> So little in size—so little in size,—
> What may they not be? and what may they not do?
> The first in the nation were once such as you.

The hopeful schoolmaster then proceeded to make some sanguine predictions as to the distinctions which his pupils might be expected to achieve in their maturity. For the most part, prediction was based more on the laws of versification than on those of probability. Some of the prognostications were so general, however, that the prediction that success, at least locally, would be within his pupils' reach was not very risky:

> While any profession, or high social place,
> *Eliot, Higginson, Lyman,* or *Lowell* may grace,

When it came to the future of young Holmes Mr. Sullivan seems to have put his principal reliance on the laws of inheritance:

> While of versatile power in all paths to excel
> The inherited talent in *Holmes* we foretell.

In the following year Mr. Sullivan gave his ten-year-old pupil a letter of introduction to be delivered to Epes Sargent Dixwell, headmaster of the Private Latin School on Boylston Place:

Boston, Sept. 29th 1851

To

E. S. Dixwell Esq.

Dear Sir,

O. W. Holmes, jr., the bearer, whom, (like his cousin J. T. Morse,) I take delight in calling my young friend, has been for four years under my charge as a pupil. He has been uniformly docile, thoughtful, amiable and affectionate. Young as he is, his habits of application are confirmed, while his proficiency in all the English branches, and his love of study are remarkable for his age.

Yours respectfully

T. R. Sullivan.[7]

Mr. Dixwell, a graduate of Harvard College in 1827, after reading law in the office of Holmes's grandfather, Judge Jackson, and spending three years in practice, had in 1836 been named headmaster of the Boston Latin School. With the years he had acquired the reputation of being "the most eminent classical scholar in the community." [8] He had married the daughter of Nathaniel Bowditch, the renowned author of the *Practical Navigator,* and of the six children of the marriage Holmes was destined in 1872 to marry the eldest, Fanny Bowditch Dixwell. Mr. Dixwell, a Cambridge resident, had left the Boston Latin School in the spring of 1851 when a city ordinance was adopted requiring that every member of the teaching staff of the School should reside in Boston. In the following fall he had opened his own Private Latin School on Boylston Place in Boston. Holmes was a pupil there until his admission to Harvard in the autumn of 1857.

Of Holmes's work at Mr. Dixwell's school no record survives. It is entirely evident, however, that the marrow of the educational process as Mr. Dixwell saw it was rigorously classical. One who knew his regime at the Boston Latin School described it as a "classical grind-mill," in which the methods were bad, and the standards low.[9] Upon other pupils, however, the impression of Mr. Dixwell as teacher was more favorable. President Eliot of Harvard, who had studied under him at the Boston Latin School, described him as "a delightful teacher" of the classics who took his pupils beyond the texts before them into the surrounding world of arts and letters.[10] Senator Lodge, who followed Holmes by a few years at the Private Latin School, respected Mr. Dixwell for the rigor of his gentlemanly discipline and for his impatience with "slovenliness of mind." [11] A letter which Mr. Dixwell wrote to his son-in-law when the former pupil was named Associate Justice of the Supreme Judicial Court in 1882 gives the impression that the relationship between master and pupil had not been entirely formal. Mr. Dixwell recalled "our first acquaintance, yours and mine, and . . . those childish days when you used to wait after school to walk along with me and talk of all topics as I went home. It was a very pleasant relation we then held and is still alive with me." [12]

Whatever views one may take of the merits and of the shortcomings of an education centered in the classics there can be no doubt that imaginative instruction by a classical scholar of distinction can carry students well along the paths of cultivation. The paths which Mr. Dixwell felt it to be his responsibility to open for his pupils were, of course, narrow, but the assumption of Mr. Dixwell's generation that education was to be acquired at home as well as in the schoolroom was fully justified, at least when the boy's household was presided over by Dr. Holmes. One must remember, furthermore, that the immediate goal towards which Mr. Dixwell's pupils were directing their energies was admission to Harvard College. For entrance there success in examinations in Latin, Greek, Ancient History, and Mathematics was the sole requirement when Holmes became a member of the freshman class. The College apparently was indifferent to the fact that his studies at Mr. Dixwell's school had included French, German, English, and Modern History. John T. Morse, Jr., Holmes's lively and long-lived contemporary and cousin, who had himself attended Mr. Dixwell's school, described the feeling for the school which prevailed in the Harvard community in the fifties. "For some inscrutable, indefinable reason a lad" from the Boston Latin School or from Mr. Dixwell's school, "seemed to touch the appreciation of the Harvard examining board a little more deftly than an applicant from any other place seemed able to do." [13] If there was a narrowness in the Dixwell schooling it was largely the result of the standards and objectives set by Harvard College.

Fortunately, perhaps, those standards could not distort the pressures of childhood's normality. If the classical training left its permanent mark in the satisfaction which Holmes in his maturity found in rereading the literature of Greece and Rome, there survived also the recollection of less rigorous experience in the world of letters. Lines from Ann and Jane Taylor's *Original Poems for Infant Minds,* "one of the English books on which children in my day were brought up," took on a meaning in manhood not fully appreciated in childhood. "A little boy," wrote Holmes describing the verses entitled "Never Play with Fire," "wakes in the night with a neighboring fire—he thinks to himself—

> 'My heart dismayed—last night I played
> With Tommy lighting straws.'

I always recall these verses when I get up in the morning a trifle squiffy." [b] Perhaps the poems of Ann and Jane Taylor, designed to "steadily inculcate good morals and manners, and quicken the gentler emotions," [14] did not, with Holmes, achieve their full purpose but, at least they left a sediment of meaning. The prose morality of Samuel Griswold Goodrich in his Peter Parley stories—particularly his *Short Stories for Long Nights* [15]—was evidently a part of education no less familiar to Holmes than to innumerable other children of his generation.

No companion of Holmes's youth was closer to him than his

[b] Autograph letter to Baroness Moncheur, Feb. 25, 1912. (Harvard Law School.) The whole verse from which these lines were taken was as follows:

> "Some burn, some choke with fire and smoke
> But ah! what was the cause?
> My heart's dismayed—last night I played
> With Thomas lighting straws."

The author of these particular verses was Adelaide O'Keeffe.

cousin John T. Morse, Jr., whose mother was sister of Mrs. Holmes. Morse was one year his senior but that small difference in age was no barrier to the intimacy which brought them together as school-mates under Mr. Sullivan and Mr. Dixwell, and bound them together, though a year apart, at Harvard College. When the Civil War came, Morse, a Copperhead in politics, remained a critical civilian while his cousin joined the Union forces. Their different political loyalties did not, however, disrupt the friendship. In 1932, when Morse was ninety-two and Holmes ninety-one, the elder friend recalled the occasions after Holmes's wounding at Ball's Bluff when "I used to come and dress (after a fashion) your wound—your first wound—in your chamber, where you lay amid flowers and candies purveyed by all the beauties of Boston." [16] In his last years Holmes also liked to remember his reply to Morse's envious inquiry why Holmes's wartime effort to grow a moustache was so much more successful than his own: "Mine was nourished in blood." [17] As the years passed Morse abandoned the legal profession to devote his considerable literary skill and historical sense to biography. In 1897 he published the *Life and Letters of Oliver Wendell Holmes,* a book which he later came to think failed to do justice to "the serious value" of Dr. Holmes.[18] Morse was one of those Bostonians, like Henry Adams, who realized that he never achieved what his capacities would have permitted him to accomplish. But he was unlike Adams in having no serious regrets that his abilities were not driven by ambition. His humor and his skepticism did not permit bitterness to color his regret that he had achieved less than he might have. When Holmes was about to be ninety years of age his old friend wrote to him:

Ninety years! It's a long time! Only nineteen such periods since our blessed Saviour was laying down those rules which have guided you to distinction,—and me to nothing in particular. . . . Well, the game is played to an end now, and while I write, so gladly, your praise, I confess that I don't *much* regret my own non-performance. I suppose it is in the nature of a misfortune for a man to be devoid of ambition. I *ought* to feel a bit of shame at having loafed through 90—(91) —years and wasted abilities which would have enabled me to do a *little* something. But, in fact, I do not care much. . . . Horses, and dogs, and boats help one through the job of life pretty well.[19]

Morse always followed the successes of Holmes with affectionate and humorous interest. When Holmes became Chief Justice of the Massachusetts Court in 1899, Morse wrote to him to express

a certain gratification in the thought of kinship—somewhat as a poor old pasture in the distant corner of the Calumet and Hecla township may rejoice that it is within the same municipal girdle. People look at the useless field and wonder whether there might not be copper in it, if it were exploited; none is ever found; but the field, in its gravelly heart, rejoices in its neighborhood to the great mine.[20]

The understanding sympathy of old age, as we have seen, had its roots in boyhood, when it had been "Leany" Holmes and "Fatty" Morse.[21] In 1921 Holmes wrote to Morse that "after teaching me all the evil I knew as a boy you still lead me along the pleasant paths of age." [22] And in their eighties and nineties the two men turned to recollections of childhood. Holmes recalled

the terrors that you instilled when we were boys. The Mauthe dog, the man that Wallace (?) saw walking on the battlements with his head under his arm, and whatever you got from the appendices to Scott used to make me feel afraid of the looking glass in my bedroom and the shadow on the front door. Once you told me that the dog that followed us a little was the Mauthe dog and I at least half believed you. And do you remember how you swindled me in an exchange—I forget what I gave—by telling me that your father said that a paving stone you contributed, was a precious stone? Well, I will be more merciful than Heaven and forgive the sins of your youth.[23]

On Morse's side there was recollection that in boyhood "you were Bruce and I was Wallace" and that Holmes, "already a casuist," upset Morse's ideas of right and wrong.[24] That upset, one suspects, occurred on the occasion when "Leany," at seven years of age, on the Boston Common asked his friend whether it was ever right to tell a lie. "Fatty," well trained in the maxims of morality, promptly replied, "Of course not." "Pointing to the path along which they were walking, Holmes said: 'Suppose a man came running along here with terror in his eyes and panting for breath and hid in the thicket . . . and the pursuers came along and asked us if we had seen him. Which would be better, to give the man away or to tell a lie?' " "Fatty" Morse was compelled to admit that in such circumstances it might be better to tell a lie.[25]

The enthusiasm with which Holmes in boyhood lost himself in the world of Walter Scott did not diminish in maturity. The boy's indulgence of a taste for tales of heroic deeds and noble aspiration was not simply the expression of a youthful longing for a more romantic world than that which lay around him in Boston, but bespoke a fundamental quality of mind and temperament—a quality which he believed gained strength from the fact that the simplicities of an earlier day lingered in the memory if not in the environment of the society in which he came to maturity. After rereading *Ivanhoe, Old Mortality,* and *The Fortunes of Nigel* in 1911, Holmes wrote to a friend:

> Just now I am having one of my periodic wallows in Scott. He also is dear to most people, I suppose—but the old order in which the sword and the gentleman were beliefs, is near enough to me to make this their last voice enchanting in spite of the common sense of commerce. The same belief was what gave interest to the South, but they paid for it by their ignorance of all the ideas that make life worth living to us. But when you see it in costume, with people who could not have heard of evolution, belated but in its last and therefore articulate moment, Oh what a delight it is.[26]

The capacity to combine enthusiastic comprehension of the ideas of the twentieth century with ardent sympathy for the feelings of an earlier age was one of Holmes's unusual gifts. Comprehension of that capacity would be incomplete, however, if it were not remembered that the feelings, as distinguished from the ideas, of his own time, were, by and large, no more sympathetic to him than were the ideas (again as distinguished from the feelings) of the times of which Scott wrote. The skepticism of his mind, unlike the romanticism of his feeling, was characteristic of the age of his maturity. His aesthetic judgment was responsive to older modes of expression and earlier moods of feeling than those which were dominant at the *fin de siècle* and later, yet his mind found its principal nourishment in the thought of his own times, and was generally impatient of those who believe that yesterday's insight is adequate for the needs of today. To Holmes it was in the world of ideas, rather than in the world of feeling, that "one agreeably patronizes the simplicity of the ancients," [27] and it was principally to that world of ideas that he referred when he said that "it is a humbug to bother boys with the great men of the past. I think one should begin with books which have our own emphasis. . . ." [28] When, however, matters of taste and feeling were in issue his standards were largely those of an age which had passed.

The normalities of alert boyhood found many satisfactions in the world of Walter Scott, and evidently uncovered equal satisfaction in other realms of less artistic making, such as Captain Marryat's *Children of the New Forest*.[29] To Holmes, as to other boys, the artistry was obviously less important than was the story, for Holmes remembered that after reading Sylvanus Cobb, Jr., the first American to produce blood and thunder on an assembly line, he had confessed to his schoolmaster that he could not see why Cobb was not as good as Scott.[30] Somewhat above the level of Cobb, if still lower than that of Scott and Marryat, were Mayne Reid's *Rifle Rangers and Scalp Hunters*, and G. P. R. James's historical novels. If Mr. Dixwell and Mr. Sullivan endeavored to confine the minds of their pupils to the narrow channels of classical scholarship and Unitarian morality there were, after all, broader rivers of literary experience available to those whose enthusiasm and curiosity were lively.

When Dr. Holmes asked Henry James, Senior, whether he did not find that his sons despised him,[31] the question was laden with implications. Upon the basis of those implications and of other suggestions in the remarks of father and son [c] it would be easy to

[c] Describing his labors in assembling scattered papers of his father's, Holmes said that he would, as a result, "have a large representation of my papa in the form of his original writings and feel a sort of filial duty performed. . . . I have an agreeable sense of having sold my governor, as he never realized that I would take any trouble to do him honor, I not spending my time in adoring him when he was alive. He even suggested to me making a little worm of a nephew his literary executor,

construct a thesis that there was an antipathy of the son to the father so intense that the son's character and achievements were molded by its influence. The subtleties of family relationships, however, are such as to make hasty acceptance of the thesis as inappropriate as dogmatic denial of its validity. Undoubtedly there were occasions, perhaps seasons, in the son's youth when antipathy was strong, but it was surely neither the first nor the last time that family life has produced such tension. The elder Henry James was scarcely speaking for the average father of average boys when he answered Dr. Holmes's inquiry with the somewhat complacent assurance that, "no, he was not bothered in that way." [32] Some may see in Dr. Holmes's suspicion that his sons despised him a reflection of his vanity. Others may take it as evidence of his alert perceptiveness. Whether it revealed a failing or a gift, it bespoke a quality quite different from the easy confidence of the elder Henry James.[d] Not only were Dr. Holmes's feet more firmly planted on the ground of reality than were those of James, but his mind and his eye were fixed more attentively on the world, or at least on the community around him, than were the faculties of his friend. The complacency which Dr. Holmes so happily achieved was that of the provincial; the complacency of James was the attainment of a mystic. Dr. Holmes, if not in all aspects an enthusiastic provincial, was at least the contented representative of a special tradition—John T. Morse, Jr. would have said the best example of the New England race.[33] Whatever label one may choose for him it is clear that his quality was largely shaped by the community in which he lived and, loving that community, he classified many of its limitations as its virtues. To a son of differing temperament, eager to escape the limitations of the New England way, the father's loyalty to its principles was inevitably a cause of irritation.

Though Dr. Holmes was, perhaps, the embodiment of provin-

whatever that may be. But I told him Not Much, and intimated that perhaps after all I might be trusted not to belittle his reputation." Autograph letter to Lady Scott, Aug. 22, 1908 (Harvard Law School).

[d] Readers of Leon Edel's *Henry James: The Untried Years 1843–1870* (Philadelphia, 1953) will wonder if the elder Henry James knew the hearts of his children with true intimacy.

cialism, the New England province, with Boston as its capital, was a center of unusual capacity and energy. During the years when Dr. Holmes was its most satisfied and articulate representative, it contributed Lowell, Longfellow, Hawthorne, and Henry James the younger to letters; Emerson, Chauncey Wright, and William James to philosophy; Theodore Parker and William Ellery Channing to religion; Charles Sumner, Wendell Phillips, and William Lloyd Garrison to politics; Motley and Parkman to history; and Louis Agassiz and Asa Gray to science. Dr. Holmes was not only the embodiment of the community's energetic spirit but contributed distinctive elements to its vitality. He was the one man of letters whose education in the sciences had been rigorous and professional; he was the one scientist whose cultivation in the humanities was lively and alert; and in whatever capacity he spoke he allowed humor to color his criticism of society and affect his appraisal of the universe. This is not to say that as scientist, as artist, or as critic he was a figure of major importance. It is simply to give him credit for a comprehensive capacity which served to make his significance as the embodiment of the Boston spirit considerable.

That spirit, as it existed in the middle of the last century and later, has mystified many observers. The clue which Henry James suggested is surely not sufficient to solve the whole mystery, yet it emphasized contrasting elements in the character of Boston which have been generally overlooked. James saw in the face, manner, and character of one of his teachers at the Harvard Law School "those depths of rusticity which . . . underlay the social order at large and out of which one felt it to have emerged in any degree but at scattered points." [34] The Puritan capital, said James, might "spread and take on new disguises" yet it affected him

> as a rural centre even to a point at which I had never known anything as rural . . . Boston was in a manner of its own stoutly and vividly urban, not only a town, but a town of history—so that how did it manage to be such different things at the same time? That was doubtless its secret—more and more interesting to study in proportion as, on closer acquaintance, . . . one felt the equilibrium attained as on the whole

an odd fusion and intermixture, of the chemical sort as it were, and not a matter of elements or aspects sharply alternating. There was in the exhibition at its best distinctly a savour—an excellent thing for a community to have, and part of the savour was, as who should say, the breadth of the fields and woods and waters, though at their domesticated and familiarized stage, or the echo of a tone which had somehow become that of the most educated of our societies without ceasing to be that of the village.[35]

Is it not fair to suggest that the rustic and urban qualities which James found to be chemically mixed in the character of Boston were similarly blended in the character of Dr. Holmes—the town's most ardent representative? A young Bostonian of the mid-nineteenth century, anxious to transcend his father's limitations, not unnaturally would seek to reject the rustic strain in his inheritance. He might come to seek the satisfaction of a man of the world, to turn his eyes with expectation from the Boston scene to some brighter spectacle beyond its borders. There were Boston contemporaries who, making a similar effort, gave their energy to the nation's destiny, whether in politics, in railroads, finance, or industry. When Holmes, rejecting his father's provincialism, turned to other pastures than those of Beacon Hill he found that his tastes were more responsive to the traditions of English civilization than to the challenge of American life. Perhaps it was partly because his friend Henry James was similarly drawn to the European scene that Holmes was somewhat offended by James's "recurrence to the problem of the social relations of Americans to the old world." If Holmes, however, had totally conquered the self-satisfied provincialism of a Bostonian he might not have found "a touch of underbreeding" in James's "drooling on the social relations of important Americans with the old world." [36]

Dr. Holmes sadly doubted whether he could ever get "the iron of Calvinism" out of his soul.[37] "The curse of ages of incompetent, nay, inhuman thinking, filtered through the brains of holy men and the blood of tender-hearted women, but still acting like a poison to minds of a certain quality and temper, fell upon me when only the most thoroughly human influences should have helped me to bud and flower."[38] The desire to free himself from the rigidities of his father's precepts and inheritance was intense but never fully realized. "I show the effects of a training too often at variance with all my instincts."[e] In this admission that the effects were visible may well lie a partial explanation of his suggestion to the elder James that his children "despised" him. In 1908 when Justice Holmes was going over some of his father's papers he wrote to a friend: "I feel a humorous filial piety, and, by the by, chuckled to come on a letter or two from *his* father to him at school inculcating virtue in the same dull terms that he passed on to me. If I had a son I wonder if I should yield to the temptation to twaddle in my turn."[39] Certainly it is possible that differences in temperament and times would have prevented the Justice from repeating the mistakes of his father and grandfather, yet one cannot help wondering whether the validity of the humorous generalization of Dr. Holmes concerning the relationship of parent and child might not have been realized once more.

> Civilized men as well as savage races live upon their parents and grandparents. Each generation strangles and devours its predecessor. The young Feejeean carries a cord in his girdle for his father's neck; the young American, a string of propositions or syllogisms in his brain to finish the same relative. The old man says, "Son, I have swallowed and digested the wisdom of the past." The young man says, "Sire, I proceed to swallow and digest thee with all thou knowest."[40]

These reflections are applicable not only to the son's rejection of the Doctor's tenets but to the Doctor's efforts—less than completely successful though those efforts may have been—to rid himself of the early influence of his Calvinist father, the Reverend Abiel Holmes. The "string of propositions and syllogisms" with which the young American customarily seeks to destroy his father had evidently been used by the Doctor himself, for he spoke of "those *enfant terrible* questions" which in his youth he had put to

[e] To Harriet Beecher Stowe, Nov. 17, 1867; Morse, *Life and Letters of Oliver Wendell Holmes,* II, 224. Perhaps it was training rather than instinct which led Dr. Holmes to lecture his brother John when the latter was eighty "as if there were danger to his morals when he took a glass of brandy and water." Autograph letter, OWH to Baroness Moncheur, Feb. 6, 1911 (Harvard Law School).

his father and which the poor pious gentleman had found "so much harder to answer than anything he found in St. Cyprian and Tarrentin." [41] Having discovered in boyhood the effectiveness with which the old orthodoxy could be attacked he continued in maturity courageously to offend against its rigid proprieties. *Elsie Venner* and *The Guardian Angel* may not be artistic successes yet they unquestionably are forceful polemics against a form of Calvinism which not only disgraced the Christian tradition but insulted the intelligence of mankind. In demanding that the notion of original sin be cast aside he asked for something more than the rejection of a dogma of theology; he urged that it was an obligation of humanity to let sympathy and science combine to control our moral judgment. The inadequacy of his philosophical understanding led him, perhaps, to do less than justice to the significance of Jonathan Edwards as a creative mind,[42] but the humanity of his common sense persuaded him that the surviving influence of Edwards upon the faith of the orthodox was almost wholly bad.

The Doctor's emancipation was not sufficiently complete to let him read novels before sundown on Sunday,[43] and his weekday standards of morality set somewhat rigid boundaries to appreciation. He considered that the realism of Flaubert and Zola had added to the territory of letters "swampy, malarious, ill-smelling patches of soil which had previously been left to reptiles and vermin." [44] To the extent that this harsh judgment was based on canons of good taste the son might not contest its validity, for he, in his turn, came to speak of "the French literary men" as "rather ill smelling." [45] Discussing Flaubert's *L'education sentimentale,* the younger Holmes said that he agreed that "an artist may realize his spontaneity by expressing what he damn chooses, but when he comes into the market the consumer is the only person of importance, as with other wares. This consumer does not care for the complexities of the ignoble." [46] On another occasion, after reading a novel of somewhat emancipated realism, he expressed the same distaste more humorously: "I didn't much care for . . . the felicities of the copulative conjunction." [47] In Holmes's mind these judgments were the reflections of taste, not the expressions of moral principle. The Doctor's condemnation of the realists, by contrast, was based not only on his canons of taste but was explicitly justified by "the laws of decency." [48] When aesthetics were discussed among the Holmeses—as surely they were—it is likely that the Doctor sought to reinforce his canons of taste with the heavier artillery of morals. It was to this tactic that the son presumably objected. He had no greater liking for the realism of Flaubert and Zola than did his father, yet he believed that Casanova, whom his father considered to be "one of the basest" of writers, had written "one of the great books of the world." [49] Doubtless the judgment of each was affected by a personal standard of taste which was not dissimilar, but the Doctor's was strengthened by a set of moral precepts which retained their vitality for him though they had lost their persuasiveness to a younger generation.

The general insufficiency of Dr. Holmes's emancipation from inherited pieties might have disappointed or irritated any rebellious member of the younger generation. As his eldest child came to maturity he found one limitation in the Doctor's emancipation peculiarly disturbing. Despite his training in science Dr. Holmes never permitted its methods to control his consideration of the ultimate questions of philosophy as fully as his son considered that he should. From his medical education in Paris, and particularly from Pierre Louis, the inspiring teacher of a generation of young American medical students, Dr. Holmes had learned the necessity of "modesty in the presence of nature" and had come to accept the principle "not to take authority when I can have facts, [and] not to guess when I can know." [50] If his son's judgment was accurate, however, it would seem that Dr. Holmes was less willing than he should have been to consider all problems, even those which are unanswerable, scientifically. In suggesting to Morris Cohen what influences had encouraged his own basic skepticism, Justice Holmes in 1919 spoke of the predominant influence as

> the scientific way of looking at the world. . . . My father [he said], was brought up scientifically . . . and I was not. Yet there was with him, as with the rest of his generation, a certain softness of attitude

toward the interstitial miracle—the phenomenon without phenomenal antecedents, that I did not feel. . . . Probably a sceptical temperament that I got from my mother had something to do with my way of thinking. . . . But I think science was at the bottom. Of course my father was by no means orthodox, but like other even lax Unitarians there were questions that he didn't like to have asked—and he always spoke of keeping his mind open on matters like spiritualism or whether Bacon wrote Shakespeare—so that when I wanted to be disagreeable I told him that he straddled, in order to be able to say, whatever might be accepted, "Well, I always have recognized," etc., which was not just on my part.[51]

Recognizing that the son found his father's emancipation incomplete, it would nonetheless do the Doctor an injustice to overlook the fact that his intellectual loyalty was dedicated to free inquiry. He saw the American's obligation to reëxamine every article of faith, whether political or religious, as persistent and inescapable.

To think of trying to waterproof the American mind against the questions that Heaven rains down upon it shows a misapprehension of our new conditions. If to question everything be unlawful and dangerous, we had better undeclare our independence at once; for what the Declaration means is the right to question everything, even the truth of its own fundamental proposition.[52]

When a household's presiding officer is of that conviction and when his greatest pleasure is in conversation, any tension which may have existed between the alert father and the emancipated son must have been somewhat alleviated by intellectual companionship. Though William James, after dining with the Holmeses in 1873, reported to his father that "no love is lost between W. *père* and W. *fils,*" [53] there was evidently enough filial loyalty in the young Holmes to resent the hostility of third persons to his father. In 1866 when he was in England he met Andrew Lang, Scottish mythologist and man of letters. In 1923 he described the meeting in these words:

Introduced. "Are you the son of Oliver Wendell Holmes?" "Yes." "Well, I don't like him." Exit. How I have regretted that I was not quick enough with rapier or bludgeon to hand him one back before he vanished. I had read some of his books and thought them dull before. Since, I have taken pleasure in thinking his *Joan of Arc* poor stuff.[f]

To say that Holmes and his father knew intellectual companionship is not to say that the Justice thought either that his father's versatile capacities matched his reputation or that he made the most of the abilities with which he was endowed. The most complete and characteristically detached statement of the Justice's estimate of his father's gifts and accomplishments is in a letter written in 1914:

I think my father's strong point was a fertile and suggestive intellect. I do not care as much as he would have liked me to for his novels and poetry—but I think he had the most penetrating mind of all that lot. After his early medical work, which really was big (the puerperal fever business) I think he contented himself too much with sporadic aperçus—the time for which, as I used to say when I wanted to be disagreeable, had gone by. If he had had the patience to concentrate all his energy on a single subject, which perhaps is saying if he had been a different man he would have been less popular, but he might have produced a great work.[g]

[f] *Holmes-Laski Letters,* I, 491–492. Perhaps it was this same instinct to protect his father's name from criticism which led him to say that Parrington in his *Main Currents in American Thought* had "missed . . . what I think the fact, that although my governor was largely distracted into easy talk and occasional verse, he had the gift of an insight that was capable of being profound." Autograph letter to Felix Frankfurter, June 26, 1928 (Harvard Law School).

[g] Autograph letter to Clara Sherwood Stevens, July 26, 1914 (Harvard Law School). Holmes's nephew, Edward J. Holmes, writing to Mr. Chief Justice Stone in 1944, described the relationships between Dr. Holmes and his eldest son in the following passage: "During every winter for eight years from the time I was thirteen until grandfather's death [1894] I used to see both of them, sometimes together and sometimes separately, at least once a week, and heard the most brilliant conversation that I have ever heard or ever expect to hear, with absolutely fair give and take and only one criterion, the skill in presentation of the argument. Father admired son and son admired father and the same was true of the other members of the family. . . . Years after Grandfather's death Uncle Wendell said to me apropos of the Saturday Club which comprised as you know pretty much everyone who counted in New England at that time: 'As I look back on it I think the old man had the most profound philosophical mind of them all.'" (Copy, Harvard Law School.)

There is some danger of reading more into the phrase concerning the Doctor's "penetrating mind" than his son intended, but one cannot help feeling that he would have concurred in the opinion which John T. Morse, Jr. expressed in a letter to Senator Lodge:

As for my uncle Doctor . . . I have always had a sort of indignant feeling that his serious value has never been appreciated; and I am conscious that I did not do my full duty to him and his reputation in my book. . . . He was the most intelligently observant man that I have ever known; and every little thing that he observed was at once taken in to be carefully examined by his most ingenious and original mind. He was as logical as Jonathan Edwards, and understood evidence like Sidney Bartlett. His contemporaries fancied him an impractical humorist; in fact he was shrewd, sagacious, prudent. . . . He thought as deeply as Emerson and more clearly; and with an independent audacity that would have made Motley and Lowell shiver.[54]

It is suggestive that the son's estimate of his father was critical with respect to the Doctor's achievements and admiring with respect to his capacities. The son's disappointment that "independent audacity" was frustrated by the Doctor's unwillingness to concentrate all his energy on a single subject" was a Puritan's judgment with respect to character. It reflected the conviction that accomplishment is a duty and high ambition an inescapable moral responsibility. It may not be an exaggeration to suggest that, however rebellious the son may have been against his father's liking for the inculcation of virtue in dull terms, the standards of morality by which in the end the son judged the father were as puritanical as the father's precepts. In any case, the son's disappointment in his father's achievements was surely a factor contributing to the Justice's persistent resolution to direct his own efforts and energies to one end—achieving distinction in the law. Not having been blessed (or cursed) with his father's exuberant versatility the temptation to scatter his talents was probably less compelling, but the son's literary, philosophical, and artistic interests were certainly of sufficient intensity to have made diffusion of his energy a real possibility had not the example of his father given warning of the damage which may result from that diffusion. If example had that effect, the Doctor's contribution to his son's moral education, however ineffective it may have been when he yielded to the "temptation to twaddle" on virtue, may have been more substantial than the son realized. The father's "failure" stirred the embers of those Puritan instincts in the son which demanded seriousness, industry, and direction of effort. The instincts had evidently begun to show themselves as early as 1866 for during that year, while Holmes was in England, his mother urged him not to feel "as you did at home that you must accomplish just so much each 24 hours." [55] It is ironic, perhaps, that the urging came from her, for speaking, in later years, of his inability to "be content with pleasure" Holmes suggested that the incapacity was derived from his mother's temperament which told him that "without some feeling of accomplishment" it was time to die.[56]

The impact of the Doctor's best qualities must also have been considerable. Of all those qualities it is likely that his extraordinary talent for talk—if not for conversation—exerted the most vivifying influence on the whole of his household. Doubtless his confessed "tendency to *linguacity*" [57] was irritating to children who were scarcely less eager than he to express themselves. Holmes's younger brother testified that Holmes found ways of competing: "Wendell," he said, "ends every sentence with a 'but' so as to hold the floor till he can think of something else to say." [h] The Doctor's nephew and biographer, John T. Morse, Jr., might have agreed with Holmes that the *Autocrat* "talked book talk not talk talk," [58] but he suggested that from its pages some notion of the charm of the Doctor's talk may be obtained. Yet, Morse said, the Doctor "talked better than he wrote. . . . His thoughts, his humor his sim-

[h] Edward J. Holmes to Mr. Chief Justice Stone, *supra*, note g. "My brother used to say that at table I ended every sentence with a 'but' to keep hold of the table." Autograph letter to Baroness Moncheur, Oct. 7, 1928 (Harvard Law School). President Eliot in acknowledging a letter from Holmes congratulating him on his ninetieth birthday referred to the table-talk at the Holmes household. "Is it true," he asked, "that when the Holmes family sat down to breakfast together they all talked at once without really expecting to be listened to? Your father once gave me a very amusing picture of that performance, which he seemed to have always enjoyed." Autograph letter, March 28, 1924 (Harvard Law School).

iles rose as fast, as multitudinous, as irrepressible, as the bubbles in the champagne, and nothing could prevent their coming to the surface." [59] Other persons than the Doctor's relatives and biographers could easily be vouched as witnesses to support the judgment of Edmund Gosse that "no man of modern times has given his contemporaries a more extraordinary impression of wit in conversation" [60] than did Dr. Holmes. His respect for talk led him to believe that "talking is one of the fine arts,—the noblest, the most important, and the most difficult." [61] Perhaps the education which he gave his children in other arts was inadequate, but one can feel confident assurance that it was not deficient with respect to that most subtle art. Those who knew the Justice's conversation would be the first to testify that if early training in conversation sharpens the talent for exciting talk the Justice's training must have been marvelously successful. Lord Haldane was no less qualified to judge the talent than was Edmund Gosse, and Gosse's estimate of Dr. Holmes's gift for talk was matched by Lord Haldane's dictum that Justice Holmes was one of the three best talkers he ever knew.[62]

The flow of the Holmeses' talk reflected not only the fluency of their tongues and the nimbleness of their wit, but it bespoke the nature of their inquiring minds. The similarities of those minds and of the style in which their qualities were reflected are as striking as the dissimilarities between the temperaments of the two men and are made notably apparent in the dicta of each on matters of fundamental importance to both. Dr. Holmes's conviction that "a man may fulfil the object of his existence by asking a question he cannot answer, and attempting a task he cannot achieve" [63] is reëchoed in the Justice's assertion that "no man has earned the right to intellectual ambition until he has learned to lay his course by a star which he has never seen,—to dig by the divining rod for springs which he may never reach." [64] When Justice Holmes said "if you want to hit a bird on the wing, you must have all your will in a focus, you must not be thinking about yourself, and, equally, you must not be thinking about your neighbor; you must be living in your eye on that bird. Every achievement is a bird on the wing," [65] he was restating in a strikingly similar style a conviction expressed by his father that "every event that a man would master must be mounted on the run, and no man ever caught the reins of a thought except as it galloped by him." [66] When Dr. Holmes in this same passage from *The Professor at the Breakfast Table* went on to say that a man, mounting these thoughts as they hurry by, "can only take his foot from the saddle of one thought and put it on that of another" and to the inquiry,—"What is the saddle of a thought?"—answered, "Why, a word, of course," one is reminded of the Justice's familiar phrase, "a word . . . is the skin of a living thought." [67]

Dr. Holmes frequently insisted, as his son persistently did after him, that it is the intelligent man's responsibility to look beneath the surface of words, and their accumulated connotations, to the ideas which they represent.

> When a given symbol which represents a thought has lain for a certain length of time in the mind, it undergoes a change like that which rest in a certain position gives to iron. . . . The word, and consequently the idea it represents becomes polarized. . . . I think, myself, if every idea . . . could be shelled out of its old symbol and put into a new, clean, unmagnetic word, we should have some chance of reading it as philosophers, or wisdom-lovers ought to read it.[68]

The Doctor's special eagerness was to have the words of the Bible and of conventional religion "depolarized." Was not that desire much like the Justice's wish that the language of the law should be washed "with cynical acid"? [i] When the Justice urged that "we must think things not words" [69] and defined a right, for legal purposes, as "the hypostasis of a prophecy," [70] he was reiterating his father's distrust of "Epeolatry"—the word-worship which leads us to spiritualize "our ideas of the things signified." [71] One of the son's favorite phrases—fire in the belly—was also a favorite of the father.[72]

The problem with which Dr. Holmes was so frequently con-

[i] "The Path of the Law," Holmes, *Collected Legal Papers,* 167, 174. Holmes was not unaware of his father's concern to depolarize our language: *Holmes-Laski Letters,* I, 688.

cerned and round which the story of *Elsie Venner* turned—the problem, that is, of imposing responsibility, either moral or legal, upon persons whose acts may in fact have been determined by physical causes beyond their control—concerned his son almost as intensely.

> What have we [asked the Justice], better than a blind guess to show that the criminal law in its present form does more good than harm? . . . Do we deal with criminals on proper principles? . . . If the typical criminal is a degenerate, bound to swindle or to murder by as deep seated an organic necessity as that which makes the rattlesnake bite, it is idle to talk of deterring him by the classical method of imprisonment.[73]

It is scarcely to be believed that in making this reference to the rattlesnake the Justice did not have consciously in mind his father's thesis in *Elsie Venner* that his heroine's "wrong" was not morally distinguishable from the act of the rattler by whom Elsie's mother, in her pregnancy, had been bitten.

Characteristic Bostonian that Dr. Holmes was, he failed in one respect to conform to the pattern of his type. He never showed the ardor for reform—particularly for associated efforts to improve the lot of man—which other spokesmen of the Boston tradition felt it to be their obligation and privilege to indulge.

> I hate the calling of meetings to order [he said]. I hate being placed on committees. They are always having meetings at which half are absent and the rest late. I hate being officially and necessarily in the presence of men most of whom, either from excessive zeal in the good cause or from constitutional obtuseness, are incapable of being *bored*. . . . I am not in love with most of the actively stirring people whom one is apt to meet in all associations for doing good.[74]

At no time was he a pacifist or a prohibitionist, and until the outbreak of the Civil War he was neither an abolitionist nor a crusader against slavery. Refusing to join the ranks of the reformers, he was charged with a hopeless conservatism by James Russell Lowell. He denied that charge indignantly, saying that "the idea of my belonging to the party that resists all change is an entire misconception."[75] One feels quite sure, however, that he would, like his son, have said, "I do accept a rough equation between isness and oughtness."[76] Though the Doctor's reluctance to become a crusader did not derive from the same vigorous skepticism which led his son, after the Civil War, to take no part in "causes," the same instinctive preference for the independent decision to the co-operative action characterized the point of view of the two men. Justice Holmes said of himself that he was "an 'unconvinced conservative' or I might say as well a sceptical radical."[77] Would not the same selection between appropriate labels have been suitable in the case of his father? It is unlikely that the Doctor would have carried his desire to think "hardly"[j] as far as his son did when he asked his friend Dean Wigmore: "Doesn't the squashy sentimentality of a big minority of our people about human life make you puke?" That minority, he said, included pacifists and others "who believe in the upward and onward—who talk of uplift, who think that something particular has happened and that the universe is no longer predatory. Oh, bring me a basin."[78] Though the Doctor's language might have been less blunt, his dislike of the "do-gooder" was not dissimilar to his son's. Finally, one cannot help feeling that the Doctor would not only have shared the opinion of his son, but would have liked himself to have shown his wit when the Justice described some of his reforming friends as "dear little proper geese that follow their propaganda."[79]

The father and the son shared a willingness to ask questions which their contemporaries were reluctant to consider. Each sought to approach the problems of morality and philosophy with the detached spirit of the scientist, and each found that within his realm of faith and conviction science left settled values undisturbed. Dr. Holmes spoke of the unsuccessful efforts of materialism to make "protoplasm master of arts and doctor of divinity"[80]

[j] Writing to Felix Frankfurter, Holmes spoke of his satisfaction that Agnes Repplier in some of her essays "thinks *hardly*, as against the sentimental way which is more in vogue. . . . I like to see someone insist . . . that the march of life means a rub somewhere. As they used to say about saddles in the army, one strained the man—another galled the horse." Autograph letter, Sept. 5, 1916 (Harvard Law School).

and said that "we do not find Hamlet and Faust, right and wrong, the valor of men and the purity of women, by testing for albumen, or examining fibres in microscopes." [81] The Justice, in his turn, sadly observed the tendency of science to pursue analysis "until at last this thrilling world of colors and sounds and passions has seemed fatally to resolve itself into one vast network of vibrations endlessly weaving an aimless web, and the rainbow flush of cathedral windows, which once to enraptured eyes appeared the very smile of God, fades slowly out into the pale irony of the void." [82] To the Doctor, skeptical as he was of the faith of his father, "a faith which breeds heroes is better than an unbelief which leaves nothing worth being a hero for," [83] and for the Justice "high and dangerous action teaches us to believe as right beyond dispute things for which our doubting minds are slow to find words of proof. Out of heroism grows faith in the worth of heroism." [84] The Doctor was not reluctant to express serious convictions in light verse, and if it is fair to read "The Deacon's Masterpiece"—the One-Hoss Shay—as an attack, not simply on Calvinism, but on the sufficiency of logic for the mastery of human problems one may even read its concluding line, "Logic is logic. That's all I say," as the condensed forerunner of the son's most famous utterance: "The life of the law has not been logic; it has been experience."

At the highest levels of their common interest one can discern a striking similarity. Each was, in intellectual matters, essentially radical, yet the radicalism of neither led him so far as to repudiate the conventions or traditions of his own time and place. Dr. Holmes carried his scientific methods to the outermost point at which his temperament told him that they were serviceable. That point surely lay beyond the limits to which earlier generations had extended science. When that point was reached he allowed other methods and other capacities to control inquiry. Beyond the limits of science the Doctor found his guidance in religion and in the precepts of morality. The son, perhaps because his training was not in science, came to believe that if the methods of science at some point failed as the instrument of curiosity it was there that inquiry should cease. To cut off inquiry, however, was not to destroy concern, and what he substituted for his father's religion and his father's morality was a romantic conviction that his own standards needed no other justification than their vividness. Those standards were not in their essentials different from those prevailing in the community where he grew up; they were not, in other words, significantly different from his father's. His refusal to claim that the values which he esteemed were accredited by a higher authority than their own intensity did not lead him to deny their force or to reject, for himself, their validity.

The sympathy if not understanding by which Henry James and his children were united did not bind Dr. Holmes and his eldest son. The evidence of strain is too clear to permit the belief that their considerable similarities of conviction, taste, and style overcame fully the antagonism of disparate temperaments. Holmes, however, later said of his father that he "certainly taught me a great deal and did me a great deal of good." To that word of gratitude, he added, however, a comment on the habit of his father (perhaps characteristic in New England parents) to run down rather than to exaggerate the natural blessings of his children. Holmes wondered whether his father had not done him in his boyhood some harm "by drooling over the physical shortcomings of himself and his son and by some other sardonic criticisms. At least," he acknowledged, "it made it difficult for his son to be conceited." [85] One wishes that the son had stated more specifically what "physical shortcomings" his father found in the boy; surviving photographs would certainly suggest that in looks, at least, he was peculiarly blessed. Perhaps the father's regret that he could not consider himself equally fortunate led him to visit his shortcomings on his child. The tension between the father and son, however, must have been eased from time to time by the father's humor. In the son's middle thirties, after he had written a note to the Doctor which evidently in form or substance was somehow unsatisfactory, the Doctor replied in the following note:

My dear Son,

Your mind has evidently not yet recovered its balance. I have consulted Dr. Tyler, late of the Somerville Institution and he suggests a method of treatment which he thinks will bring order out of the mental chaos which has betrayed itself in the singular note you have sent me.

He says: "let him rub a little *goose-grease* over the hollows in his skull corresponding to the phrenological organs of the principal intellectual faculties. This is the nearest approach to and best substitute for the natural secretion, in *his case.*

"His diet should consist largely of *asses' milk,* as this food will require little or no labor of assimilation.

"Let him avoid *pudding;* it goes to the head, and he has had more than was good for him already."

So speaks this wise physician and I hope you will heed his counsel. . . .

Your affectionate parent
O. W. H.[86]

It is hard to think that a relationship, colored by such gaiety, was intensely strained.

The quality of Dr. Holmes's mind so affected the structure of his son's that it is hard to see the mother's hand as a shaping influence upon her boy. Even in the Doctor's affairs she appears as nothing more arresting than a figure of gentle benevolence. Her talent as wife, like that of many other women of her generation, was for giving unobtrusive aid to her husband's career and quiet sympathy to his vanities. "She gave him every day the fullest and freest chance to be always at his best, always able to do his work amid cheerful surroundings." [87] Her talent as mother, so far as one can estimate it on the basis of the scantiest evidence, was of the same sort. The few letters to her eldest son which have been preserved indicate clearly that her consuming interest was in her family. When she was forty-eight she asked her boy of twenty-five, "What does a woman of my age care as much for as her children, what they are and what they will be? I assure you," she continued, "that I give more thoughts to them than to anything else in this world. . . . I suppose I bother you sometimes—but I love you very much." [88] Her task, like that of other women, was so to balance a wife's with a mother's devotion as to provide the family as a whole with that tranquillity of affection on which household peace so largely depends. She did not claim credit for the achievement, but her testimony that "we are as happy a little household as you will meet with" [89] would indicate that her task was fulfilled with success. Her son's reticence and his act of destroying the bulk of his letters to his parents makes it virtually impossible to find expressions of his feeling for his mother. The intensity of affection which is shown in his Civil War letters to her bespeaks, however, a dependent intimacy which the tension and crisis of war perhaps intensified but surely did not create. "Goodnight my loveliest and sweetest" are scarcely the words of a son who is unresponsive to his mother's affection, and "bestest love to Dadkin" [90] hardly the phrase of a boy who despised his father. In the last analysis one feels that the influence of Mrs. Holmes upon her son was neither intellectual nor moral—that is, that she did not, like his father, either contribute the perspective of a critical and enlightened point of view to his understanding or provide him with an example of achievement which, by repulsion or attraction, would set the course of his own ambition. Instead she gave him, as she did her husband, that sense of security which nothing can more effectively provide than unselfish devotion. That devotion the son was fortunate enough always to know—first in her, and later in his wife.

The mother's significant contribution to her son's inheritance was not a gift from her alone, but from the family which had reared her. Her people were the merchants of New England. Their concern had been more with the affairs of this world than with the problems of the next.[91] Dr. Holmes, to be sure, was more interested in the color of life than in the shadows of the unknown, but the devotion of his father had been to a somber ministry and an austere scholarship. Mrs. Holmes, on the other hand, had grown up in a household where religion and scholarship were, at most, peripheral. Mrs. Holmes's father, Charles Jackson, had been an Associate Justice of the Supreme Judicial Court for some ten years, but the central concern of his professional career had been with the private affairs of men of power and position rather than with the public affairs of the Commonwealth. The influence of this background had importance not only in the worldly security which it afforded to the Doctor's family—the house on Montgomery Place was given to the young couple by Mr. Justice Jackson —but, more significantly, in the extension of the family's social affiliations. The natural intimacies of Dr. Holmes were with men of letters and of science, perhaps one might say with the unfashionable scholars of Cambridge rather than with the fashionable merchants of Boston. Those of Mrs. Holmes were precisely the opposite. The two worlds met, of course, at many points and their fusion often came about by other means than mixed marriages, but the children of such marriages grew up, if not with divided loyalties, at least with a division of alternatives. The young Holmes was as much at home with the children of merchants and bankers as with the offspring of ministers and professors. Perhaps it is not a distortion to suggest that when he traced his own skepticism to his mother's influence he implied that a part of him found the worldliness of men of affairs more attractive than the somberness of the clergy. Perhaps it was his mother's inheritance that led him to believe that "an ounce of charm is worth a pound of intellect." [92]

To emphasize the worldly affiliations of Holmes is not to assert that the position of his mother's family brought him into relationship with the expansive energies of nineteenth-century America. The Boston merchants were concerned with the large affairs of the New England region, with the larger problems of the continent, even with financial activities of international scope, yet these manifestations of Boston's energy did not make themselves felt in the household of Dr. Holmes. This household lived its life largely unconcerned with the cruder tendencies of the world by which it was surrounded. Its security was more fundamental and more formative of character than that which came in those days from financial means and economic power. The Bostonians who possessed those means and that power became familiar with the risks and the brutalities which are their accompaniments. The family of Dr. Holmes, associated by blood and friendship with those who were giving direction to the economic destiny of their region and their nation, succeeded in separating themselves from the tumultuous expansion which surrounded them. Clearly they were among the privileged of their time and place, but they used their advantages for the preservation of a way of life which had its roots in other soil than that of privilege, which found its nourishment in the traditions of scholarship rather than the accidents of power. As a result of this isolation from the pressures of the world of affairs and of American commerce, Holmes always found himself to some extent a stranger in his own land.

The conflicting strains in Holmes's inheritance had revealed themselves in something more decisive than contrasting tendencies. His paternal grandfather, Abiel Holmes, in 1829 was the pastor of the First Church in Cambridge. He had remained true to the Calvinism in which the churches of New England had been founded while the majority of his parishioners had taken the Unitarian way of Boston. The conflict between the shepherd and his flock not only concerned the spirit but involved the hard realities of property.[93] Should the meetinghouse in Cambridge remain in the control of the pastor and the faithful minority or should it be transferred to the emancipated majority? The victory was with the Unitarians and went to them because the Supreme Judicial Court, with Holmes's maternal grandfather among its concurring members, had determined that the property of a Congregational church was subject to the control of the majority of the parishioners, even though that majority had abandoned the faith in which the church had been founded.[94]

To suggest that when the faith of the Puritans was subjected to the law of the land New England's spiritual tradition had fallen victim to Boston's worldliness would be to distort the elements in the conflict. Yet it is fair, perhaps, to see in the positions of Justice Jackson and Abiel Holmes a reflection of those contrasting strains which made up the inheritance of their grandson. The Jackson Court believed that no faith, no matter how deeply rooted it might be in the soil of New England, should enjoy an irresponsible and perpetual tenure. Abiel Holmes, on the other hand, believed that the law should support the truths of Calvinism against the variable whims of democracy. To the New England traditionalists, like Abiel Holmes, it seemed clear that Mr. Justice Jackson and his associates had allowed either their Unitarian inclinations or a prevailing indifference to truth to determine their judgment. Quite possibly neither ground of criticism was wholly justified, but it is evident that the fervent certainties of Abiel Holmes were not shared by the Court which permitted ecclesiastical authority to pass from the heirs of Calvin to New England's heretics. Though Dr. Holmes had joined the heretics he was the son of orthodoxy; Mrs. Holmes, by contrast, was the daughter of heresy. It was, perhaps, for these reasons among others that Holmes thought of his skeptical inclinations as an inheritance from his mother.

Doubtless the usual preoccupation and concerns of childhood left their mark on the temperament and character of Holmes. There are some indications, however, that less than the normal amount of the boy's energy was given to sports and outdoor life. At fifty he referred to the "futile shrinking from new things" [95] which, in his youth, had kept him from skating, riding, and dancing, and we know that it was not until the Civil War that he became a horseman.[96] Yet it is evident that the seven summers of country life at Pittsfield in the years from 1849 to 1856 were seasons of outdoor contentment. Dr. Holmes reported to a friend in 1854 that his thirteen-year-old son spent his time there shooting, fishing, swimming, and drawing [97]—in general laying the groundwork for the reflection of his old age that "what we most love and revere generally is determined by early associations. I love granite rocks and barberry bushes, no doubt because with them were my earliest joys that reach back through the past eternity of my life." [98] Yet for nature, Holmes's feeling never seems to have been intense. Writing of a friend's enthusiasm in the face of nature's great spectacles he said, "I respect it not without envy. Such things work more gradually and unconsciously upon me. I think about them (or something else) instead of seeing them." [99] And again, "It is my misfortune not quite to get ecstasy out of nature. It makes me no wiser and I can't paint." [100] After spending two months at Niagara Falls in the summer of 1888 Holmes said that "it was like living on intimate terms with the prophet Isaiah," [101] suggesting once more that his satisfaction in nature was more intellectual and speculative than emotional and poetic. Though the forces of nature in their most dramatic manifestations moved him, it was, in general, to the inner rather than the outer stimulus that Holmes's feelings were responsive. "I have said that the great emotions that I have known from external events was [*sic*] due to the Swiss mountains, a storm at sea, a battle, and a total eclipse of the sun." [102] With time there evidently came a feeling for the simpler regularities of nature, for in his later years he systematically recorded such signs of the spring's coming as the appearance of the first crocus on the White House lawn and the voice of the bullfrog along the banks of the Potomac.

It was because nature seemed to Holmes to make him no wiser that his energy in maturity was given to other concerns. And from the scattered indications of the preoccupations of his boyhood it seems that the habits of maturity were built upon the practices of his youth. The "futile shrinking from new things" which kept him from skating and dancing with his contemporaries gave his hungry curiosity about the oldest problems opportunity to seek an outlet in speculation and satisfaction in books. In 1921, after reading *Du côté de chez Swann,* he suggested something of the mood of his boyhood. Proust, he said,

> seemed to call up all the melancholy of youth—the vague horizons—the changing associations with the old—the enchantment of the country and the spring—my folios and my old prints, some of which I have had since my teens and many of which I grew up among. . . . They had been part of my whole life, and other melancholy and lonely lads had had the same futile yearnings.[103]

The loneliness and melancholy were again suggested in his description of the Boston of his youth where "though I didn't get Hell talk from my parents" the shadows of damnation were in the air, particularly on Sundays. "Oh, the ennui of those Sunday morning church bells—and hymn tunes—and the sound of citizens' feet on the pavement—not heard on other days. I hardly have recovered from it now." [k] Elsewhere Holmes described the years of his boyhood as "a weary time," lived in "barren surroundings," mitigated only by the teachings of contemporaries "in the rudiments of crime—ringing doorbells, and playing devils tricks at back doors —a weary time of waiting for 'some divine, far-off event.' " The barren surroundings were those of "a Boston with no statues, few pictures, little music outside the churches, and no Christmas." [104] Was this aesthetic barrenness an aspect, perhaps, of that rusticity which Henry James observed in the atmosphere of Boston? Urbanity of the mind was coupled with rusticity of the spirit and a boy of artistic inclinations who "pored over a dictionary of engravers by one Shearjashut Spooner—'Phoebus, what a name! '—" [105] until he could recognize prints by their remembered description, found little in the Puritan atmosphere to invigorate those inclinations. "[B]ad statues are better than no statues. They are points of interest, and give you something to think about." [106]

The boy's first approach to "the vague horizons" of youthful thought and feeling was evidently literary and aesthetic, rather than religious or philosophical. His boyhood's enthusiasm did not stop with Walter Scott and Sylvanus Cobb but included Lamb's *Dramatic Poets* [107] and *The Prometheus of Aeschylus*.[108] His first exploration of the borderland between religion and philosophy was in the pages of Vaughan's *Hours with the Mystics,* a book which, he said, marked "my transit from boy to young man, before I went to college " [109] and in which he saw the rationalist's dislike of romatic extravagance and the moralist's distrust of ecstasy. He evidently had begun to hope that systematic inquiry would provide answers to the questions of philosophy which a somewhat melancholic nature had come, rather early, to appreciate. When, at seventeen or eighteen, he took up Plato he did so "expecting to find the secrets of life revealed." [110]

The story of that expectation is, however, a part of the life of the young man, not of the boy.

[k] *Holmes-Laski Letters,* I, 154. On another occasion he expressed the same mood: "The Boston of my youth was the still half-Puritan Boston, with the 'unutterable ennui' of its Sundays and the church bells which I still affectionately hate." Speech at the Tavern Club, Nov. 1902 (MS, Harvard Law School).

2

Harvard College

In January 1860, Francis Bowen, Alford Professor of Natural Religion, Moral Philosophy, and Civil Polity in Harvard College, acknowledged that Darwin's *Origin of Species,* which had just been published in America, was "making a great sensation." He believed, however, that a review of the work in the July issue of the *North American Review* was inadvisable. "The interest in such a matter so quickly passes away . . . that it will all be used up before July, and it would hardly be worth while to recur to it then." [1] Professor Bowen in making this complacent prophecy did not, of course, speak officially for Harvard, and there were, fortunately, some in that community of scholars whose prediction would have shown a somewhat more sensitive awareness of the direction of Western thought. Yet Bowen's hope that the stream of "licentious and infidel speculations which are pouring in upon us from Europe like a flood" [2] could be diverted by a rigorous education in the orthodoxies was more characteristic of the spirit of Harvard College in the sixties than the conviction of its radicals that inquiry is legitimate though it fails to confirm inherited belief. The Harvard world to which Holmes moved as a freshman in the fall of 1857 and in which he remained until his graduation in 1861 was, in truth, a world dominated by traditions of oppressive stuffiness, and organized with the authoritarian energy suitable for a reform school for young, but already morally delinquent, gentlemen. A college contemporary of Holmes's seems to have spoken substantial truth when he described the College as being rather a primary school, on a grand scale, than the first University in the country. . . . The system of marks is too absurd to require condemnation; the system of discipline too puerile to call forth anything but contempt; the standard of scholarship required to obtain a degree, so low that any fool can have the distinction of graduating with full honors from the University. . . . Almost all instruction has become dry and mechanical, tutors and professors rather striving to maintain a wooden old-maidish dignity than to inspire any generous sympathy with their separate studies.[3]

Henry Adams said that although Harvard College "taught little, and that little ill," it none the less "left the mind open, free from bias, ignorant of facts, but docile." [4] It seems unlikely that the ruling authorities were as pleased that the openness resulted from their method of instruction as that their discipline had nourished an appropriate docility. The irritation of Henry's elder brother was, perhaps, more human and less subtle when he spoke of the Harvard methods of instruction in the fifties as "simply beneath contempt." Charles Francis Adams, however, did the majority of the Faculty full justice when he described them as "a set of rather eminent scholars and highly respectable men [who] attended to their duties with commendable assiduity, and drudged along in a dreary, humdrum sort of way. . . ." [5]

The philosophy of education by which the College was inspired while Holmes was a student was accurately reflected in its grading system. An elaborate mechanism of points had been devised for measuring the achievements of the students. For perfect recitations 8 points were earned; for perfect written exercises 24 points were awarded—and so on through an elaborate "scale of merit." At the end of each term and of each year the score of the student was computed by totaling the points which he had accumulated in each of his courses. An unusually gifted and faithful student might in a single term earn more than 1000 points in a single course. Upon Holmes's graduation he had accumulated 20,192 points—a total which was so petty as to prevent him from securing any form of honorable mention.

In itself this cumbersome system of measuring achievement

was not, perhaps, worse than others which later generations have devised for appraising the effectiveness of higher education. The aspect of the system which most significantly reflected the prevailing conception of education was the procedure by which moral and intellectual standards were measured on the same scale of merit. Points earned through intellectual effort were lost by moral delinquency. The student who on Monday earned 8 points for a perfect recitation on the *Tusculan Disputations* would lose them on Tuesday if he were late to morning chapel. The student who, like Holmes in his senior year, was twice publicly admonished for his delinquencies might find, as he did, that all credits earned for studies in Greek—*The Clouds* and *Alcestis*—were canceled out by the mathematics of immortality. A generation of teachers that was committed to the doctrine that natural and revealed religion, philosophy, and science all proclaim the validity of Christian morality, not unnaturally treated its responsibility to impart knowledge as simply an aspect of its obligation to enforce the standards of that morality. In New England that generation had come to believe, furthermore, that ignorance in those to whom knowledge was made available was sinful, and correct understanding virtuous. To such a generation it was obviously appropriate that the intellectual achievements and the moral delinquencies of those being trained in the philosophy and the practice of Christianity should be measured on a single scale.

That company of scholars, the College Faculty, was compelled by the logic of their principles of education to devote an extraordinarily large part of its time to sitting as a police court for the imposition of sentence upon offenders against the code of parietal regulations. On at least one occasion they interrupted their judicial deliberations to go forth, *en masse,* under Presidential command to capture offenders red-handed.[6] The regular meetings of the Faculty, however, were almost wholly given over to the less exciting duty of hearing charges and entering judgments against wayward students. "Voted that Runkle, Senior, be privately admonished for bringing a cigar into the choir, and ordered to sit down stairs for the future, and that H. P. Tobey, Junior, be appointed to blow the organ in his place": "Voted that Garrison and Holmes, Freshmen, be fined one dollar each for writing on the posts in Tutor Jennison's room": "Voted that Swinerton, Senior, be privately admonished for playing on a violin and smoking in the Yard": "Voted that Magenis, S. M. Weld, Sherwin and Skinner, Seniors, be privately admonished by the President, for galloping around the Yard on Friday": "Voted that Hayes, Freshman, be privately admonished for blasphemy in the Latin recitation room," and, the most pathetic of all, "Voted that Bradlee and Willard, Seniors, be privately admonished for throwing reflections of sunshine about the College Yard." [7] It is not surprising that a Faculty that in general was willing to devote its time to such adjudications found it appropriate on the retirement of President Walker, in January 1860, to supplement its general expression of gratitude for his services in promoting the University's "intellectual, moral, and religious improvement" with the more specific commendation of the "efficiency with which he has maintained order and discipline, so essential to its prosperity." [8]

For the future health of the College it was fortunate that its students did not, for the most part, submit meekly to discipline. A healthy and unruly few considered it to be their special responsibility to make life as miserable as possible for the Faculty. Edward Pearce, Tutor in Mathematics, in January 1859, described to President Walker a recent incident, not at all unusual in character, in which he had been vigorously involved. A student was discovered in an attempt to imprison Pearce in his room by sealing its door with screws. The student and the Tutor came to blows. "He did not strike me a second time," reported Pearce, "though he endeavored to use his teeth for the purpose of freeing himself from the hand by which I held him." At this point the Tutor called loudly for the police to assist him, to which appeal the student, releasing the hand which fed him mathematical learning, bitterly protested: "If that isn't a scrubby trick to call for the police in a college matter!" [9] In the age of Walker a relatively small proportion of college matters seem to have been academic matters. It is not surprising that a student who described the Cambridge atmosphere as one of constant warfare between the Faculty and students, in his diary proudly recorded the fact that on November 13, 1857, "I broke my 17th window this evening." [10] Had hostilities been less vigorously carried on by the students, the Faculty's burden of enforcing discipline might have been supportable and the tradition of respectable piety might have become a habit so oppressive as to stifle the growth of a freer way of academic life. As it was, however, President Eliot, who as a junior member of the Faculty had sat for many years as police magistrate with his learned associates, was able to speak with convincing authority when he discussed problems of discipline in his Inaugural Address in 1869.

> The petty discipline of colleges attracts altogether too much attention. . . . It is to be remembered that the rules concerning decorum, however necessary to maintain the high standards of manners and conduct which characterizes this College, are nevertheless justly described as petty. What is technically called a quiet term cannot be accepted as the acme of university success.

He concluded his reflections on this theme with the mild understatement that "the Statutes of the University need some amendment and reduction in the chapters on crimes and misdemeanors." [11] One may well doubt whether such hopeful promises of reform would have been made if Holmes's generation of students had submitted without resistance to the edicts of the authorities who ruled over them.

So far as the records indicate, Holmes's freshman year was largely uneventful. He lived then, as he did in his subsequent college years, in the private rooming house of Mr. Danforth on Linden Street, just off the College Yard. Perhaps the decision to live there rather than in a dormitory bespoke a desire to stay relatively clear not only of the police state within the Yard, but of the obligation to participate in resistance. Whatever the motive may have been, it seems probable that by living as he did he was able to indulge his relatively quiet tastes without the same distractions to which they would have been subjected had he lived within the

Yard. At Mr. Danforth's there were other student roomers—all of them New Englanders, and most of them Bostonians of the same circle in which Holmes had spent his boyhood.[12]

The freshmen in 1857–58 were not active participants in college affairs outside the classroom. Tradition made their most intimate contact with upperclassmen as a group an annual football match or, more accurately, battle with the sophomores.[13] (In Holmes's freshman year his class was defeated.) Exclusion from student organizations postponed their effective participation in undergraduate affairs until they had been admitted to the upper classes. In such circumstances college life, at least for those living outside the Yard, must have revolved principally round the prescribed routine of study and round such personal friendships as individual temperament and opportunity might encourage. Although Holmes moved in a circle of familiar Boston names and faces there were a few from beyond New England with whom he established an early intimacy.[a] No classmate was a closer friend in college or in later years than Norwood Penrose Hallowell, a Philadelphia Quaker, who, with Holmes, turned soldier on the outbreak of the Civil War. During the years when Holmes was an undergraduate, a Bostonian was unlikely, however, to broaden his understanding of national character by his college friendships.

The curriculum required of freshmen in 1857–58 did not open new fields of knowledge to one who had received his preliminary schooling under Mr. Dixwell. Greek and Latin, Mathematics, Ancient History, and Rhetoric (Orthoepy, the science of pronunciation, was the subject in the first term) were studied much as they had been studied in school. In Greek, readings from Isocrates and *The Odyssey* supplemented drill in grammar. The instructor's name, his Olympian appearance, appropriate to one who was born, as he was, at the foot of Mount Olympus, made Tutor Evangelinus Apostolides Sophocles a most impressive reality. It was Longfellow

[a] In a freshman class of 99, 80 students came from New England. One of Holmes's classmates came from Honolulu, four from Ohio, one from Missouri, and one from Wisconsin. The South was represented by three classmates from Mississippi, South Carolina, and Kentucky.

who said of him that he "makes Diogenes a possibility." [14] Apparently Sophocles found the academic regulations unsound, for when it was reported to him that a student had been caught cheating in one of his examinations he replied, "It make no matter. I nevare look at his book anyway." His judgment of the qualifications of applicants for admission to college was, evidently, somewhat jaundiced. "X and Y were among the candidates for admission examined in a group, and *viva voce,* as was the custom then. The next day X asked his grade. 'Passed,' said Old Sophy. 'And Y?', said X, though certain that his friend had failed. 'Passed,' was the reply: 'It is unfair to discriminate. You all do know nothing.' " [15] Instruction by such a figure must have opened vistas which even parietal regulations could not entirely conceal. In later years, Holmes looked back upon the scholarship of Sophocles with admiration,[16] and his election of courses in the classics, when election became possible in his last two years, suggests that study under Sophocles could bring substantial satisfaction. Instruction in other freshman subjects was more pedestrian. The routine of recitation, written exercise, and final examination did little to enliven Livy or make Algebra, Geometry, and Ancient History more stimulating than they had been in Mr. Dixwell's school. During the first term, daily attendance at morning chapel, required for all students in the college, was supplemented for freshmen by a course of Religious Instruction based upon an elementary text of Archbishop Whately, *Introductory Lessons on Morals and Christian Evidences.* The volume, edited by Frederic Dan Huntington, Preacher to the University and Plummer Professor of Christian Morals who was soon to astound his Unitarian associates by joining the Episcopal Church, was introductory indeed. Its first two hundred pages were given over to the statement and justification of the generalizations of Christian morality, making them seem both marvelously simple and beautifully rational. The second part of the volume on Christian Evidences gave to the young Christian the arguments by which he might in disputation either with Mohammedans or with Western skeptics establish the truth of the Christian religion. The arguments were not new and merely endeavored to put in simple form the case for Christianity which Butler and Paley had previously developed to the satisfaction of the orthodox. That case was founded on the contention that the prophecies of the Old Testament were realized in the birth of Christ, that the miracles performed by Jesus must have had their origin in the Divine will, and that internal evidence in the New Testament makes it irrefutably clear that the Apostles were not impostors and knew as reality the events which they related. Such elementary lessons in orthodoxy could hardly be labeled philosophical, but one whose nature was either speculative or skeptical might well step from that introductory text to the fundamental perplexities which its simplicity endeavored to conceal.

A freshman coming to Harvard with a mind uninitiated to inquiry and a temperament unaccustomed to skepticism would not have been likely to have either his habit of mind or the bent of his temperament affected by his first year's curriculum. He had no opportunity in his formal studies to consider critically the problems either of method or of substance with which science was challenging conventional belief. His instructors included no such members of the Faculty as Asa Gray and Jeffries Wyman who were willing, and even eager, to let inquiry carry them beyond the limits of orthodox conviction. The only world of letters to which the attention of freshmen was officially directed was that of antiquity and it was, for the most part, examined with the grammarian's precision rather than revealed with the artist's feeling. A young man with an already matured intelligence accustomed to inquiry could scarcely find in such a curriculum as this a freshening stimulus for his capacities. There is every reason, therefore, to suppose that the significant influences and the productive interests which colored Holmes's freshman year came from other sources than his curriculum and its discipline. The one suggestive intimation of the young man's predominant interest during that year is found in the list of the family's withdrawals from the Boston Athenaeum. The books taken out included Vasari's *Lives of the Painters,* Northcote's *Life of Titian,* Lady Morgan's *Life of Salvator Rosa,* and Ruskin's *Pre-Raphaelitism* and *Stones of Venice.* From the College

Library Holmes's one withdrawal in the same year was Haydon's *Autobiography.* That fact offers some confirmation for the belief that the books on art taken from the Athenaeum were for the freshman's use rather than for his parents or his younger brother and sister. There is ample evidence to show that Holmes's lifelong interest in art—particularly in prints—was at its liveliest in his youth.[17] A few drawings done when he was a young man survive to show a considerable talent.

In December 1858, there was published in *The Harvard Magazine,* an undergraduate literary periodical, an anonymous essay, "Books," [18] which was the first of a number of papers which Holmes contributed to its pages. Published in the middle of his sophomore year, it reflected views which must have been developing during the first year of college study and in the summer vacation after the freshman course was completed. If its style suggests that of an elderly gentleman of rather priggish enlightenment, it was neither the first nor the last undergraduate essay to have that quality. That this first piece of published writing suggested opinions which were reiterated and redefined on innumerable later occasions gives it, however, a rather special interest.[b]

The highest conversation is the statement of conclusions, or of such facts as enable us to arrive at conclusions, on the great questions of right and wrong, and on the relations of man to God. And so we all

[b] Among the rules for intelligent reading which Holmes prescribed in this first of his published essays was one which in later years he persistently violated. In 1858 he quoted approvingly "a great reader" for the saying that "As soon as you forget the color of the heroine's hair, lay down the book." Holmes went on to endorse that advice: "[W]e must read no longer than we are perfectly engrossed in our subject." In 1924 he described his own habits in reading: "A real reader I think doesn't bother about beginning at the beginning or reading more of it than he wants. He rips out its guts and passes on. But I have to begin with the first word and scrupulously go on to the end and then put it down in my list like a good little boy, neither can I read down the page, a paragraph at a glance, as did Horace Gray and do Laski and Reginald Foster. I read word by word, or at most line by line." Autograph letter, OWH to Mrs. John C. Gray, Sept. 17, 1924 (Harvard Law School). In the back of Holmes's diary for 1867 the following entry appears in his hand: "Mem: Father reads 27 pp. [of] 270 words in 1 hour = 7290 words. I read 36 or 37 office paper pages written middling small. I read 22.1 Law Rev. printed pp. [in 1 hour]." There were some 400 words on a normal page in the *American Law Review.*

know the difference, in our various associates, between him who lives only in events, and can relish nothing but the College gossip of the day, and him who feels that this is well enough, but that he can find higher food for thought, and who, while still young, passes restless hours longing to find someone who will talk to him of better things. Those, then, who have somewhat higher aspirations than the mass of their companions, and who in the ranks of boyish insipidity find none who meet or satisfy their desires, must as an alternative take to books. . . .

. . . But more important than all this, we must at once in some shape understand the questions of the day. Just as one man implies humanity, so the history of the struggles of one period implies eternity. And though there always is a fight and crisis, yet are we not in a peculiarly solemn position? Books and papers, within a century or two only accessible to the common people, have had their effect. A hundred years ago we burnt men's bodies for not agreeing with our religious tenets; we still burn their souls. And now some begin to say, Why is this so? Is it true that such ideas as this come from God? Do men own other men by God's law? And when these questions are asked around us,—when we, almost the first of young men who have been brought up in an atmosphere of investigation, instead of having every doubt answered, It is written,—when we begin to enter the fight, can we help feeling it is a tragedy? can we help going to our rooms and crying that we might not think? And we whistle or beat on our piano, and some—God help 'em!—smoke and drink to drive it all away, and others find their resting-place in some creed which defines all their possibilities, and says, Thus far shall ye think, and no farther. No, no; it will not do to say I am not of a melancholic temperament, and mean to have my good time. It will not do for Ruskin to say, Read no books of an agitating tendency; you will have enough by and by to distress you. We *must,* will we or no, have every train of thought brought before us while we are young, and may as well at once prepare for it.

. . . And so I say again, we must study the present to know the past. Emerson, who probably takes about as large a view of man and events as any one we could point out now living in America, gains much of this breadth by the peculiar direction of his studies. . . . We encourage a hot-bed operatic taste that requires a strong stimulus to excite it, and consequently the delicacy of the noblest and calmest books is to us insipidity. The great secret of all delight in literature is preserving this fineness of taste, and Emerson understands it, and not only reads the great works of our own tongue, but he studies all the great inspired books of all the great literatures. He knows and reverences Shakespeare, Montaigne, and Goethe; but he has also penetrated into Plato and Confucius, into the Bhuddist and Zoroastrian sacred books, which we contemn on the authority of others, without ever having looked into them ourselves. . . . It seems to me there is nothing in literature so elevating as these volumes; and we cannot help feeling how infinitely better were our time spent in really learning these, than in reading book after book of puzzling and involved commentary on a book which bears on its face that it was written for all if for any. Yet books are but little seeds after all, seeming insignificant enough before the merest weed of real life; but they lie soaking in our minds, and when we least expect it, they will spring up, not weeds, but supporters that will be our aid in the sorest struggles of our life.

Holmes began his sophomore year with an undistinguished but better than average academic record behind him. For the mild disgrace of being privately admonished, with fourteen others, for creating a disturbance in the Yard after his last freshman examination he had lost 32 points on the scale of merit, but even with that deduction, and others for smaller offenses such as tardiness, he had accumulated 4933 points and ranked 22nd in a class of 96.[c] His record, in any case, was considered sufficiently worthy to entitle him (along with 29 others) to a "detur" (*Detur Digniori:* "to the more worthy let it be given") consisting of a copy of Bryant's

[c] At the end of his sophomore year Holmes ranked 30th in a class of 84. In his junior year he stood 13th and secured an average of 82, the highest average in the class being 97. With respect to grades awarded in particular subjects throughout Holmes's college course it appears that they were average or less in Philosophy, Mathematics, History, Chemistry, and Physics. The subjects in which his grades were among the highest awarded to his class were in Greek (particularly in the advanced work of his senior year), Latin, German, and Rhetoric. The talents which were reflected in grades were thus more literary than scientific and were those which he indulged in his extracurricular pursuits. He succeeded in securing the honor of election to Phi Beta Kappa in his senior year and thus received credentials of capacity no less significant than those which the Faculty provided through its Scale of Merit.

Poems. The natural relief which he may have felt in having the freshman year satisfactorily behind him must have been somewhat colored by the prospect of a less arid curriculum in his second year. Most of the same fields were there again (only History disappeared from the course of study), but new subjects were required. These were Chemistry, Botany, and Anglo-Saxon (under the compendious rubric "Rhetoric"). The Professor of Chemistry, Josiah Parsons Cooke, was affiliated in thought and temperament with the conservative element in Harvard, and looked upon Darwinism with the same alarm as did his better-known and more eloquent associate in science, Louis Agassiz.[19] Botany, on the other hand, was taught to the sophomores by Asa Gray, Darwin's most ardent champion in Cambridge, and his most effective supporter throughout the scientific world in America.

The loyalties of students, like those of their teachers, were divided between the cause of orthodoxy and the cause of "liberalism." An organization of students, The Christian Brethren, had been formed to support and advance the conservative cause among the undergraduates. Its constitution provided that

> no person shall be admitted as a member to this Society who does not heartily assent to the fundamental truths of the Christian religion, particularly the doctrines of depravity and regeneration, the existence of one God in three persons, Father, Son, and Holy Ghost; the atonement and mediation of Christ; and also furnish to himself and others satisfactory evidence of a saving change of heart.

It is significant of the condition of undergraduate opinion that in the fall of Holmes's sophomore year a rival organization, The Christian Union, was established. Although its purposes were far from radical—"to secure the moral and religious improvement of the members; to elevate the standards of morality in College; and to spread among us Christian sentiments"—it was specifically stated in the constitution that those sentiments should be "unsectarian and liberal." Furthermore, its membership was to be upon a base notably broader than that of the Christian Brethren. "All students of good moral character, without distinction of sect, claiming to believe in the truths of Christianity, may be elected members of the Society." [20]

Towards the close of his sophomore year Holmes joined the Union. It would appear from the minutes of its meetings, however, that his affiliation was purely nominal, for his presence at its regular meetings is nowhere recorded. At those meetings the members discussed and debated selected topics of morality and belief: "Is Prejudice Averse to a Good Influence?", "The Best Method of Spending the Sabbath," "How Far Are We Justified in Participating in Vice, in Order to Fortify Ourselves against It, or Rescue Our Friends from It?" The comfortable direction of the members' beliefs is indicated by the minutes of a meeting held in the fall of Holmes's junior year when the subject under discussion was the question whether any danger to religion was to be apprehended from the scientific tendencies of the age. The secretary's record of the meeting indicates that most of the members present "seemed inclined to answer the question in the negative."

In his sophomore essay, "Books," Holmes had expressed dissatisfaction with undergraduate conversation, which too seldom was concerned with "the statement of conclusions, or of such facts as enable us to arrive at conclusions, on the great questions of right and wrong, and on the relations of man to God." One might have supposed that, holding this conviction, he would have been among those members of the Christian Union who attended its formal debates and deliberations. Perhaps what kept him away was a temperamental hostility to solemnity—particularly to organized solemnity. Or it may have been the feeling that the conversation of undergraduates was so colored by "boyish insipidity" as to make books a more satisfying source of stimulation. The only statement of the reasons which prompted him to join The Christian Union is in the autobiographical sketch which he wrote in the Class album at the end of his senior year. That statement suggests that his membership in the Union was based more on a desire to indicate by the act of affiliation where his loyalties lay than to become an active participant in its program. He there said: "I was, while in College a member of . . . the 'Christian Union'; not that I considered my life justified belonging to [it], but because I wanted to bear testimony in favor of a Religious society founded on liberal principles in distinction to the more 'orthodox' and sectarian platform of the 'Xtian Brethren.' " The affiliation, however nominal it may have been, justifies the assumption that at this intermediate stage in Holmes's college career his skepticism had not gone so far as to make him unwilling to be labeled as one who believed "in the truths of Christianity." Though he may well have claimed the right to determine for himself what those truths were, association with The Christian Union did, at least, suggest that no complete repudiation of the Unitarian faith in which he had been brought up had yet occurred.

That it was the solemnity of the Union, not the simple fact that it was an organization, which made Holmes's affiliation purely nominal is suggested by his active membership in social clubs—the Institute, the Hasty Pudding, the Porcellian, and the Alpha Delta Phi. In each of these he seems to have been an enthusiastic and companionable member, giving the gayer elements in his nature a chance to indulge themselves rather more freely than they could have if his one concern in College had been in securing moral and intellectual education through serious conversation and books.[21] In 1912 the Alpha Delta Phi (then the A. D. Club) gave a dinner in Holmes's honor. In his remarks on that occasion he glanced for a moment at the Club as he had known it as an undergraduate.

> In my days, after having been saved from extinction by two members of the Class of 1860, it used to meet, I think rather oftener than elsewhere in my room, at Danforth's in Linden Street, which had the advantage of being outside the College Yard. If I am not mistaken, the last meeting that I attended before this was there in 1860 or 1861. In those days the Club used to listen to essays by its members before the business of the bottle began.[22]

Had the serious-mindedness of some of Holmes's undergraduate writings represented the whole of his temperament he might well have become an ally of his reforming classmate Wendell Phillips Garrison, who did his abolitionist name and inheritance something more than justice when he sought through persuasion to abolish smoke and drink from the extracurricular habits of his fellow-students, and generally belabored them in the pages of *The Harvard Magazine* for their frivolity and intemperance. Holmes, to be sure, was capable of scolding his fellow students in those same pages, but when he rebuked them he did it with a relatively mild severity. At the Harvard-Yale boat-races at Worcester in July 1860, the supporters of the Cambridge victors celebrated their successes with some exuberance. In the issue of *The Harvard Magazine* of the next September Holmes published the following unsigned comment on undergraduate manners: [23]

Now, without undertaking to express a belief that when young men meet together all will or should be members of the Temperance Society, and not forgetting that to the natural ebullition of animal spirits on such an occasion some license may be allowed, as it certainly will be taken, still we cannot but protest against such behavior as was shown at Worcester, on the two grounds of the advantage and the honor of the students. . . . In brief, while we believe that these troubles were the result of thoughtlessness rather than of deliberate malice, and consequently have perhaps received too harsh a treatment in some of the papers, it is clear, on the other hand, that, if the gentlemanly feeling and the morality of the collegians does not suffice to stop a repetition of the trouble expediency tells them the continuance in such ways insures inevitably the interference of the authorities and the speedy stopping of the cause of the offence.

Holmes has testified that he was of a more reforming nature in his youth than he was in his later years: "I can remember the time," he wrote in 1928, "before the Civil War when I was deeply moved by the Abolition cause—so deeply that a Negro minstrel show shocked me and the morality of Pickwick seemed to me painfully blunt." [24] However active the capacity to give himself to causes may have been in his undergraduate days, it was never sufficiently vigorous to make him the humorless preacher to undergraduate contemporaries which his classmate Garrison became. In 1925 Holmes said, "I value enthusiasm but not enthusi*i*sm" [25] and in the statement expressed a temperamental hostility to the dedicated reformer. One whose feelings were of that sort was not likely to give disproportionate attention either to the purification of human nature or to such an unrelenting pursuit of knowledge that the graces of living would be neglected. Had his qualities been those of Garrison, he would not have been chosen to write the class poem for the sophomore banquet in the spring of 1859, and it is unlikely that if Garrison had, by some strange chance, been selected to fulfill that responsibility he would have written the verses which Holmes produced for the occasion:

> Two years have passed since fair Harvard received us,—
> Two years touched the face of our smiling young earth,—
> She, who with many a pang has conceived us,
> Two years from now will give some of us birth;
> And we shall love her,
> Our bountiful mother,
> We shall all love her wherever we go,
> Both for her motherhood,
> And for our brotherhood,
> We shall all love her, wherever we go.
>
> Babies in life, we shall play with its roses,
> Boys, see their opening; men watch their decay;
> But the beauty departing a higher discloses,
> And we find the fruit just as the flower drops away.
> Then drink to our mother,
> Our bountiful mother,
> For we shall all love her, wherever we go;
> Both for her motherhood
> And for our brotherhood
> We shall all love her wherever we go.

When in Holmes's senior year a fellow member of the Porcellian Club died suddenly, Holmes prepared an obituary record for the Club and in his description of his friend left an indication of his own qualities as well.[26]

Francis Lowell Gardner, our late Secretary, and beloved Brother and friend, died on the 10th of February 1861.

Endowed with virtues which made him the delight of his domestic circle, he also possessed those manly qualities and livelier graces which compelled respect while they won the love of his companions.

An only son, he was brought up with a tender solicitude which served to make more refined and thoughtful his naturally fine and considerate disposition; this those who knew him best most deeply appreciated, for they saw it working in every action of his life; but it needed not intimacy to feel the courage and courtesy which never deserted him, even when most tried, but which always walked hand in hand; his high breeding restraining all needless display of his bravery, and that, in turn, giving to his manners dignity and weight.

His graceful bearing and the beauty of his features harmonized singularly with the rare qualities of his spirit, and combined with them to mark and signalize him among his fellows.

But he is gone from us whom, as a man, we honored, as a brother we loved. In the social circle, and in the walks of friendship we shall feel the void which he has left unfilled, yet we shall recall his memory rather with pleasure than with pain, as one who did honor to his College, his Class, his Club, as a truly chivalrous gentleman.

A college boy who honors the livelier graces and courteous chivalry in a friend reveals his own inclinations. In Holmes's tribute to Gardner one may feel that the emphasis upon the delicacies of breeding reflects the limitations of a snob, and that the grief of a boy for a friend's death was translated into the mourning of a young gentleman. The formalities which made an obituary record appropriate affected, of course, the shape of expression, and Holmes's tribute was designed to satisfy the formalities. It surely is not surprising that one who came from a community which saw refinement as the child of breeding and the mother of restraint, should esteem a friend's fidelity to that tradition. It is doubtless an oversimplification to suggest that the Harvard undergraduate who came from Holmes's background had to make a choice, in his day, between two destinies—that of the snob or that of the prig. Some of Holmes's classmates, like Garrison, chose the latter. Holmes avoided that. The path that he followed as an undergraduate did not mean the renunciation of his inheritance, it did not significantly broaden his understanding of America and its people, yet it allowed the "livelier graces" some indulgence. Had his inclinations been rebellious he might have separated himself from the young men with whom he had grown up. He could have rejected entirely the easy familiarities of the Harvard clubs and by that rejection, perhaps, have broadened the foundations of his experience. Had he turned in the direction of solemnity he might have satisfied the ghost of Abiel Holmes, but in doing so he would have betrayed the sprightlier elements in his own nature. He seems to have made a happy compromise which permitted his concern for the durable mysteries to find expression in unrequired reading and his taste for the livelier graces to fulfill itself in the easy gaieties of undergraduate life. The extent to which he participated in the social life of Boston and Cambridge while he was at college we do not know. It is clear, however, that by the end of his student days he was the intimate friend and perhaps the ardent admirer of more than one of the eligible young ladies of the community. It is hard to believe that his later pleasure in their company and liking for their admiration was not revealed in his youth.

Holmes's advice to his fellow-students that they should disregard Ruskin's caution against "books of an agitating tendency" was in all probability disapproved by the majority of his teachers. John Fiske was publicly admonished for reading Comte during Sunday service, and the desire of President Felton, Francis Bowen, and Josiah Cooke to make the penalty more severe was doubtless based not on the fact that reading in church deserved a higher punishment but on the principle that the agitating tendency of the author compounded the felony of the reader.[27] The one "agitator" on the Faculty under whom Holmes studied was Asa Gray; in his scientific studies in his junior year Professor Cooke still was his guide through Chemistry and in the same year his introduction to Physics was under the auspices of Joseph Lovering, a professor who later expressed his unreconstructed conservatism by insisting on the continued use of an outmoded textbook "because it was behind the times," and by dismissing the increased interest in electrical engineering with the comment, "It's only a spurt." [28] It was not, therefore, in the prescribed studies that Holmes found encouragement for the inquiring mind which the expanding world of science and the temper of his father's household proclaimed to be essential for a civilized intelligence.

From whatever source the impulse to face the questions which Harvard was so reluctant to recognize may have come, it is quite evident that Holmes's reading during his last three years in college was increasingly of "an agitating tendency." Although the college curriculum had given him no taste of philosophy, save as its problems had been implicit in the freshman course of Religious Instruction, two volumes of Plato's *Dialogues* had been taken from the Boston Athenaeum in the spring of Holmes's sophomore year and were most probably in his hands during that period. It was in the course of his junior year that his reading in philosophy seems to have turned to contemporary works in which the fundamental issues of the times were being squarely faced. Lewes's volume on *Comte's Philosophy of the Sciences* was taken from the Athenaeum once in 1859 and again in 1860. Cousin's *Modern Philosophy,* which Holmes had withdrawn from the College Library in his sophomore year, was taken from the Athenaeum in the spring of 1860, as was Lewes's *Biographical History of Philosophy,* a volume passionately concerned to show the validity of Comte's thesis that speculation had passed through its fruitless eras—the theological and the metaphysical—and was about to enter the era when thought would find its salvation in science—the age of Positivism. That Holmes was not entirely persuaded by Lewes's conviction is indicated by his renewed withdrawals of Plato's *Dialogues,* and his subsequent, though nearly contemporaneous, reading of Fichte's *Contribution to Mental Philosophy,* Butler's *Ancient Philosophy,* and Vaughan's *Hours with the Mystics.* During his senior year the withdrawal of Spencer's *Scientific Essays* from the Athenaeum suggests, however, that current thought stirred his philosophical interest as much as did that of the ancients.

This catalogue of readings acquires some significance when one looks at the three essays which Holmes published in his senior year and in which the direction of his thought is indicated. That direction was determined not only by the quality of his temperament and the nature of his capacities, but was evidently influenced by his current reading and associations outside the Harvard community. In his sophomore essay, "Books," he had testified to his admiration for Emerson and in later years he referred to the days of his youth when "Emerson set me on fire," going on to say, "he could impart a ferment—a thought which I believe Father appropriated from me in his book." [29] It is probable that Holmes's conversation with Emerson concerning the spirit with which one should first read Plato occurred during Holmes's junior year, for it was at that time that the *Dialogues* were so frequently taken by a member of the Holmes household from the Athenaeum. It was with great hopefulness that Holmes first turned to Plato. In 1924, referring to a recent return to the *Dialogues,* he said, "You no longer take up Plato as I did at 17 or 18 expecting to find the secrets of life revealed." [30] Emerson, to be sure, had cautioned the young man against carrying his expectations too far. " Hold him at arm's length," he advised. "You must say to yourself: 'Plato, you have pleased the world for two thousand years: let us see if you can please me.' " That Holmes followed Emerson's advice to do his reading critically is indicated by the essay, "Plato," which Holmes contributed to the *University Quarterly* in the fall of his senior year.[d] When the essay, either in an earlier draft or in its published form, was shown to Emerson, the sage's comment must have been a little discouraging to his youthful admirer. "I have read your piece. When you strike at a king, you must *kill* him." [31]

Neither the degree of Holmes's success nor the vigor of his criticism need concern us. What is more significant is the position from which he starts and the standards by which he measures Plato's genius. Holmes's inclination to accept the traditions of

[d] *University Quarterly,* II, 205 (Oct. 1860). This periodical was an intercollegiate publication with its editorial offices at New Haven. For the essay on Plato Holmes was awarded the *Quarterly*'s prize of $20 for the best undergraduate essay published in its pages in 1860. The judges awarding the prize were George Ticknor and George S. Hillard. In Holmes's copy of the essay the following penciled notation appears on the first page in his handwriting: "Took the prize for the year 1860. Written in the summer vacation 1860."

empiricism is indicated in his assertion that he does not "feel sure that each man's own experience is not always to be that which must ultimately settle his belief." [32] It is evident, furthermore, that his conviction that the instruments of philosophy are to be found in the methods of science was in process of development. "[I]t is only in these last days," he wrote, "that anything like an all-comprehending science has embraced the universe, showing unerring law prevailing in every department, generalizing and systematizing every phenomenon of physics and every vagary of the human mind." [33] Though Plato was denied the enlightening advantages with which science has endowed philosophy, he anticipated its basic principle when he recognized "the fatality attaching to matter. With it the law of cause and effect is absolute; if we know the data, the results are inevitable." [34] Plato's failures were not in genius but were ordained by the deficiencies of scientific knowledge throughout the ancient world. The philosophical sinners have been the later metaphysicians who treat as persistent mysteries questions which science has answered. They have failed to recognize "those accumulations of new material and consequent correction or annulling of old results and methods in every branch of knowledge, which, with the steady advances of civilization, each eager generation continually makes." [35]

Holmes's youthful reflections on Plato clearly foreshadow the convictions of his maturity. They include, however, a few passages which indicate that the logic of empiricism had not yet carried him as far as it was destined to. Insistent as he was in 1860 on the merits of scientific empiricism, he had not yet come to reject or even perhaps to question the belief that there are "necessities" in the universe. "[A]s long as we have faith in reason we must believe in the truths of mathematics and the like as existing in the nature of things." He was willing, at this stage of his intellectual pilgrimage, to accept an "intuitive faculty" as a reality and even to assume that by means of that faculty we come to know those "necessary ideas" which permanently exist "in the mind of the Creator." [36] These acknowledgments were more than argumentative concessions and reflect a moderation in his empiricism which time and experience were to destroy. One other phrase in the essay suggests that the skepticism in his temperament had not yet led him to question the legitimacy of the settled standards of propriety. He mentioned occasional instances in which Socrates developed principles which were "shocking to sound morality," [37] and in doing so spoke more in the voice of his father than in the voice that later was to become so unmistakably his own. These conventional phrases, like the detailed criticisms, reflect a stage in the intellectual development of Holmes. The mood of the essay reveals something no less important—an aspect of the critic's temperament. It was not only the intellect of Holmes which found the achievement of Plato of absorbing interest. His spirit found inspiration in the passion of Plato's effort and in the nobility of his aspiration. "[T]o see a really great and humane spirit fighting the same fight with ourselves . . . fills my heart with love and reverence at one of the grandest sights the world can boast." [38] The stilted language is that of an undergraduate, the reverent mood that of a romantic youth. Holmes's style later came to a polished maturity, but he never lost the young man's capacity to find unquestioning inspiration in "manly and heroic conduct." [39] The Civil War did not create but confirmed and accentuated a temperamental willingness to admire, if not to glorify, heroism and manliness.

During Holmes's sophomore year his reading had been centered around the history and the interpretation of art. In his junior and senior years it was more concerned with philosophy. The essay on Plato suggests that the transition from art to philosophy came easily to Holmes and that he saw his two predominant intellectual interests as intimately related. Though he rejected Platonism in metaphysics he accepted it in aesthetics.

> [I]n separating man the idea, from man the concrete, how completely Plato has anticipated the best art by dividing the accidental from the real. How deeply would he have felt the difference of the plodder, who, professing nature as his model, puts before him a flower, and copies every corrosion and chance stain upon its leaves, . . . and the great artist, who, seizing the type of plant, paints that upon his canvas, and leaves the rest in the subordination in which it belongs.

When the admirable artist of the *White Captive* said that in every man and woman he tried to see their face and form as it would have been if it had descended from Adam, still characteristic, but free from the marks of sin and sickness, he was talking pure Platonism and true art.[40]

The essay on Plato expressed Holmes's conviction that the genius of a philosopher may find adequate justification in his discovery of a fundamental principle of aesthetics. In the year when that essay was published Holmes contributed to *The Harvard Magazine* his paper "Notes on Albert Dürer" in which he dealt with the philosophy of a great artist.[41] If the essay on Plato suggested that Holmes found artistic validity in philosophical speculation, the "Notes on Albert Dürer" make it abundantly clear that his enthusiasm for art was grounded in the conviction that its significant insights are philosophical. A distinguished critic and historian of art has recently written of Holmes's undergraduate comments on Dürer and has described the essay as a "magnificent . . . piece of precocious writing." He states that Ruskin's comments on Dürer "sound hazy and ephemeral when compared with Holmes's sure and methodical approach, his conciseness, deep understanding and modest restraint." [42] The "Notes" are devoted, in part, to matters of the engraver's technique and to critical consideration of particular engravings, but the heart of the paper is in its passages of generalization.

The men of the fifteenth and sixteenth centuries, it seems to me, had one advantage not likely to be soon possessed again. Without stirring the dogmas of the Church, it is clear that a noble philosophy will suffice to teach us our duties to ourselves and our neighbors, and some may think also to our God. Some may take satisfaction in basing their moral obligations on this foundation, and in contemplating the future construction of an abstract religion on the same general ground; it is certainly now true, however, that the weaker faith of the majority of mankind prefers for these pure abstractions a clothing of more concrete fact, and demands the stimulus of a story and a life to excite their souls, sluggish to receive the highest truth; and that this demand will not remain to the end of time is by no means sure. But however this may be, certainly the growth of civilization increases our faith in the natural man, and must accordingly detract from the intense and paramount importance attached in darker times to the form of the story embodying the popular religion. Thus, while it has come to pass, that nowadays we see that duty is not less binding had the Bible never been written, or if we were to perish utterly to-morrow; on the other hand, the story that once made corporeal, and fit subject for the painter, man's highest religious conceptions,—that dramatized philosophy,—is now regarded in so far a different light, that those scenes, once wrought out with such loving faith, have now, I fear, passed from the province of art. . . .

But, however much may be lost to art when the religious stories become matter for reasoning and scholarly dispute, in place of the old reverence for the letter, art does not finally depend for inspiration on religious form. The ideal spirit may be influenced by circumstances, but it is the great gift of humanity, not of a sect; it inspired the philosopher Plato, the artist among thinkers, as well as the Christian Dürer, a thinker among artists. This it is that sees the eternal disguised in the visible form, in the particular event; and I notice that its highest results with Dürer, after all, are not found in even the profound pathos and grand tenderness of the *Passion* and the *Life of Christ,* but in conceptions more remote from the contact of history. The mortal figures there portrayed were personal and ephemeral, but the MELANCOLIA sits forever, an undecaying and immortal thought.[43]

Holmes's search during his college years was for the "noble philosophy" which in itself would provide justification for ideals and give assurance that behind the pettiness of particular events lay some undecaying verity. Science, he had come to believe, had rendered the traditional assurances of religion and of metaphysics illusory, and yet he was unwilling to abandon hope that assurance somehow could be found. The Emersonian confidence, partly romantic and partly mystical, was confirmed for Holmes in the artistic genius. It would not do, of course, to take Holmes's undergraduate essays as systematic formulations of belief; they are, however, suggestive indications of an attitude and a tendency in process of development. The direction of that tendency was sufficiently clear, at least in the "Notes on Albert Dürer," to arouse the indignation of an orthodox classmate, William A. Holbrook, who was later to serve in the Episcopal ministry. In the December issue of *The Harvard Magazine* Holbrook contributed a highly critical review of Holmes's essay.[44] His complaint was that Holmes was an imitator and follower of Emerson, that though he seemed to be at home "in a dreamy, transcendental, artistic religion," his ideas were "barbarous in the province of reason and practical piety." He concluded his criticism with an appeal to Holmes not to be "so unscholarly, so feeble as to think that you are to abuse 'the meek and lowly Jesus,' and injure the cause He came to advance by obscure and flippant hints at a beautiful new kind of religion, that has become the light of the world since the fifteenth and sixteenth centuries." Holmes, who was then one of the three senior editors of *The Harvard Magazine,* published Holbrook's protest without comment.[45] It would be surprising, however, if he was not pleased that his essay had rubbed the pieties of The Christian Brethren the wrong way.

If Holmes's essay was displeasing to an orthodox contemporary, it is probable that it was read by the Faculty with small enthusiasm. A letter from President Felton to Dr. Holmes written shortly after the "Notes on Albert Dürer" was published indicates how precarious were the rights of undergraduates to publish opinions distasteful to their teachers.[46] The President, to be sure, made no direct reference to Holmes's essay, but his appeal to the Doctor that he should use his parental authority to prevent his son and his associates on the board of *The Harvard Magazine* from speaking too freely may well have seemed to imply dissatisfaction with unorthodoxies of every sort. The President's specific complaint was that a recent issue of *The Harvard Magazine* had contained an undergraduate comment on Professor Huntington's resignation from the Faculty and that this comment was "disrespectful in tone and language." The anonymous contribution, it appears, was written by Holmes's reforming classmate, Wendell Phillips Garrison, but Felton did not indicate that the identity of the author was known to him.[47]

> An attack upon a retiring professor, by those who have been more or less under him, and who are still members of the College and under College laws, under circumstances that make any reply on his part impossible, cannot be excused or palliated. I am told there are other things equally objectionable: and I repeat that if they continue, I have no doubt the Faculty will forbid the continuance of the work. . . . No one objects to criticism of course; but printed or oral acts of disrespect by students, are alike inconsistent with their relation to the College and the Faculty, and printed as well as oral acts of this description I am sure the government will not permit.

It is greatly to be regretted that the reply of Dr. Holmes to the President's plea and warning has disappeared. A year before, he had permitted a testimonial over his signature to be published in the first issue of the *University Quarterly,* the undergraduate periodical conducted on an intercollegiate basis, in which he had warned the editors that they had difficulties ahead: "A venerable President will shake his head, and the little Olympus of little pismires over which he presides will tremble to its foundations." [48] Now that the Harvard ant-hill was trembling, it was hardly wise for the venerable President to turn to Dr. Holmes for aid, and one can only wish that the Doctor's response had been preserved.

Holmes's other published undergraduate writings tell much less of his intellectual development than do the essays on Plato and Dürer. A brief paper on Pre-Raphaelitism which was published in the June issue of *The Harvard Magazine* [49] and would have been read as an Exhibition Part in May, 1861, had Holmes not been at that time in uniform, reflects attitudes towards painting similar to those which had been carefully developed in the essay on Dürer. There is the same emphasis upon the conviction that the "noble work" is the highest art and the same demand that the artist should seek to "combine the highest art with the noblest truth." [50] Though Holmes expresses sympathy with the aims of the Pre-Raphaelites he also indicates that their performance is frequently disappointing to the critic who seeks not only for enlightened aspiration but technical proficiency. Of several book reviews which he contributed to *The Harvard Magazine,*[51] one has a quality and style of some interest. In reviewing a recent novel, *Marion Graham; or, "Higher than Happiness"* by Meta Lander,[52] Holmes placed the book in "that class of vulgar novels, and what is worse, vulgar novels by women, which are one of the afflictions of our day." Perhaps the fact that the cast of male characters was overweighted with ministers was a special source of irritation. "Ministers," Holmes complained, "are as thick throughout the book as salamanders after a rain; and a new one creeps out from under every leaf we turn over." At the close of the review there is a sentence expressing a characteristic inclination of Holmes's taste. "Now in all this," he says, "there is a certain purity of tone that is really much better than the hot, bad atmosphere of some books of more ability. . . ." Thus again appears the demand of art, as of philosophy, that its tone should be colored by nobility.

In his senior year Holmes studied for the first time under Francis Bowen, that stalwart champion of Harvard's brand of orthodoxy. During the first term Bowen's texts were Thomson's *Laws of Thought* and his own volume on metaphysics and ethics. The full title of Bowen's volume—*The Principles of Metaphysical and Ethical Science Applied to the Evidences of Religion*—accurately described the purpose of the book. Bowen did not purport to write a history or treatise which should be concerned with metaphysical and ethical thought in general. His object, he said, was "to consider those objections and difficulties in the way of the believer which are of recent origin, or have grown out of recent discoveries and speculations in science and philosophy, as well as the important additions to the Evidences of Religion which have been derived from the same source." [53] His energies were directed not only against modern scientists who had come to acknowledge, for man, "fraternity, or a common pedigree, with the reptile and the brute," [54] but against the Emersonian effort to merge conventional religion "in the practice of a sublime but rather indefinite morality." Of the Emersonians, he said, "reverence of their own nature seems . . . quite as just and proper as reverence of the Deity, and a glowing though vague conception of virtue takes the place of religion as a guide of life." It was Bowen's insistent conviction that morality cannot itself "find anywhere a sure and permanent support except in a recognition of its dictates as the commands of God." [55]

While Holmes was receiving instruction in these principles from Professor Bowen, *The Harvard Magazine* appeared containing Holmes's assertions that "a noble philosophy will suffice to teach us our duties to ourselves and our neighbors," and that "duty is not less binding had the Bible never been written." Perhaps when President Felton wrote to Dr. Holmes of the "objectionable" contributions to *The Harvard Magazine,* he knew neither that the piece on Dürer had been published nor that it had been written by the Doctor's son, but it is virtually certain that the son knew from his father of the President's threat to suppress the periodical. It is tantalizing that we know nothing more of an incident, or series of incidents, which occurred during the second term of Holmes's senior year than is contained in the records of the Harvard Faculty for April 21, 1861: "Voted that Hackett and Holmes, Seniors, be publicly admonished for repeated and gross indecorum in the recitation of Professor Bowen." Is it not distinctly possible that the repeated indecorum consisted in a stubborn refusal to omit from recitations a critical comment on Bowen's orthodoxies? President Felton had gone out of his way to tell Dr. Holmes that it was not only the printed act of disrespect which would necessitate action by the Faculty, but that the government of the College would not permit "oral acts of this description." It is certainly a possibility that indecorous acts towards Professor Bowen had already been committed by the young Holmes when the President wrote to the Doctor.

During the term when the public admonition occurred, Holmes was no longer studying natural and revealed religion under the name of Metaphysics and Ethics but he was then taking Professor Bowen's required course in political economy. Work in the subject consisted entirely in recitations on Bowen's own *Principles of Political Economy*. This treatise, whole-heartedly devoted to the principles of a laissez-faire society, could not, being Bowen's, escape a theological flavor. The ultimate justification for the laissez-faire economy, in Bowen's mind, lay in natural religion. He admitted that the doctrine of noninterference by government seemed to leave the economic interests of society in the hands of selfish and often ignorant individuals. It was nonetheless proper to let their impulses guide the general course of development.

> Society is a complex and delicate machine, the real Author and Governor of which is divine. . . . Man cannot interfere with His work without marring it. . . . *Laissez-faire;* "these things regulate themselves," in common phrase; which means, of course, that God regulates them by His general laws, which always, in the long run, work to good. In these modern days, the ruler or governor who is most to be dreaded is, not the tyrant, but the busybody.[56]

In Bowen's text on political economy the conviction that economic policy is fashioned by Providence was blended with a belief that the wisdom or folly of man may make substantial differences in his economic destiny. Much of his effort was to discover the laws of God which govern political economy,[57] but a considerable energy is given to the somewhat inconsistent task of showing that man is the master of his own fate. Perhaps his most notable endeavor was that of showing that the dogmas of British and European economists are not applicable to the United States. In emphasizing his belief that laws of political economy, possibly valid for Europe and England, have no application in the New World, he characteristically found that the strength and promise of American prosperity is derived principally, not from the wealth of America's physical resources, but from the moral quality of her people and her institutions.[58] His optimism, grounded in this conviction that the morality of our ideals and of our political system is purer than that of any other people, led him to reject the gloomy forebodings and despairing fatalism of Malthus. Bowen acknowledged that Malthus may accurately have predicted the destiny of a European civilization which refused to effect such alterations in its institutions as might destroy the privileges of the few, but he found in American morality justification for the belief that our destiny must be an increasing prosperity for all. In the same breath in which he credits Americans with so much, he indicates, however, that the basic Malthusian error sprang from its misinterpretation of the law of God.

> In those facts which appear so alarming to the Malthusians, I see only indications of a beneficent arrangement of Providence, by which it is ordained that the barbarous races which now tenant the earth should waste away and finally disappear, while civilized men are not only to multiply, but to spread, till the farthest corners of the earth shall be given to them for a habitation.[59]

No contemporaneous record indicates either directly or indirectly how Holmes in his senior year responded to the economic teachings of Bowen. It is hard to believe, however, that the antipathies which were so evident between the philosophical principles of the teacher and of the pupil did not carry over to the class in political economy. If Holmes's later admiration of Malthus—he described himself as "a devout Malthusian" [60]—may be taken as an indication of the predilections of his senior year, it may well be that some of his indecorous classroom behavior occurred during recitations to Professor Bowen in political economy. Bowen's tendency to nourish his hopes with comforting interpretations of the decrees of Providence and his confidence that nature respects the rules of Christian morality would hardly have been sympathetic to a young man who found Providence impersonal and Christian morality debatable. Furthermore, Bowen's entire willingness to dismiss as "monstrous" a scientific theory which seemed inconsistent with the religion of Harvard [61] must have been peculiarly distasteful to a student who was coming to doubt that the happiness of pious and instructed men was the end towards which all nature moved. It was the optimism of Bowen's belief which gave it what significance it had as an influence (perhaps wholly negative) in the development of Holmes's thought. In his later years Holmes was often to find himself in disagreement with younger friends whose hopes were greater than his own. Their hopes, of course, were not founded on the presuppositions of Francis Bowen, but it is not impossible that an early revulsion against the tendency of the Harvard which educated him to see pious men as masters of a favorable fate survived in Holmes as distrust of social optimism. It is important to remember, however, that there is a vast difference between the cheerfulness of Emerson and the optimism of Bowen. Holmes rejected the latter, but embraced the former. To that Emersonian quality of temperament the scientific point of view added the conviction that science demands of mankind a greater degree of humility in the face of nature than his teachers possessed.

While temperament, reading, and thought were leading Holmes to this persuasion, the nation's political and moral crisis was reflected in the affairs of Harvard and of Boston. During his senior year Holmes evidently became increasingly concerned in that crisis. The brief question in his sophomore essay on Books—"Do men own other men by God's law?"—suggests that early in his college career he held slavery in abhorrence. In later years, as we have already seen, he spoke as if the cause of abolition had moved him deeply in the years before the outbreak of the Civil War. Few indications of the extent of his commitment to that cause survive, yet there is evidence to show that the commitment carried him beyond theory to action. In 1926, referring to events of his senior year, Holmes described himself as having been at that time "a pretty convinced abolitionist" who was "one of a little band intended to see Wendell Phillips through if there was a row after the meeting of the Anti-Slavery Society just before the war." [62] Among Holmes's papers is a document which seems to refer to the occasion which Holmes thus recalled and which suggests that he was a participant in exciting events in Boston on January 24, 1861. The document in question is a letter from Richard Price Hallowell, the elder brother of Holmes's classmate Norwood Penrose Hallowell. The elder Hallowell was a Philadelphia Quaker, turned Boston merchant, and one of the small group of abolitionists who, during the winter of 1860–61, made themselves responsible for securing the physical safety of Wendell Phillips against the threats of the Boston mobs.[63] "Ruffians in broadcloth and ruffians in rags" [64] had made it their systematic business to break up abolitionist meetings and gatherings of any kind at which Wendell Phillips was to speak. A number of his youthful supporters not unreasonably felt that his life was in danger. They accordingly took steps to assure that a bodyguard of followers would give him protection which the Boston police seemed unlikely to provide.[65]

In December 1860, and in the opening weeks of the next month increasing national tension led to mounting strain in Boston. The annual meeting of the Massachusetts Anti-Slavery Society was to take place in Tremont Temple on January 24 and 25 and the members of the Society were to hear addresses by anti-slavery leaders, including Phillips, James Freeman Clarke, Edmund Quincy, and Emerson. Mayor Wightman, recently elected to office, was something less than friendly to the abolitionists, and the police force of Boston was under his control. It was clearly an occasion on which trouble might flare up and pass out of hand, and those who had been fearful of mob violence against the radicals saw the need for preparation. It was in these circumstances that R. P. Hallowell wrote the following letter to Holmes.[66]

Boston, Jany 23^d –61

Dear Wendell,

I am sorry not to be able to meet you as arranged. Our meeting will organize at 10 o'c and an *imperative* duty will oblige me to be engaged from 9 o'c to 10 o'c. If you call at our store you can obtain the William[e] our young man promised you. I do hope you will not receive personal injury tomorrow and trust you will not use a weapon except as a last resort. I will see you at the meeting. If you will visit our Festival at Music Hall this evening I will explain everything fully. Hoping to see you I am sincerely yours,

R. P. Hallowell

Although no further contemporaneous record established that Holmes did attend the meeting of the 24th his letter of 1926 would seem to make it clear that he was on hand at Tremont Temple when the Anti-Slavery Society convened. One bit of evidence indicates that he may have met with Hallowell on the evening of the 23rd. That was the evening on which the "Liberty Women"

[e] This reading of the word is clear. The meaning has not been ascertained.

2. The Holmes children: Edward Jackson, Amelia, and Oliver Wendell, Jr., about 1855

3. The Holmes family: Edward Jackson, Mrs. Holmes, Amelia, Oliver Wendell, Jr., and Dr. Holmes, about 1859

4. September 1861

5. November 1862

6. April 1862

7. January 1864

Holmes during the Civil War

had their levee or Festival at the Music Hall as a preliminary to the next day's gathering and at which Hallowell suggested that Holmes might meet him. The occasion was entirely tranquil; the radical ladies and gentlemen "circulated in groups, exchanging greetings, and talking cheerfully of martyrdom." [67] In *The Liberator* for February 15, 1861, there was published a list of persons who had made financial contributions at the Festival of the 23rd. Among the contributors listed is O. W. Holmes, Jr.[68] Was it the poverty of a college student or the instinct of a Yankee which led the young abolitionist to limit his contribution to the sum of 25 cents? One cannot, of course, answer that question, but the inclusion of Holmes's name on the list of contributors suggests that he met with Hallowell on the evening of the 23rd in order to secure instructions for his conduct at the meeting of the next day.

We know that Wendell Phillips's friends were seriously alarmed about the likelihood of violence. They had good reason to believe that the police would do little to protect the radicals and they had received fair warning that murder might be done.[69] Phillips was resolved, however, to exercise what he considered to be his constitutional rights of speech. Those who were committed to his cause had no alternative but to support him in his fortitude, and to support him by any means which might prove to be necessary. His bodyguards were, therefore, armed and more than ready to meet violence with force. At the opening meeting the floor and platform of the auditorium were filled with resolute friends of the abolitionists, the balcony and doorways crowded with ruffians "full of whiskey and blasphemy. . . . The contrast between the galleries and the floor and platform of the Temple was as great as could be exhibited between vice and virtue, mental imbecility and the highest intellectual development, moral degradation and spiritual growth, measureless vulgarity and the most perfect refinement of manners." [70] As each of the speakers gave his address the crowd in the balcony persistently sang, hooted, and cheered. The placid orators, however, poured their inaudible message into the hearts of their converts on the floor. It is impossible to determine whether the abolitionists' fears of violence were justified, for public authority intervened after a morning and afternoon of threatening turbulence. The mayor closed Tremont Temple to further proceedings. Protesting bitterly, the Society was compelled to conclude its convention in a private session.

The character of the public proceedings was such as to make the occasion less memorable in the annals of abolitionism than in those of free speech. Nobody could hear the message of the speakers but all could see their insistence on their right to be heard. What Phillips and Emerson were demanding, and what they failed to secure, was police protection against a mob which sought to silence them. Had the abolitionists been timid men and women they would, on learning that public authority would not sustain them, have retired into silence. Instead they came before their massed opponents and said their say, not so much in the hope that their message of abolitionism might be heard as in the conviction that they could teach a lesson in freedom by proving their fortitude. When Holmes stood guard to such speakers did he not, perhaps, learn something more important than what his Cambridge professors taught him?

Larger events than those of January quickly followed. Fort Sumter surrendered on April 14, 1861. Three days later Lincoln called for 75,000 militiamen to suppress combinations obstructing the execution of the laws in seven of the Southern states. On or shortly before April 25 Holmes enlisted as a private in the Fourth Battalion of Infantry, and on that day accompanied the Battalion to Fort Independence in Boston Harbor for guard duty and for training.[71] In the meanwhile, as the nation passed from precarious unity to civil war, the Harvard Faculty convened on April 22. On the following day President Felton reported to Dr. Holmes the results of the deliberations of his company of scholars:[72]

Dr. O. W. Holmes
Boston

Cambridge, April 23, 1861

My dear Sir:

I regret to inform you that your son has incurred a censure of being engaged in breaking the windows of a member of the Freshman

Class. Ordinarily this is regarded as a very high offence: but in this case, the Faculty were happy that they were able to treat it as of a character less serious than usual. The act was committed from the window of a classmate; and those who were engaged in it frankly and honestly confessed to the President, in order to save the occupant of the room from the responsibility, which, by the laws of the College, he is under for whatever happens in it. They also made suitable apologies for what they had done to the injured parties. Taking all these circumstances into account, the Faculty have voted a public admonition, with a fine of ten dollars each: the offence of breaking windows, which their act tended to countenance and encourage having been carried to an unprecedented extent.

They state that they have never before been concerned in this kind of mischief, and I have no doubt their statement is entirely true.

Yours very respectfully,
C. C. Felton

P.S. In every other case known to me, breaking windows has been punished by dismission from College, when detected.

I have to add that your son incurred an additional admonition "for repeated and gross indecorum in the recitation room of Professor Bowen." I hope he will not persist in this inconsiderate conduct, now that he is so near the end of his course. He is an excellent young man, but of late, under some influence to which he has not heretofore yielded, his conduct has been frequently the subject of complaint.

Evidently Dr. Holmes replied to this letter in person. Writing to Felton in June on another matter concerning his son's relationships with Harvard, Dr. Holmes stated that on the morning of April 25 he had himself called on President Felton to notify him of his son's intention immediately to sign "his name as a member of the military corps. . . . This was in the morning, and at 2 o'clock of that day he is uniformed and on his way to Fort Independence." [73] In this conversation the son's offenses against the statutes of the College may well have played a less important part than his decision to discontinue if not to abandon his college studies. President Felton in another letter to Dr. Holmes indicated that the principal subject of their conversation on April 25 had concerned the possibility that the son's performance of military rather than academic duties in his last two months of his senior year would mean the loss of his degree.[74] President Felton in the same letter suggested that Holmes had gone to Fort Independence assuming that he was no longer to be considered a candidate for the degree.

No contemporaneous record indicates what impulses and what convictions were of dominant importance in Holmes's decision to join the military forces before the conclusion of his academic course. Doubtless the hatred of slavery which drew him into the camp of Wendell Phillips played its part, as did the desire to preserve the Union from rebellion. Time cooled his capacity to dedicate enthusiasm to causes and led him to feel something approaching shame for his early abolitionist faith. Yet he never lost his confidence that the corruption of Southern manners by slavery had been profound. When his friend Senator Beveridge was writing his biography of Lincoln and sought to show that the abolitionists had grossly exaggerated the evils of slavery Holmes came to the defense of those with whom his earliest loyalties had been affiliated.

> On the matter of the relation of the whites to slave women I don't believe there is any doubt, and I have heard a most humane and tender hearted Southerner use language that made me shudder. . . . The whole implication . . . is that the abolition talk was a body of malicious lies. I think in spite of what you have said that it was true as to the women, at least.[75]

To many of Holmes's college contemporaries one of the most painful aspects of the Civil War was the fact that classmates and companions whose friendships before 1861 had been intimate, after Sumter became enemies. Holmes, quite evidently, did not find the Southerners as attractive and appealing a type as did many of his friends. Writing again to Senator Beveridge, Holmes expressed some distrust of the effort to keep alive the tradition of the Old South.

> I hope that time will explode the humbug of the Southern Gentleman in your mind—not that there weren't a few—and not that their

comparatively primitive intellectual condition didn't sometimes give a sort of religious purity of type, rarer in the more civilized and therefore more sceptical northerner. But the southern gentlemen generally were an arrogant crew who knew nothing of the ideas that make the life of the few thousands that may be called civilized.[76]

"As a matter of personal preference I do undoubtedly prefer the kind of men I saw when young to the provincially arrogant, and, in spite of your English travellers, usually half-educated Southerners." [77] Certainly it was not this dislike for the Southern type which led Holmes to go to war, but it is not unlikely that his abolitionist mood found some reassurance in the conviction that the institution of slavery had played a major part in breeding a civilization which seemed more primitive than that in which he had grown up and in which his roots of inheritance were planted.

To one of Holmes's speculative temperament periods of faltering faith were bound to come, even during the War itself. In its most strenuous phase he wrote to Charles Eliot Norton of the need he felt for knowledge of historic acts of chivalry "to help us bind our rebellious desires to steadfastness in the Christian Crusade of the 19th century." He went on in the same letter to say that "if one didn't believe that this war was such a crusade, in the cause of the whole civilized world, it would be hard indeed to keep the hand to the sword; and one who is rather compelled unwillingly to the work by abstract conviction than borne along on the flood of some passionate enthusiasm," must have his ardor rekindled by stories of earlier crusades.[78] Doubtless the conviction that slavery was an intolerable evil in a civilized society played its crucial part in Holmes's decision of April 1861. Yet other convictions and other impulses found their expression in that same decision. One who had already in published writings committed himself to a romantic faith in "manly and heroic conduct" [79] could scarcely have postponed effective action until the calendar of academic days had run its course. If the Quaker faith of his intimate friend, Penrose Hallowell, bent to the winds of the crusade and permitted him also to enlist in the Fourth Battalion, how could a young man whose religious principles included no condemnation of war stay at his books, reciting to Professor Bowen rules of morality in which he did not believe? The opportunity through action to cry defiance to a Faculty which maintained that only the believer in its orthodoxies could act with pure nobility (and which contributed but one of its members to the armed forces, and that one a German immigrant)[f] must have been appealing even to one whose inclinations were for speculation rather than for action. Holmes's published conviction that "a noble philosophy will suffice to teach us our duties to ourselves and our neighbors"[80] could be brought to the test of action. If it should meet that test not only would personal faith be vindicated but the possibility of reconciling idealism and rationalism, romanticism and science, might be established.

Below these levels of philosophic conviction lay, of course, the normal impulses of youth to participate in great and exciting events. Not all of the young men who volunteered for service at Fort Independence went there convinced that this first phase of their military career was the opening chapter in the Christian Crusade of the nineteenth century. The Harvard undergraduate, William Francis Bartlett, who was to become the most distinguished soldier of all the men enrolled in the Fourth Battalion, in the previous January had recorded in his diary the grief with which he had said good-bye to two of his Southern classmates who had left College when their states seceded from the Union.[81] "However far we may be separated or however hostile may be our respective countries we have sworn that our friendship will never grow cold." After the fall of Sumter when there was a high degree of likelihood that the Fourth Battalion, in which Bartlett was already enrolled, would be called up, he stated that he did not know what he would do if it were. "I would be fighting rather against my principles, since I have stuck up for the South all along." These early associa-

[f] Holmes's fellow-officer, Charles A. Whittier, in his "Comments on the Peninsula Campaign of General McClellan" in *The Peninsula Campaign* (Boston, 1881), contrasted Harvard's contribution of one member of its Faculty to the Union forces with the enlistment of 32 out of 35 of the Faculty at William and Mary College in the Confederate Army. The one member of the Harvard Faculty to enlist was George Adam Schmitt, a German refugee who had been Holmes's instructor in German in his junior year and who became a fellow-officer in the 20th Regiment.

tions with soldiers of unsurpassed gallantry whose principles made them doubtful of the cause for which they fought were by no means the last such associations which the Civil War was to bring to Holmes. They led him ultimately, and perhaps from the first, to the faith that "duty is not to be proved in the evil day, but then to be obeyed unquestioning," and that "high and dangerous action teaches us to believe as right beyond dispute things for which our doubting minds are slow to find words of proof." [82]

With reveille at sunrise, dress parade at six, drill for six hours during the day, lights out at 9:30, and guard duty to be performed at intermittent intervals, life at Fort Independence was somewhat more rigorous than it had been on Linden Street. Those who shared the new experience, however, entered upon its mild severities with common advantages behind them. The officers and men who made up the Battalion were the sons of Boston and of Harvard. Those, like Holmes, who were privates might differ in military rank from their officers but the community of militiamen was a community of friends. Boston, furthermore, was not far away and the rigors of camp life were broken from time to time by visits from ladies and gentlemen of Boston to see friends and relatives in the romantic role of soldiers. It was entertaining to spend a Sunday outside the walls of the Fort on Castle Island listening to Gilbert's Band from Boston play gay airs to the soldiers and their visitors, and it was doubtless a moving ceremony when the ladies of Boston presented a banner to the Battalion. On Tuesday, May 30th, a salute was fired in honor of Charles Francis Adams who sailed that day from Boston to his post of Minister in London, leaving his second son, Charles Francis, Jr., among the troops at the Fort. Perhaps the Minister's third son, Henry, who was on shipboard with his father, took the salute as symbol of the opening of a new chapter in the endless process of his education; certainly the young men on Castle Island who primed the piece, thumbed its vent, and fired it were beginning in pleasant circumstances a phase of their education which for many was soon to end in death and for others was to leave indelible impressions on mind, spirit, and body.

The tour of duty on Castle Island, to everyone's regret ("we had just begun to enjoy ourselves"),[83] came to an end on Saturday, May 25. The Battalion boarded the steamer *Nellie Baker,* and crossed the harbor to Long Wharf where it was received with acclamation by its reserve members who had not volunteered for service at the Fort. The Battalion then marched through "a series of cheers and clappings" to the Parade Ground on the Boston Common where it was honored by the first public performance of a new air, "The Fourth Battalion Quickstep."[84] The tour of duty ended with waving handkerchiefs, pride in knowledge gained, and an exciting uncertainty as to what duties and what opportunities lay ahead.

When Holmes enlisted in the Fourth Battalion, he had supposed not only that his connections with Harvard were severed but that when he had had his basic training he would go South as a private.[85] When the Battalion returned from the Fort it had become clear, however, that it would not be sent to the theater of operations and would make no other demands on its members than occasional drill at the armory.[86] Those young men who wanted to see active service took immediate steps to secure commissions in the volunteer regiments which were in the process of organization by Governor Andrew. The Governor's aide, Colonel Henry Lee, who was cousin of Holmes, was the person to whom Holmes turned in his effort to secure a commission. Twenty-three years later Colonel Lee recalled Holmes's application to him as he was "strolling along the path between Massachusetts and Harvard Halls" and his own first feeling of "pity for your youth and delicacy."[87] The Colonel, however, could not let pity control him and the solicitation of his interest gave good assurance that the application would soon be allowed. Until that time came there were the concluding formalities of graduation to be observed. Since Harvard was willing to let her sons who had joined the Fourth Battalion return to Cambridge, with no other penalty than loss of points for accumulated absences from the recitation room and Chapel, and since Holmes had been elected Class Poet in the previous March, there was obviously good reason for him to rejoin his classmates for the concluding formalities of graduation. That he did, but evidently under some compulsion from the administration. On June 10 the Faculty voted "that Hallowell and Holmes, Seniors, be informed that they must return to College and pass the usual examination of their class as a condition of receiving their degrees." President Felton once more sat down and wrote to Dr. Holmes telling him of the Faculty's surprise "that your son has not rejoined his class since he was relieved of duty at the Fort," and instructing the Doctor that the son's attendance at the examinations was necessary if he were to be recommended for a degree. "Not knowing where he is at present," the harassed President concluded, "I must rely on you to communicate this notice to him." [88] The letter evidently brought results, for Holmes and Hallowell both appeared at their examinations, passing them satisfactorily, and thus earning their degrees.[89]

At the Class Day exercises on June 21 the Class Orator was Hallowell and the Poet, Holmes. The poem was delivered in the First Church in Cambridge, where his father's Calvinist father had been pastor until a liberal majority of the parish had evicted him. Henry Adams' description of Class Day in 1858, the year of his graduation, in all probability accurately described that which occurred three years later.

> Crowded into the large church, the students, their families, friends, aunts, uncles, and chaperones, attended all the girls of sixteen or twenty who wanted to show their summer dresses or fresh complexions, and there, for an hour or two, in a heat that might have melted bronze, they listened to an Orator and a Poet in clergyman's gowns, reciting such platitudes as their own experience and their mild censors permitted them to utter.[90]

The *Cambridge Chronicle* reported that Holmes's poem was "finely written, and listened to with much interest." The reporter's description, however, does not indicate that there was such fresh imagery in the theme of graduation as to make it a work which Holmes would have preserved with pride. "He ably compared the class just arrived at the end of its College career, to a ship well-armed and equipped launched upon the wide sea. He referred very effectively to the perils of our country and encouraged his associates to

'Be brave, for now the thunders roll.' "[91]

The poem was not preserved among Holmes's published undergraduate writings and does not seem to have survived elsewhere. Whether the Poet's poetic father found the verses satisfactory we do not know, but it is hardly conceivable that the discomfort of the son reading from the grandfather's pulpit was not increased by the consciousness that the audience listened to his performance with ears cocked to catch all strains of inherited virtue, talent, and facility. One may assume, however, that the uneasiness of that performance was quickly dissolved in the concluding festivities of the day—a "spread" under the Doctor's auspices, dancing in Harvard Hall, and finally "the farewell dance, with 'Auld Lang Syne' around the Class tree" in the College Yard.[92]

During the weeks which followed Class Day, Holmes was restlessly awaiting the results of his efforts to obtain a commission. On July 2 he wrote his autobiographical sketch in the Class Album, like others giving not only an account of his own life to date but a summary account of his ancestry. "Our family," he wrote, "has been in the habit of receiving a college education and I came of course in my turn, as my grandfathers, father, and uncles had been before me." In his concluding sentences he indicated not only the direction which ancestry had given his tastes but an indication of where he believed those tastes might, with good fortune, lead him. "The tendencies of the family and of myself have a strong bent for literature, etc., at present I am trying for a commission in one of the Massachusetts Regiments, however, and hope to go south before very long. If I survive the war I expect to study law as my profession or at least for a starting point." [93] On April 1 Holmes had withdrawn Austin's *Lectures on Jurisprudence* from the College Library and if the political crisis of the opening weeks of that month did not make its reading impossible he may have found in its pages the assurance that speculative and philosophical tastes can find satisfaction in the law. The natural next step for one who had looked into Austin would be to turn to Hobbes's *Leviathan*. We know that that step was about to be taken when an event occurred which forced its postponement. "At the beginning of July '61 I thought that I would read it," wrote Holmes in 1916. "I was walking down Beacon Street from the Athenaeum with it under my arm when as I passed the State House someone told me that the Governor had commissioned me in the 20th Mass. I returned the book and went off to Pittsfield recruiting, and thereafter into camp and to the war." [94]

This longed-for termination of the first chapter in Holmes's education apparently occurred on July 23, six days after Harvard's Commencement exercises. In view of his predominant interests at that time it is at least doubtful whether he bothered to attend those exercises and it is unlikely that he gave more than a moment's thought to the fact that the Faculty had determined that the points lost from his scale of merit while he was on his tour of duty at Fort Independence prevented his being honored either by the delivery of a "Commencement Part" or by appearing on the Commencement program among those who ranked in the first half of the Senior Class. Dr. Holmes, however, felt paternal indignation on his son's account (and, perhaps, a little on his own) and resented an application of disciplinary rules so mechanical as to disgrace a young man whose rank, had he been less patriotic, would clearly have entitled him to honors on the scale of merit. President Felton, one feels, knew the son's mind better than did the father when, in explanation of the action of the College, he said that "the faculty took it for granted that in engaging in an employment so remote from College study, for such a length of time, he had relinquished all expectation and desire of a commencement part, to secure what he considered of greater importance." [95] Although Dr. Holmes in reply stated that he had "never heard a word of complaint" from his son and that he did not suppose he had in fact bestowed "any thought upon the matter," he was far from satisfied by Felton's explanation.[96]

He left college suddenly, no doubt, but if he did not stop to kiss his Alma Mater, neither did many other volunteers stop to kiss their mothers and wives and sweethearts. He went with the expectation of going into active service, and has never ceased his military discipline and efforts to get into a post where he could serve his country. He established so good a character as a soldier that yesterday he was appointed First Lieutenant in a Company of Colonel Lee's regiment now in camp and soon to be in the field.

For his promptitude in offering his services, at the very close of his college life he is not only deprived of the honors which I know you personally wished him to obtain, as one who would not discredit the College, but is consigned to the inglorious half of the Class, standing forever on the College records as one not worthy to be named among those who had achieved a decent mediocrity. . . .

His case was entirely exceptional. Revolutions do not follow precedents nor furnish them. The enforcement of the scholastic rule in this instance seems to me harsh and unworthy of the occasion. If a great General receives an LL.D. for military services, it seems hard that a poor private or Lieutenant should be publicly humiliated,—or his friends through him,—for being too prompt in answering the call of the Commander in Chief.

In this burst of paternal patriotism, not unnatural in circumstances which clearly were more unusual than the Faculty had been willing to admit, Holmes's undergraduate association with Harvard came to its close. To that association official Harvard had contributed few values of lasting significance. In stimulating the young man's revulsion it had, to be sure, encouraged his intellectual independence and had, perhaps, hastened his effort to find a tentative formulation of his ideals. Nothing, however, had happened to lead the young man to repudiate the ideals of an inherited tradition. He had shown a desire to base those ideals on other foundations than those which New England had accepted. The ideals, however, were common to his progenitors, to his teachers, and to his contemporaries. The coming of the War offered an opportunity for their affirmation. Holmes's ideals found their strength in many elements, but not least in the young man's consciousness not only that his family had "been in the habit of securing a college education," but that those ancestors also fought in the Revolution.[97] A quotation from Plato was later used in remembrance of Harvard's dead in the Civil War; its applicability to the sons who survived is no less.[98]

Hence it is that the fathers of these men, and ours also, and themselves too, being thus nurtured, in all freedom and well-born, have shown before all men deeds many and glorious, in public and private, —deeming it their duty to fight for freedom and the Greeks, even against Greeks.

3

Civil War: Ball's Bluff through Antietam

The Twentieth Regiment, Massachusetts Volunteers, in which Holmes was commissioned on July 23, 1861,[1] was a three years' regiment, organized by Colonel William Raymond Lee, a West Point classmate of Jefferson Davis. Colonel Lee had left the Army and settled in Roxbury as a civil engineer. The Lieutenant Colonel was Francis W. Palfrey, a son of the New England historian, John Gorham Palfrey. He had been a lieutenant in Company B of the Fourth Battalion and as such had come to know something of the military qualifications of the young men who had volunteered for duty at Fort Independence. From that number Palfrey selected William Francis Bartlett and John C. Putnam as Captains. Bartlett in his turn asked for Henry L. Abbott as his 2nd Lieutenant, and Putnam requested that Norwood P. Hallowell should be his 1st Lieutenant. These officers were among the first to join the Regiment at the camp in Readville which had been set up on July 10 to receive its recruits.

The time was less auspicious for recruiting than it had been one or two months earlier, and there were serious difficulties in filling the Regiment's roster and in shaping it into an effective force. Colonel Lee later referred to a special problem which confronted the Regiment in the formative weeks at Readville: "The regiment . . . had in it elements which required strong and judicious government; the personal material which constituted its nucleus having been principally drawn from a disbanded and mutinous organization and being thus demoralized." [2] The condition of the Regiment several days after it was officially mustered into the Federal service on July 18 was so unsatisfactory that Captain Amory, the mustering officer, reported that only one third of the enlisted men were up to the standards of the average of the regiments previously mustered into the United States service. On July 23, one day after the Union defeat at Bull Run, two entire companies, officers and men, were transferred to the Nineteenth Massachusetts. It was the creation of the vacancies resulting from that transfer which brought Holmes into the Twentieth as 1st Lieutenant in Company A, under Captain Henry M. Tremlett.[3]

The Twentieth differed in significant respects from other of the Massachusetts regiments. It was not, for the most part, organized in the conventional way upon a geographical basis. In the first Massachusetts regiments each company was normally constituted of men enlisted from a single town or community. The Fifteenth, for instance, was a Worcester County regiment with companies of men from Fitchburg, Clinton, Grafton, and other towns of the county. In such organizations pride in the Commonwealth and even devotion to the nation were apt to be subordinate to the consciousness that its officers and men represented a particular locality. The healthy, if somewhat unmilitary, result was a spirit of fraternity among the officers and men. In the Twentieth, on the other hand, there was little attempt to organize companies geographically. The enlisted men came from all parts of the State and were not allocated to companies on the basis of residence. The notable exception was Company I, a group largely made up of Nantucket recruits enlisted by their fellow-townsman, 1st Lieutenant Macy, who later became Colonel of the Regiment. Insular pride led these men, on their arrival in Boston, to march to camp singing their own version of "The Raw Recruit":

> I'm a raw recruit with a bran new suit
> One Hundred dollars bounty.
> I'm going down to Washington
> To fight for Nantucket County.[4]

Two other companies, B and C, were made up entirely of German immigrants, commanded originally by their compatriots, Ferdinand Dreher and John Herchenroder. Holmes's Harvard Instructor in German, George A. Schmitt, was Captain of another company constituted in part of Germans. The somewhat conglomerate character of the Regiment as a whole was significantly qualified by the fact that the majority of its officers came from a Harvard background out of the leading families of the Commonwealth.

The basis upon which the Regiment was organized explains in large measure the special problems which troubled its whole existence. The bond of localism did not hold the Regiment together as firmly as it did so many others; Company I might fight for Nantucket County but others shared no sustaining provincialism. A distinctly mixed fidelity to the Commander-in-Chief of the Commonwealth, Governor John A. Andrew, was a poor substitute for local pride. Captain Shepard, with some exaggeration, perhaps, spoke of himself as the only officer in the Regiment who supported the Governor and the cause of the Civil War and stated that his brother officers "hated and cursed" Governor Andrew "hour in and hour out in camp." [5] To those like Hallowell and Holmes and their German fellow-officers Schmitt and Dreher, who went to war with some of the crusading temper, the Governor's ardent Republicanism and antislavery convictions gave reassurance that the wartime objectives of Massachusets were enlightened. But Captain Bartlett, whose first sympathies were with the South, and Lieutenant Abbott, who was proud to think that the Twentieth was known as the Copperhead Regiment,[6] had little reason to think of themselves as fighting for the ends which inspired their Governor. In November 1863, Major Charles A. Whittier, Holmes's fellow officer both with the Twentieth and later at the Sixth Corps Headquarters, wrote to him of the recent elections. He was eager to express his regret at the defeat of the Copperhead candidates in the different states.[7]

We have but two parties, Union (republicans, abolitionists, contractors & liberal generals promoted for merit) and Copperheads (democrats, opposers of the war, all McClellan men, commanders of departments like Schenck, Milroy & Fremont & many others whose recommendations for promotion & high places lie in military ability). I am a Copperhead.

As the War progressed, those officers who shared the opinions of Whittier, Abbott, and Bartlett developed increasing admiration for the officers of the Regular Army. The Regulars did not serve in order that they might contribute to the achievement of certain defined objectives, whether political or humane, but because they were professional soldiers who had chosen the career of arms. It was not surprising that young men who joined the Union forces as volunteers without a burning hatred of slavery, without confidence in Lincoln, and uncertain whether or not secession was lawful should make the standards of the professional soldier their own. The standards were attractive partly because tradition said they measured courage and modesty and partly because they provided a fixed point of reference. The standards were the same in times of adversity and in times of success; they did not alter as the objectives of the Government or the motives of commanders changed. Those other volunteers, like Holmes and Hallowell, who joined the Union forces because their cause was just, of necessity found larger complexities in their situation than did Abbott, Bartlett, and Whittier. Their engagement was of such a character that the course of politics and the direction of Union aspiration must affect the intensity of their commitment. This did not mean, of course, that the standards which sustained the officers who had volunteered as neutral combatants in the moral and constitutional crusade did not also strengthen Holmes and Hallowell. Surely they did. With Holmes and Hallowell, however, the standards of the professional soldier at the outset constituted, as it were, a line of defense, not a motivating force.

Though the purposes which led these young men to volunteer differed, the majority of the officers came into the service molded by similar influences and blessed by similar advantages. It was not surprising that other officers in the Twentieth who did not come from the same world as the contingent of Harvard officers saw that group as privileged. There were some who felt that Copperhead sympathies dominated the affairs of the Regiment and made it faithless to its trust.[8] General Devens warned Lieutenant Colonel Palfrey, while he was commanding the Regiment, that "the sooner you get this blue-blood notion out of your head the better for yourself and your Regiment," [9] and Governor Andrew expressed the fear that, in Colonel Lee's absence, merit, within the Twentieth, "yields to favor" and that it had become "the private property of a few neighbors, or of a mere clique." [10] The charges probably had some justification in the early years of the Regiment's existence. That they were well founded did not mean, however, that the Harvard group did not serve with extraordinary gallantry and courage. The standards by which its members measured their achievements required of each that he prove his bravery and his modesty, for in that proof might lie the refutation of the charge that privileged Copperheads did not deserve positions of command. Though Holmes was not among the Copperheads he was one of those who seemed to be favored by his commanding officer.[a] Whether he acknowledged the tendency of his group of friends to become a clique, and if he did, whether he regretted it, we do not know. It is abundantly clear, however, that as the experience of war engulfed him his greatest loyalty and his greatest admiration were given to those associates who made gallantry their ideal and who cared little for the constitutional and moral cause for which they fought.

[a] One of the most vehement critics of Regimental policies was Ferdinand Dreher, an officer of German birth who had served as a Major with the revolutionary forces in Germany in 1848. In Dec. 1862, he protested to Governor Andrew when Captain Macy, in violation of rules of seniority, was named Acting Major of the Regiment. "Since the battle of Ball's Bluff," wrote Captain Dreher, "the Regiment was officered by young men, belonging to a certain aristocratic clique. Not only we German officers in the Regiment were made to feel it, there is Captain Shepard and Lieut. Murphy . . . who have to tell the same history." He then named the officers who constituted the controlling clique. The leaders, he said, were Lieutenants Mason, Patten, and Milton, and Captain Macy. "The members of it are Captain Holmes, Lieutenant Ropes, Lieutenant Abbott, and the tools are Capt. Cabot and Lieut. Wilkins." As an ex-Prussian soldier he had small regard for the military competence of the officers whom he named. "I would take all the military sciences out of this gentlemen and put them in a private, and it would *not make* the best Sergeant we have." Executive Department Letters [State Archives], #157.

Naturally enough the official history of the Twentieth [11] says nothing of the political and social tensions by which the Regiment was distracted during its first year and a half in the field. There was heroism enough within each faction to let reciprocal suspicions be washed out in pride for what the Regiment as a whole had done. Certainly the fortitude of Captain Dreher was questioned by nobody, and, if he had small regard for the military capacities of the aristocratic young officers, he could not fairly have denied that Harvard had contributed its full share of dead and wounded to the rolls of the Regiment. Colonel Palfrey suffered such wounds at Antietam that he was compelled to leave the service and ultimately died of them; [12] Captain Bartlett, after losing a leg, left the Twentieth to become Colonel of the Fifty-seventh Massachusetts and later Brigadier General, in which capacities he again distinguished himself for bravery; Macy lost a hand at Gettysburg yet returned to duty as Colonel; Major Abbott was killed in the Wilderness, Lieutenant Ropes at Gettysburg, and Captain Cabot at Fredericksburg. The young aristocrats, however distrustful they may have been of the cause for which they fought, showed to themselves and to the world that their heroic capacities were no less than those of believing men and of men who had known fewer advantages.

Surviving records do not tell many facts of Holmes's affiliations of sympathy and friendship with the officers and men of the Twentieth. His periods of convalescence from wounds chanced to take him out of the field at times when the antagonisms were most intense and he was thus not personally involved in the disputes. His personal affection for the Copperheads Henry Abbott and Charles Whittier must have been founded on some basic sympathy, yet his friendship for the abolitionist Hallowell was equally ardent. Unfortunately, we know little of his relations with the men under his command. His admiration for his Sergeant, Gustave Magnitzky, indicates that artificial barriers of rank did not stand in the way of friendship and affection. Magnitzky, after the War, became chief clerk in Holmes's office and when he died in 1910, Holmes paid tribute to his memory.[13]

Our friendship had lasted for nearly fifty years. He was my First Sergeant when I commanded Company G of the Twentieth Massachusetts in the Civil War, he having recently come to this country from Polish Prussia and having gone into the army upon principle and because of his sympathy with the cause. We made many a heart-breaking march and were in many a battle together and his gallantry and efficiency gained him a commission in a regiment in which a sergeant had to be a fighting man to keep his chevrons and an unusual man to gain the shoulderstraps. . . . Quiet and steady under fire, quiet and effective in camp, modest, distinguished in bearing and soul, Captain Magnitzky was a type of the great regiment in which he served.

The day on which Holmes was commissioned 1st Lieutenant in the Twentieth, July 10, 1861, was the day on which the first elements of the Regiment pitched their tents at Camp Massasoit in Readville. Holmes evidently did not join his Company at once, but was sent to Pittsfield as recruiting officer.[14] There Holmes was among friends, for Pittsfield had been the scene of his boyhood summers for seven years, and now in the family of Robert Pomeroy there were two daughters, the elder of whom, Agnes, was evidently a particular favorite of the Lieutenant's. She was destined, however, to become the wife of his fellow-officer, William Francis Bartlett. Regimental records do not indicate when Holmes joined the Regiment at Readville, though they tell us that on July 22 he was ordered to join Company A under Captain Tremlett.[15]

The duties to which Holmes was assigned when he joined his Regiment at Readville were those of quickly putting the unorganized unit into shape for active duty. The ranks were still thin and the men but slightly trained.[16] One of the enlisted veterans of the Regiment thirty years after the war described the arrival of himself and other recruits at Readville in terms which suggest that the men of the Twentieth had much to learn.

After We Got our Uniforms and went into boston and had Quite A time and When We Went back We Ware put in GH but was thair only a few howrs When orders Came if any of the 20th Rigt was thair to Release them as the had orders to send us to the Frount the was about 25 Recutes of Us thair for the 20 Mass. . . .

In his reminiscences the old veteran went on to say that later he learned that Captain Abbott was "a Verry fine Soldier . . . and so was Holmes that is now Judge in Boston. . . . The both of them liked to fight." [17] By mid-August the ranks were still thin and untrained, yet the Regiment was put on the alert for orders to follow other Massachusetts regiments to Washington. An occasional leave and visits from family and friends provided hurried interludes in a busy and strenuous routine.

On September 2 the expected orders came, directing the Regiment in two days to proceed to Washington. At four o'clock on the afternoon of the 4th "the Regiment was drawn up in line of battle on the parade ground, and Mr. H. B. Sargent in the stead of Governor Andrew, gave us a standard and made us a long and tiresome speech, not quite so bad as the one Col. Ritchie made when he presented the 4th Bat. at Fort Independence with a flag in behalf of the Ladies of Boston . . . [but] close to it." [18] Unlike other regiments, the Twentieth did not have the opportunity of parading on the Boston Common before entraining for the South, but immediately after Mr. Sargent's speech, boarded the train at Readville. A member of Company H there announced that "he proposed to throw his New Testament from the car window to the first pretty girl he should see." Though the Regiment later passed through New York and Philadelphia it was not until it reached Wilmington, Delaware, that the soldier felt compelled to make his sacrifice to beauty.[19] At Groton, Connecticut, the Regiment was transferred to the steamer *Commodore*. The following day it disembarked in New York where a dinner for the Regiment was provided by the Sons of Massachusetts at the Park Barracks.[20] Governor Andrew was on hand to greet the Regiment with the speech which he had been unable to deliver at Readville. He evidently did the Commonwealth proud.[21]

He kept the house in a complete tempest, and when he referred to even the possibility of Baltimore, Philadelphia and New York yielding, and of our men giving away, and said that in such an event Massachusetts would entrench herself behind the hills of Berkshire and make the Switzerland of New England the rampart of freedom, the whole mass came up to their feet and made a response that drew men from Broadway up on to the iron railings to see what was going on in the Park Barracks at that particular time.

Some of the officers, inculcated, perhaps, with Harvard's indifference, showed less concern for oratory than did the passers-by on Broadway. "The room where the officers were to dine was filled with vulgar looking reporters" and Holmes, with other friends, dined in greater privacy and luxury at Delmonico's.[22] One of the special responsibilities of the officers seems to have been to inspect the canteens of the enlisted men and to empty in City Hall Park all which contained whiskey.[23] The precaution, though it may have made the journey to Philadelphia easier for the officers than it might otherwise have been, did not solve the problem permanently, for when the troops arrived at an enthusiastic reception in Philadelphia, a number of the soldiers "got exceedingly drunk." [24] From there, where undoubtedly Holmes had at least a glimpse of the Hallowell family which was to offer him so many hospitalities in later and grimmer stages of the war, the Regiment moved on to Baltimore by train. Since the Sixth Massachusetts had been fired on by a mob on April 19, all Regiments marched between the railroad stations with some uneasiness. The Twentieth was no exception; it passed through the city "with our state flag unfurled and rifles loaded." [25] With the exception, however, of two or three boys who gave faint cheers for General Scott, "everything was totally quiet." [26]

Arriving in Washington by cattle cars, the Regiment spent its first hours at the Soldier's Retreat near the Capitol, then marched out Pennsylvania Avenue to Camp Kalorama at Georgetown Heights. From there Holmes wrote to his mother telling of the trip from Readville and of his first hours in and about Washington. The passage, he said, "was very long and there was very little sleep or food," but, despite fatigue he had rather enjoyed it. The future, he thought, looked propitious and, either in his innocence or in a desire to encourage those at home, said that he thought the Regiment had "seen the worst of hardships, unless on special occasions." [27] The young man's thoughts, in recent weeks, had evidently not been of war only, for at some interlude in his hurried weeks of training he had found the opportunity to write a sonnet which he asked his parents to send on to the Pomeroys in Pittsfield and to his classmate Charles M. Walton of Philadelphia. Among the Civil War letters which Holmes preserved there is a sonnet, in his handwriting, which seems probably to have been the poem referred to in this letter. If it is, one can see why his classmates had believed his talents qualified him to be Class Poet in the previous June.

> Lost and long-wandering at last I brake
> From a deep forest's sullen-opening jaws,
> Where hungry junipers stretched bony claws
> Like traps of devils, baited with a snake—
> And all around the dark rocks seemed to take
> Forbidden shapes of things that man outlaws,
> Speckled like toads, and patched with all the flaws
> Of stormy days, and lichen-ringed, and black—
> Then wearied out—"Is there no hope?" I cried—
> Hearken—A soft melodious rapture thrills
> As from the forest's deepest heart replied
> Their hermit—and the music multiplied
> And rose reechoing upward far and wide
> From the dark valleys to the sunlit hills—

Having begun to settle in some comfort at Camp Kalorama on the 7th and 8th, the Regiment on the 9th was ordered to move back closer to Washington, and accordingly packed up and marched again, this time to Camp Burnside on Meridian Hill overlooking the city. Holmes's letter to his mother from there gives an account of the circumstances at Camp Burnside and indications of how briefly the Regiment was to be permitted to enjoy its interlude of tranquillity.[28]

Camp Burnside
Washington
Sept. 11, 1861

My Dear Mother

We are right in the midst of the work now—all sorts of camps around us—military discipline—and a regular soldier's life. We officers live on what we can get, buying milk, eggs, and lots of pies; (peach & apple, price—12½) now getting meat & again not. On the whole we have had a very comfortable time however. Last night we pitched our tents here, the most beautiful place we have been at either here or in Mass. Tomorrow morning we have marching orders again with one ration in the haversacks. Destination will be known after we have started. We are under Gen. Lander (a first rate man they say). . . .[29] The Col. is ranking Co. & it is said will be made Brig. General—this is not settled to my knowledge. Bartlett, just come in, says we are to support Genl Lander's HeadQr's on this side the River who asked for our Reg't (a big compliment). This may be changed however.

In sight of where we are is the unfinished Capitol & from the neighboring Camp we hear the Bugle calls going all day.

Today we heard cannonading for 4 or 5 hrs & it is said there has been an engagement.——Now in comes Tremlett & gives another story of our destination. So I guess it's nowhither in particular. In the meanwhile I feel *very* well & in *very* good spirits and I think I am learning as I certainly am trying—I wish I could write details of our life but I am too impatient & have too little time to write long letters. However, God bless you my darling. I love you just as much as if I talked more with my mouth. God bless daddy too & love to the babbies.

I write again soon.

Yours my dear
O. W. Holmes, Jr.

On the day after Holmes wrote this letter the Regiment started on the contemplated march to join General Lander in Stone's Corps of Observation. Captain Bartlett in a letter to his family told of the fate of that march.

We had tents struck, baggage packed, and knapsacks slung, and had reached the foot of the hill on which our camp was pitched, when an aide-de-camp of General Lander rode up at full speed, and asked for the Colonel. I directed him, and in a moment the word came down the line, "Column halt!" The order for crossing the river there had been countermanded, and we were to start for Poolesville, up the river towards Harper's Ferry. We countermarched, and started up the main road. . . . We made about nine miles over an uneven road, and at night bivouacked under the starlit skies.[30]

The march to the northwestward from Washington to Poolesville took three days, giving the Regiment its first mild taste of conditions in the field. The complement of two wagons to each company, in which were carried "trunks, iron bedsteads, mattresses, mess chests, bath tubs, and many other absurdities" had not yet been reduced to its later limit of one wagon for each regiment.[31] It is doubtful, however, whether on the march to Poolesville wagons were emptied of their more luxurious contents. "It now began to look more like my idea of an army on the march," wrote Captain Bartlett of the second day's progress, "now fording a shallow stream and now climbing a long, steep, and rocky hill." [32] At length, and after a false alarm that rebel cavalry had crossed the Potomac, the Regiment reached Poolesville on September 14 where it joined other units under the command of General Stone. The chief responsibility of the forces at Poolesville was to keep an eye on the activities of the Confederate forces across the river in the neighborhood of Leesburg. Lieutenant Edward G. Abbott, of the Second Massachusetts which passed through Poolesville a day after the Twentieth arrived, wrote to his father telling of the visit he had paid to the Twentieth and to his brother Henry. As a member of an older Regiment he looked down his nose a little at the younger, but his description of the condition of the Twentieth is probably substantially accurate.

They had an air of neatness and discipline, which appeared very soldierlike. They did look as if they had been sent off in a hurry though. I think the officers were dressed pretty scrubbily. Some of them even had on citizens clothing. . . . The officers are all green and appear as I have no doubt we appeared when we first came on thinking a fight was going to take place every five minutes. They actually believed that they were going to march to meet 30,000 men that very night.[33]

Within the Twentieth, however, there was ample confidence in its generally superior quality. The officer who described a captain in the Second Regiment, New York Volunteers, as "a vulgar, illiterate brute from New York City" had not lost the Bostonian's pleasing sense of superiority.[34]

The duties of the Twentieth in its camp at Poolesville, in addition to making up for lost training time, included outpost and picket duty on the banks of the Potomac near Edwards Ferry. The firing between the opposing pickets, for the most part, seems to have been done in the friendliest spirit and the occasional death or wounding of a picket on either side might have been considered almost accidental. Not only were the home papers of the respective forces exchanged midstream, but invitations to dine with the enemy were tendered and accepted: "I just learned," wrote one of the pickets in the Fifteenth Massachusetts, "that one of the Mississippians is coming over in a boat to take dinner with the Leominster boys today." [35] Casual as hostilities may have been, the duties of the Regiment were more exciting than any previously assigned to it, and there was always the likelihood that war would begin in earnest. Holmes's response to these first experiences on the brink of combat is revealed in his letter to his mother of September 23.[36]

My Dear Mother

This has been an eventful week to me as it has been the first that really looked like biz. Last Wednesday we (our company & Bartlett's) were suddenly ordered to fall in, pack up blankets & overcoats, received a number of rounds of cartridges and after a brief speech from Gen. Lander were sent marching off, we didn't know whither. The General merely signified we had a post of honor & must do our duty. Well we first tramped off a couple of miles to Edward's Ferry and then across country—couldn't find the place—so back to ferry—circumbendibus by night—arrive at last at an advanced battery of ours (Rhode Island) whence firing had taken place the day before. In silence we settle in a grove and lie down to pass the night as best may be. I had carried my invaluable carpet bag, Whittier [37] his blankets which we shared. A drizzle & brief rain increased the liveliness of this first experience as groundlings (we had out our bedsteads on the march from Washington to where we now are, you remember). But we were very tired & slept pretty well. Well, to cut it short, for, as usual, I irk the lengthened tale when told with pen—we stayed at the place till Saturday evening doing duty as an outpost near to the river, our pickets extending down to it & communicating with those of a Minnesota Reg. stationed along the banks of the muddy Potomac. The first morning my eager eyes descry one man in a straw hat sitting unconcernedly on his tail, apparently a guard on duty for the seceshers. Men & horses are seen from time to time from the tops of the trees and within cannon shot off to our right grows up from day to day an encampment with earthworks and what may be a heavy gun or so but of the last we are not sure. But firing across the river is forbidden so we sit & look & listen to their drums. . . . To the rear of our hill & woods is a secesher's house where we eat & paid (.37) for delicious dinners of goose & icecream &c, but the artillerymen hooked his pigs, geese, &c (for wh. their Lieut. commanding had to come down pretty well & got a reprimand to boot). This secesher has since been arrested for signalizing by lights from his house but evidence seems inconclusive & I guess he'll be released. The last night we were there we slept in our boots & kept a horse saddled but though an attack would have used us up I think we were about as safe in their intentions as you were.

Capt. Crowninshield's Co. & that of Capt. Walleston [38] relieved us, unwilling to leave goose & laziness, on Saturday evening—I had that day a touch of diarrhea from drinking to [*sic*] much milk on guard the night before—which soured on my stomach & did not improve the results of wet & lying on the ground without a blanket—an experiment you need be at no fears of my repeating. I'm as well as ever now though. Flour & water is an excellent & safe specific. This was a mere touch & before & since I've been *very* well—& weigh 136 lb. Last night (Sunday), or rather in the afternoon about four o'cl'k, we again bundled down—this time the whole reg't except the aforesaid two companies—to Edwards Ferry—there being news that the Rebels had crossed—we slept in our clothes at the Ferry all night—most of the officers at a buggy (bed—& spider) house, I in the middle of the road—Tremlett leaving me in charge. I secured a convenient slant & took a canteen for pillow but it was cold as the tenth circle of Inferno. It seems wonderful though that I mind the exposures little as I do—I get on as well as the average of the men I should say. They were jumping round at a great rate to get warm. I had a conviction there'd be no trouble & there wasn't so at 5 A.M. this morning home we pack again. All these things you see give reality to the life but I don't expect any fighting for the present—It seems so queer to see an encampment & twig men through a glass & think they are our enemies & hear some of our pickets talking across & so on. But I must get some sleep tonight, to make up for last & it gets late. I long for letters—write all of you all the time. The mails are irregular & the last I got was the one containing C. Walton's letter. You ask me if I like letters like yours. I delight in 'em. They are my great pleasure. Remember once for all that all details like those I've written of our actual or probable movements are strictly private as we are strongly forbidden to write about such things.[39] Love to everyone. Bestest love to Dadkin—also to A & N. Let them write. . . .

Goodnight my loveliest & sweetest

O. W. Holmes, Jr.

Later in the War Holmes liked to startle the young ladies of Boston by describing war as "an organized bore." [40] In the first weeks at Poolesville there surely was sufficient organization of the training activities to justify the adjective in Holmes's aphorism. Men who shut their eyes when they pulled the trigger had to be taught the advantages of vision; men, and officers too, had to be taught that after taps the rule of silence was to be observed; and the sixty-three recruits who had joined the Regiment since it left Massachusetts had to be taught the school of the soldier which their predecessors had begun to master.[41] Colonel Lee was a vigorous disciplinarian who demanded of officers and men something of the proficiency and precision to which he had become accustomed in his days in the Regular Army. Yet he was sufficiently understanding of the concern of parents to write to Dr. Holmes on October 9 telling him of the "fortitude, patience and cheerful submission to privation" which "the boy officers" had shown. "Within the last hour," he concluded, "I have visited an outpost—Ricket's Battery supported by Company A—near the river, where I was greeted by your soldier boy with one of his pleasant smiles." [42]

It is doubtful whether during these first weeks in the field Holmes found the military life the bore which later he proclaimed it to be. The picket from the Twentieth who, not recognizing General Stone as the man making a reconnaissance along the canal, bawled out: "God damn you! If you don't come back and give an account of yourself, I'll blow your damned head off," [43] was undoubtedly a nuisance to his commanding officer, but organization had scarcely become a bore at that stage of regimental growth. Doubtless Holmes would have preferred to be living in times when duty did not require the devotion of his energies, as pupil and teacher, to military training, yet his letters suggest that there was some excitement and some interest to be found in the uncertain novelties of life at Poolesville.

While routine was following this not unpleasant course the storm of war broke with fury upon the Twentieth. The battle of Ball's Bluff was, to be sure, a distinctly minor engagement. It was a needless and a mismanaged encounter in which no significant objective would have been gained had it succeeded and which, in the losing, cost the raw Union troops casualties far exceeding the value of the lesson which the battle taught them. Had it been less disastrous it might not, of course, have been the last of the amateur battles,[44] and it may, therefore, have had a ghastly utility. The engagement was brought on by the Union effort to learn whether there was truth in the rumored departure of the Confederate forces from Leesburg on the west bank of the Potomac. A detachment of the Fifteenth Massachusetts, under Colonel Devens, supported by Companies I and D of the Twentieth, on October 20 crossed the Potomac a few miles above Edwards Ferry. At the point of crossing, Harrison's Island lay in midstream, affording a useful steppingstone across the river. With completely inadequate boats to support the forces, other elements of the Twentieth, together with Colonel Baker's California Regiment (of Philadelphia) and the Nineteenth Massachusetts and Tammany Regiments, piled across the river, no one knowing with any accuracy what forces were opposed to them, and took up their positions in an open field at the top of the steep bluff on the western bank of the Potomac. On October 21 "at two o'clock the officers of the Twentieth were all assembled, and sat smoking under a tree . . . telling the story of the morning's work; when, all of a sudden we heard a shot fired, and Captain Dreher, experienced in war, said, 'Well,

Gentlemen, I advise you all to go to your companies,' which we did at once." [45] The companies fell in, with Company A in the front rank.

> Col. Baker, a fine old man, acting Brigadier, Senator from Oregon . . . rode up on a large horse, looking so nobly and said: "Where's Col. Lee—Col. Lee I congratulate you on having a chance to meet these fellows at last. Boys, how are you? Are you ready for work?" "Yes, Yes," was the answer on all sides. . . . Here we were in the open field & the rebels all out of sight completely protected, nothing to cover us. Behind us a bank going to the river, abrupt, rocky, woody . . . , and only one boat capable of carrying 40 or 50 men.[46]

Captain Bartlett's account of the battle tells details of an engagement which became one of the most vivid in the memories of its survivors.[47]

> Well the first volley came and the balls flew like hail. . . . The whizzing of balls was a new sensation. I had read so much about being under fire that I was curious to experience it. I had a fair chance. . . . The men now began to drop around me; most of them were lying down in the first of it, being ordered to keep in reserve. . . . One poor fellow near me was struck in the hip while lying flat, and rose to go to the rear, when another struck him on the head and knocked him over. I felt that if I was going to be hit, I should be, whether I stood up or lay down, so I stood up and walked around, stepping over them and talking to them in a joking way, to take away their thoughts from the bullets, and keep them more self possessed. I was surprised at first at my own coolness. I never felt better, although I expected of course that I should feel the lead every second, and I was wondering where it would take me. I kept speaking to Little [Abbott], surprised that he was not hit amongst this rain of bullets. I said two or three times "Why Lit., aren't you hit yet?" I remember Macy was lying where the grass was turned up, and I "roughed" him for getting his coat so awfully dirty. Lit. was as cool and brave as I knew he would be. The different companies began to wilt away under this terrible fire. Still there was no terror among the men; they placed *implicit confidence* in their officers (I refer to our regiment particularly), and you could see that now was the time they respected and looked up to them.
>
> We were driven back inch by inch, towards the top of the

bank. . . . General Baker was standing near me at about four o'clock; he seemed indifferent to bullets. He said it was of no use, it was all over with us. A few minutes after, he fell, struck by eight bullets *all at once;* so you can judge by this how thick they flew. No one took command after he fell; in fact the battle was lost some time before. At this time I came upon Captain Dreher; he was shot through the head in the upper part of his cheek. . . . The field now began to look like my preconceived idea of a battle field. The ground was smoking and covered with blood, while the noise was perfectly deafening. Men were lying under foot, and here and there a horse struggling in death. Coats and guns were strewn over the ground in all directions. I went to the Colonel who was sitting behind a tree, perfectly composed. He told me there was nothing to be done but "surrender and save the men from being murdered." Most of the men had not got down the bank. I thought it over in my mind, and reasoned that we might as well be shot advancing on the enemy, as to be slaughtered like sheep at the foot of the bank.

It was after an hour of active combat that Holmes was wounded. In after years he mentioned the fact that he was "a devilish sight more scared in later engagements" than he was at Ball's Bluff "when one was keyed up to meet the unknown." [48] Perhaps the example of Bartlett and Abbott contributed also to Holmes's fortitude. Lieutenant Whittier of Holmes's Company wrote of the battle to Dr. Holmes on the day after its close.[49]

The California Brigade behaved poorly, and in the thick of the fight as I look around, I see none in action but ourselves. I am standing close by the Colonel. Wendell is 6 or 8 feet from me. He falls over but rises immediately. Has been struck by a *spent* ball in the stomach. Nothing. He goes on. We advance, fire, fall back & load on our bellies. The Capt. [Tremlett] calls me. His coat is torn open right on the heart. His too, thank God, is a spent ball & no damage is inflicted. Soon Wendell is struck in the breast, twice, I believe & is carried off. Dr. Revere sees him & he is carried back to the island. Firing continues—I can tell you little more. . . . We carried twenty-two officers to the battle. 9 returned unharmed.

The further activities of the Regiment and of Captain Bartlett and Lieutenants Abbott and Whittier who managed not only to escape the battle unscratched, but to see that some eighty enlisted men of the various regiments got safely back to Harrison's Island, need not concern us. Their good fortune and their prowess became traditions of the Twentieth. The capture of Colonel Lee removed him from his command until the spring of 1862, and thus put the Regiment in charge of Lieutenant Colonel Palfrey.

The officers and men wounded on the Bluff, when taken to Harrison's Island, were carried from chaos to confusion. Temporary hospital facilities had been set up in two abandoned houses on the Island and there Nathan Hayward, Surgeon of the Twentieth, and Dr. Haven of the Fifteenth did what they could for the stream of wounded which began to flow in upon them in the middle of the afternoon. Dr. Hayward in a letter to his father told of the problems with which the doctors were confronted.[50]

Our greatest difficulty was to induce men to carry the wounded to the river. The Tammany men behaved disgracefully. . . . The Musicians on the 15th Mass. Regt. also showed the white feather, refused duty and ran away. . . . It was thought the Secessionists might shell the Island at daybreak, and it was therefore desirable to remove all the wounded to the Maryland shore before morning. By tearing down all the doors in . . . two houses we succeeded in getting litters enough to take every wounded man down to the shore. . . . All those employed in the early part of the evening to move the litters took the opportunity of crossing themselves, and did not return. No order or discipline existed in the boats; they were filled with the strongest and most impudent, and started leaving the poor wounded behind. When I reached the shore, there lay 16 poor wounded fellows, including three of our own officers, who had been lying, some of them, two hours in a drizzling rain. We succeeded in getting a boat, and putting all our 16 into it, having laid straw in the bottom of the boat which was wet and muddy. . . . It was necessary to show my revolver to keep off intruders. . . . And many a man of our side, that day, was threatened by his officers and in some instances struck with the sword. We reached the Maryland side without difficulty, pulling the scow over by a rope which had been stretched across. . . . When we reached the shore . . . we could get none of the lazy Pennsylvanians, who occupied the bank, to lift a hand to help us, in spite of objurgations. . . . We got them at

8. *Undated pencil sketch by Holmes, probably about 1860*

9. Major Henry L. Abbott

length into a canal boat which lay in readiness with Dr. Bryant [Assistant Surgeon of the Twentieth] on board. . . . Once on board the canal boat, we got down to Edwards Ferry without difficulty.

After reaching Edwards Ferry it was but a relatively short journey overland to Camp Benton near Poolesville where more adequate hospital facilities were available. It was from there that Holmes sent his mother his own first report of the events of two days before.[51]

[20th Regiment Hospital, Camp Benton]
"*Wed:* Oct. 23 1861

My Dear Mother

Here I am flat on my back after our first engagement—wounded but pretty comfortable. I can't write an account now but I felt and acted very cool and did my duty I am sure—I was out in front of our men encouraging 'em on when a spent shot knocked the wind out of me & I fell—then I crawled to the rear a few paces & rose by help of the 1st Sergt; & the Colonel who was passing said "That's right Mr. Holmes—Go to the Rear" but I felt that I couldn't without more excuse so up I got and rushed to the front where hearing the Col. cheering the men on I waved my sword and asked if none would follow me when down I went again by the Colonel's side. The first shot (the spent ball) struck me on the belly below where the ribs separate & bruised & knocked the wind out of me—The second time I hope only one ball struck me entering the left & coming out behind the right breast in wh. case I shall probably recover and this view is seconded by finding a ball in my clothes by the right hand wound—I may be hit twice in which case the chance is not so good—But I am now so well that I have good hopes—The first night I made up my mind to die & was going to take that little bottle of laudanum as soon as I was sure of dying with any pain—but the doctors told me not to take it, and now seem to think I have a fair *chance*. God bless you and all my friends. Whatever happens I am very happy in the conviction I did my duty handsomely—Lt. Putnam is dead, Capt. Putnam lost his right arm. Hallowell fought like a brick but wasn't hurt—Schmidt [*sic*] badly wounded—Lowell wounded—Colonel Major & Adjutant probably prisoners, Babo & Wesselhoeft probably dead [52]—Dreher shot through the head—Sergt Merchant shot dead (in the head). From a third to a half of our company killed wounded & prisoners.

I have written a few details if you can read 'em [53]—Men are concentrating in all directions and fighting still going on—They begun by cutting up the 20th. Only 8 officers out of 22 in our Regt got home unhurt. I hope we'll lick 'em yet though—I was hit in the beginning of the fight,

Yours Always
O W Holmes Jr

I can't send a good looking note lying on my back—But I believe Whit. has written you [54]

The son's report was quickly followed by other encouraging letters to Dr. and Mrs. Holmes. General Banks on the 24th had visited the hospital at Camp Benton and found young Holmes "so patient, so cheerful, and withal so full of manly spirit" that he had given the General "quite an elevation—in Yankee phrase 'a lift.' " [55] On October 26 Lieutenant Colonel Palfrey wrote of favorable progress: "Today I found him smoking and deriving much satisfaction from the contemplation of the photographs of certain young ladies. He declared that to look at the portrait of Miss Agassiz was like having an angel in the tent." [56] Despite the manifest seriousness of his son's wound, Dr. Holmes must have found satisfaction in all personal expressions of admiration for the bravery that his boy and his boy's regiment had shown. Nor was the Doctor likely to regret the public recognition that the young man bearing his name had behaved gallantly. When The Lounger in *Harper's Weekly* pulled out the stops of northern pride Dr. Holmes may well have preened himself.[57]

Through the tears with which friends and lovers read the story of Edwards's Ferry they can still smile upon the bravery of the Massachusetts boys. In the front of fearful fire, with no means of retreat, with every chance against them, those young men stood serene, each man a hero. . . . Lieutenant Holmes, said the first brief despatch, "wounded in the breast": not in the back; no, not in the back. In the breast is Massachusetts wounded, if she is struck. Forward she falls, if she falls dead.

Good news of progress made parental pride a legitimate indulgence. On October 31 the son was moved to the house of the Hallowell family in Philadelphia,[58] and a few days later Dr. William Hunt wrote a detailed letter to Dr. Holmes giving medical facts in the greatest detail concerning the wound. Probably the Doctor's professional understanding kept him from worrying unduly over the account, but it is doubtful whether Mrs. Holmes was able easily to disregard the gruesome features of Dr. Hunt's account.

> The cavity, when I first saw it [was] filled with venous blood, (probably from oozing) which on pressure was discharged through the opening to the left. Pus and a small quantity of clotted blood have now replaced the blood above spoken of. . . . Ausculation & percussion indicate no involvement of the thoracic viscera. Now Sir you can judge from this description what a narrow escape your son has had from immediate death, and also what trouble may yet occur, as the cavity of which I speak is separated from important parts by a very thin partition.[59]

Though Dr. Hunt advised the father that he saw no need for him to come to Philadelphia, the Doctor could not be kept away. On November 8 he wrote to Mrs. Holmes from Philadelphia to reassure her that he "found W. looking finely—fat and in good spirits." After consultation with Dr. Hunt it was decided that the trip could safely be made to Boston, with a stopover at the Fifth Avenue Hotel in New York. The Doctor closed his letter with the suggestion that the wounded son should on his arrival have his sister's room.[60] On the same day a telegram to Mrs. Holmes told her that husband and son had safely reached New York and would arrive in Boston on the next afternoon and that a coach should meet them at the Worcester depot.[61]

In later life Holmes spoke of Dr. Hayward's division of the world into external and internal men.[62] Stories of battles and of gallantry are likely to leave the impression that their heroes are what the regimental surgeon would have classed as external men. If the college career of Holmes reveals anything of his quality, it indicates that his most telling capacities were those of that other type—the internal man who believes "that ideas are more interesting than things." [63] War did not make any fundamental change in Holmes's character. The letters to his mother which have already been quoted do not, to be sure, indicate that Holmes was reflecting seriously upon the validity under fire of the principles of conduct which he had begun to formulate as an undergraduate. Young men, particularly perhaps, young New Englanders, do not easily reveal such reflections to their parents, and it is not surprising that in the first letters to his mother Holmes wrote of nothing but the external aspects of his experience. He reserved for a private Diary, kept sporadically during the Civil War but evidently somewhat later than in its opening months, the record of the inner aspects of his ordeal.[64] The story of Ball's Bluff which he there recorded is a far more interesting story of the battle and its immediate aftermath than any which the military histories relate. As an account of the response of a young mind to the tests which sudden disaster had put upon philosophy, it is an extraordinarily vivid piece of autobiography. Holmes left behind him no other writing which speaks with such simplicity of the relation of conduct and faith, of practice and of theory.[65]

There are a great many things of course,—thoughts, occupations & events—of which I wish I'd kept Memoranda during my past life—But I wish especially that after the military affairs—battles etc. in which I've been concerned I had noted many of those facts which so rapidly escape the memory in the mist which settles over a fought field.

Wound at Ball's Bluff.

Not to speak of while the fight was actually going on, I have been struck with the intensity of the mind's action and its increased suggestiveness, after one has received a wound—

At Ball's Bluff, Tremlett's boy George told me, I was hit at 4½ P.M., *the heavy firing having begun about an hour before, by the watch*—I felt as if a horse had kicked me and went over—1st Sergt. Smith grabbed me and lugged me to the rear a little way & opened my shirt and ecce! the two holes in my breasts & the bullet, which he gave me. George says he squeezed it from the right opening. Well—I remember the sickening feeling of water in my face—I was quite faint—

and seeing poor Sergt. Merchant lying near [b]—shot through the head and covered with blood—and then the thinking begun. (Meanwhile hardly able to speak—at least, coherently) Shot through the lungs? Lets see—and I spit. Yes—already the blood was in my mouth. At once my thoughts jumped to "Children of the New Forest" (by Marryatt) which I was fond of reading as a little boy, and in which the father of one of the heroines is shot through the lungs by a robber. I remembered he died with terrible haemorrhages & great agony. What should I do? Just then I remembered and felt in my waist coat pocket—Yes there it was—a little bottle of laudanum which I had brought along. But I won't take it yet; no, see a doctor first. It may not be as bad as it looks. At any rate wait till the pain begins—

When I had got to the bottom of the Bluff the ferry boat (the scow), had just started with a load—but there was a small boat there. Then, still in this half conscious state, I heard somebody groan. Then I thought "Now wouldn't Sir Philip Sydney have that other feller put into the boat first?" [c] But the question, as the form in which it occurred shows, came from a *mind* still bent on a becoming and consistent carrying out of its ideals of conduct—not from the unhesitating instinct of a still predominant & heroic *will.* I am not sure whether I propounded the question but I let myself be put aboard.

I never have been able to account for the fact that bullets struck in the bank of the island over our heads as we were crossing. Well; the next question was how to get me from the ferry to the hospital—this I solved by another early recollection—the "Armchair." Two men crossed their hands in such a way that I could sit on 'em & put my arms round their necks—& so they carried me. The little house was filled so I was taken into the large building which served as a general hospital; and I remember the coup d'oeuil on which I closed my eyes with the same

[b] Sergeant John Merchant of Pittsfield had enlisted in early August, and had perhaps been recruited by Holmes when he was in Pittsfield at that time.

[c] Holmes was not the only person who thought that the figure of Sir Philip Sidney had relevance. John Lothrop Motley in Vienna heard of Holmes's wounding at Ball's Bluff and wrote to Dr. Holmes. "I do not regret that Wendell is with the army. It is a noble and healthy symptom that brilliant, intellectual, poetical spirits like his spring to arms when a noble cause like ours inspires them. The race of Philip Sidneys is not yet extinct, and I honestly believe that as much genuine chivalry exists in our Free States at this moment as there is or ever was in any part of the world, from the Crusaders down." *Correspondence of John Lothrop Motley* (Curtis, ed., N.Y., 1889), II, 42.

sickening which I had felt on seeing poor Merchant. Men lying round on the floor—the spectacle wasn't familiar then—a red blanket with an arm lying on it in a pool of blood—it seems as if instinct told me it was John Putnam's (then Capt. Comdg Co H)—and near the entrance a surgeon calmly grasping a man's finger and cutting it off—both standing—while the victim contemplated the operation with a very grievous mug. Well presently old Hayward approached and inspected me. "How does it look, Doctor, shall I recover? Tell me the truth for I really want to know" (It seemed then and does now as if I was perfectly rational but Whittier says that when he saw me later I was very light headed.) Hayward in his deliberate way—"We-ell, you *may* recover—Gen. Shields did." [d] Shields! I'd thought of him before and got small comfort from that. We all thought that night that I had a couple of bullets in my lungs—& I bled from them (at the mouth) very freely. "That means the chances are against me, don't it?" "Ye-es, the chances are against you." Meanwhile he picked something from the left opening—I thought it was bone till he told me it was a bit of flannel—again I felt for the laudanum and again determined to wait till pain or sinking strength warned me of the end being near. I didn't feel sure there was no chance—and watching myself did not feel the hand of death upon me beyond a hope—my strength seemed to hold out too well.

After this my recollection of events is confused. I remember poor Willy Putnam's groans—and his refusing to let the Dr. operate on him, saying he knew the wound was mortal and it would only be more pain for nothing. I remember hobnobbing with the man who lay near me, and when to my astonishment John O'Sullivan (Whit's & my servt.) appeared, telling him to help my neighbor too, and feeling very heroic after that speech. (By the way Hayward had turned me on my breast & this may have helped a good deal of the wound to heal almost by first intention.) I remember being very sleepy—(some enlisted man has since told me he gave me some coffee and my face flushed and I went right off—) & presently a Doctor of (Baxter's?) Fire Zouaves coming in with much noise & bluster, and oh, troops were crossing to the Virginia side, and we were going to lick, and Heaven knows what not. I called him and gave him my address and told him (or meant &

[d] Major General James Shields in the battle of Cerro Gordo, in the Mexican War, had been hit by grapeshot which entered his chest, passed through his lung, and came out near his spine. The wound had been treated by drawing a silk handkerchief through it with a ramrod.

tried to) if I died to write home & tell 'em I'd done my duty. I was very anxious they should know that—and I then imparted to him my laudanum scheme. This he dissuaded and gave me a dose of some opiate—he said it wasn't laudanum, but I guess that was a white lie—and when I slumbered I believe he prigged the bottle.

Pen [e] before I was moved came in & kissed me and went away again. Whittier came & saw me too, though I'm not sure if I remember it—and Sturgis [f] of whom anon. I think I remember the confusion when some bullets struck the house—and the story that the enemy would shell the island. But all these recollections are obscure and the order of their occurrence uncertain.

Much more vivid is my memory of my thoughts and state of mind for though I may have been light-headed my reason was working—even if through a cloud. Of course when I thought I was dying the reflection that the majority vote of the civilized world declared that with my opinions I was *en route* for Hell came up with painful distinctness. Perhaps the first impulse was tremulous—but then I said—by Jove, I die like a soldier anyhow—I was shot in the breast doing my duty up to the hub—afraid? No, I am proud [g]—then I thought I couldn't be guilty of a deathbed recantation—father and I had talked of that and were agreed that it generally meant nothing but a cowardly giving way to fear. Besides, thought I, can I recant if I want to, has the approach of death changed my beliefs much? & to this I answered—No. Then came in my Philosophy—I am to take a leap in the dark—but now as ever I believe that whatever shall happen is best—for it is in accordance with

[e] Norwood Penrose Hallowell.

[f] Henry H. Sturgis was 2nd Lieutenant in Company H.

[g] General Lander when he heard that the Confederates asserted that fewer Massachusetts officers would have been killed at Ball's Bluff had they not been too proud to surrender, wrote stirring verses defending the pride of the Bay State:

> "Aye, deem us proud, for we are more
> Than proud of all our mighty dead;
> Proud of the bleak and rock-bound shore,
> A crowned oppressor cannot tread.
>
> . . . . .
>
> "*Pride,* 'tis our watchword; 'clear the boats,'
> 'Holmes, Putnam, Bartlett, Pierson—Here.'
> And while this crazy wherry floats
> 'Let's save our wounded,' cries Revere."

The entire poem is printed in Bruce, *Twentieth Regiment,* 64–65.

a general law—and *good* & *universal* (or *general law*) are synonymous terms in the universe. (I can now add that our phrase *good* only means certain general truths seen through the heart & will instead of being merely contemplated intellectually. I doubt if the intellect accepts or recognizes that classification of good and bad.) Would the complex forces which made a still more complex unit in *Me* resolve themselves back into simpler forms or would my angel be still winging his way onward when eternities had passed? I could not tell. But all was doubtless well—and so with a "God forgive me if I'm wrong" I slept. But while I was debating with myself Harry Sturgis bulged upon the scene—I don't remember what I said—I know what I wanted—it was the cool opinion of an outsider—a looker-on—as a *point d'appui* for resistance or a *που στω* from which to spring aloft, as the case might be; at any rate a foreign substance round which my thoughts could crystallize. Sturge I hear says I was very profane, to this effect—"Well Harry I'm dying but I'll be G. d'd if I know where I'm going." But I doubt it although a little later I swore frightfully—to the great horror of John O'S. who tried to stop me, thinking I was booking myself for Hell rapidly. Sturge thereat with about his usual tact, begun "Why—Homey—you believe in Christ, don't you" etc. with a brief exposition of doctrine argumentatively set forth. I gave him my love for Pen whom I'd not yet seen, & the same message home which I subsequently gave the Fire Zouave Surgeon and Sturge departed. Later I only can recall, in a general way, being carried across the Island in a blanket—lying on the bank comatose, being ferried across to the Md. shore with some hitch (we came mighty near being upset I heard afterwards)—swearing terrifically as I've said—and finally after being put in the hold of a canal boat and the hatches or scuttle or whatever you call it tumbling in and nearly all but smashing me & one or two others into sudden death, that I muzzed away the time till we got to Edwards Ferry.

N.B. I forgot to mention on the second page of this account, that I believe it was while I was being taken down the Bluff—that I said to myself in rather grim pleasantry—"Whittier Brevet First Lieutenant."

I was taken from the Canal boat and put into one of the two wheeled ambulances which were then in vogue as one form of torture—Captain Dreher was my companion—shot through the head & insensible, but breathing heavily. The Ambulance was broken—the horse baulked and the man didn't know how to drive—whenever we came to a hill, & there were several, there we stopped head downward, till some of the men along the road gave us a boost & started our horse forward again—I suffered much in mind—for what with the rough riding & my momentary expectations of being upset I hardly thought to reach camp alive. There was a piece of road which Sturge had built & on which he prided himself not a little; my aching bones told me when we reached that Via Mala. Fortunately I directed our driver to go to the Regt. instead of to Poolesville and we got to the Hospital at early dawn. There were many commiserating exclamations—Hibbard [h] (then pr. H. Co. A.) who was there, sick, insisted on turning out and giving me his bed. Then for the first time I saw Dreher—a ghastly spectacle. Two black cavities seemed all that there was left for eyes—his whiskers & beard matted with blood which still poured black from his mouth—and a most horrible stench.

The Hospital Steward—a cockeyed Dutchman who afterwards stuck me certain shekels for his services—looked at my wound and conjectured the true state of affairs—bound me round with an infernal bandage (which Hayward cut as soon as he saw), having first rammed plugs of lint into the holes, and then left me uncomfortable but still exceedingly joyful, for he had told me I should live—I could have hugged him for that. After this—whiskey—lightheadedness—laudanum & a request (the old idea still haunting me) to Peter Wilkins [i] to get me a quart of laudanum—which, he has told me, he did, more or less—Peter like!

I remember Hayward's saying "It is a beautiful face," or something of the sort & looking up & seeing Willy Putnam, calm & lovely, and being told or knowing he was dead. I was soon moved to a Wall Tent with John Putnam where all was quiet (Tremlett here astonished me with his tenderness & even Wollaston [j] [*sic*] when he returned from Boston had tears in his eyes as he looked on John). Maj. Gen. Banks came in (see his letter home), Gordon & Andrews of the 2nd [k]—Mr.

[h] Sergeant Lansing E. Hibbard, later 2nd Lieutenant, had enlisted from Pittsfield in August.

[i] Probably Henry E. Wilkins who later was commissioned 1st Lieutenant in the Twentieth. See "My Hunt after 'The Captain,'" *Works of Oliver Wendell Holmes*, VIII, 16, 26.

[j] Captain Edmund A. Walleston had been on leave at the time of the battle. He resigned from the Regiment in Nov. 1861.

[k] George H. Gordon was Colonel, and George L. Andrews Lieutenant Colonel of the Second Regiment, Massachusetts Volunteers.

Hovey[l] etc. and things went smoothly barring my impatience till I started for Phila. with Bill Hallowell[m]—memorable time when my temper gained me his lasting dislikes. He was only too kind to me.

Notes to account of my first wound

1. At first I only intended to show the rapidity of thought & queer suggestions which occur when one is hit, but as I always wanted to have a memorandum of this experience—so novel at that time to all & especially so to me from the novelty of the service and my youth—I have told the whole story from time I was hit until apprehension had left me.

2. I must add one more confession. While I was lying on the island, one of the thoughts that made it seem particularly hard to die was the recollection of several fair damsels whom I wasn't quite ready to leave.

3. Charley Pearson told me when I saw him in Washington after my wound at the 2nd Fredericksburg, that a gentleman told him that visiting Harrison's Island and looking round for a relic he came on a blood-stained handkerchief marked "Lt. O W Holmes Jr." "20th Regt. Mass. Vols." which he pouched & preserved.

4. It is curious how rapidly the mind adjusts itself under some circumstances to entirely new relations. I thought for awhile that I was dying, and it seemed the most natural thing in the world. The moment the hope of life returned it seemed as abhorrent to nature as ever that I should die.

5. Curious time on arriving at Georgetown by canal. Bill H. got a ramshackle vehicle—one horse & negro driver which both went to sleep whenever we stopped—I, my trunk & John O'S. in rear part. On getting to the White House I wanted to see it & our equipage boldly drove in & by the door. We had the greatest difficulty in finding a place at any Hotel—Willard's full but an officer offered his room which of course I didn't take. "Mr. Brown" (*Metropolitan* now, then called Secesh) "says he *won't* have him"—another says yes but finding he's mistaken the man backs out—finally at the National we were kindly entreated.

At the Battle of Ball's Bluff Holmes was a boy of twenty; at the close of his military service he was a young man of twenty-three.

[l] Not identified.

[m] William P. Hallowell, brother of Richard P. and Norwood Penrose Hallowell, was at this time a civilian.

Although the written account of the Battle and of his wounding was more nearly contemporaneous with the end than with the beginning of his service it vividly reflects the boy's spirit. The qualities in that spirit which seem notable were various. Confronting death, his chief concern was that his friends and family should know that he had done his duty, that facing violence and pain for the first time in his life, he had shown a soldier's fortitude. The child of cultivation, he interpreted his situation, as it were, in literary terms, and gained strength by seeing himself as under a historic obligation to follow in the manly footsteps of Captain Marryat, Sir Philip Sidney, and General Shields. There is no indication that he reinforced a faltering spirit by recollection of the cause for which he had run the risk and suffered his wound; instead, he sought strength by an effort to realize in his own conduct those qualities which he had admired in his fellow-Porcellian, Francis Lowell Gardner, the classmate who had died before the outbreak of war. "Courage and courtesy . . . high breeding restraining all needless display of bravery"; the qualities of "a truly chivalrous gentleman," were those to which Holmes looked for sustenance as he lay wounded after Ball's Bluff.

In many other young men of Holmes's generation these traditional sources of fortitude were buttressed by religious belief. When Colonel Wilder Dwight, another young Harvard officer, lay dying on the battlefield at Antietam, he found strength for his final ordeal in a soldier's reserve: "It's a pretty little wound," he commented after being struck by the ball that killed him. Giving directions for his burial, the young civilian in uniform observed that "I have lived like a soldier, I die a soldier, I wish to be buried as a soldier." He then summoned the Chaplain, who asked, "Colonel, do you trust in God?" "He answered with ready firmness and cheerfulness, 'I do.' 'And in the Lord Jesus Christ, your Saviour?' 'I do.' . . . He died as he had lived, a brave, gallant, noble man, a hero, and a Christian. . . ." [66] Belief and hope accompanied most of Holmes's friends upon the battlefields, and he had wondered whether without their sustenance he could show their gallantry. As death hovered over him on Harrison's Island the boy's "first impulse was tremulous," for if his lack of faith should have the consequences which orthodoxy ascribed to it the black continent in the cosmography of Calvinism would lie before him. He had not avoided the war to evade its dangers. Could one who was seeking now to show himself a soldier properly avoid the miseries of unrepentant death by renouncing the doubts which science had instilled in his mind? "I die like a soldier . . . I am proud." These were the answers which the heart gave to the crisis of death and they were reinforced by the very principles of science and its philosophy. "[W]hatever shall happen is best, for it is in accordance with a general law, and *good* and *universal* (or *general law*) are synonymous terms in the universe." Thus the boy had discovered that he had within his spirit resources of courage and within his philosophy resources of doctrine sufficient to carry him, without flinching, to the precipice of life. No discovery, in youth or in maturity, had larger moment than that.

To assert that Holmes was seeking to prove that the standards of an aristocracy had, as it were, an aesthetic value in a democratic society would be to interpret his conduct in terms which did not occur to him. Yet it well may be that his admiration for the unadvertised gallantry of the gentleman,[n] and his confidence that fortitude might be derived from other sources than religion, reflected the hope that those who stood outside their society, isolated from its effusive vulgarities and its sentimental comforts, might ultimately be its leaders. Many other young men of Harvard had volunteered for service, confident that they could justify the advantages which had been theirs by participating unostentatiously in the common dangers of their times. Few who tested themselves in that way sought, with Holmes, to assess the capacity of resolution, when unsupported by belief, to survive the strain of war. He endeavored to prove by conduct that his standards and those of his friends were self-sufficient and shone with the same vitality

n "I learned in the regiment and in the class the conclusion, at least, of what I think the best service that we can do for our country and for ourselves: To see as far as one may, and to feel the great forces that are behind every detail; . . . to hammer out as compact and solid a piece of work as one can, to try to make it first rate, and to leave it unadvertised." "The Class of '61," *Speeches,* 95, 96.

whether nurtured by the faith of religion or by the rationalism of science. If there was danger of arrogance in this aristocracy of breeding and this aristocracy of doubt there was pride and dignity.

Arrived at Charles Street on November 9, and occupying his sister's room, Holmes found some consolations for his suffering. During November, his mother kept a list of "Visitors to the Wounded Lieutenant," [67] and on the very day of his homecoming he had three callers, including his boyhood friend and cousin John T. Morse, Jr. On his second day at home the wound was probed by Dr. Bigelow, but thereafter the doctors left the healing to nature.[68] On the succeeding days the list of visitors grew to remarkable lengths and the names of the young ladies of Boston and Cambridge appeared with recurrent frequency. On November 12 Miss Ida Agassiz (the angel of his hospital tent) appeared at Charles Street in person, and was followed on other later days by her father, Professor Agassiz. On the 14th President Felton stopped in to see the young man—for once, it may be assumed, not to admonish but to commend. Charles Sumner, the senior Senator from Massachusetts, called on two occasions and in all probability spoke privately, as he was then speaking publicly, of the true cause of the disaster at Ball's Bluff—slavery.[69] The wounded Lieutenant, though he may still have shared the basic conviction of the abolitionists, may already have begun to mistrust such facile generalization as the Senator's and to dislike that "emotional state" in the temperament of the militant reformer which "catches postulates like the influenza." [70] Sumner may also have taken the occasion to inquire of Holmes whether he knew anything of the complaints which had begun to reach him of Captain Macy's conduct in surrendering fugitive slaves to their Maryland owners.[71] In late November Anthony Trollope, then visiting Boston, stopped by to see the wounded veteran. Ice cream, flowers, grapes, pears, and butter were brought to the bedside of the young hero. At regular intervals Mrs. Holmes put on her list the mysterious entry: "The 'Unknown'—Flowers." Dr. Holmes's description of his convalescent son was surely accurate: "Wendell is a great pet in his character of young hero with wounds in the heart, and receives visits *en grand seigneur*. I envy my white Othello, with a semicircle of young Desdemonas about him listening to the often told story which they will have over again." [72] Mrs. Dixwell, wife of Holmes's old schoolmaster who himself called on November 14th, sent flowers to the Lieutenant on the 13th, and her daughter Fanny called twice (accompanied by her mother), on one occasion bringing flowers. It is possible that she, his future wife, was "The Unknown," but there were many others who would gladly have played that romantic role. By November 29th Dr. Holmes could report that his son was thriving well and able to walk,[73] and on December 7 Mrs. James T. Fields, a few doors down the block on Charles Street, had Charles F. Browne ("Artemus Ward"), Dr. Holmes, and the wounded Lieutenant to breakfast. "The young lieutenant," she reported, "has mostly recovered from his wound and speaks as if duty would recall him soon to camp. He will go when the time comes, but home evidently never looked half so pleasant before." [74]

It was not until late March that Holmes returned to his Regiment. During part of the winter he was evidently on recruiting duty in Boston and in Pittsfield, seeking to fill the vacancies which had resulted from the casualties of Ball's Bluff.[75] Those duties were not, however, so arduous as to prevent Holmes from pursuing other interests. Perhaps it was during this winter, rather than after his later woundings, that he revived his concern with engravings. The Francis C. Gray collection of prints had recently been bequeathed to Harvard University and Louis Theis was in charge as curator. In 1918 Holmes recalled that when he was "a soldier in the Civil War and at home with wounds" he went to Cambridge to see Theis and the collection.[76] On Holmes's arrival the old curator "opened his arms and embraced and kissed me and produced a bottle of wine and cigars. I had good times with him and with a queer old collector at the South End of Boston with whom I used to sit up till all hours." [77] There were other interests, however, which convalescence permitted him to follow. Once more Lewes's *Biographical History of Philosophy* was drawn from the

Athenaeum, but that was the one philosophical work to be taken out while Holmes was in Boston. The young officer was, after all, still in uniform and still committed, for a term, to the profession of arms. The consciousness that he was still a serious soldier is indicated by a group of books taken from the Athenaeum in quick succession during November and December—MacDougall's *Campaigns of Hannibal,* MacDougall's *Theory of War,* the *Life of Sir Charles Napier,* Napier's *History of the Peninsular War.* Problems of political theory evidently concerned someone in the Holmes household at the turn of the year, for in December, January, and February, Mill on *Representative Government* and Tocqueville's *Democracy in America* were charged to the Holmes family on the Athenaeum's records.

During the months of Holmes's convalescence all was expectantly quiet along the Potomac. The expectancy and the quiet resulted from the peculiar gifts of General McClellan which, as they gradually unfolded themselves, made him the idol of his men and the anathema of the radicals. His regiments of volunteers, held inactive in the environs of Washington, saw inactivity as their opportunity to become an army. The fire-eaters saw it as time wasted. The nation had learned that victory would not come easily and McClellan was teaching it that while he was General-in-Chief it would not come speedily. To Lincoln, delay was tolerable only because of the hope that when McClellan moved it would be with decisive and terminating force, ending the rebellion and bringing peace to the nation. That McClellan disappointed the President's hope was owing as much, perhaps, to the clumsy interferences with McClellan's command by civilian authority as it was to the failings of the General. Wherever the blame lay it left in its wake the corrosion of distrust.

When Holmes left Boston in late March of 1862, it was apparent to all the country that the time for large-scale operations had arrived and that even General McClellan could no longer prevaricate. Whether his operations would be based on Washington or whether the Army of the Potomac would be moved by water to the mouth of Chesapeake Bay and from there launch its attack on Richmond was a much-discussed military secret. No one doubted, however, that McClellan's forces would soon see action. When Holmes had journeyed south in September there was a color of cheerful uncertainty in his mood; his first letter had enclosed a sonnet singing of the hermit thrush.[78] His first letter to Charles Street in March of 1862 closed with the caution: "Whatever happens keep up your pluck." [79] Experience of war had made pluck, not poetry, seem the first necessity.

The condition of the Regiment had not been happy during Holmes's absence. Personal irritations had developed into jealousies, and political disagreements had encouraged suspicions. Lieutenant Colonel Palfrey had not handled the problems of the Regiment skillfully and Holmes reported from Washington on March 25 that he did not "like the look of things under Palf.—wish Lee was here." [80] Lieutenant Henry Ropes, brother of John C. Ropes, Boston lawyer and distinguished historian of the Civil War, who had been commissioned during Holmes's absence and had joined the Regiment in December, already was forming his opinion of the officers with whom he was associated. One of the captains who was not of the Harvard group he found "remarkable for his obscenity and licentiousness"; Lieutenant James Jackson Lowell, a cousin of Holmes who had also been wounded at Ball's Bluff, he described as "a shockingly bad officer," and he added, "they say Holmes is as bad." He acknowledged, however, that Lowell and Holmes were liked and were "in the best set of course." He went on to give the basis for his low regard for Lowell and Holmes as officers: "The more I study of an officer's life, the more I see the need of energy, and business ability, qualities which neither possess." [81] There is little reason to suppose that Holmes would have felt greatly injured by Ropes's cavalier judgment; he stated himself that "I have a very modest opinion of my merits as a soldier," [82] and never in his letters home, or elsewhere, showed pride in his military capacities as such but only satisfaction that he had been able, despite his speculative bent of temperament, to stand in the evil day. Ropes's prejudgment of Holmes's capacities as an officer appears, furthermore, to have been modified after the two fought together, for on Holmes's return to the Regiment after his second wounding Ropes spoke not only of the pleasure which he was finding in his companionship but stated that the condition of the Regiment had been much improved as a result of Holmes's return.[83] Henry Abbott, similarly, seems first to have felt that Holmes, like the other officers who had been away from the Regiment after Ball's Bluff, was "most thoroughly & amazingly deficient in military knowledge" [84] but came later to describe him as "a very good officer" and to say further that he had come to be considered "a remarkably brave and well instructed officer." [85]

Two days after Holmes's return to duty, the Twentieth found itself moving by water with the Army of the Potomac to Fortress Monroe, at the mouth of the James River. The nation finally had good reason to believe that the grand advance and final assault on Richmond was about to open and Northern optimists had some reason to hope that a successful conclusion of the War was in sight. The rigors of the Peninsula Campaign were not long postponed. During the weeks of April, the Twentieth moved up the peninsula between the York and the James rivers as an element in General Sedgwick's Division of the Second Corps. Much of the Army's energy was given to the laborious effort of advancing on roads which had turned to rivers of mud and over which artillery pieces, wagons, and baggage trains must be moved. "It's a campaign now and make no mistake," reported Holmes to his parents. "No tents, no trunks—no nothing." [86]

McClellan's critics in Washington, still demanding a quick victory, and persistently denying him the additional forces that he had been promised, might taunt the General with soured reflections on his strategy—"spades is trumps"—but his troops still saw him as their inspiring leader. While his forces made their oozing advance, reconnaissance uncovered rebel troops, and skirmishes were sharp and frequent. The combat in which Holmes now found himself engaged was totally different from that which he had tasted at Ball's Bluff; this was made up of a series of small and isolated engagements in which men fell by ones and twos and not by companies. He wrote to his parents that "the notion now seems to be that McClellan is trying to out-general and catch 'em if possible without a big fight" and added that all was "exceedingly well except the fewness of letters and diminishing chance of a fight." [87] All in all, he found himself "in good spirits, though of course I despise the life in itself outside of special circumstances and principles." [88] One of the sources of satisfaction at the outset of the campaign was that Holmes was in the Company commanded by Pen Hallowell—that, he said, "makes all the difference in the world." [89] That special association, however, was shortly to end, for word was received from his family that the Boston newspapers had reported that Holmes had been promoted to a captaincy. Before receiving official notice of his promotion he said he would not accept it, since the promotion had occurred without the knowledge of Lieutenant Colonel Palfrey,[90] but the matter was evidently straightened out, or decided over his head, and in the principal engagements in the Peninsula campaign Holmes was Captain commanding Company G, filling a vacancy which had resulted from the resignation of another officer.

Letters which Henry Abbott wrote to his family indicate that some persons believed that Holmes had not acted entirely creditably in accepting a promotion which would have gone to Lieutenant George Perry if the normal rules of seniority had been followed. Abbott, who himself had refused to accept the promotion to the vacant captaincy because of his desire to stay with his own Company,[91] defended Holmes's conduct, saying that it was assumed by all of the officers that Perry, who had been taken prisoner with Colonel Lee at Ball's Bluff, had been assigned to a skeleton regiment and therefore stood no longer on the rolls of the Twentieth at the time when the promotion had to be made. The Governor, acting on the same assumption, had "filled the vacancy for Captaincy by the next name on the roster, without Holmes doing anything in the matter." [92] It would appear from Holmes's letter to his parents that Abbott's understanding was entirely correct and that Holmes had done nothing to secure advancement for himself.

During the last two weeks of April, the Regiment was encamped below the Warwick River within sight and shot of the Confederate lines. It was while commanding a picket line on this sector that Captain Bartlett of the Twentieth was gravely wounded and thus compelled to leave the Regiment to which he had contributed so much in valor and leadership.[93] The pause of the Union forces on the south bank of the Warwick was occasioned by McClellan's decision to lay siege to Yorktown on his right flank before turning east towards Richmond. It was not surprising that the enemy took the opportunity which this delay offered to strengthen their lines, and by May 4, when the Twentieth entered an evacuated Yorktown, the Union forces had opposite them not only the stubborn terrain east of Richmond but an alert and reinforced foe. Holmes's Regiment escaped the unfortunate Battle of Williamsburg in which many elements of the Second Corps were involved on May 5. Instead, it was ordered to proceed by boat with other units to West Point where the waters of the Pamunkey and Mattapony rivers join to form the York River. Thence the Regiment moved through muds and marshes for a distance of some ten miles to the southwest, crossing the Chickahominy at a point about three miles distant from Bottom's Bridge. By May 30 the Regiment was encamped with the rest of the Second Corps seven miles or so east of Richmond, but north once more of the Chickahominy.

General Johnston, then commanding the opposing forces, realized on the 30th that the situation of his enemy, precariously "astride a fickle river," [94] afforded him an opportunity for offensive action which must be seized. Nature enlisted her forces in his support by filling the Chickahominy with torrential rains on the night of the 30th. When Johnston struck on the next morning against those Union forces which had crossed the river, McClellan's difficulties in bringing up reinforcements were almost insuperable. Among the troops that were ordered to advance were those of General Sumner's Second Corps, including the Twentieth. On the afternoon of the 31st, infantry troops made a precarious crossing of the river. "As the solid column of infantry entered upon the bridge, it swayed to and fro to the angry flood below or the living freight above, settling down and grasping the solid stumps by which it was made secure, as the line advanced. Once filled with men, however, it was safe till the corps had crossed; it then soon became impassable." [95] Writing to his parents on June 2nd, Holmes described the part which he and the Regiment played in the Battle of Fair Oaks after the crossing had been made. Following a preliminary encounter

the order was given: Forward in line, Double Quick. At this point . . . I threw away my haversack containing all my food, my dressing case, my only change of stockings, my pipe and tobacco—which I have vainly lamented since. . . . When we got to the road the right wing entered the wood firing hard, and the left wing (I am next the colors on the left of the color company . . .) advancing more slowly to avoid getting fired into by our own men. A company of rebels, trying to pass out of the woods, was knocked to pieces, and thus we soon took the final position of the first day. . . . Here we blazed away left oblique into the woods till we were ordered to cease firing and remained masters of the field.[96]

Throughout the night and following day the Regiment remained on the field in this position, forming a "square to resist an expected attack of cavalry in the afternoon—OWH in the front rank . . . handling a sword and pistol, and were fired at several times during the day by sharpshooters. A bullet has a most villainous greasy slide through the air." [97] The Battle of Fair Oaks, however, had run its bloody course, leaving in its wake seven thousand Confederate and five thousand Union casualties. "It is singular," wrote Holmes, "with what indifference one gets to look on the dead bodies in gray clothes which lie all around. . . . As you go through the woods you stumble constantly, and, if after dark, . . . perhaps tread on the swollen bodies, already fly blown and decaying, of men shot in the head or bowels." Yet Holmes was grimly satisfied by the experience. "[W]e licked 'em and this time there was the maneuvering of a battle to be seen—splendid and awful to behold, especially as the dusk allowed us to see clearly the lines of flames from the different Regiments as they fired." [98] Furthermore, he was able to report that he found the duties of a captain preferable to those of a lieutenant, that his men appeared to like him, and had, in fact, cheered him after the fight.[99] The exhilaration of what appeared to have been a victory was qualified, however, by the admission that Holmes and his men were "worn by fatigue and privation as well as mental anxiety." [100] That he had not gone into battle with light-hearted gaiety or indifference to the gentler world which he had left behind him is indicated by a request to his parents which he smuggled into the closing paragraph in his letter of June 2. "If I am killed," he wrote, "you will find a memorandum on the back of a picture I carry which please attend to." [101] Nothing survives to identify the subject of the picture, but it is probable that it was the photograph of one of the girls at home from whom Holmes was receiving welcome letters with some frequency. Among his most regular correspondents was Fanny Dixwell. Yet nothing tells us that it was the picture of his future wife that Holmes carried into battle.

Holmes was, in a sense, justified in saying that at Fair Oaks "we licked 'em." The Second Corps had stopped Johnston's offensive and turned what might have been a grave defeat of the Union forces into a stalemate. The exhaustion of the opposing forces held them in their positions while the two commanders took stock of the situation. General Lee, now commanding the Southern army in place of the wounded Johnston, put the interlude to bold and imaginative use; McClellan wasted time in fidgeting uncertainty. For some ten days the Twentieth held its advanced position, doing picket duty on short rations, standing in the mud by day, and sleeping in the mud and rain by night. On June 11, however, the Regiment was relieved in the front line and moved to dry land in the rear. There Holmes reported to his father that "many of the officers, including your beloved son, have discovered themselves to have been attacked by body lice—(caught perhaps from the men, perhaps from the dirty places we have been forced to live in or enter)." He added the comment that "it's queer that I stand this exposure and hard work better than many a stout fellow who looks more enduring than I." There was no expression of concern as to how the Union forces might capitalize upon their success in stopping the Confederate offensive. The one explicit protest to his father was against the unfairness of the newspaper accounts of Fair Oaks, in which "*local* regiments, like the 10th and 15th get cracked up like thunder" while the Twentieth is denied its "due credit." "After all," he added, "it makes very little difference except for the sake of justice and one's friends." His letter concluded with a word of reassurance: "I am always well and—as things are—contented." [102]

On June 26 came the end of tranquillity. The Union forces then realized that General Lee had made good and well-concealed use of the interlude and had brought forces under Stonewall Jackson down from the Shenandoah Valley to attack McClellan's right flank from the north. Instead of meeting this threat by turning again on Richmond, McClellan decided to withdraw his forces to a new base on the James River, southeast of Richmond and from there, at a later date, resume his advance on the Southern capital. The Twentieth was not engaged in the encounter at Gaines's Mill where the Union forces were defeated on June 27. The retreat towards the James, for the Twentieth, commenced two days later. From the 29th through July 1, however, the Regiment was in the thick of the confused fighting which made up the series of engagements known as the Seven Days' Battles. In later life while rereading *The Odyssey* Holmes came across the passage in which Ulysses, longing to start for home, looks in the skies to see if the sun is yet setting. "It made me think," wrote Holmes, "of the Seven Days in '62, when I would wonder if that damned sun ever would go down—a dispirited army fighting by day and marching for the James by night." [103] The first word that reached Charles Street from the front was brief but reassuring. It was in an undated note, probably written on July 4 from Harrison's Landing, whither the Army of the Potomac had withdrawn.[104]

[July 4, 1862
Harrison's Landing]

Dear Mother

We have had hard work for several days—marched all night—lain on our arms every morning, and fought every afternoon—eaten nothing

ing—suffered the most intense anxiety and everything else possible. I'm safe, though, so far. But you can conceive the wear and tear. Lowell is probably dead, bowels cut.[105] Patten wounded leg.[106] Abbott wounded arm. Miller wounded and probably prisoner.[107] Our Co. had 9 or 10 wounded and some missing out of 37.

Give my love to all my friends & remember me in your thoughts and prayers.

Your loving son
O. W. Holmes, Jr.

The fuller account was written on the following day, and tells of the events of June 29 and 30 (the Battle of Glendale) and of the notably successful battle of July 1 at Malvern Hill, the last engagement in the disheartening Peninsula campaign.[108]

July 5, 1862
[Harrison's Landing]

My dear Mother and Father

June 29 we started from the trenches on our retreat—at Fair Oaks passed Rocket Guns & great quantities of stores wh. had to be destroyed. Went a little further & formed in line. Cos. I & B (the R. & Left Cos.) went out as skirmishers & my Co. as support Our own side fired shell & cannister into us (hurt no one luckily) and the 5th N. H. Regt. behaving badly I had to fall back on the Regt. Afternoon marched to Savage's Statn. where lots more stores were destroyed and a hospital stood where all the wounded had to be left to the enemy. Here the enemy shelled us—several men hurt, none of our Co. . . .

Marched all night, rested at early dawn—marched and rested in woods noon—afternoon terribly thirsty (hardly any water to be had) came up double quick onto field of action (knapsacks on backs)—Nelson's Farm. Forward in line (whole battalion front) better than the Regt. generally does it on drill—*Whang* goes a shell. Two men drop in Co. G. "Captain! Noonan's hit." "No Matter, Forward Guide Right." We go forward passing a deserted battery, the dead lying thick round it and then begins the deuce of a time. The Mich. 7th on our left breaks & runs *disgracefully* (private), they lay it to Col. Grosvenor who they say showed the white feather. Not a waver in our Regt. Our Co. behaved admirably (better than most I may say) till Palfrey (Lee comm'ded the Brigade & Dana the Divn. pro tem.) gave the order to march double quick in retreat. We were flanked & nearly surrounded and that saved us. After that we couldn't avoid confusion and what with stragglers of other Regts &c. didn't form a good line. In our Co. the loss in those known to be wounded was 1/5 and 1/4 the Co. not counting the missing of whose fate we are ignorant nor those temporarily disabled only—as one man stunned by a piece of shell for instance & knocked out of fighting. The guns got so hot & dirty we couldn't load or fire more than 2/3 of 'em. That night June 30 we marched again (all this time I only eating about 3 pieces of hard bread a day & not wanting more hardly sleeping at all & never washing). We started about, I suppose, as father was writing to me. The next morn'g a splendid line of battle (of the whole army) at Malverton where the Rebs. shelled us (our brigade) hard. The shell & Round Shot bounced round lively. At midnight started and marched through terrible rain & mud till we reached the James the next afternoon. The anxiety kept pretty lively only getting down when on the last of our march I was told by cheerful birds like Tremlett & co that we *must* surrender or be cut to pieces within 36 hours.

Poor Lowell was hit just as Willy Putnam was & had to be left behind—beyond doubt dead. Patten hit in leg. Abbot flesh w'd in arm. Muller wounded & missing. Palfrey bruised not hurt. N. P. Hallowell cut on the side not hurt. I was awfully frightened about him. I'm in comm'd of E. & G. I'm too tired, that is too mentally inefficient, to write well but I've sent 2 notes before including a leaf of my pocket book written some time ago to you in case I was ever killed. . . .

My love to all. All write please—

It was the thought of you dear ones sustained me in terrible trials—Hereafter Allen's Farm, Savage's Station, Nelson's Farm, Malverton are added to my list of actions. The hardest seems over now—at any rate I'm ready—

God bless you all
Goodbye
O W H, Jr.

Show this if you wish to any of my particulars, Ellen Hooper[109] or any one—understanding it's *private* & not to be quoted—Keep all letters that are at all historical as I've no diary to speak of. . . .

Licking its wounds, the Army of the Potomac remained at Harrison's Landing until mid-August. Despite the disappointments and frustrations of the Peninsula campaign it spent the midsummer weeks in a state of high confidence. On August 10, Lieutenant Ropes wrote to his brother from Regimental headquarters reporting that "our army is in splendid fighting trim and ready for anything. . . . [I]t is healthy, well fed and confident. I fully believe that we shall *utterly crush* the rebellion before cold weather." [110] When Ropes spoke thus confidently he evidently did not realize that some few days earlier General McClellan had received an order directing him to transfer the Army of the Potomac from the James to Aquia Creek on the Potomac, an order which has been described as "the greatest single disaster of the war." [111] In the eyes of McClellan and his supporters this decision to abandon the earlier strategy reflected the triumph of radical politicians over conservative soldiers. When Lincoln had appeared at Harrison's Landing on July 8 McClellan had handed him a document in which the General set forth his opinions and recommendations concerning the conduct of the war. What he asked, in essence, was that the army's responsibility should be narrowly confined to the achievement of military objectives, and that it should not be made an instrument of social reform in those Southern communities where its successes forced upon it the responsibilities of government. In particular, McClellan urged that emancipation of the slaves should be effected only when military necessity required such action and then only upon the payment of compensation. The futility of McClellan's plea for moderation in the radicals and for wholehearted support of the contemplated drive on Richmond was quickly apparent. On July 14, with blustering shrillness, General Pope assumed command of a newly constituted force, the Army of Virginia, which lay south of Washington. On July 23 General Halleck was named General-in-Chief of the Union forces. Favorites of the Congressional Committee on the Conduct of the War, Pope and Halleck, believed that while McClellan's forces remained in the neighborhood of Richmond, Washington was in constant danger. They added the prestige of apparent military competence to the cause of the radicals, and Lincoln, bending to the winds of politics, allowed their judgment to prevail over that of McClellan and his staff.

It was on August 16 that the Twentieth started its march to Newport News and on the 25th that it embarked for the journey up Chesapeake Bay and the Potomac to Aquia Creek. While it was moving from one camp to another in the neighborhood of Washington the Regiment heard heavy cannonading in the distance and learned on the 31st that General Pope had suffered a devasting defeat at Bull Run—the site, for the second time, of Union humiliation. General Lee, taking quick advantage of his victory, between the 4th and 7th of September crossed the Potomac and entered Maryland, establishing his base near Frederick City. Meanwhile, on September 1st, Lincoln, recognizing the almost total demoralization of the Union forces, restored McClellan to the highest field command and gave him the responsibility for the defense of Washington. For once moving with dispatch, McClellan advanced into Maryland and put his forces between Lee and the capital. As the Union army moved forward the Twentieth was assigned to the Second Corps, as it had been on the Peninsula, and thus came once more under the command of General Sumner. It was not engaged in the successful action at South Mountain on September 14, but by then had advanced with the right wing of the Union line and had on that day moved north out of Frederick. When on the 15th the Second Corps reached Antietam Creek it found Confederate forces massed on the other side. There, McClellan decided, they should pause.

At three in the morning on September 17, just before the opening shots in the Battle of Antietam were fired, Holmes sat down by candlelight and wrote to his mother and father.[112]

Dearest Parents

I'm comparatively well though last night rain set me off again as usual. Never since the terrible exposures of Fair Oaks have I been myself. I can digest hardtack or tacks or shingle nails but one damp night recalling those dreary times plays the deuce with me. . . . Write just as regularly (as you have *not* lately) whether I answer or not—I want letters. Just rec'd Ned's & Dad's Sept. 13. All of us feel a deuced sight more like a fight than in that forlorn peninsula. I don't talk seriously for you know all my last words if I come to grief. You know my devoted love for you—those I care for know it. Why should I say any more? It's rank folly pulling a long mug every time one may fight or may be killed. Very probably we shall in a few days and if we do why I shall go into it not trying to shirk the responsibility of my past life by a sort of death bed abjuration. I have lived on the track on which I expect to continue travelling if I get through—hoping always that though it may wind it will bring me up the hill once more. With the deepest love

love to A. & N—
Your Son W.

Before the letter arrived in Boston a telegram was delivered to Dr. Holmes. It had been sent by William G. LeDuc from Hagerstown, Maryland, and, as thousand of readers of the *Atlantic Monthly* were to learn when they read the issue for December 1862, it contained the brief message: "Captain Holmes wounded shot through the neck not thought mortal at Keedysville." [113] The battle of Antietam was over and Holmes, who had gone through the Peninsula campaign unscratched, was once more, as after Ball's Bluff, so seriously wounded that the gravest alarm was justified.[o] The losses in Sedgwick's Division of which the Twentieth was a part were of staggering dimensions—2255 casualties, of whom 355 were killed. The details of the battle which was counted a Union victory need not concern us; it is enough to know that General

o Among the forces with which the Twentieth was engaged at Antietam was the Thirty-fifth North Carolina Regiment. One of the officers of that Regiment was a fifteen-year-old boy, Lieutenant Walter Clark. In later life Clark became Associate Justice and Chief Justice of the Supreme Court of North Carolina, gaining, as such, distinction for a dissenting liberalism, comparable in some ways to that which Holmes achieved as Associate and Chief Justice of the Supreme Judicial Court of Massachusetts. It was Clark who found Holmes's commanding officer, Colonel Palfrey, lying wounded on the battlefield at Antietam and brought him behind the Confederate lines. So far as we know fate never brought Holmes and Clark into more intimate and less precarious relationships than those which they briefly enjoyed on Sept. 17, 1862. See Aubrey Lee Brooks, *Walter Clark: Fighting Judge* (Chapel Hill, 1944), 9.

Sumner had permitted Sedgwick's Division to be marched into an ambush, that, flanked and attacked from the rear, the Division had been mowed down and in a state of disorder left the battlefield. As Holmes described the part of the Twentieth in the engagement, Sumner had moved his reserves "up so close to the front line that we could have touched them with our bayonets, and we got hit about as much as they did, but of course could do nothing, and when the enemy broke through on our left we were surrounded with the front. Whereas had we been a little further back they would have got a volley." [114] In a speech delivered to the Regimental Association thirty-five years after the battle Holmes was able to speak of the occasion with some levity: "We have stood side by side in line—we have charged and swept the enemy—and we have run away like rabbits—all together." Yet he felt it fitting to add to his own copy of those remarks a footnote saying, "This would do among ourselves. To an outsider it would be necessary to explain that the 20th never ran except by orders of General Sumner at Antietam." [115]

It was evidently shortly after the Confederates broke through on the left of Sedgwick's force that Holmes was struck in the back of his neck. "When I was hit we were getting it all round and I remember chuckling to myself as I was leaving the field, to remember that *Harper's Weekly* was flamboyant on my first wound at Ball's Bluff—about Massachusetts hit in the breast, etc. I thought to myself, this time I am hit in the back, and bolting as fast as I can—and it's all right—but not so good for the newspapers."[116] On the day after the battle he wrote briefly to his parents, presumably from Keedysville, Maryland, where LeDuc had stated that he was located.[117]

Sept. 18

My Dear Parents

. . . Usual luck—ball entered at the rear passing straight through the central seam of coat & waistcoat collar coming out toward the front on the left hand side—yet it didn't seem to have smashed my spine or I suppose I should be dead or paralyzed or something. It's more than 24 hours & I have remained pretty cocky, only of course feverish at times—

and some sharp burning pain in left shoulder. Pen & I, singular to say, are the hardest hit officers. He, I think, will lose his left arm—bone smashed above elbow. We lay together for a while in a little house on the field and were one time within the enemy lines, heard their orders etc. (they were all round us) but they fell back and we escaped.

Only one doctor, Haven, the Surgeon of 15 Mass has yet looked. He glanced hastily yesterday and said it wasn't fatal. I shall try to get home as soon as possible but have no plans yet.

I shall write again soon. . . .

Your loving
O W H, Jr.

This summary account of the events of the previous day is supplemented in the account which Hallowell gave in his reminiscences of the doings in the first place of shelter where he and Holmes found themselves after they were hit.[118]

Before long I gained the little farmhouse marked on the maps as the Nicodemus house. The yard was full of wounded men, and the floor of the parlor, where I lay down, was well covered with them. Among others, Captain O. W. Holmes, Jr., walked in, the back of his neck clipped by a bullet. The baggage train had not been up for many a day, so that I had replenished my wardrobe by appropriations of chance clothing from various sources. It so happened that I wore on that day the light blue trousers and dark blouse of a private soldier. When the rebels, a little later, were busy in the yard, paroling some and taking others to the rear, paying marked attention, of course, to officers, I was glad to have taken the precaution to remove my shoulderstraps and to conceal them with my sword under a blanket.

The first Confederate to make his appearance put his head through the window and said: "Yankees?" "Yes." "Wounded?" "Yes." "Would you like some water?" A wounded man always wants some water. He off with his canteen, threw it into the room, and then resumed his place in the skirmish line and his work of shooting retreating Yankees. In about fifteen minutes that good-hearted fellow came back to the window all out of breath, saying: "Hurry up there! Hand me my canteen! I am on the double-quick myself now!" Some one twirled the canteen to him, and away he went.

. . . For a while the farmhouse appeared to be midway between the opposing forces. Shells broke the window panes, and ploughed up the wounded in the yard, but not a shot went through the house.

During some fifteen or twenty minutes only we were within the rebel lines. Late that afternoon ambulances carried us off to Keedysville.

One other bit of evidence survives to tell of the period of uneasy waiting in the Nicodemus house. In a scrapbook of Civil War items Holmes preserved a slip of paper with a penciled note written on it in a faltering hand: "I am Capt. O. W. Holmes 20th Mass. Son of Oliver Wendell Holmes, M.D. Boston." Beneath the slip in a firm postwar hand is the entry: "I wrote the above in a little house on the field of Antietam which was for a while within the enemy's lines, as I thought I might faint & so be unable to tell who I was." [119] The identification of his father, perhaps, had no different significance from that which might be found in any other similar note written by another son in a moment of equivalent emergency, but one cannot help wondering whether Holmes did not give the identification in the hope that it would have special meaning to a passing Samaritan.[p]

In Holmes's letter of September 18 he told his parents that Dr. Haven of the Fifteenth Massachusetts had said that the wound "wasn't fatal." One piece of evidence suggests either that Holmes was giving a brighter picture to his parents than the facts as he saw them justified, that Dr. Haven was deceiving the Captain, or that

[p] Fifty-seven years after Antietam Holmes recalled another incident in the Nicodemus House. "Fifty seven years ago today I was nearly killed at Antietam. A shot through my neck just dodged the spine and carotid artery but gave me neuralgia for a very long time. I don't believe I ever told you of a curious evidence of how a man's mind works when he thinks he is finished. My great friend [Hallowell] and I lay on the floor of a little house close to the line of battle—for a time inside the enemy's lines. When they had fallen back a doctor came down and my friend's arm being shattered he wanted the doctor to cut it off. The doctor said that if he could get a thin piece of board he could save it. I said if you look behind the looking glass in that clock you probably will find one—which he did, and my friend kept his arm till he died—a few years ago. . . . If I hadn't been at high pressure under the belief that I had my dose I don't suppose that I should have thought of it." Autograph letter to Lady Ellen Askwith, Sept. 17, 1919. (Copy, Harvard Law School.)

another doctor took a more serious view of Holmes's condition. For William G. LeDuc, the officer from General Dana's staff who telegraphed news of the wound to Dr. Holmes, at a later day put down in writing his recollection of the situation of the wounded Captain when he took him in charge. LeDuc had found Holmes unattended, presumably in or near Keedysville, identified him as Dr. Holmes's son, and in his desire to have the Doctor an indirect beneficiary of humane conduct, had a surgeon look at the wound. The surgeon, LeDuc reported, "shook his head when I urged him to give attention to Holmes, and said his duty was to try to save those who had a chance of recovery—that Holmes had none." LeDuc then persuaded the doctor to tell him what he might do as an amateur. "Wash off the blood, plug up the wound with lint, and give him this pill of opium . . . and have him keep quiet," the Doctor replied.[120] The energetic LeDuc then demanded and secured accommodations for his patient at the house of Mrs. Kitzmuller in Keedysville[121] and administered to his needs before sending off the telegram to the anxious family in Boston. The gaiety of the patient persuaded the attendant that the hopeless diagnosis of the doctor with whom he had spoken was not justified. In any case the doctor proved to be a poor prophet. On September 20 a young officer, "evidently wounded, as he had a bandage around his throat and was walking very languidly," appeared in the streets of Hagerstown, Maryland, *en route,* quite evidently, to the loving attentions of home. A fourteen-year-old boy, deputized by his mother, stepped forward to ask if there was anything that could be done for the young officer. The result of the inquiry was that Holmes stopped off in Hagerstown as the guest of Mrs. Howard Kennedy, a faithful Unionist whose house had become a port of refuge for Union soldiers equivalent, almost, to that of Morris Hallowell in Philadelphia.[122] The friendly household of Mrs. Kennedy included, at the moment, a visitor from Philadelphia, Miss Ellen Jones, by whose hand the following letter was written to Boston on September 22, over the signature of the wounded Captain.[123]

Per commissimam formosissimamque amanuensem haec parentibus meis.[q]

Tho unheard from I am not yet dead but on the contrary doing all that an unprincipled son could do to shock the prejudices of parents & of doctors—smoking pipes partaking of the flesh pots of Egypt swelling round as if nothing had happened to me.

I pulled up in good quarters at Hagerstown with most charitable people of whom more anon & not feeling quite inclined to undertake the journey homeward immediately alone—I decided to remain here a few days from which determination my having a good time here did not much detract. In a day or two however I shall start & I may remark I neither wish to meet any affectionate parent half way nor any shiny demonstrations when I reach the desired haven.

Out of charity for you I will state plainly that I am really disgracefully well that I walk about all day & am in no respect in the condition of one who has been hit again within an inch of his life. I will be with you shortly for another jollification in Boston.

Your loving Son
O. W. Holmes, Jr.

I only use an amanuensis from sheer laziness as I can write perfectly well my left arm only being a little paralyzed from the effects of my wound—. . .

Holmes's request that an affectionate parent should not run to his side was natural. He remembered how Dr. Holmes had appeared in Philadelphia after Ball's Bluff and had taken him in charge. Then Holmes was a mere boy and it was, perhaps, pardonable in a parent to treat his wounded son as a sick child. Now, however, the boy had become a veteran and believed that he was able to take care of himself. To have his father once more appear by his side and lead him tenderly back to the family hearth would amount to a denial of the emancipation which had taken place. The request, therefore, that no one should meet him half way was

[q] Mrs. Kennedy's daughter has told of the occasion on which Holmes dictated this, or a similar letter, to Miss Jones: "He dictated in Latin, a letter to his father; but she understood Latin as well as he did, as she confessed when she cautioned him that he was becoming a little too personal concerning herself in moods and tenses." Anna Howard Kennedy Findlay, "Where the Captain Was Found," *Maryland Historical Magazine,* XXXIII, 109, 118 (June 1938).

seriously intended. It was, however, quite ineffective, for before the letter was written, Dr. Holmes was on his way to find his wounded son. On the morning of the 18th, Dr. Holmes had set forth from Boston in search of the Captain. When he chattily told the readers of the December issue of the *Atlantic Monthly* of his disappointments, his adventures, and his final success in "My Hunt after 'The Captain,' " Dr. Holmes, at the climax of his account of the search flavored sentiment with a dash of New England reticence. He had finally learned that his son would be on the Hagerstown-Philadelphia train on September 25, and he boarded it at Harrisburg. "In the first car, on the fourth seat to the right, I saw my Captain; there saw I him, even my first-born, whom I had sought through many cities."

"How are you, Boy?"

"How are you, Dad?" [124]

This was the published version of the meeting of father and son, and there is no good reason to doubt that it accurately recorded the words of the two men and the mood of the father. It is not unlikely, however, that the reticence of the son concealed something other than affectionate gratitude, and that in the unrecorded conversation which followed the terse salutations the Captain asked for some explanation of the Doctor's disregard of the request that this time he was not to be met half way. The Doctor, not having received the request, doubtless felt that he could justify his action. Furthermore, he might have pointed out that it was not unusual for parents, friends, and family physicians of men wounded in the War to rush to the battlefield as soon as the fighting was over, and there attempt to give the aid and comfort which the Army was incapable of providing. The instincts of the doctor and of the father were natural, as also was the irritation of the son with what may well have seemed in the circumstances to be excessive solicitude. Did the son, knowing the father, also fear that from the father's concern and the doctor's interest might later grow the Autocrat's hope that a lively account of personal drama in a setting of national crisis would please the readers of the *Atlantic Monthly?* We cannot know. If that suspicion hovered in the mind of Captain Holmes, the Doctor showed wise discretion as a reporter in not recording the conversation on his return journey to Philadelphia and Boston.

In Philadelphia the Captain paused for two nights at the Hallowell house, where not only his friends Pen Hallowell and Edward Hallowell had already arrived from Antietam but where Lieutenant Colonel Palfrey, seriously wounded in the same battle, was being cared for. Beds were so full of the wounded that Dr. Holmes had to stay with his son's friend, Charles Walton, cousin of the Hallowells. There Dr. Holmes bubbled with almost more than his usual fervor, describing his host's small Negro servant as "a huckleberry with features," [125] and skipped about the city to see its sights and to compare them with Boston's. On Saturday the 27th, thanks to the kindness of the president of the Philadelphia, Wilmington and Baltimore Railroad (brother of President Felton of Harvard), a couch, specially prepared for the wounded Captain, was ready in the railroad car to carry him to New York. Once more the father and son stopped off at the Fifth Avenue Hotel—the father taking the opportunity to look New York over with the critical eye of the Bostonian—and on Monday, took the train to Boston.

> Fling open the window-blinds of the chamber that looks out on the waters and towards the western sun! Let the joyous light shine in upon the pictures that hang upon its walls and the shelves thick-set with the names of poets and philosophers and sacred teachers, in whose pages our boys learn that life is noble only when it is held cheap by the side of honor and of duty.[126]

The son's wish that no affectionate parent should meet him half way had been frustrated; one cannot help wondering whether the companion request that there should be no "shiny demonstrations" on his arrival was fully observed.

No personal record like that which Holmes made after his wounding at Ball's Bluff survives to tell us in what new way the Peninsula campaign and the Battle of Antietam tested or developed his spiritual resources. After Fair Oaks and before the Seven Days, he had sent with a letter to his parents a note in which he recounted something more than the external events of combat, a memorandum, evidently, "to show [his] feelings." When in later life he went over his Civil War letters he destroyed that memorandum, noting as the reason for the act the fact that it was "rather pompous." [127] To speculate about the contents of the note would not be a fruitful effort, yet it may be well to suggest a few of the elements which made of the Peninsula campaign a very different experience than Ball's Bluff had been. The brief encounter on the Potomac had tested the boy's capacity to respond manfully to sudden, intense danger. To pass that test with credit was a considerable achievement, yet the brevity of the ordeal limited its significance. To measure a boy's courage is not to assess a man's fortitude. When Holmes advanced with his Regiment at Fair Oaks he tested and proved once more the qualties that he had shown at Ball's Bluff, but the testing and the proof were incidental to the larger ordeal of the whole campaign. To sustain the prolonged effort something beyond the courage sufficient for a battle was needed. Some of Holmes's friends found their strength in the cause for which they were fighting, others found it in the common commitment of their Company, their Regiment, their Army, and their friends. To assert that Holmes's strength during the Peninsula campaign came entirely from the fact of the commitment and not at all from belief in the cause would not be justified. It is clear, however, that one of the principal sources of his strength was his pride in and ambition for the Twentieth. It was hot resentment, not a balanced sense of justice, which led him to protest against the greater credits that the newspapers gave to other regiments than his. It was loyalty to the Army of the Potomac and not merely devotion to General McClellan which led him to resent civilian control and criticism of military operations. Perhaps Holmes found an added source of strength in a surviving conviction that the Northern cause was "right," yet as the task of defining the cause in other than military terms became increasingly difficult, it is hard to believe that he had found the fortitude for the Seven Days in that conviction. He had discovered, perhaps, that their sufficiency was to be found in their own honor.

4

Civil War: The Later Years

It was six days after Antietam that Lincoln issued his preliminary Emancipation Proclamation announcing that all slaves would be declared free in those states still in rebellion on January 1, 1863. Two days later he abolished the writ of habeas corpus. In the eyes of the radical Republicans it seems that the President had finally recognized the nature of the crusade that he was leading. The Union armies, now carrying the sword of righteousness into battle, would fight, not in the stultifying name of law, but in the vivifying name of Justice. Governor Andrew of Massachusetts spoke for the radical wing of his Party when he insisted that "Republicans must make it *their* business to sustain this act of Lincoln. . . ." Looking forward to the November elections he announced that "we will drive the 'conservatism' of pro-slavery Hunkerism and the reactionaries of despotism into the very caves and holes of the earth. The conquest of the rebels, the emancipation of the slaves, and the restoration of peace founded on liberty and permanent democratic ideas! Let this be our platform." [1] Conservative Republicans, Democrats, and other cautious spirits responded to Lincoln's Proclamation with shouts of indignant protest. The "Hunkers and reactionaries" met in a People's Convention at Faneuil Hall on October 7, 1862. There General Devens, Holmes's future associate on the Supreme Judicial Court, received the nomination as Governor. A resolution was adopted in which the services of General McClellan were acclaimed and a note of warning added: "Let all irregular and irresponsible intermeddling with General McClellan's command of the army, whether in high places or low, by letter-writers in camp or Governors in convention, anywhere and everywhere, henceforth cease." Leading figures in the People's Convention were Josiah Abbott, father of Holmes's intimate friend of the Twentieth, "Little" Abbott, and Judge Joel Parker, his future Professor of Constitutional Law at the Harvard Law School.[2] When Lincoln, on November 7, removed McClellan from his command, replacing him with General Burnside, all political groups, whether they were radical, conservative, or reactionary, saw the action as the consequence of the political decisions which Lincoln had made when he issued his Proclamation of September 22.

In determining how Holmes, convalescing in Boston, responded to these developments, the authentic evidence provides little guidance. A few things we know with certainty. In one of his Civil War Scrap-Books he preserved a printed flyer listing the candidates whom the "Union Republicans," headed by Governor Andrew, were offering to the electorate in the November elections. Beside the flyer Holmes wrote the notation "1st ticket I ever voted." [3] This would seem to indicate that Holmes believed that the radical policies of Andrew and his supporters were preferable to the more cautious program of his opponents. An intimation that a similar belief had been held by Holmes on the eve of Antietam may be found in the letter which he had written to his father on September 17 when, speaking confidently of the military prospects, he had burst forth indignantly: "Damn the N. Y. Herald." [4] Although the *Herald* currently was optimistic about the military prospects, and for that aspect of its policy did not deserve the curses of Holmes, it was bitterly opposed to the Jacobin critics of McClellan.

These items of evidence indicate that in the fall of 1862 Holmes still accepted the principles which Charles Sumner, Wendell Phillips, and Governor Andrew had, in their several ways, defended from the first. The persistence of that loyalty might lead one to suppose that Holmes shared their disgust with McClellan's lukewarm attitude. Yet there is other evidence indicating that Holmes, like most of the other officers in his Regiment, held McClellan in high regard.[a] In December 1862, after Holmes had returned to the front to find demoralized forces serving under the incompetent command of Burnside, he wrote to his father in some despair concerning the possibility of military success and complained that "it is maddening to see men put in over us & motions forced by popular clamor when the army is only willing to trust its life and reputation to one man." [5] It is perfectly clear that it was of McClellan that he spoke.[b] Governor Andrew, for whom Holmes had voted in the previous November, had significantly contributed to the clamor which had forced McClellan's removal. Had Holmes in December abandoned the beliefs which he had accepted in November? It seems unlikely that such a basic change in conviction had occurred in the span of a little more than a month. What seems likelier is that Holmes, during this period, had become increasingly aware of the division of his loyalties. On the one hand, he remained convinced that the Union's cause was not merely self-

[a] There is one comment of his later years that might seem to suggest that during the War Holmes was not an admirer of McClellan. When he read Samuel Eliot Morison's *Oxford History of the United States* in 1928 he said that Morison's account of the Civil War had led him "to modify my old impressions of MacLellan [*sic*]." (*Holmes-Laski Letters,* II, 1075.) Professor Morison's appraisal of McClellan is so balanced that it is difficult to say with confidence whether it was his respect for the General's good qualities or his recognition of his egregious faults that led Holmes to modify his earlier impressions. In general, it may be said that Morison gave McClellan greater credit than did most other historians. The passage in Holmes's letter may, therefore, be read as an indication that he had not fully shared the pro-McClellan sentiments of his fellow-officers. This interpretation finds some support in his explosive outburst against the New York *Herald.* On the other hand it is not at all improbable that the "old impressions" of McClellan to which Holmes referred in 1928 were those which he had formed after the War was over. During that period such a close friend and expert military historian as John C. Ropes, brother of Henry Ropes, had recognized and exposed the military shortcomings of McClellan. See, Ropes, *The Story of the Civil War* (N.Y., 1898), II, *passim.*

[b] In the spring of 1863, Major Whittier wrote to Holmes, then returning to Boston, reporting on conditions in the Army of the Potomac after Chancellorsville. "What do you think of Hooker? What do you think of McClellan?" he asked. He went with this warning: "Now . . . don't permit your dark friends at home to drive you from George B. [McClellan]. He seems to me to be the only man now to bring good out of the Army of the Potomac." Autograph letter, May 15, 1863 (Civil War Scrap-Book, #1, Harvard Law School).

preservation but the abolition of slavery within its old borders. On the other hand, he had come to see that a modern war is a ghastly enterprise in which the fighting soldier's principal concern is with military victory rather than the triumph of civilization. Those with whom he was most intimately associated in the Army were better suited by temperament than he to a soldier's life, and their respect for McClellan as a commander told him that military success could best be achieved under his leadership. A Northern victory in the field might make possible a civilized society, but the achievement of that possibility rather than the attainment of that society was the Army's responsibility. The conflicting loyalties—one to his past, the other to his present affiliations—brought, of course, the misery of confusion and doubt.

Lincoln, perhaps, had been more sensitively aware than any other American of the differing responsibilities of the Army and of the Government. It was that awareness which led such radicals as Charles Sumner and Governor Andrew to distrust his leadership. When he issued the Emancipation Proclamation they believed that he had seen the light and at long last responded to it. Those in the Army who saw its responsibility as limited and believed that McClellan was best qualified for the fulfillment of that responsibility supposed that when emancipation was proclaimed and McClellan removed from his command the Army's task had been made impossible. It was not surprising, in these circumstances, that Union officers did not look upon Lincoln as the great and heroic figure of the War. We know that Holmes did not come to recognize his greatness until later years. "Few men in baggy trousers and bad hats are recognized as great by those who see them." [6] Holmes admitted frankly that he was not among the admirers. "[U]ntil I was middle-aged I never doubted that I was witnessing the growth of a myth. Then the revelation of some facts and the greatness of some of his speeches—helped perhaps by the environing conviction of the later world—led me to accept the popular judgment—which I do, without a great deal of ardor or very great interest in the man." [7]

The conflicting loyalties with which Holmes returned to the

field in November 1862 bred necessarily the misery of doubt. On November 19, the day after he had rejoined his dispirited Regiment, the note of misery found expression in a letter to his sister. He then said that he had "pretty much" made up his mind that the South had achieved its independence.

I am almost ready to hope that spring will see an end. I prefer intervention to save our credit. But believe me, we shall never lick 'em. The Army is tired with its hard and terrible experience and still more with its mismanagement, and I think before long the majority will say we are vainly working to effect what never happens—the subjugation (for that is it) of a great civilized nation. We shan't do it—at least the Army can't.[8]

Dr. Holmes evidently saw this letter or another in which his son expressed similar views. He appears to have replied in some sadness, intimating that the Captain was losing his faith in the ends for which the War was being fought and that he overlooked significant successes. The son's answer was written on December 20 at a moment of supreme despair, just after the disastrous slaughter at Fredericksburg and while Holmes was recovering from the dysentery which had kept him from participating in that engagement.[9]

I never, I believe, have shown, as you seemed to hint, any wavering in my belief in the right of our cause—it is my disbelief in our success by arms in which I differ from you. . . . I think in that matter I have better chances of judging than you—and I believe I represent the conviction of the army—& not the least of the most intelligent part of it. The successes of which you spoke were to be anticipated as necessary if we entered into the struggle. But I see no farther progress. I don't think . . . you realize the unity or determination of the South. I think you are hopeful because (excuse me) you are ignorant. But if it is true that we represent civilization which is in its nature, as well as slavery, diffusive and aggressive, and if civilization and progress are the better things, why they will conquer in the long run, we may be sure, and will stand a better chance in their proper province—peace—than in war, the brother of slavery—brother, it is slavery's parent, child and sustainer at once. At any rate, dear Father, don't, because I say these things imply or think that I am the meaner for saying them. I am, to be sure, heartily tired and half worn out body and mind by this life, but I believe I am as ready as ever to do my duty.

This same letter concluded with a request that his father should send him the new American edition of J. E. Cairnes's *The Slave Power*. It is not improbable that Dr. Holmes in the missing note to which the son's letter of the 20th was responsive had either made explicit references to Cairnes's volume or taken its thesis for granted.[c] A central part of Cairnes's effort had been to show that the slave power of the South was in its nature expansive and that its aggressiveness found its natural satisfaction in war. Professor Cairnes had expressed small sympathy with the die-hard abolitionists who had been willing to surrender the Union if they could purify themselves by disassociating the free states of the North from the slave states of the South, and made the somewhat less righteous but no less passionate principles of Charles Sumner his own. Holmes's letter to his father quite clearly indicates that he was in agreement with that position and suggests that however much the constitutional cause of union may have commanded his loyalty he was convinced that the evil of slavery was the issue of supreme importance. That he was still eager in the black winter of 1862–63 to read the ablest argument against the slave power suggests that despair of military success had not chilled the ultimate conviction for which he fought.

The return journey which Holmes and Abbott had together made from Boston to their Regiment was neither easy nor uneventful, and if they had possessed the energies and talents of

[c] Writing in 1864 to Holmes's friend of Antietam, Colonel LeDuc, Dr. Holmes made some reflections on slavery and the South which probably bespoke his point of view throughout the war. "I have often noticed that there is something child-like in many Southern minds. They seem to have the simplicity of old world peasants of the lower order of Catholics who believe what the priest tells them and have a holy horror of all heretics, as our Southern people have of Boston 'infidels.' Slavery is to a nation what gin is said to be to a child; it keeps a people stunted so that they never seem full-grown intellectually. Unfortunately the arts of war may be practiced very knowingly by people otherwise not well instructed, and these fellows have fought well beyond question." Letter of May 7, 1864. (Copy, Harvard Law School.)

Dr. Holmes they might well have written of their trip under the title "Our Hunt after 'The Twentieth.'" [10] A short stopover in Washington—"that modern Gomorrah"—was sufficient to persuade Holmes that it was "absolutely loathsome" and "stinks of meanness." [11] His glimpse of the capital in wartime, a train trip from there to Warrenton, Virginia, after a stopover in Alexandria, and the discouraging prospect of ever finding the Twentieth led him to draw a moral in a letter to his sister.

> While I'm living *en aristocrat* I'm an out-and-outer of a democrat in theory, but for contact, except at the polls, I loathe the thick-fingered clowns we call the people—especially as the beasts are represented at political centers—vulgar, selfish and base. . . . [T]here are only two civilized places in America—Boston, known for its State House and some cultivation, and Philadelphia, celebrated for the Hallowells, cold slaw, and large-grained hominy.[12]

Leaving Washington as quickly as they could, Holmes and Abbott set out to find their Regiment, which by the last accounts that had reached them was stationed at Warrenton, Virginia. Arriving there they were told that they would find the Twentieth at Warrenton Junction; there they were advised that Sumner's Corps had passed through town two days before on the way to Fredericksburg. The two officers

> started cross country for [the] main road to Fredericksburg. Went on spite of warning of some soldiers (pickets) about "gurillas" likely to pick us up. At dark (rainy) struck a nigger hut, but no road. . . . [On the next morning, November 17, they set out again and] walked over 20 miles stopping occasionally at Secesh houses & finally put up . . . at a good house with a motherly old gal who advised us to go home and get stronger. The women are freer in their expressions than the men & swear the South will stick it out to the end. . . . This morning [November 19] went on the dreary march, roads already getting muddy & cut up—passed soldiers who of course quietly sneered at us as straggling officers (a rare and disgraceful sight) & had got on about 5 miles when we were accosted by an old fella and lo! on t'other side of road THE REGIMENT.[13]

During the next few weeks the Twentieth was stationed in Falmouth while inadequate preparations for the crossing of the Rappahannock and the assault on Fredericksburg were undertaken. The morale of the Regiment was evidently at its lowest ebb; Colonel Lee, worn out and broken by his imprisonment and battles, had just returned from sick leave in Boston but was clearly unable to resume command; Lieutenant Colonel Palfrey, wounded at Antietam, was permanently disabled, and the officers entitled by seniority to command in their stead were disliked and distrusted by their fellow officers. Fortunately, just before Fredericksburg the efforts to disregard the rules of seniority succeeded, and the command was given to Captain Macy, acting as Colonel. Had Holmes not been on the sick list of December 13, he would presumably have filled the position of Acting Major which fell to Abbott as the next ranking Captain in the Regiment. Holmes, however, for some time before the engagement had been stricken with dysentery [14] and was lying in the Regimental Hospital outside Falmouth where he could see the battle of Fredericksburg spread out below him. From there he wrote of the events in which the Twentieth was most honorably engaged.[15]

Dec. 12. 1862.
Near Falmouth Va.
Hospl 20th Mass. V.

My Dear Mother . . .

These have been very trying times for me I assure you. First after being stretched out miserably sick with the dysentery, growing weaker each day from illness and starvation, I was disappointed in getting my papers sending me to Philada. . . . Then yesterday morning the grand advance begins. I see for the first time the Regiment going to battle while I remain behind—a feeling worse than the anxiety of danger, I assure you. Weak as I was I couldn't restrain my tears. I went into the hospital—the only tent left here—listless and miserable. They were just moving out a dead man—while another close to death with the prevailing trouble (dysentery &c.) was moaning close by. In the hospital all day with no prospect of being moved or cared for, and this morning we hear the Regiment has been in it. Exaggerated rumors; then it settles down that poor Cabot is killed—and several, among them my 2nd Lt., wounded. The cannonading of yesterday hasn't recommenced this morning but the day is young and I expect before night one of the great battles of the war. I was on the point of trying to get down there but found I was too weak for the work. Meanwhile another day of anxious waiting—of helpless hopelessness for myself, of weary unsatisfied questioning for the Regt. When I know more I will continue my letter. I have no books I can read. I am going to try to calm myself by drawing, but now four days have passed in disappointed expectations. . . .

Dec. 13. Quiet all yesterday. . . . This morning there's heavy cannonading and just now there's a very lively musketry practise going on—and many a nice fellow going off, I doubt not. Still the popping keeps lively but somehow it doesn't seem to settle down to a good steady roll—but it's brisk—Today will settle I fancy whether we fight more or not; if not whether it shall be one or two.

Dec. 14. Today begun with a smart rattle but later the quiet has been oppressive—They fought all yesterday till after dark with great determination. Lt. Willard . . . & I climbed a neighboring hill & saw the smoke of the musketry; the flash of the shell as they burst; & the rest. We couldn't see the men but we saw the battle—a terrible sight when your Regt is in it but you are safe. Oh what self reproaches have I gone through for what I could not help and the doctor, no easy hand, declared necessary. And in it again the Regt has been. Scarcely anyone now left unhurt, Macy & Patten (Adjt.) Abbott & Murphy—these are all, as far as I can hear. The brigade went at an earthwork & got it with cannister.

Dec. 15. Last night a sharp volley probably from some Regt. wh. got scared on picket—I rejoice to hear that in addition to the four mentioned as safe Mason & Ropes are all right, also Perkins; Half my company is wounded but none killed I judge from the serg't's report—Lt. Alley, Abbott's 2nd Lt., is killed. . . . Hayward they say looked like a butcher, red up to the chin & elbows. . . .

I shouldn't think we'd gained much as yet, unless Franklin has driven back their left a little.—I hear the Rebs. have warned our wounded out of Fredsburg & sure enough the shelling on one side or both has just begun. This is afternoon—you see I write a little from day to day; it will be an interesting diary of one of the most anxious and forlornest weeks of my military experience. . . .

Well—yesterday the fellow I spoke of as near death the day of my going to Hospital, perished & there's another candidate now—Poor devils—there's little enough comfort in dying in camp except it be that one gets accustomed to it (as an Irishman might say) and has plenty of company. But it's odd how indifferent one gets to the sight of death —perhaps, because one gets aristocratic and don't value much a common life. They are apt to be so dirty it seems natural—"Dust to Dust." I would do anything that lay in my power but it doesn't much affect my feelings—and so I'll stop for the present. . . .

The Regt. has been relieved I hear & is on this side—

Afftly
O W H, Jr.

The events which Holmes had observed from his sickbed included those in which the Twentieth achieved its most memorable distinction. Serving in Colonel Hall's Brigade of the Second Division, the Twentieth, with the Nineteenth Massachusetts, Seventh Michigan, and other selected Regiments, had been assigned the task of crossing the Rappahannock, establishing a bridgehead in Fredericksburg, and clearing the city of the enemy. Some fifteen hundred men were on hand to defend it, and concealed in cellars, yards, and gardens within the city were supported by artillery on Marye's Heights, behind Fredericksburg. Burnside, lacking a plan, threw his troops "over the river in a sort of blind hope that so splendid an army, in such overpowering numbers, would somehow achieve a victory." [16] When a precarious bridgehead had been established, the Twentieth was called upon, on the 11th, to clear a passage into the heart of the city. Macy commanding, and Captain Abbott, in the absence of Holmes acting as Major, led the Regiment up the street. "Macy says quietly, 'Mr. Abbott you will take your first platoon forward.' To which A.: 'First Platoon, Forward —March!' and walks quietly ahead. His first platoon is knocked to pieces . . . instantly. 'You'll have to put in the second,' says Colonel Hall. '2nd Platoon, Forward!', and A. leads them into the storm with the same semi-indifferent air that he has when drilling a battalion." [17] In his report of the occasion Colonel Hall stated that "I cannot presume to express all that is due the officers and men of [the Twentieth Regiment], for the unflinching bravery and splendid discipline shown in the execution of the order. Platoon after platoon was swept away, but the head of the column did not falter. Ninety-seven officers and men were killed or wounded in the space of about 50 yards." [18] The courage at the bridgehead had unfortunately made it possible for fresh troops to cross the river before nightfall on the 11th. Had the Twentieth failed in its mission perhaps the bewildered stubbornness of Burnside would have been deflected from its tragic course.

On the 12th the Union forces, holding their bridgehead, waited for General Burnside to decide what course he should follow. It would have been pleasant if the Confederates had abandoned their strong positions and surrendered the battle to Burnside. The General seems to have sustained himself for twenty-four hours on that hope. It was on the 13th that he ordered that some five thousand men of the Second Corps should advance against the forty thousand Confederate troops entrenched on Marye's Heights behind the city. The ghastly consequence—twelve thousand casualties—found the Union forces back on the north bank of the Rappahannock, a demoralized and defeated army.

It is little wonder that the cool courage of "Little" Abbott at Fredericksburg became a legend of his Regiment. For Holmes who would have filled Abbott's post had illness not stood in the way it had a special significance. Accident had made this test another's when it should have been his. That other, until he died in the Wilderness, took persistent pride in his opposition to the cause for which the radicals insisted that the war must be conducted. Abbott who fought at Ball's Bluff, Fair Oaks, the Seven Days, Antietam, Fredericksburg, Chancellorsville, and Gettysburg, applauded heartily the New York rioters who defied the draft in the summer of 1863. Putting his case against the radicals in terms of law he expressed the conviction that ultimately the courts would condemn the Conscription Act as illegal. "The vilest rowdies in

New York have shown the fruit of Lincoln's teachings and if resistance to tyranny is to come only from them, why then despotism will surely triumph as preferable to anarchy. . . . Hurrah for the time when we shall have our heels on [the radicals'] necks, particularly in Massachusetts." [19] Writing in August 1863, Abbott spoke in bitter terms of Dr. Holmes who had delivered a patriotic address in Boston on July 4: [20]

> As for Holmes Senior, I agree with you fully that he is a miserable little manikin, dried up morally and physically, and there is certainly nothing more aggravating than to have such a little fool make orations and talk about traitors and the man who quarrels with the pilot when the ship is in danger. . . . But for all that, his son is a good fellow and remember is *six* feet high.

In his address, Dr. Holmes had described the legalistic critics of Lincoln as men who are "busy holy-stoning the quarter-deck, while all hands are wanted to keep the ship afloat," [21] and in doing so doubtless had in mind such Democrats as Abbott's father, conveniently overlooking the fact that two of Judge Abbott's sons were in the Union forces where they both lost their lives.

Holmes, who had entered the war a radical and had clung to his convictions despite accumulating doubts realized that had he been called upon to perform Abbott's duties at Fredericksburg he might have failed. Would his conviction have sanctified his failure? Had Abbott's doubts diminished his triumph? Surely it was clear that success or failure in these matters did not depend upon conviction. "[T]he faith," said Holmes, "is true and adorable which leads a soldier to throw away his life in obedience to a blindly accepted duty, in a cause which he little understands, in a plan of campaign of which he has no notion, under tactics of which he does not see the use." [22] Startling and even shocking as this pronouncement may sound in the ears of a generation which has forgotten the politics and heroism of the Civil War, it stated the feelings of one who had seen his closest friends die in a war mismanaged by generals and committed to objectives in which they did not believe.

The exact date when Holmes was released from the hospital is not known. On December 17, 1862, Captain Abbott spoke as if Holmes would soon rejoin the Regiment.[23] On the 21st, when Colonel Lee was finally compelled to leave the Regiment, his departure was marked by an address expressing the feeling of those who had served under him. It was written by Holmes.[24]

The officers of the Twentieth here present, in behalf of themselves and their absent brothers, earnestly desire to express to their Colonel who is now retiring from the post he has so long held with such honor to himself and his regiment, their affection and appreciation, and their regret for the necessity which compels him to leave them.

Entering the regiment as strangers, your constant and truly parental kindness begot in us an almost filial love. Your example taught us more perfectly than we could learn elsewhere to strive not only to acquire the discipline of soldiers, but the high feelings and patriotic self-sacrifice of chivalrous gentlemen. How could we, young and with comparatively little to leave behind, repine at any self-denial when we saw our Colonel, leaving wife and children, constantly endure without thought of self, hardships which tested the strength of the strongest, and face without shrinking, danger which tried the courage of the bravest hearts.

It moved us at once to admiration and to sadness, to see you defying with indomitable will, the sickness and exhaustion to which any other would have yielded, and returning again and again in spite of failing strength to lead your regiment or command the brigade through every hard fought action.

And now, sir, that the ill health against which you have so nobly borne up compels you to resign the command of the regiment whose fame is identified with your own, you will not be less present to our hearts and remembrances as a tender friend and gallant commander, than when you were present to lead us forward in the field.

In January Holmes secured the leave which had been denied him just before Fredericksburg, and he went, as so often before, to the hospitable Hallowell house in Philadelphia to recover fully from the dysentery.[25] There his parents came to see him. While there he saw the Philadelphia poet and playwright, George H. Boker, whose poem "The Crossing at Fredericksburg" gave

Holmes an anonymous notoriety. One wonders whether it was the Captain or Dr. Holmes who gave Boker the facts on which poetic fancy played with such patriotic fervor.[26]

I lay in my tent at mid-day,
Too full of pain to die,
When I heard the voice of Burnside
And an answering shout reply.

I heard the voice of the General,—
'T was firm, though low and sad;
But the roar that followed his question
Laughed out till the hills were glad.

"O comrade, open the curtain,
And see where our men are bound,
For my heart is still in my bosom
At that terrible mirthful sound."

. . . . .

"O to go, but to go with my comrades!
Tear the curtain away from the hook;
For I'll see them march down to their glory,
If I perish by the look."

. . . . .

"O, help me, help me, comrade!
For tears my eyelids drown,
As I see their starry banners
Stream up the smoking town.

"And see the noisy workmen
O'er the lengthening bridges run,
And the troops that swarm to cross them
When the rapid work be done.

"For the old heat, or a new one,
Flames up in every vein;
And with fever or with passion
I am faint as death again.

"If this is death I care not!
Hear me, men, from rear to van!
One more cheer for Massachusetts,
And one more for Michigan!"

Even the most patriotic of poets would have found it hard in the weeks after Fredericksburg to hear the soldiers' shouts responding to the voice of Burnside. Lieutenant Henry Ropes on January 13 described to his brother an occasion on which Burnside, with the Divisional commander, General Howard, had reviewed his troops at Falmouth. After elaborate preparations

> Burnside rode by. Here and there a feeble cheer was raised. I really felt sorry for him when he took off his hat as he rode down our front, but there was dead silence, and he put it on again. When he got through, General Howard thought he must get a little enthusiasm out of the poor frozen men, and riding in front, called out: "Now, three cheers for General Burnside! One! Two! Three!" But not one single shout was raised, not a single voice, and he rode back apparently much vexed. I heard at a late review, probably of a less disciplined Corps, the men yelled: "Butcher!" at Burnside, as he rode down.[27]

"Little" Abbott reported that on the evening of January 18 the men of the Twentieth passed their time "groaning Abe Lincoln and cheering Jeff Davis in the most vociferous manner." [28] Contemporaneously Henry Ropes reported that the "state of the Army is shocking. . . . They have no confidence whatever in their leader. . . . What with constant fighting, poor food, no pay, innumerable hardships, and defeats in battles . . . officers of high rank are squabbling and almost talking treason." [29] Until January 28, when Burnside was relieved of his command, the Army of the Potomac, as Holmes later said, was "as flabby as a dead jelly fish." The selection of Hooker to replace Burnside had, however, an amazingly prompt effect on morale. "[I]n a week men who had never seen him, got a swagger on and believed they could do things." [30] Holmes's suggestion of the previous month that the Army was "only willing to trust its life and reputation to one man"

—McClellan—was shown for the moment, at least, to have been something less than accurate. Improved as the situation appeared to be under Hooker, there were, however, many who were uneasy about what might lie ahead. Henry Ropes's loyalty to McClellan remained unshaken: in the middle of April he wrote to his brother saying that he did not expect "to see the Rebellion put down until General McClellan is in Halleck's place and is left with full control for at least 18 months. Perhaps we must wait until he is in Lincoln's place." [31] Towards the end of the month and shortly before the futile efforts at Chancellorsville he wrote again predicting that "if General Hooker should meet with an overwhelming defeat and the Rebels should take Washington, and Congress and the President escape to Philadelphia and the whole country be thrown into panic, then every eye would turn to McClellan. The President and Halleck would fall on their knees and beg him to save them." [32]

During the winter weeks of readjustment and preparation the Twentieth, in recognition of its distinguished service at Fredericksburg, had been given the assignment of Provost Guard at Army Headquarters in Falmouth. Holmes was appointed Provost Marshal of the town. His duties as such brought him into pleasant and intimate relationship with officers outside of the Twentieth. His old associate and intimate friend, Charles A. Whittier, had left his Regiment to serve as aide-de-camp to the commander of the Sixth Corps, General John Sedgwick. Letters which Whittier wrote to Holmes during the war indicate that Sedgwick took a notable liking both to his aide and to his aide's friend. An officer in the Regular Army, Colonel Norman J. Hall, also was an increasingly close friend of Holmes. These associations brought satisfaction not only in their assurance that Holmes himself was respected by such men, but that the Twentieth was seen by these officers of the Regular Army to have qualities about it that most other volunteer regiments lacked. The soldier's familiar pride in his "outfit" was by no means missing in Holmes. Passages from two letters to his father, written in March 1863, reveal the feeling of satisfaction.[33]

March 18, 1863
Falmouth Va.

". . . Since I was last at Sedgwicks to see Whit. (HdQrs 6th Corps) Sedgwick said to Whit. "Tell Capt. Holmes he must come over again soon I want to hear him talk" or words to that effect. Likewise if a certain party didn't get a Comm'n as Major and go on his staff he asked Whit. how would the Captain like the place to which W. very properly responded that I wouldn't take it. But from this . . . I fancy old John rather likes me & you must know that John Sedgwick is one of the biggest Maj. Genls. now in our army. Today it was suggested to me (as it has previously been also to Ropes (Lt.)) that I should take Provost-Marshalship of Corps wh. also I politely declined. I should like a good staff appointment but I wouldn't leave the Regiment. I tell you these things because you like to hear 'em & Sedgwick's talk did tickle me a little (though it only showed personal liking). The latter merely came from Maj. Mallon who is now Provost-Marshal 2nd Corps & Lt. Potter (son of Bishop) who wanted some one & knew that the 20th were A.1. and that our crowd was a pleasant one.

Yr Loving Son
O W H, Jr.

Falmouth Va.
Mar. 29—'63

My Dear Old Dad

I had my blowoff in one of my last and now let bygones be bygones —if *you* will—for I fear I was somewhat in the mood wh. would have led to sass had I been at home—Imprimis—I send two sketches of Fredsburg by Col. Hall who, thank the Lord, has returned to the Brigade—also a rough one of Fair Oaks which he surveyed & mapped out— [34]

What a joy it is to have a man thoroughly educated to his biz. well-bred, knowing what's what & imparting his knowledge in place of one who tells you his Regiment (not such a remarkable one except for a Penn. Regt) has been in 42 battles & other unending blowing about himself, it, and the transcendent merits of both . . . I was talking to Hall about this *blowing* being something I didn't much like or understand & he said "Yes your Regiment is more like old times" (meaning thereby the old Regular Army where Officers *were* Gentlemen) "than anything I have seen in the Army." which in connection with other remarks about the perfection of their present condition and their behavior in the Field rather pleased me. He said "The 20th have no poetry in a fight" and there *is* about as little excitement & hullabulloo on those occasions as may be. . . . I really very much doubt whether there is any Regiment wh. can compare with ours in the Army of the Potomac. Everyone says this, perhaps, who belongs to a good Regiment but still I fancy I am right from the evidence of many things.

Now I fancy the time is counted by days almost, rather than by weeks, before we move—and by weeks only before we fight.

Ah well, I am trying to see things straight in my own mind before it all begins so as to be ready and cheerful.

I am a little totty bit melancholy just now but that will soon be gone as it is only a passing cloud. It's very well to recommend theoretical porings over Bible & Homer. One's time is better spent with Regulations & the like and any connected study situated as I am is rather impossible. What I do read is chiefly connected with War and Fiction.

The discretion of his middle and later years led Holmes to destroy a number of his own Civil War letters as well as all those which his parents and family wrote to him while he was at the front. The recent "blowoff" to which he referred in the opening of this last letter seems to have been sacrificed to that later discretion, and only surmise as to its cause is possible. Perhaps it was the condition of things in the Army of the Potomac; more probably it concerned some preachment of his father's, relating to war objectives and his son's falterings of faith as to their attainment. The Doctor's suggestion that spare time before the opening of the spring campaign might be devoted to the Bible and Homer hardly bespoke an imaginative understanding of the interests of a young volunteer whose concern at that particular moment was largely given to the establishment of friendly working arrangements with officers of the Regular Army.

Among the letters which Holmes preserved is a brief note from his friend Pen Hallowell which, standing as it does alone and without collateral documents or other evidence to add perspective, can justify little more than tantalizing questions. On January 26, 1863, Governor Andrew had been authorized by the President to recruit a regiment of volunteers made up of "persons of African descent," to be commanded by white officers. Robert Gould Shaw accepted the Colonelcy and Hallowell, the sole abolitionist officer in the Twentieth, had accepted the Lieutenant-Colonelcy.[35] It was of this matter that Hallowell wrote to Holmes.[36]

State House, Boston
Feb. 7th (?) [1863]

Dear O. W.

By a power as irresistible as fate I am drawn into the colored regiment (54th) as Lt. Col. Would you take the majority? not that it would be offered to you certainly, but your name would command attention. Bob Shaw has accepted the Colonelcy.

Difficulties of every kind rise up. One by one they will be overcome. I retain my position in the 20th for the present.

Thine affectionately
N. P. Hallowell

Holmes's reply has not, apparently, survived, and the records of the Fifty-fourth tell nothing of whether Holmes's name was ever considered by Colonel Shaw and the Governor. It is possible, of course, that Holmes indicated a willingness to accept the commission and that the application was rejected.[37] That decision, however, seems unlikely and it is probable that it was by his own choice that Holmes remained with the Twentieth. He had already rejected suggestions that he should accept transfer to more attractive posts. Hallowell, to be sure, was willing to leave the Regiment, but his fidelity to abolitionism, sustained not only by religion but by the commitments of his entire family, had not weakened.

The single fact of which we are certain—that Hallowell suggested that Holmes might secure the Majority in the Fifty-fourth—supports one significant probability. That is that Holmes's convictions as to the purposes and ends for which the war was being fought were sufficiently similar to those of Hallowell to make him seem a suitable man to fill an important post in the colored regiment. On January 30 Governor Andrew had written to Colonel Shaw's father setting forth the standards which he proposed to follow in the commissioning of officers of field grade.

I am desirous to have for its officers . . . young men of military experience, of firm anti-slavery principles, ambitious, superior to a vulgar contempt of color, and having faith in the capacity of colored men for military service. Such officers must necessarily be gentlemen of the highest tone and honor; and I shall look for them in those circles of educated anti-slavery society which, next to the colored race itself, have the greatest interest in this experiment.[38]

When Hallowell expressed his desire to propose Holmes for the Majority he surely had in mind the standards of selection prescribed by the Governor. The letter from Hallowell clearly suggests that Holmes, despite the effort of his other friends in the Twentieth to make him a good Copperhead, had not lost all of the crusading spirit. If he rejected Hallowell's proposal one of the considerations which led him to that decision may well have been the doubt whether one whose idealism had chilled should participate in an enterprise of idealism. The Negro regiment, it must be remembered, was to be enlisted as much to prove the radicalism of the Northern cause as to strengthen the military forces of the Union. Though Holmes in 1863 might still have rejoiced if the proof were made, it is not surprising that he found reasons to stand personally aside from the process of proof.

The brief confidence which General Hooker imparted to his men carried the Army of the Potomac into the Battle of Chancellorsville with eagerness and enthusiasm. It even served to make the needless defeat seem something less than the disaster which it was. The Twentieth had not lacked enthusiasm before the unsuccessful effort was launched, for in April when it was suggested that a direct assault against Fredericksburg might be repeated, despite the December failure of Burnside, Macy, then commanding the Twentieth, was asked whether his Regiment would lead in the "desperate assault." Henry Ropes reported that Macy "has, of course, accepted." [39] Fortunately for the Twentieth, however, plans were changed and it was not included with the forces under Sedgwick which, with comparative ease, took Fredericksburg from the south on May 3. The twentieth on the same morning crossed the Rappahannock without opposition, passed through the streets which four months previously had witnessed their most heroic efforts, and moved out of the town along the River Road towards Chancellorsville. Held up by the demolition of bridges, the Regiment paused in an open field within the range of Confederate artillery on Marye's Heights. The events which then occurred were described in Holmes's letters to his parents.[40] The first was written in pencil on a battered slip of paper.

May 3. [1863]

Dear Mother

Ned Paine arrived here last night & is at present occupied in his maiden battle—if not killed.[41] Pour moi I'm already hit in the heel—bullet from spherical case—

Pleasant to see a d'd gun brought up to an earthwork deliberately brought to bear on you—to notice that your Co. is exactly in range—1st discharge puff—second puff (as the shell burst) and my knapsack supporter is knocked to pieces. . . . 2nd discharge man in front of me hit—3d whang the iron enters through garter & shoe into my heel—

They have been firing hard ever since & as the stretcher is waiting for me I stop.

Your loving
O W Holmes, Jr.

later I've been chloroformed & had bone extracted—probably shant lose foot

May 4, 63

Dear Father

I've written two or three epistles wh. I suspect will not reach you & so write again. I'm hit in the heel—ball (from sperical [*sic*] case) buried in Os Calcis—chloroformed & ball extracted—foot didn't have to come off as was feared—

I shall start for Phila, as soon as I can get my leave.

Love to all
O W Holmes, Jr.

Murphy flesh wound in arm
No one else hurt

The casual references to the possibility that Holmes's wound would necessitate the amputation of his foot concealed a desire which he expressed at the time and which he recalled in later years, but which he did not mention in the quoted letters. Writing to Holmes on May 13, ten days after the wounding, his friend Whittier quoted Dr. Hayward, who had first attended to the wound, as reporting that "Holmes seemed to be rather sorry that he wasn't to lose his foot." [42] Seventy-one years later Holmes vividly recalled his prayers after the wounding that he might lose his foot in order that duty might not a third time compel him to return to the front.[43] The letters to his parents spoke cheerfully, but the mood behind them was of despair that the end of strain and suffering might not even yet be in sight.

After the customary stopover in Philadelphia Holmes returned to Charles Street for the longest period of convalescence which he experienced during the war. On May 25 his father described to Dr. Hunt of Philadelphia, who had once more cared for the wounded Captain en route to Boston, how things were going with his patient.[44]

> Wendell has been doing very well, but of course without any notable change. There has been very little pain, no mark of inflammation, nothing but what belongs to the healing process. . . . He is in excellent spirits, not at all nervous, as when he was last wounded, is very reasonably tractable, avoids stimulants, smokes *not* enormously, feeds pretty well, and has kept tolerably quiet until today, when Dr. Bigelow let him ride out, and is, on the whole, a quite endurable patient. . . .
>
> Dr. Bigelow has done nothing but keep the wound open as you did. He makes him use a little plug of *carrot* for that purpose, which is handy enough, and seems to agree very well with the wound. . . . I pinched W's heel a little the other day and asked him into what vegetable I had turned his carrot. No answer.
>
> Why, into a Pa's nip! was my response.

No other wit could make that particular sally, but the Captain was so frequently the subject of a more obvious, if less elaborate, effort of his visitors and friends that it taught him a lesson in psychology which he never forgot. "I early realized the illusion of personality in the really mechanical action of the mind. When I was wounded in the heel, I would see man after man approach with self-gratulatory smile as he made a reference to Achilles. Each had the feeling of personal achievement while he really was moving along the path of least resistance. . . ." [45]

The extended period of recovery not only gave Holmes a fuller opportunity than had the earlier Boston interludes to see his friends, but it gave him the chance to do some of that more serious reading—though not in the Bible and Homer—which his father had thought suitable for spare hours on the Rappahannock. War had not appreciably altered the direction of the intellectual interests of his undergraduate years, and there was need to catch up with the current of English scientific and philosophical thought. Herbert Spencer's *Social Statics,* in its devotion to the dogma of laissez-faire individualism, must have seemed a strangely doctrinaire piece of theorizing to one who was supporting in war his government's refusal to allow the Southern states to follow the path of their own choosing. In Spencer's *First Principles* Holmes, who did not read Darwin until 1907 [46] found the Darwinian formula so skillfully applied to the institutions of human society that its thesis was thereafter a fixed element in his own thought. Holmes spoke for himself as well as for his generation when he said to Sir Frederick Pollock that "I doubt if any writer in English except Darwin has done so much to affect our whole way of thinking about the universe" as Spencer.[47] Convalescence brought indulgence not only of the interest in sociology but of the old enthusiasm for philosophical inquiry. James Mill's *Analysis of the Human Mind,* John Stuart Mill's *Logic,* and, once more his *Dissertations and Discussions,* as well as Plato's *Dialogues* and Herschel's *Essays* were all among the books taken from the Athenaeum during the period of convalescence.

From his friends at Falmouth Holmes received frequent letters telling him of regimental gossip. On June 8 Lieutenant Henry Ropes told him of the inadequacies of Colonel Paul Revere, who had recently been given the command of the Regiment, and of the great promise which Holmes's cousin, Lieutenant Sumner Paine, was showing in his first weeks of military life. "Everything dull enough," he reported, adding an expression of hope that "we shall break up the monotony soon and do something or go somewhere." [48] One month later, when the Battle of Gettysburg had come to its bloody conclusion on July 3, among the Union dead were Colonel Revere, Lieutenant Paine, and Lieutenant Ropes. For Holmes the greatest of these losses was Ropes, the young soldier who had fought heroically for the Union doubting that its cause should be the abolition of slavery, and who met his death, incongruously enough, seated under a tree on the battlefield reading Dickens.[49] His elder brother, John C. Ropes, disqualified by physical disability from serving in the Army, became one of the most distinguished military historians of the war and offered Holmes invaluable guidance and encouragement in his first years at the Boston bar. When the body of Henry Ropes arrived in Boston his brother wrote to Holmes asking him if he would serve with two other officers of the Twentieth as pallbearers at the funeral. He suggested that Holmes might prefer not to visit the undertaker's to see the body. "It is, I am grieved to say, not in a state to be seen. It would not do to open the coffin. All that can be seen through the glass plate is the breast, which is bare, and in which is a fearful wound in the region of the heart, which must have caused instant death. . . . It is a sad and shocking sight. Nothing of the face can be seen but the chin, round which is a handkerchief." [50] Holmes had escaped the dangers of Gettysburg but not its tragedy.

During the period of his convalescence Holmes was forced to face a problem of his future course of conduct which caused him great uneasiness of mind. As a result of the death of Colonel Revere at Gettysburg it became evident that Lieutenant Colonel Macy should be promoted from Lieutenant Colonel to command the Regiment. By right of seniority Holmes, in the normal course of events, would succeed to the Lieutenant Colonelcy, but he was at home, as was Macy, for an uncertain period while their friend Abbott, holding a Captain's commission, acted as Colonel. Just after Chancellorsville Holmes had suggested to Abbott that if the situation which in fact developed after Gettysburg should ever occur it would be his inclination to waive promotion in favor of his friend.[51] During the summer while Holmes was in Boston he evidently repeated the proposal to Abbott. His friend, however, resisted the suggestion.[52] Whether it was Abbott's plea, the desire of his parents to see him advance in the normal course, or a final determination that such magnanimity would be quixotic which led Holmes to consent to the promotion we do not know. We do know that in the end Holmes notified the Governor's aide that he would accept the Lieutenant Colonel's commission if it were issued,[53] that he received the commission, and that Abbott considered that his friend's impulses in the whole matter were characterized by the highest generosity—"a voluntary attempt at self-sacrifice." [d] In late September 1863, the rumor reached Abbott that, disgusted by the slowness of his recovery, Holmes was considering quitting the service. Abbott's objection to any such course of conduct was vigorous and immediate.

No matter if you have to stay at home six months longer, if you will then be well, stick to it. I want to ask you in the earnestest manner possible not for a moment to be influenced by any idea that in staying at home while you are unable to come out, you are keeping others out. All that is damned nonsense. I tell you we can't afford to lose you. . . . I tell you, my dear Oliver, that when we heard that rumor that you

[d] Autograph letter, Henry L. Abbott to Josiah G. Abbott, Sept. 18, 1863 (Houghton Library). In this same letter Abbott, sympathetic with his father's strong Copperhead inclinations, came to the defense of Holmes. "I am glad," he wrote, "you are going to take Holmes under your wing. His father, of course, one can't help despising. But Oliver Junior, though you have an instinctive dislike to his speculative nature, is infinitely more manly than the little conceited Doctor. I am very confident, that he is worthy of your friendship, because a man here in the hardships and dangers of the field can easily detect what is base in a man's character, and it is particularly trying to Holmes who is a student rather than a man of action. But since I have seen him intimately, he has always been most cool, cheerful, and self sacrificing. And I think his action in regard to my commission is simply, entirely a gratuitous act of generosity that would not be seen in any other regiment. He is considered in the army a remarkably brave and well instructed officer, who has stuck to his work, though wounded often enough to discourage any but an honorable gentleman."

talked of leaving us, we all felt alike. . . . Don't be frightened by any sixty day order & be assured that it will be long in the future before you hear any complaints from a single officer in the regiment, & complaints, you know, always begin long before justice demands. If any impudent stay-at-home wide-awake asks you when you are coming back, punch his head.[54]

In a letter of October 8 Abbott expressed the warmest satisfaction in Holmes's final decision to return to the Regiment. In expressing his delight, Abbott said: "I believe you have done not only what is agreeable to yourself and us, but what is thoroughly right & proper, instead of absurdly wasting yourself before the shrine of the great nigger." [55] This blunt language suggests the possibility that Holmes had once more been asked to take a commission in a colored regiment and had once more rejected the proposal. Colonel Shaw of the Fifty-fourth had been killed and Major Edward N. Hallowell had been gravely wounded at Fort Wagner in July, and there had been heavy casualties among the officers of the Fifty-fifth Regiment under the command of Norwood Penrose Hallowell. It is by no means unlikely that one of the Hallowell brothers had again sought to persuade Holmes to fill a vacancy among the field officers in one of those regiments.[56]

In August Holmes had begun to learn to ride, against the day when he should return to his Regiment a field officer and no longer lead a company into action afoot.[57] At that time he also had in mind the possibility of accepting the suggestion of his friend Whittier, aide to General Sedgwick, that he should obtain at least temporary appointment to a staff position in Sedgwick's corps—the Sixth. For such a post, of course, horsemanship was an essential requirement and in letters from Whittier the suggestion is clear that Holmes's efforts to become a horseman were related to the real possibility that Holmes, instead of rejoining the Twentieth, would accept a staff appointment.[58]

Not until January 3, 1864, was Holmes's wound sufficiently healed for him to return to the Regiment. When he went back, however, the situation there was such as to make his stay exceedingly brief. Commissioned Lieutenant Colonel of the Regiment by Governor Andrew, he could not be mustered into service with that rank but could only fill the shoes of a captain—and there were captains already commissioned and mustered in for each company. The impossibility of his being mustered in at the new rank resulted from the fact that Macy, though commissioned Colonel, had not yet been mustered as such, and therefore still filled the Lieutenant Colonel's position. Abbott, however, had been both commissioned and mustered as Major. Dr. Holmes wrote to Senator Sumner in a state of some indignation, asking that steps should be taken to have the confused situation straightened out by arranging that Macy should be mustered in as Colonel, thus breaking the log jam by which Holmes's effective advancement was stopped.[59]

> Yesterday Lieut. Co. Holmes went back to the army [wrote the distressed Doctor]. There he will find that Abbott has been *mustered* in as Major, but as he himself (O W H Jr.) has not yet been mustered in, what will be his position?
>
> My son will find himself practically under his inferior officer—being a Lieutenant Colonel by commission, but in fact only a Captain.
>
> Now he has the highest opinion and personal liking for Abbott, but he was Abbott's senior, and cannot after receiving his commission in due order of promotion, serve under him—nobody would expect him to do so.
>
> The consequence is he will feel compelled to leave a regiment with which he has been identified from Ball's Bluff to Fredericksburg, and try to get appointed to some staff or other. . . .
>
> Can nothing be done to right this wrong?

It is uncertain how accurately the Doctor's indignation represented the feelings of his son. One suspects that the indignity of serving under a junior officer meant less to Holmes than it did to the Doctor; the practical situation resulting from the fact that there was a captain commissioned and mustered for each company made difficulties of a more substantial sort than those which Dr. Holmes emphasized. In any case, the situation was so confused that it is no wonder that Whittier's earlier suggestion that Holmes should secure a staff position in the Sixth Corps bore fruit. By Special Orders of January 29 General Sedgwick directed that Captain Holmes should report for temporary staff duty at the Headquarters of General Horatio G. Wright, divisional commander.[60] By those orders Holmes's association with the Twentieth was, as a practical matter, brought to its end.

The condition of the nation and the condition of the nation's forces had undergone significant changes in the months which had passed between Holmes's wounding before Chancellorsville and his return to duty. The Conscription Act of July 1863 reflected the public's recognition that victory would not come in a quick and dashing campaign. Although the currents of battle and even the tides of war had turned in the Union's favor at Gettysburg, it was seen that the voyage to reunion must be prolonged. The spokesmen of New England radicalism, Andrew and Sumner, retained their political authority; the President's Northern critics, led by Vallandigham in Ohio, kept dissension alive, and when Lincoln, in December 1863, outlined his forgiving plan of reconstruction, the North was compelled to reconsider and redefine its war aims. On the military side the successes of Grant in the west brought home to the nation the ugly fact that victories were to be won by "sanguinary war," and when in March 1864 he was assigned to the command of the Armies of the United States it was clear that a new phase of Northern strategy was about to open. On March 27 Henry Abbott wrote to his mother of the prospects of the Army of the Potomac. "We shall have by long odds the greatest battles ever fought on this continent. Every battle grows worse and as this corps lost 45% at Gettysburg, it will probably lose 50% this time. . . . It makes me sad to look on this gallant regiment which I am instructing and disciplining for slaughter to think that probably 250 or 300 of the 400 which go in, will get bowled out." [61] Throughout the month of April, Grant was at the headquarters of the Army of the Potomac at Culpeper planning his offensive. It was on May 4 that the campaign of forty bloody days began, taking the Army of the Potomac through the Wilderness, Spotsylvania, Cold Harbor, and up to the gates of Petersburg. The

War was not concluded, the Union effort had failed, yet the army of Grant remained confident of its commander and of its ultimate success. These weeks of service were Holmes's last experience of war.

The closing months of Holmes's military career, though they took him out of the line, by no means took him out of action. The duties of a staff officer during a campaign as vigorous and bloody as that which General Grant fought in the Wilderness and at Spotsylvania were scarcely less dangerous, and no less demanding, than those of a combat commander. Another staff officer with the Sixth Corps described with accuracy the duties which fell to him and his associates to perform.[62]

> The troops are going wearily into camp. "Major, we march to Frying Pan Shoals tomorrow, about twenty miles: this map is wretched. Go there, acquaint yourself with the road and the best places to halt for water, and be back here by daybreak." Then, on another horse, through the dark woods, through the blinding rain, with a colored man for guide, nothing but blackness visible, which is well for no guerrillas will be abroad, I press on all the lonely night, and take my place in the marching column again at dawn, to traverse again the same road. Staff duty was no sinecure, though no doubt it seemed so to our brethren of the line, as we dashed by on good horses, sometimes guilty of a "boiled shirt," and often attaining a square meal at a farmhouse distant from the column while our orderlies kept watch and ward. But our duty was never finished. When the regimental officers were lying down by the fire and smoking a last pipe before turning in, we were on our way to some other corps or to army headquarters to get or give information, or we were making ready in various ways for the march and fight tomorrow.

In the Diary which Holmes kept while on General Wright's staff the incessant strain, the exhausting tension, and the constant demands which duty put upon nerves and body stand out even more clearly than in the intermittent letters written from the Twentieth in the earlier campaigns. The entries describing Holmes's impression of the Battle of the Wilderness—"a battle which no man saw or could see"— [63] are characteristic.[64]

May 6 [1864]—(Hot but fine day)

A simultaneous attack was tried at 5 a.m. advanced some way—not much effected however—a marsh, abattis & battery in our front—General W. managed to keep himself & staff pretty well in range of their shells—Lost some prisoners stuck up to waist in marsh, in their attempt to charge—Seymour tried to advance 7:40 a.m. but found himself outflanked.

Our H.Q. were exposed all day to pretty sharp arty. practice from 3 different directions partly drawn by the sight of our horses—several horses & men hit.

At dusk after a brief picket fire & just as Gen. Sedgwick was expressing apprehensions and sending to reinforce the right, the enemy flanked & broke Seymour & Shaler—& there was a stampede of these Brig-s. back to plank road—Seymour prisoner, Shaler missing.

We all tried to rally the troops but in vain. . . .

(Mem. May 16. I see the papers, esp. Tribune mention very complementarily conduct of Staff of Gens Sedgwick & Wright.)

May 7.

Up all night in the saddle—establishing new line—our right (Russell) resting on plant road—Gen. Neill on right of the road—Cavalry sent up the road, but got stampeded & mizzled—About 4 a.m. Farrar & I fell in with McCartney's Batty. on the road and he gave us a wash & a breakfast—Found Gens. S. and W. just afterwards—No fighting, except picket firing on line of 6th Corps. Horse got his only feed for 36 hours in the a.m.—

Not much except picket firing today—

Orders to march at 8½ P.M. postponed to 9½ P.M. Were on the road all night.

This day was very fatiguing—my heart beat strangely & I felt somewhat as I remember doing at Harrison's Landing—

Lee started within an hour of the time we did, they say, & we taking all night to make Chancellorsville L. was enabled to get to Spottsylva. Ct. Hs. just ahead of us, marching by a parallel road—I suppose the "Brook Road"—I think this was discreditable to us—

May 8.

At daylight made Chancellorsville passing 9th C. & Burnside. Road crowded with (Supply) Trains and a long line of Ambulances. . . .

Stopped at Piney Br. Church for troops to breakfast—Advanced turning to left at church. After going a mile or 2 found woods afire & bodies of Rebs. & our men just killed and scorching—just as we were forming a line of battle Warren sent word he was hard pressed & Gen. W. sent forward all but Upton Brig. of his Div. Arty. remained behind—I was sent to notify Gen. Sedgwick—looked in vain for him at H.Q.A.P. & got snubbed by Gen Meade—After seeing Gen S. returned to front so tired I could hardly sit up. . . .

May 9.

. . . Morn'g 1st Div. passed from Warren's right to his left to rejoin Corps—We had just arrived when Whittier rode up to Gen. W. with news that Sedgwick was killed—we had been with him a moment before—he was in an exposed angle between Warren's front & ours & had just been chaffing a man for ducking at the bullets of a sharpshooter; saying "Why man they couldn't hit an elephant here at this distance"—he was struck on one side of the nose & sunk senseless & soon died—McMahon & Whittier were with him at the time—

Gen. Wright took the Corps by commd. Gen Meade although Ricketts ranked him—Nothing in particular except advancing pickets —reconnaisances &c I believe during today. . . .

In such a hurried account of events in the Wilderness on the 6th there was no place to record an occurrence which more than any other went to Holmes's heart. On that day "Little" Abbott, commanding the Twentieth in place of Macy who had again been wounded, finally met his death. Twenty-one years later the feeling of personal loss was still a vivid reality, and no passage in Holmes's Memorial Day Address of 1884 was as heartfelt as that in which he spoke of Abbott's memory.[65]

He entered the army at nineteen, a second lieutenant. In the Wilderness, already at the head of his regiment, he fell, using the moment that was left him of life to give all his little fortune to his soldiers. I saw him in camp, on the march, in action. I crossed debatable land with him when we were rejoining the army together. I observed him in every kind of duty, and never in all the time that I knew him did I see him fail to choose that alternative of conduct which was most disagreeable to himself. He was indeed a Puritan in all his virtues, without the Puritan austerity; for, when duty was at an end, he who had been the master and leader became the chosen companion in every pleasure that a man might honestly enjoy. . . . He was little more than a boy, but the grizzled corps commanders knew and admired him; and for us, who not only admired, but loved, his death seemed to end a portion of our life also.

Holmes paid another tribute to his friend a few months after the Wilderness in a sonnet which appeared anonymously in the Boston *Evening Transcript* in October 1864. Its feeling and its form show that the war had not destroyed the instinct and the talent which Holmes possessed at its opening.[66]

H. L. A.

Twentieth Massachusetts Volunteers

He steered unquestioning nor turning back,
Into the darkness and the unknown sea;
He vanished in the starless night, and we
Saw but the shining of his luminous wake.
Thou sawest light, but ah, our sky seemed black,
And all too hard the inscrutable decree.
Yet, noble heart, full soon we follow thee,
Lit by the deeds that flamed along thy track.
Nay, art thou hid in darkness, shall we say,
Or rather whisper with untrembling lips;
We see thee not, yet trust thou art not far,
But passing onward from this life's eclipse
Hast vanished only as the morning star,
Into the glory of the perfect day.

The details of the persistent pressure of Grant's drive towards Richmond, of the "bloody angle" at Spotsylvania where after twelve days and nights of fighting the dead of both sides were "piled in the trenches 5 or 6 deep—wounded often writhing under superincumbent dead," [67] and of the slaughter at Cold Harbor in the opening days of June need not concern us. Holmes's part in them can be pieced together from the hurried jottings in his Diary. One incident, however, which he never forgot and of which in later years he spoke with special delight, occurred on May 29, when General Wright directed Holmes to carry a dispatch to General Russell at divisional headquarters, and not to spare his horse.[68]

> When I turned from Plantation Road into Lane, Upton's boyscout came riding along back full tilt & sung out to me not to go on; he had been fired at by 2 rebel cavalrymen. Dilemma. Concluded must go on. Picked up a straggler (infty) an unarmed man on a mule, a sick officer, and the boy and was starting when I saw 2 or 3 cavalry foragers. Got them, & sent back rest except Upton's boy whose head is level. Trot to place where boy was shot at—then gallop to where the road bends to right. Bang—Whiz—"Halt," "Surrender" from about 20 rebels in line. I thought it was a mistake & they were friends & begun to pull up, but saw the gray jackets & clapped the spurs to my horse—much shooting—presently a fellow comes down the road. "Surrender!" He hadn't got his carbine quite unslung & I put my pistol to his breast and pulled trigger—missed fire—then he and others on right of road do shooting, I lying along the side of horse Comanche fashion. 2 of my men got through with me.

It was not only the excitement and the success of his mission that gave Holmes satisfaction. Writing to his mother some ten days later, he spoke a second time of the incident and said,

> fortunately I have a jewel in the head of this campaign in the shape of my adventure of Sunday week ago. For let me tell you . . . that, although I am not aware of the General's knowing the particulars, the staff to whom I spun my yarn intimated that they thought it rather a gallant thing, & it was I think myself, to get the order through & not knock under or turn back.[69]

It was after the cruel failure at Cold Harbor that Grant, changing his strategy, moved the Army of the Potomac from the Chickahominy, across the ill-starred Peninsula, to the James River. It had now been determined that Petersburg, lying some fifteen miles to the south of Richmond on the Appomattox, must be taken before initiating the drive on the Confederate capital. Lee's success in bringing reinforcements to the defense of Petersburg again defeated the Union effort and it was clear, during the first days of

July, that the siege of Petersburg would be a long-drawn-out affair. Northern outcries against "Butcher" Grant, radical attacks on the administration and its generals, and uncertainty at home concerning the possibility of victory increased throughout the month of June and the opening days of July. Lee, seeking to take advantage of Northern discontent, as he had when the Army of the Potomac had earlier found itself immobilized in the Peninsula, again let loose a threat on Washington—this time by Jubal Early. The threat seemed more than diversionary when Early took Frederick, Maryland, and moved rapidly south towards Washington. On July 10 "a scarecrow army," [70] nothing more, stood on trembling guard around the city as Early's forces came within sight of the Capitol. The city's fortifications, to be sure, were formidable enough to present real obstacles. At Fort Stevens, in particular, there was Union strength and Early hesitated to advance in force against it. It was well for him that he proceeded cautiously for as he arrived within sight of his objective the Sixth Corps, dispatched by Grant from the Army of the Potomac to aid in the defense of Washington, reached the capital and marched in haste to Fort Stevens.

The Diary of John Hay tells us that General Wright and his staff reached Washington on July 11. It also describes briefly a visit which Lincoln made to Fort Stevens on the afternoon of that day.[71] Lincoln told Hay that while he was at the Fort he had gone onto the parapet to observe the terrain on which Early's skirmishers and sharpshooters had already appeared. The President told his secretary that as he stood there scanning the scene "a soldier roughly ordered him to get down or he would have his head knocked off." [72] Apparently the President accepted the advice and departed. Whether Holmes was at Fort Stevens when Lincoln made his visit to the Fort on July 11 we do not know. The probabilities are that he accompanied General Wright to the Fort, but that they were there after the President had left.[73] General Early on the morning of Tuesday, July 12, realized that reinforcements made a full-scale assault on the capital impossible, but he could not resist the temptation, being thus near to Washington, to keep his enemies on their toes. The dignitaries of Washington, appreciating the opportunity which Early had given them of seeing the spectacle of battle, gathered at Fort Stevens on the 12th. Again the President appeared, this time with Mrs. Lincoln, anxious once more to see the defenses and encourage the defenders of the capital. Again he ascended the parapet. Nearby stood a surgeon of the Sixth Corps, who had joined the company of distinguished sightseers. When a Confederate bullet struck the surgeon in the thigh "Old Abe ordered our men to fall back." [74] The President, however, remained to see the course of battle. With his stove-pipe hat upon his head he stood, an imperturbable target for the sharpshooters. As General Wright recounted the events, Lincoln stood his precarious ground after the surgeon was shot and after the parapet had been cleared of all others. Thus he remained, said Wright,

> until I told him I should have to remove him forcibly. The absurdity of the idea of sending off the President under guard seemed to amuse him, but in consideration of my earnestness in the matter, he agreed to compromise by sitting behind the parapet instead of standing upon it. . . . After he left the parapet he would persist in standing up from time to time, thus exposing nearly one-half of his tall form.[75]

In varying shapes, some grossly inaccurate in accompanying details,[76] others authenticated by unimpeachable authority, the story has been made familiar of the encounter between Holmes and Lincoln on the parapet at Fort Stevens.[77] In their most reliable version the facts would seem to be these. Possibly on the afternoon of July 11, but more probably during Lincoln's visit to Fort Stevens on the following day, Holmes's eye was caught by the outrageous sight of a tall civilian blandly surveying the battlefield while bullets smashed into the Fort. In the heat of the moment Holmes shouted "Get down, you damn fool, before you get shot." At the moment when the explosive order came from his lips Holmes "was wholly unaware of who it was [that he addressed]" but "a sharp look after his exclamation made him aware." [78] If the incident occurred on July 11 it is probable that Holmes was the "soldier" who by Lincoln's account to Hay had roughly ordered the President to get down, and who thus removed him from danger. If, on the other hand, the events occurred on the 12th it would seem from General Wright's account that it was by his order, rather than by that of an aide, that Lincoln was persuaded to retire to a position of greater safety. In any case, the Captain seems to have treated the Commander-in-Chief with some impetuosity and in doing so, incidentally, to have expressed the conviction that the fighting of wars was something more serious than a spectacle produced for the benefit of civilians.[e]

As Holmes, accompanying the Sixth Corps, moved north towards Poolesville, his mind must have gone back to the fall of 1861 when he had made the same march with Ball's Bluff the destination. The wheel had gone full circle and he found himself at the point of his beginning. Three years had passed since he had been commissioned, thrice he had been wounded, and many more than three friends had died. The War, however, was not over, and it was hard to see a favorable end in sight. Yet soon after Holmes left Washington he knew that for him the War was virtually over —that in a few days he would return to civilian life, leaving his Regiment with the Army of the Potomac on the Appomattox and his new friends of the Sixth Corps prepared to fight their way down the Shenandoah Valley.

So far as is known, Holmes left no statement explaining the reason for his ultimate decision to leave the service upon the ex-

[e] A problem of collateral interest concerns the fact that though Holmes frequently visited Fort Stevens and described the scene as he recalled it, there were many instances when his description made no reference to his "order" to Lincoln. He spoke only of the refugees upon the roads, of the gunfire from the opposing forces, and of Lincoln standing in his stove-pipe hat upon the parapet. Alexander Woollcott has suggested that Holmes told the story but rarely because of a reluctance to pose as Lincoln's savior. (Woollcott, "Get Down, You Fool," *Long, Long Ago,* 3, 9–10.) The tale, even in its most dramatic form, does not, however, impute glory to the rough soldier. If Holmes seldom recounted the story it is more probably because he did not see it as a significant event. It remains surprising, however, that Holmes who was generally not reluctant to repeat to one friend a Civil War story that he had told to others did not, so far as I have discovered, tell this story to more than a very few persons out of the many who accompanied him to Fort Stevens.

piration of his three-year term. In a few letters that survive, however, there are indications of the course which his doubts and his resolutions followed during his tour of duty on General Wright's staff. On April 17 he had written to Charles Eliot Norton from the headquarters of the Sixth Corps expressing gratitude and appreciation for Norton's kindness in sending him a copy of the *North American Review* containing an essay-review of Norton's on St. Louis and Joinville.[79] In the letter Holmes said that the story of Joinville had come "most opportunely now when we need all examples of chivalry to help us bind our rebellious desires to steadfastness in the Christian Crusade of the 19th century. If one didn't believe that this war was such a crusade," he went on to say, ". . . it would be hard indeed to keep the hand to the sword; and one who is rather compelled unwillingly to the work by abstract conviction than borne along on the flood of some passionate enthusiasm, must feel his ardor rekindled by stories like this." Holmes went on to speak of his prospective service. "In all probability from what I hear of the filling up of the Regiment I shall soon be mustered in for a new term of service as Lieutenant Colonel of the 20th and so with double reason I am thankful to read of the great dead who have 'stood in the evil day.' No—it will not do to leave Palestine yet." [80]

In the surviving record the next indication of Holmes's plans for his future service is found in a letter to his parents written on May 6 after the Wilderness and Spotsylvania, and after the death of "Little" Abbott and General Sedgwick. "[T]hese nearly two weeks," he wrote, "have contained all of fatigue & horror that war can furnish. . . . [N]early every Regimental officer I knew or care for is dead or wounded." The strain of these events had altered the plans that he had outlined to Norton. "I have made up my mind," he said, "to stay on the staff if possible till the end of the campaign & then if I am alive, I shall resign." In explanation of this decision he went on to say: "I have felt for some time that I didn't any longer believe in this being a duty & so I mean to leave at the end of the campaign, as I said if I'm not killed before." [81]

There were technical considerations which doubtless facilitated this decision against returning to the duties of the line. The Twentieth Regiment in which he still held his commission had been enlisted for three years, and all officers and men whose three years of service had expired were entitled to be discharged. The delays that had prevented Holmes from filling the post of Lieutenant Colonel, delays for which he had not been responsible, had kept him from holding the post to which he was entitled. Now he held a position elsewhere and his services with General Wright were appreciated. A return to the Twentieth would have brought him back to a Regiment largely reconstituted and haunted for him by the ghosts of dead friends. Without regard to Holmes's mental and physical exhaustion, there were, therefore, strong reasons which favored the decision to stay on General Wright's staff.

Holmes's announcement of his decision did not, however, make its precise nature clear. When he spoke of leaving the service at the end of "the campaign" it was possible to read his words as an indication that he would leave before many months, or even before many weeks had passed. Evidently his parents so read his announcement, for on May 30 he wrote to them once more, this time in response to their surprised and apparently disapproving comment on such a premature departure from the service. "I am sure," wrote Holmes, "I cannot have conveyed the idea, rightfully, that I intended resigning before the campaign was over (i.e. next winter just near the end of my term of service)—then I probably shall for reasons satisfactory to myself. I must say I dislike such a misunderstanding, so discreditable to my feeling of soldierly honor, when I don't believe there was a necessity for it." [82] In view of the ambiguity in Holmes's earlier letter his irritation with his parents for their interpretation of his announcement was scarcely justified. Legitimate or not, his protest clearly reflected a struggle in his own spirit between duty and inclination. His insistence that no other reasons than those which satisfied him were needed to support his decision was, perhaps, an assertion of his independence from parental authority. It also reflected some personal doubt whether his decision could be so explained as to satisfy the world that it was "right." Despite the indication to his parents that he felt no obligation to give reasons for his decision, Holmes went on in the same letter to state why he intended to leave and why his father should notify Governor Andrew that he should commission new field officers in the Twentieth.

I am convinced from my late experience that if I can stand the wear & tear (body and mind) of regimental duty that it is a greater strain on both than I am called on to endure. . . . I talked with Hayward the mentor of the Regiment & told him my views on the matter. I am not the same man (may not have quite the same ideas) & certainly am not so elastic as I was and I *will not acknowledge the same claims upon me under those circumstances that existed formerly.*[83]

A week later Holmes came back to the same subject, but this time without irritation. He now asked his mother to believe that

I was not demoralized when I announced my intention to leave the service next winter if I lived so long. I started this thing as a boy. I am now a man and I have been coming to the conclusion for the last six months that my duty has changed. I can do a disagreeable thing or face a great danger coolly enough when I *know* it is a duty—but a doubt demoralizes me as it does any nervous man—and now I honestly think the duty of fighting has ceased for me—ceased because I have laboriously and with much suffering of mind and body *earned* the right which I denied Willy Everett to decide for myself how I can best do my duty to myself, to the country, and, if you choose, to God. I believe that Governor Andrew understands my determination to waive promotion. . . . The ostensible and sufficient reason is my honest belief that I cannot now endure the labors & hardships of the line. Nothing further need be told abroad. I hope that this will meet your approbation—you are so sure to be right. At all events I have tried to decide conscientiously & I have decided.[84]

There is, perhaps, no occasion to probe beneath the surface of this statement. A sufficient reason for Holmes's decision may well have been his physical and nervous exhaustion. In the language of today it might truthfully be said that Holmes had determined to leave the line because he was suffering from "battle fatigue." The medical officer at the Sixth Corps in June told Holmes that he was keeping himself going not by the strength of his constitution but by the daily pressure of necessity.[85] Such a diagnosis of his condition would surely have made it folly for Holmes either to accept the Lieutenant Colonelcy or to return as Captain in the Twentieth. Holmes, however, gave his parents additional reasons than these for his decision. That further effort to explain his conduct introduced elusive elements. He contrasted his course of action at the outset of the War with that of his contemporary, William Everett, who had apparently solved his problem of responsibility in purely personal terms. When war broke out Everett had insisted on the right to make up his own mind as to the nature of his duty and had not allowed the convictions of the nation or the community to affect his independent judgment. That had told him that he should spend the Civil War in graduate study in England. Holmes had joined the Union forces not merely because he believed it was his duty to do so but because the community of which he was a part had established the measure of his responsibility. After three years of service, however, Holmes felt that he had earned the right—perhaps even inherited the obligation—to decide for himself the scope of his duty. A boy's humility and a boy's conviction had combined in 1861 to make Holmes a volunteer. A man's responsibility and a man's doubts led him three years later to reconsider and redefine his duty.

At the time when Holmes made his decision not to return to the Twentieth he expected to continue to hold his Captaincy and to remain as aide to General Wright, at least until the winter. This was his plan as late as June 21st.[86] After the Sixth Corps had been separated from the Army of the Potomac and dispatched first to Washington and then to the Shenandoah Valley, he decided to secure his final discharge. It was on July 8 that he broke the unexpected news to his mother that about the 17th he would leave for home and would do so with finality.[87] He had apparently learned that if he remained on the staff of General Wright he would do so under the constant risk of being transferred back to his Regiment as Captain. Since he had already decided to leave the line it was clear to him that the occasion of the Sixth Corps's separation from the Army of the Potomac was a suitable time for him to secure his final discharge. He spoke, however, of the possibility of later seeking a commission from the President if that course should seem appropriate. These were the elements which gave structure to the problems of discharge.

In his later years Holmes indicated that he had come to question his decision to leave the service. In 1917 he said that he agreed that "now I should allow less than I did . . . 50 years ago to the consideration of the special faculties that one may attribute to oneself as a ground for not taking the chances of war." [88] This reminiscent comment would indicate that he came to feel that in 1864 he should have made no claim that he had earned the right to decide for himself the scope of his duties. Near the War's end he had come to make the same mistake that Willy Everett had made at the beginning; he had applied an inner, personal standard to measure his obligation. Instead he should have let the external standard of the community define his duty.

Another possible factor in his decision deserves attention. When serving in the Twentieth Regiment Holmes was but one member of a group of young officers, coming in general from the same background, and committed to each other and to their men. Each officer was therefore strengthened by the others. Serving on the staff of General Wright an officer's position was far more isolated. If there was any weakness of conviction as to the cause for which one fought other sources of strength were not at hand. When Holmes found himself a staff officer he found himself far more alone than he had been before. If he had returned to his decimated Regiment he might again have acquired strength in the old loyalties to comrades. Would those loyalties be the same, however, when the old comrades had gone? Surely it was not surprising that an exhausted spirit and a doubting mind found reasons to justify a decision that would make warfare and battle ugly memories instead of impending realities. Nor is it surprising, perhaps, that when the exhaustion was over uncertainty would come as to the rightness of that decision.

On July 17, 1864, at Petersburg, Virginia, Holmes was given

his discharge. The document stated that "said O. W. Holmes, Jr. was born in Boston, is 23 years of age . . . and by occupation, when enrolled, a gentleman." [89] On its back it carried the penciled endorsement of Holmes's friend, Whittier: "Approved. Citizen Holmes will proceed at once to Boston and take drinks accordingly. C. A. W." Two days later Holmes reached Boston and on the following evening attended a dinner of the Class of '61 at Young's Hotel. Though Whittier's orders had both been carried out, Holmes did not forget what lay behind him or disregard the nation's future. Asked by his classmates to speak again as the Poet of '61 he read these verses to his companions: [90]

How fought our brothers, and how died, the story
You bid me tell, who shared with them the praise,
Who sought with them the martyr's crown of glory,
The bloody birthright of heroic days.

But, all untuned amid the din of battle,
Not to our lyres the inspiring strains belong;
The cannon's roar, the musket's deadly rattle
Have drowned the music, and have stilled the song.

Let others celebrate our high endeavor
When peace once more her starry flag shall fling
Wide o'er the land our arms made free forever;
We do in silence what the world shall sing.

5

Harvard Law School

In July 1861, Holmes had written in his Class-Book that it was his intention, if he survived the War, to study law as his profession "or at least as a starting point." [1] Older men who had either come to know him personally, or had heard from others of his talents and capacities, thought of him in the war years as a young man whose promise was principally along literary and artistic lines. Thomas Hughes, the English writer whom Holmes came to know with some intimacy in 1866, had heard enough of Holmes by 1865 to be able to describe him as "poet, artist, Greek scholar [and] virtuoso." [2] Many reasons lead one to believe that when Holmes enrolled in the Harvard Law School in the fall of 1864 he did so with some misgivings, and without a settled confidence that he would make the law his profession. In 1932 he told friends that when he came back from the war he had not made any decision about his career—that his head was full of thoughts about philosophy and that the study of medicine was among the possibilities that he considered. He said, however, that his "Governor" would not hear of that last possibility "and put on the screws to have me go to the Law School—I mean he exerted the coercion of the authority of his judgment." [3] On another occasion Holmes said that he was "kicked" into the law by his father,[4] and in putting his apathy in such terms gave support to the belief that his own instincts did not impel him to the profession in which his great distinctions were to be achieved. That his father, who had tried quite unsuccessfully to interest himself in his studies when he was enrolled at the Harvard Law School in 1829–30, should have urged his son to make the same effort may seem surprising. Yet it must be remembered that if the father considered that a literary career might, in the end, be that which his son would prefer, there was nothing to lead him to feel that the study of law would be a wasted preliminary. From his own experience he may have learned that to pursue both medicine and literature was a difficult task. A number of the men of letters, however, with whom Dr. Holmes was intimately associated had studied law: Motley, James Russell Lowell, Longfellow, H. H. Brownell, the Civil War poet, even Emerson, had each in his youth studied law.

Another special consideration which may have had an influence upon the judgment of the father and possibly of the son related to family traditions and inheritance. Dr. Holmes's younger brother, John, the charming and humorous recluse of Appian Way, whose horizon of interest extended no farther than the Cambridge Common but whose springs of subtlety and perception were deeper, perhaps, than his brother's, had not only studied law but briefly practiced the profession in Boston.[5] The special affection in which his nephew always held him may have been one of those imponderable elements which persuaded the young man that knowledge of law did not necessarily destroy the capacity to live artistically. To Dr. Holmes the recollection of the fact that his grandfather, Oliver Wendell, a prosperous merchant with no training in the law, had nonetheless attained distinction as Probate Judge of Suffolk County may have seemed to make a career in the law the natural thing for his namesake to seek. The far more telling instance of the ancestor who had distinguished himself in the law was that of Mrs. Holmes's father, Charles Jackson.

The realities of inheritance are likely to be distorted if the qualities of a single ancestor are treated as peculiarly significant to one of his descendants. The career of that ancestor, however, may bespeak the traditions not only of a family but of a community as well. In that sense the professional life of Mr. Justice Jackson has a special bearing upon the career of Mr. Justice

Holmes.[a] It is of more than coincidental interest that grandfather and grandson sat upon the same court. The fact of significance is that Holmes, through this personal affiliation with the most critical period in the growth of American law, was in a sense made heir to the oldest traditions and continuing problems of the common law. Certainly the meaning of those traditions and the seriousness of those problems had a special vividness to one whose grandfather had studied with Theophilus Parsons, had been friend of Joseph Story, and had sat on the bench in Doctors Commons as guest of Lord Stowell. Jackson's capacities and convictions seem, furthermore, to have been characteristic of the ascendant qualities of the civilization in which he lived—qualities which were so effective that they largely determined the character of the New England world in which his grandson was to come to professional maturity.

Charles Jackson was born in Newburyport in 1775, and died in 1855 when Holmes was a boy of thirteen. After a notably active and successful career at the Boston bar, he served as Associate Justice of the Supreme Judicial Court of Massachusetts from 1813 to 1823. At the time of his appointment to the Court Theophilus Parsons was Chief Justice, and it was under Parsons, in whose Newburyport office John Quincy Adams had been trained for the bar, that Jackson had studied law. In 1864 Jackson's grandson began his legal education at Harvard under the son of Parsons, Theophilus, Jr. The elder Parsons, preëminent leader of the profession at the turn of the century, had predicted that Jackson would "prove himself the American Blackstone." [6] That prediction was not realized, but Jackson's career showed him to be a man of forceful talents, learned in the British and American antiquities of the law, sensitive to the currents of European thought, and responsive to the demands of justice in a new nation. In another person or in other times, learning equivalent to his might easily have blended with conservative instincts to produce a frosted en-

[a] It has been said that Mrs. Holmes considered that the career and character of Mr. Justice Jackson had an appreciable influence on her husband. (Conversation with Mr. Justice Felix Frankfurter.)

thusiasm for static law. Had his qualities of mind and temperament been slightly different he might well have contested Chancellor Kent's claim to the title which Parsons had predicted would be Jackson's. Whether Jackson ever seriously considered the publication of *Commentaries* comparable to those of Blackstone we do not know, but there is reason to doubt whether he had either the passion for preservation which inspired Kent or the capacity for constructive generalization which distinguished Story. In 1828, after his retirement from the Court for reasons of health, Jackson's erudition produced his treatise on Real Actions, in which he proved himself to be a master of the logic of special pleading and of the intricacies of such ancient writs as those of Ayel and Besayel and of Entry on Disseism in the *quibus,* in the *per,* in the *per* and *cui,* and in the *post.* There were lawyers who considered that this indulgence of an ingenious capacity for the logic of special pleading contributed little of concern to Massachusetts practitioners. Jackson, however, defended himself by reiterating his conviction "that the system of real actions established by the common law needed only to be known, to be universally approved," [7] and regretted the charge that he was too much concerned with technical nicety. Such criticism tends "to excite among the younger members of the profession an unfounded and unjust prejudice against this branch of our law" which "is distinguished no less by its completeness as a whole, than by the symmetry of all its parts." [8] The interest which inspired the production of the treatise seems, however, to have been more that of the antiquarian than of the reactionary. In 1836 Jackson's hospitality to change led him to recommend to the legislature the total abolition of the real actions.[9] It is good evidence of a disinterested nature when the expert favors, however reluctantly, the destruction of the subject matter in which his *expertise* has been most notably developed.

The qualities of Jackson which today seem most significant were, in large measure, the qualities of his time, his place, and his class. Those qualities had given a peculiar direction to New England's Federalism. The Essex Junto, of which Charles Jackson's father, Jonathan, and his uncle, Nathaniel Tracy, were active members spoke for the men of means who had wanted a national government strong enough to protect American property and encourage American ambition, but who were unwilling to accept such a government when it gave no preference to New England's property and New England's ambition. They had accordingly toyed with the idea of secession. During many of the years of Charles Jackson's active life the issue between state and nation was a living reality and in that period his political loyalty was principally to New England's special brand of Federalism. After the defeat of that cause the loyalty of New England sons to the memory of their father's faith persisted. But, for their peace of mind, the sons were compelled to mold the memory to suit the new alignment of political forces, and to deny that their fathers had sought and encouraged disunion. When John Quincy Adams in 1828 charged the early leaders of New England's Federalism with a virtually treasonable disloyalty to the nation, Jackson, with other first sons of the "prigarchy," [10] came indignantly to the defense of those who had controlled the Hartford Convention and had done their best to obstruct the successful prosecution of the War of 1812.[11] Instead of pleading in confession and avoidance of old errors, they sought to deny the undeniable facts of history. In choosing this course they tacitly acknowledged that the destinies of Massachusetts must be those of the United States and that New England must cast its lot with the nation. This did not mean that Jackson and his associates in protest had become Jeffersonian Republicans. They remained ardent conservatives in economic and political matters. It is well to remember, however, that the spokesmen of the Federalist tradition, conservative as they were in their articles of political faith—particularly in those which concerned the distribution of power among the classes of American society—did not close their minds against all the fresh winds of America. Jackson shared with other New England Federalists an energy of temperament which made its imprisonment by dogmatic convention impossible.

At the bar and on the bench of the Supreme Judicial Court, he was inevitably involved in the issues of international and domestic policy with which the American courts were so persistently concerned in the first quarter of the century. While our law was still in its formative stage, before American decisions were reported and precedent had established the extent to which decisions of the English courts were to be taken as conclusive, the legislative responsibility of lawyers and judges was far more apparent than it was in later years. It was as clear to laymen as it was to lawyers that the nature of American institutions, whether economic, social, or political, was largely to be determined by the judges. In such a period questions of private law were considered as questions of public policy. On the Massachusetts Court which in 1812 had advised the Governor that it was for him and not for the President of the United States to determine whether the exigency of an invasion required the calling out of the State militia,[12] Jackson was associated with judges who saw themselves not only as citizens but as nationals of Massachusetts affiliated by somewhat tenuous ties to the Government of the United States. When Parsons, in accepting the office of Chief Justice of the Massachusetts Court, spoke of the Commonwealth as "our country" [13] he expressed a point of view which greatly influenced the attitude of judges and lawyers to their professional responsibility.

One healthy aspect of the provincial pride of the early Massachusetts judges must not be overlooked. In treating the Commonwealth to the fullest extent possible as an independent nation, capable of establishing its own law, the judges assumed an enlarging responsibility. The horizon of their interest was extended to the limits of their ambition for Massachusetts. This meant that the law which it was their responsibility to declare—perhaps even their pleasure to make—had broad and extensive dimensions. The greatness of their British contemporary, Lord Stowell, it has been said, was made effective by the fact that he came to the Court of Admiralty at a time when there were no English precedents in the prize law by which he was controlled or from which he could even seek guidance. Daring fully to discharge his responsibility he played the role of lawmaker rather than merely filling the office of judge.[14] The forceful judges of Massachusetts assumed a responsibility analogous to that of Stowell, but in a field of law much broader than that with which Stowell was principally concerned. The Massachusetts judges would undoubtedly have shared the opinion of their South Carolina contemporary, Abraham Nott, Presiding Judge of the Court of Appeals, when in 1826 he announced that "the great object of courts ought to be to fix principles, and not merely to decide cases." [15] While Jackson sat on the Supreme Judicial Court he and his associates laid the foundations of the whole law of the Commonwealth and in doing so drew upon all sources available to industrious men of learning. The admiration of Jackson and his associates for British institutions, and their distrust of the despotism of France were not so compelling as to make them inhospitable to the law of the Continent. If the pride of Massachusetts at times approached disloyalty to the nation, that pride was not parochial, but as it was expressed in the impulse of the Federalist bench and bar sought to invigorate the law of Massachusetts with the wisdom of other nations. As a result, the later generation of Massachusetts lawyers and judges, to which Jackson's grandson belonged, fell heir to a professional tradition which was in no sense provincial.

One of the most striking qualities of the American judges of the generation of Jackson and Story was their small concern with the philosophical problems concerning the foundations of law. Had Story been as familiar with German writing as he was with French, perhaps he would have been compelled to take serious notice of the theoretical issues with which Savigny in 1814 had challenged the complacencies of the rationalists. In Savigny's denial that reason alone was adequate to determine and define the legal order, in his insistence that law is found and not made, he compelled those who would listen to him to reëxamine the basic assumptions on which the legal philosophy of the eighteenth century had been built. The American bar and the most distinguished American judges, however, for some fifty years seemed hardly to know that the challenge had been made. Their indifference to the philosophical issue was largely owing to their absorption in the day-to-day tasks of creating bodies of law for the states and for the nation. Men confronted by such a demanding task were so absorbed in the immediacy of that responsibility that they had no time for the reconsideration of the theories of law and legislation which were their inheritance. Brought up, furthermore, in the natural law tradition, Anglicized by Blackstone and Americanized by Kent, they were able to escape the problem which troubled continental jurists—the definition of boundaries between law and morality—in their comforting certainty that morality was part of the law of nature and the law of nature part of the common law.[16] American lawyers and judges, in other words, were living their professional lives on the philosophical assumptions of the eighteenth century and were so busy deciding cases and enacting statutes that they could not pause to reconsider the justification of those assumptions. When Bentham championed codification he felt it necessary to do so under the philosophical banner of utilitarianism; when David Dudley Field took up the same cause in the 1840's he felt no need to base his program of reform upon a philosophy; reform was called for not by reason of theory, but by reason of practical convenience. It was not until the second half of the century that the issues of theory over which the jurists of England and the Continent had been struggling since 1800 were considered by American lawyers as relevant to the problems of American law. That Story and Jackson, Marshall and Shaw, were not philosophers may, in some ways, have been unfortunate for the growth of American law. Yet that deficiency did not prevent them from making momentous contributions to the American legal inheritance. Their achievement stood recorded in treatises and decisions; the beginning of full maturity for American law was, however, postponed until the birth of a generation of lawyers capable of reëxamining the philosophical foundations of law which its predecessors had taken for granted.

Those traditions which, for the Holmes family, were embodied in Charles Jackson, for the Harvard Law School were embodied in Mr. Justice Story. Story had been the dominant figure on the Law School Faculty from 1829 to 1845, and twenty years after his death the highest aim of his successors at Harvard was to follow in his footsteps. That aim was not easily to be achieved, for few men could be expected to match the energy of a teacher who, while fulfilling his academic duties and the judicial responsibilities of a Justice of the Supreme Court of the United States, was able to produce massive treatises on the Constitution, on Equity, Conflict of Laws, Negotiable Instruments, Agency, and Bailments. In later years of the nineteenth century the Harvard Law School Faculty had departed sufficiently from its old reverence to permit Professor Gray to describe Story as "a man of great learning, and of reputation for learning greater even than the learning itself." [17] In 1864, however, when Holmes entered the School, such an intimation that Story's genius had limitations would have challenged the institution's most sacred traditions. The Faculty was then made up of three men, Theophilus Parsons, Joel Parker, and Emory Washburn. Their varying talents suggest that they had been selected in the hope that if the judicial experience of Parker, once Chief Justice of New Hampshire, the productive scholarship of Parsons, author of numerous treatises, and the statesmanship of Washburn, former Governor of Massachusetts, were brought together in the Law School, Story's spirit would survive in legal education.

Although a faculty selected in such hopes as these is unlikely to prove successful, the triumvirate which ruled the Law School in the middle years of the century was by no means undistinguished. "Character was . . . all over the place, as it could scarce fail to be when the general subject . . . had become identical with the person of all its votaries." [18] Each of the three professors was a person of considerable capacity in his own right. Their faults derived principally from their common conviction that legal education should follow the course which earlier generations had found effective. It would be true only within limits to say that the inadequacies of the College which Holmes had left in 1861 permeated the Law School of 1864. No one of the triumvirate seems to have possessed the impressive stuffiness of Francis Bowen, and the Faculty at the Law School proceeded on the assumption that the students would lead a more fruitful academic life if they were free from the terrors of parietal discipline. The assumption was carried to such lengths that the students were not required to be examined on their studies and were awarded their degrees if they paid tuition and put in an occasional appearance in the classroom. Though a college degree was not required for admission, the School was administered as if it were a graduate school for men of responsible maturity.

Joel Parker, as Royall Professor, stood at the head of the Faculty, fulfilling the administrative duties which nowadays would fall on the shoulders of the dean. Parker's technical competence was the admiration of the ablest students and the dread of the less talented. For the less competent he was evidently a bewildering teacher; for the unusually gifted an excellent instructor; for all a singularly dull lecturer. The discerning eyes of Henry James, unhappily and briefly committed to legal studies, saw Parker as the embodiment of

> dryness and hardness, prose unrelieved, at their deadliest—partly perhaps because he was most master of his subject. . . . [W]hat mainly comes back to me of him is the full sufficiency with which he made me ask myself how I *could* for a moment have seen myself really browse in any field where the marks of the shepherd were such an oblong dome of a bare cranium, such a fringe of dropping little ringlets toward its base, and a mouth so meanly retentive, so ignorant of style, as I made out, above a chin so indifferent to the duty, or at least to the opportunity, of chins.[19]

Holmes later spoke of Parker as "one of the greatest of American judges, . . . who showed in the chair the same qualities that had made him famous on the bench." [20] Those qualities were of the highest grade when tested by purely professional standards of learning and analytical capacity, yet they would scarcely seem to have been so notable as to justify the rank among American judges which Holmes, in oratory, gave him. He suffered, apparently, from what Leslie Stephen somewhere called "scholar's paralysis," an instinct for perfection which kept him from making any large contribution to the literature of the law. Yet as a teacher whose example would show to students the importance of accuracy in detail and caution in generalization he was, perhaps, more effective than either of his associates. A perceptive law student said that Judge Parker, as teacher, "ever had a luminous method of exposition which grew more luminous as the subjects grew more abstruse" and that "under his teaching a legal mind was formed." [21] It was the lawyer's love of the letter, not the Copperhead's impulse to complain, which led him, a vigorous supporter of the war, to oppose Lincoln's measures of emancipation and suspension of habeas corpus.[22] When involved in political controversy, he showed little of the caution which tradition associates with the temperament of a judge and the office of a teacher. Replying in public print to certain "lax" constitutional views expressed by Congregational ministers, he said that "it is quite time that they should be exposed as the 'all-sufficient, self-sufficient' persons which they make themselves, and the 'insufficient' personages which they really are. If any of them have D.D. attached to their names, that does not disqualify them from being also ASS, and mischief-makers besides." [23] In his class in Constitutional Law he felt no reluctance vigorously to express the views of a strict constructionist, and the presence in the classroom of Lincoln's eldest son, Robert Todd, who was a first-year student with Holmes, did not, apparently, lead him to caution in his criticism of the President's theories of constitutional law.[24]

The difference between the temperament of Parker and that of Parsons was reflected in the conflicting points of view of the two men as to the issues of the Civil War. Parker, the precise lawyer, opposed with conscientious integrity the means which Lincoln had chosen to defeat the rebellion. Parsons, the ardent champion of the cause of the Union, did not let the political impulses of his heart fall under the control of the lawyer's mind. He did not simply follow the maxim *inter arma silent leges,* but proceeded on the assumption that the Constitution permits the application of a special body of law to the affairs of a people engaged in suppressing a lawless rebellion.[25] The hesitant caution which restrained Parker from writing legal treatises never bothered Parsons. He wrote law books with a fluency that almost matched Story's. Although his treatise on Contracts was for many generations the leading American treatise on its subject, it was hardly a book of distinguished excellence. Parsons, however, possessed considerable charm both as teacher and as author, and was the most generally liked professor in the Law School. Henry James saw Parsons as

> an *illustrative* figure, . . . with all the marks one might have wished him, marks of a social order, a general air, a whole history of things, or in other words of people. . . . [H]is tone, his unction, his homage still to some ancient superstition, some standard of manners, reached back as to a state of provincialism rounded and compact, quite self-supporting, which gave it serenity and quality, something comparatively rich and urban. . . .[26]

Parsons was of that breed of teacher which considers that the personal anecdote, the apt recollection of a departed giant, or the simple bit of professional gossip contributes to a student's education. In his treatise on Maritime Law, the field in which he had achieved his principal distinction as a practitioner, he showed himself to be a master of a difficult and elaborate field of law, to which, unfortunately, Story had contributed no systematic treatise but which in judicial decisions he had made a coherent and living body of law. The achievement of Parsons in his work on maritime law was principally that of translating the decisions of Story into the ordered form of a treatise.

As to Emory Washburn the judgment of one of his more alert students, John Fiske, was, perhaps, a little severe. After reading some 350 pages of Washburn's treatise on Real Property, Fiske wrote to his fiancée: "Washburn is detestable. His style is clumsy, obscure, inelegant, ungrammatical and ambiguous. While his thinking is but little more lucid than his style." [27] Although Fiske nowhere suggested that other qualities in the teacher made up for these defects in the author, the bulk of the students seemed to have had a warm affection and admiration for Washburn; the affection was stimulated by a friendly and genial temperament which made him always willing to give time and interest to the problems of individual students.[28] Contrasting the simple rusticity of Washburn with the richer urbanism of Parsons, Henry James found that Washburn

> was of a different, but of a no less complete consistency—queer, ingenuous, more candidly confiding, especially as to his own pleasant fallibility, than I had ever before known of a chaired dispenser of knowledge, and all after a fashion that endeared him to his young hearers, whose resounding relish of a frequent tangle of his apologetic returns upon himself, quite, almost always, to inextricability, was really affectionate in its freedom.[29]

Reading this estimate it is hard to escape the suspicion that the student saw in the mind and manner of his teacher qualities which later if not then characterized the student's own style of expression, perhaps of thought. Holmes's admiration for Washburn came from the first realization which the teacher gave the student of the meaning of "the enthusiasm of the lecture room." His "kindly ardor," said Holmes, did more "than the learning of Coke and the logic of Fearne" could have done to make the subject of Real Property comprehensible.[30] Shortly after graduating from the Harvard Law School, Holmes described Washburn both as teacher and author as "untiring, laborious, enthusiastic." [31]

When Holmes enrolled in the Law School Professor Parker asked him what he had read "in the way of law." Holmes "answered with some satisfaction 'Benét's *Court-Martial.*' " [32] The pride in the fact that he, unlike most of his fellow-students, had already seen a grimmer side of life than his teachers had ever known, that he had learned by reading, and perhaps by practice, something of the working of the machinery of military law, was not unnatural. Nor was it surprising that he did not tell Professor Parker that he had at least dipped into Austin's *Jurisprudence* for he had naturally looked upon that as a work of general rather than professional relevance. With enrollment, however, began the extensive and intensive reading of treatises round which the course of legal instruction revolved. Election of courses was so freely allowed, and Law School records were so meager that it is impossible to say with any certainty what lectures Holmes attended while he was at the Law School. A course of study was suggested but not prescribed by the Faculty. It was recommended that those men who planned to attend the School for two years should elect to follow lectures in a certain order, but each man was entirely free to decide for himself whether he should, for instance, go to Professor Washburn's lectures in Conflict of Laws before he had heard Professor Parker's on Pleading. It is not unlikely, however, that Holmes followed the recommendations of the Faculty. If he did so it meant that in the first year of his study he went to the lectures in Agency, Pleading, Equity, and Constitutional Law given by Parker, to those on Blackstone's and Kent's *Commentaries,* Contracts, Evidence, and the Law of Nations by Parsons, and to Washburn's lectures on Real Property, Arbitration, Wills, and Criminal Law.

An important part of the Law School's curriculum consisted of the argument of cases in the Moot Courts, which were organized both officially by the Faculty and unofficially by student clubs. The archives of the Law School contain but one document recording Holmes's participation in a Moot Court argument. The case concerned a plaintiff's claim for damages which he had suffered from the defendant's digging of a ditch on lands adjacent to the plaintiff's. The case was argued in November 1865, before Professor Parker, with Holmes and his associate, representing the plaintiff, being at least partially successful in their effort.[33] Many years later Holmes wrote of the occasion and of how excitement stirred the embers of his Antietam wound.

> I am converting misfortune into a source of satisfaction. For some years I have had trouble with my teeth on the left side of my mouth and I remember that as long ago as when I was in the Law School when I was getting up my first case to argue before old Parker, being much excited and having got a case for a skiandhu with which to stick the enemy in the guts, I had a neuralgia in the same side of my face. My wife tells me that the doctor had told her that the disturbance of a great nerve by my wound at Antietam, when I was shot through the neck and for some weeks couldn't get my left arm away from my body, sooner or later would be likely to give me this sort of trouble. So I at least can pretend to myself that my discomforts came from that source and inwardly swagger.[34]

It seems probable that Holmes, like many others of his Law School contemporaries, preferred to acquire the moot court experience in the more informal atmosphere of a Law Club, in his case the Marshall Club, than in the Moot Courts organized by the Faculty. The records of the Marshall Club indicate that once in his first year and again in his second year he sat as judge in cases argued by other students. The study of law, in other words, involved other less arid occupations than reading treatises. Holmes later recalled the occasions on which, with another student-veteran, he laid "the dust of pleading by certain sprinklings" which he and his companion "managed to contrive together." [35]

There was, however, a moral obligation to study law in books. An "imperfect list" of books read during this period, which Holmes made in 1866,[36] would indicate that he diligently followed the suggestions which the Faculty published in the Law School's catalogue as to a course of reading. All the standard treatises on the first-year subjects appear in Holmes's list, Stephen on Pleading, Greenleaf on Evidence, Parsons on Contracts, Jones on Bailments, Byles on Bills—such titles as these were the required fare. A few titles indicate that he made some effort to go behind the treatises to the decisions. The list includes two volumes of the American edition of Smith's *Leading Cases,* parts of Tudor's *Leading Cases on Real Property and Conveyancing,* and the first two volumes of Allen's *Massachusetts Reports.* His professional reading, however, was primarily of that conventional sort which the Faculty recommended to the students.

It would do the triumvirate of Law School professors less than justice to suggest that they chose an unimaginative course of reading in preference to another recognized alternative. Training in the law, even comprehension of its principles and methods, was still unaffected by the changes in the aspirations of scholarship, philosophy, and science which had so altered the intellectual habits of the Western World in the middle years of the nineteenth century. Blackstone's complacency continued to set the tone of legal scholarship. Harvard might have suggested to its students that Bentham had had something significant to say as to that complacency, and for not doing so it may be blamed. It might also have recommended that an antidote to Kent's *Commentaries* be at least tasted in Walker's treatise on *American Law,* in which a rather crude but none the less vigorous Benthamism controlled the author's standards of judgment.[b] The Faculty might, above all, have shown an awareness that a lawyer's education must reach beyond the symmetries of the common law to the disturbing confusion of statutes. When Judge Parker spoke of "those devices of ignorance, called Codes," [37] he expressed the bitterness of a generation which saw in legislative reform a threat to the ingenious and graceful artificiality of a legal system conceived in reason and nourished by logic.

The triumvirate's failure in imagination had the compensating advantage which characterizes conservatism. It was not concerned with horizons but with traditions. The Faculty believed that rigorous concern with the systematic elements in law developed its students' capacities and not only qualified them for a vocation but also equipped them for a profession. The Faculty believed that in fulfilling its dual responsibility of imparting knowledge and training intelligence it would produce men of learning. Maitland's aphorism concerning legal education in the later Middle Ages might, without distortion, be applied to the Harvard curriculum in law: "it was not academic; it was scholastic." [38] For Holmes there were, undoubtedly, difficulties in accepting these limiting objectives of study, yet he came to believe that a law student does well to keep his philosophical inclinations in check while he is laying the groundwork for his career. Asked whether he had "found a lawyer the worse for being a philosopher," he replied that "I have known some young lawyers who I thought were the worse for their liberal interests. It made them unwilling to tackle the details." [39] Holmes's law professors would probably have given

[b] That Holmes was aware of a point of view different from Blackstone's and Kent's is indicated by the inclusion in his list of readings of Bentham's *Defence of Usury* and Walker's treatise. Eleanor N. Little, "The Early Reading of Justice Oliver Wendell Holmes," *Harvard Library Bulletin,* VIII, 163, 169 (Spring, 1954). Holmes evidently had a high regard for Walker's volume: see his anonymous review of a volume of the Iowa Reports, *American Law Review,* III, 357 (Jan. 1869).

the same answer to the inquiry had it, by chance, been directed to them.

In view of the extent to which Holmes later committed himself, at least temporarily, to the historical approach to law it may seem surprising that his list of earliest readings in the law contains none of the conventional volumes on legal history which the Faculty recommended to the students. In neglecting the histories of English law by Crabb, Hale, and Reeves, Holmes did not escape those currents of historical scholarship that later were to move him, for in their pages the history of law marched with formal dignity through the empty streets of time. The jostling presence of a society that set the procession's course was overlooked. Though a student in observing such an ordered succession in the annals of the law might discover shapes that otherwise would escape his notice he was unlikely to see the forces beyond the law that determined its structure. In 1911 Holmes looked back upon the opportunities which professional education had offered to the young man of speculative tastes when he had been a law student.

> When I began, the law presented itself as a ragbag of details. The best approach that I found to general views on the historical side was the first volume of Spence's *Equitable Jurisdiction*. . . . The only philosophy within reach was Austin's *Jurisprudence*. It was not without anguish that one asked oneself whether the subject was worthy of the interest of an intelligent man. One saw people whom one respected and admired leaving the study because they thought it narrowed the mind; for which they had the authority of Burke. It required blind faith—faith that could not yet find the formula of justification for itself.[40]

It is, perhaps, significant of the altering dimensions of Holmes's interests between his days at the Harvard Law School and his first years of scholarship after graduation that he did not read Spence's volume on the history of equity until 1868. The Faculty included the work on its list of suggested reading, yet Holmes before he turned to Spence had sought by three readings of Adams on *Equity* to master the details of the existing system. It was only after that mastery had been achieved that he gave his attention to Spence's learned history of the Court of Chancery. One title on the list of books read while Holmes was a law student does indicate, however, that the new tendencies in historical scholarship attracted his attention. That is Maine's *Ancient Law,* a volume omitted from the Faculty's list of recommended readings. When John Fiske was a law student he also had come across Maine's epoch-making volume—the first philosophical study of the history of law to reach an Anglo-American audience and the volume which more than any other single piece of work awakened the legal profession to the consciousness that the history of law is but one phase of the history of ideas. The inflammable mind of John Fiske burst into an exuberant flame when he first read *Ancient Law,* and his fiancée felt the heat of his passion when she received her lover's comment: [41]

> No novel that I ever read enchained me more. I consider it almost next to Spencer. It has thrown all my ideas into definite shape. It has suggested to me many new and startling views of social progress. It has confirmed many new generalizations which were beginning to arise in my mind as faint suspicions. . . . It is perfectly GLORIOUS. . . . O my dear! there is nothing in this world like SCIENCE, nothing so divine as the life of a scholar!

It is doubtful whether Holmes's enthusiasm equaled Fiske's, but in later years, applying to Maine the formula that he did to Emerson, he suggested that the influence of Maine's work on his own studies had been considerable, if not decisive. "He had the gift of imparting a ferment which is one of the marks of genius. . . ." In connection with this comment he went on to indicate the direction in which Maine's scholarship had led him. Maine had "brilliantly caught and popularized in the form of established propositions the ideal ends toward which more truly scientific students on the continent had long been striving." [42] There is nothing to indicate that while Holmes was a student at the Harvard Law School he became familiar with continental scholarship or even that he had come to recognize its "scientific" vitality. Maine's *Ancient Law,* however, opened vistas of learning which he later industriously explored. It may not be an exaggeration to say that the ferment of Maine's genius if it was not the proximate cause of Holmes's efforts in *The Common Law* was at least a significant influence in their structure.[43] In 1864 Professor Theodore Dwight expressed the hope that Maine "or some equally competent person, will do for the English common law" what *Ancient Law* did for the philosophical study of earlier periods and different areas of legal history.[44] That hope was encouraged when Holmes published the essays out of which *The Common Law* was built and was, perhaps, fulfilled when he brought them together in a systematic form in the volume itself.

To credit Maine with these contributions to the tendencies in Holmes's thought is not to suggest that his course of study and reading in the Law School was appreciably influenced by *Ancient Law*. Had that been the case the reading list would surely reveal a number of historical and anthropological titles. Such works do not, however, appear on the list until some years have passed and until Holmes had reread *Ancient Law*.[c] The first time that Maine's work appears it is followed immediately by Austin's *Lectures on Jurisprudence*. The influence on Holmes of Austin's analytical exposition of law was surely no less than was Maine's historical emphasis.[d] The Austinian strain in Holmes's thought was vigorous and persistent. Was it possible, perhaps, that his experience of civil war, his discovery of the conflicts between principles of political morality and the necessities of public order, had made his mind receptive to Austin's thesis that the province of jurisprudence and the domain of morals are contiguous, not overlapping territories? That receptiveness, if it had thus been aroused, was further stimulated by the Law School's emphasis upon the formal and systematic aspects of the common law. The scattered evidence which survives would, in any case, indicate that while he was a law student Holmes's loyalties had not been committed to any one school of legal philosophy. He was acquiring an increasing familiarity with

c Holmes's second reading of *Ancient Law* was in 1868. Little, "The Early Reading of Holmes," *Harvard Library Bulletin*, VIII, 163, 178.

d Between 1863 and 1871 Holmes read Austin's works five times: see Little, *id.*, 169, 177, 181, 183.

the current controversies as to the nature of law, was finding excitement in the suggestiveness of Maine, and interest in the logical niceties, the artificial reason, and the analytical precision which permeated the common law. It was temperamentally impossible for him to become a disciple of any person or any principle with an ardor equal to that which John Fiske dedicated to Herbert Spencer and his philosophy. Holmes, however, was scarcely less alert than was Fiske to the currents of thought around him.

In October 1865, writing to H. H. Brownell, the Civil War poet who had turned in his middle years from law to literature, Holmes spoke of a new insight which his reading in law and of lawyers had given him. "It is interesting," he said, "to understand how men come to prefer a professional to a general reputation—and for the sake of the former, which hardly outlives the greatest, except a few judges, will sacrifice every hope of the other." [45] The observation, of course, does not establish the fact that Holmes had finally rejected the other preference which his father had shown so early in his career—the desire to have his name known in the broad world of letters and not simply recognized in the parochial community of a profession. It is not unlikely, however, that the son had his father's preference in mind when he spoke of the new understanding which professional study had brought. It was while his father was a law student that his poetic talent gained national fame, for it was then that he wrote and published "Old Ironsides." It is doubtful whether the Doctor in any circumstances would have found the law a sympathetic profession, but the uncertainties of its postponed successes must have seemed particularly arid to a young man who could make himself a national reputation through a few eloquent stanzas. There is good reason to believe that the son during his first year in Law School knew the same temptation to which his father had submitted. Another Civil War poet, Forceythe Willson, whose "Old Sergeant" was his most famous poem and among Holmes's favorites, was living in Cambridge in 1864 and 1865, and the young Holmes had some correspondence with him. Unfortunately, the only letters that appear to have survived are a few from Willson. A letter which he wrote to Holmes in April 1865 indicates that the young law student had written to him of his poetic ambitions, and of his philosophical inclinations—suggesting, perhaps, that he was finding the study of law less than completely satisfying. "The more of an 'idealist' you may happen to be," wrote Willson, "the finer your promise as a poet. . . . Here, now, you stand before two of God's own mighty gates—Poetry and Philosophy! Whichever you may enter with that true *emprise* which only comes of habitual Self-Renunciation, Devotion, and Reverence, you shall certainly come to great good and great joy." [46]

To Brownell, whose experiences in the law might be expected to have bred a special understanding of a poetic law student's problems, Holmes wrote a letter in May of 1865 in which he spoke not only of his occasional efforts in verse but of his special labor to make the law his chief concern.

> I think my first year at law satisfies me. Certainly it far exceeds my expectations both as gymnastics and for its intrinsic interest. It is so easy and so pleasant to go from day to day satisfying yourself for not having knocked off a hundred pages of Evidence or Contracts with the thought that you have turned over a few stones in some new mind and seen all sorts of funny things wiggling, or have read some new poem or (worse) written one, and so on, that I acknowledge no caution can be given to a young man which is too great. All I can say for myself is that I know the danger well and try to avoid it. . . . Truth sifts so slowly from the dust of the law.[47]

The dust, apparently, was not so thick as to destroy Holmes's enthusiasm for the truth which it concealed. In the middle of Holmes's first year of law study John C. Ropes, young Boston practitioner and brother of Henry Ropes of the Twentieth, reported that Holmes was already showing a "fondness for talking over his points" while sipping a gin toddy and smoking a cigar, and predicted that "he will master the theoretical part easily enough." [48]

While Holmes was at the Law School he lived with his family on Charles Street participating, we may be sure, in the life of Boston. Until April 1865, the war still cast its heavy shadows over the Nation and the Commonwealth and until peace was restored the normal gaieties of a lively household must have been somewhat muted. Yet there was vivacity on hand. Holmes's younger brother was a sociable sophomore at Harvard College and his sister Amelia was a girl of twenty-one, exuberantly talkative and busily gregarious in her inclinations. Holmes himself was not one to turn his back on society or to look to his law books when the chance was offered to pass the time of day with a pretty girl. The chance was surely available quite frequently to the handsome young Captain who had returned from the War. Though Holmes's Civil War Scrap-Books contain clippings and other items that reflect a continuing attention to military and poltical events, no other records survive to indicate the degree or character of his concern with current affairs.[e] It would seem virtually certain that in the elections of November 1864 he voted for Lincoln in preference to General McClellan, the Democratic nominee. Surely Holmes's heart rose with the Union's relentless successes in the field and shared the nation's grief when Lincoln, in the moment of final victory, was killed.

On July 21, 1865, Harvard celebrated her Commemoration Day.[49] The occasion allowed the University to honor those who had fought and died in the War. As one of the survivors Holmes was on hand, again in his uniform, and once more thinking of those who had passed in his company through the gates of Harvard to a civil war from which they had not returned. The tragic chapter had come to its close, ending for many the entire story but leaving for the survivors the responsibility of reconstituting a nation and finding for themselves the thread of purpose that might guide them on their way. Harvard's ceremonies were conducted with a suitable spirit of mourning and an appropriate spirit of hope.

e Among the items in the scrapbooks are newspaper clippings and drawings relating to the assassination of Lincoln, the fall of Petersburg, and the surrender of General Lee. Noted to be gifts from John C. Gray and to have been taken from the private baggage of Jefferson Davis at the time of his capture are a $50 bill in Confederate currency and a personal calling-card of Davis'. On the same page there is a bit of red bunting described by Holmes as "part of the flag on Fort Sumter when it was taken." Scrap-Book, #1 (Harvard Law School).

Holmes's friend and fellow-officer of the Twentieth, Major General Bartlett, who had lost a leg and an arm with the Union forces, was the hero of the occasion, symbolizing by his wounds and his modesty the strength which Harvard honored. James Russell Lowell's *Ode,* less appreciated at the time than it was later, bespoke the mood of the College and of the nation. Being a local celebration it was inevitable that Dr. Holmes should read a lyric prepared especially for the occasion. His son once more may have wished that the Doctor had not spoken in public quite so personally, for by doing so before this audience he must have realized that many eyes would turn in the son's direction as the poet asked three persons to answer the question: Which is the dream, the present peace or the past war? [50]

> Tell us, O father, as thine arms enfold
> Thy belted first-born in their fast embrace,
> Murmuring the prayer the patriach breathed of old,—
> "Now let me die, for I have seen thy face!"
>
> Tell us, O mother,—nay, thou canst not speak,
> But thy fond eyes shall answer, brimmed with joy,—
> Press thy mute lips against the sunbrowned cheek,
> Is this a phantom,—thy returning boy?
>
> Tell us, O maiden,—ah, what canst thou tell
> That Nature's record is not first to teach,—
> The open volume all can read so well,
> With its twin rose-hued pages full of speech?

It would be pleasant if we could know how many "rose-hued pages" announced their interest in the Doctor's "belted first-born" as the poet read his verses to the Cambridge audience. Surely there was more than one in that audience who saw herself as the maiden to whom the Doctor put his question.

The personal intimacies of Holmes's first year as a law student which counted most to him were evidently those that he found in Cambridge. The hospitalities of the Dixwell family on Garden Street were readily available. The instincts of privacy which were so strong in Holmes and in the girl who was to become his wife in 1872 make it peculiarly difficult to achieve understanding of their early relationship. No letters which they exchanged before their marriage have survived, and the image one forms of her qualities is made largely in one's own imagination. It is clear that Holmes and Fanny Dixwell had been close friends when he went to war. In 1866 William James said that for eight years "that villain Wendell Holmes has been keeping [Fanny Dixwell] all to himself over at Cambridge." [51] There is every reason to suppose, accordingly, that they had been intimate friends when he was an undergraduate and it is not improbable that the roots of their friendship went back to their childhood when her father was Holmes's teacher. They were virtually of the same age, she having been born some three months before Holmes. She was the eldest of six children—five girls and a boy. Shortly after William James came to know her in 1866 he described her as "about as fine as they make 'em . . . A1, if anyone ever was." [52] Her family represented the complex traditions of Cambridge; cultivated, less than affluent, yet dignified by the blood of New England's worthies, they occupied a position between the fashionable world of Boston, the learned community of Harvard, and the clerical world of New England. The few authentic traces of Fanny Dixwell's youth do little to reveal the qualities which remain in the memory of those who knew her in later years. The observant eye and the playful and occasionally caustic tongue doubtless appealed to the lively temperaments of Holmes and William James. Her interest in art brought her into an area which was one of their chief concerns and her extraordinary skill in needlework, which later put her embroideries on public exhibition in Boston and New York, was known and prized at an early date among her friends.[f] A letter

[f] In Nov. 1869, the Jameses' charming cousin, Minny Temple, wrote to Henry James the younger telling him that "Miss Dixwell came to see me. I was out. I went to see her. She was to hum, and was satisfactory to me. She gave me one of her embroideries, a good one representing night and morning. This mark of favor aroused Willy's jealousy—he said she meant it for him, and would fain have taken it from me, but I brought it off triumphantly. When I told W. Holmes that she had given it to me he remarked 'good lick'—accompanied by the old familiar twinkle in the eye. I had never chanced to hear the elegant expression before. But you perceive

which Holmes wrote to William James when the latter was in Europe in 1867 indicates that beyond her talent as needlewoman lay a broader interest in art. Holmes told James that Fanny Dixwell "has suffered a good deal for some time past with her eyes —a sad disappointment as she was expecting to go into painting in good earnest. But she said yesterday that they were nearly well and that she thought she might begin her lessons before long. I wish she may, if only for her own sake to find a voice for something within her." [53]

Whether Fanny Dixwell in her girlhood found as little pleasure in "society" as she did in her middle years we do not know; it would seem probable that she found more satisfaction in the simple intimacies of Cambridge than in the more fashionable affairs of Boston. There is no indication that in her youth she had a circle of close friends and one suspects that then, as later, she shunned intimacy to such a degree that she found most members of her family singularly distasteful.[g] It is hard to believe that one who became as dedicated in all her conduct to the happiness, success, and tranquillity of her husband ever found much satisfaction in the gaieties of the world. It may be that the disappointment of her later years that she was childless [h] or an illness which, it has been suggested, left its mark on her appearance [i] led her to withdraw from a world which a natural inclination found attractive, yet it seems likely that those circumstances did no more than ac-

---

from it, that his style has not radically changed." Quoted in LeClair, "Henry James and Minny Temple," *American Literature,* XXI, 35, 43 (1935).

[g] Thomas Barbour, an intimate friend of Holmes, whose wife was a cousin of Mrs. Holmes, told the author that Mrs. Holmes had no close friends and "hated" most of her sisters. Other friends and members of the Dixwell family have testified similarly.

[h] Mrs. Edward Jackson Holmes, the wife of Holmes's nephew, told the author that Mrs. Holmes on more than one occasion spoke with profound sorrow of the fact that she had no children.

[i] In 1896 Mrs. Holmes had rheumatic fever. *Holmes-Pollock Letters,* I, 75. Mr. Arthur D. Hill suggested to the author that this illness, bringing a loss of hair, accentuated Mrs. Holmes's plainness in her middle and later years and increased her natural shyness. Early photographs would indicate that in her youth Fanny Dixwell had considerable beauty. In 1876 John Fiske described a call which he had made "on O. W. Holmes, Jr. and his pretty wife." *The Letters of John Fiske,* 357.

centuate a tendency which inheritance had implanted in her. When New England breeds women of intelligence and reserve it occasionally brightens those qualities with a dash of wit and humor and, ashamed to admit it, softens them with sentiment. The surmise that Cambridge had bred such a girl in Fanny Dixwell seems justified.

So far as we know, Holmes's path, before the War, had not crossed either that of William James or that of his brother Henry. When William, interrupting his medical studies, in March 1865, left on an expedition to Brazil with Professor Agassiz, he was already an intimate friends of Holmes.[54] A year later, after his return to Boston, William James spoke of Holmes as "the only fellow here I care anything about," and, acknowledging that his friend was "perhaps too exclusively intellectual," added that he "sees things so easily and clearly and talks so admirably that it's a treat to be with him." [55] The relationship of Henry James and Holmes in these early years of friendship was tenderly recalled by Henry in his *Notes of a Son and Brother*. One there glimpses an association of ardent spirits—the Jameses, Holmes, Minny Temple, John C. Gray—delicate in their appreciation of each other and enthusiastic in their quest for beauty. The hunger of Holmes and Gray was doubtless increased by the ugly experience of war which they had shared; the impulse of James sprang from the subtleties of his introspective nature; and the gay seriousness of Minny Temple was surely affected by the frailty of her hold on life. It was in the summer of 1865 that Holmes, by his own account, "read no end of poetry," [56] and Henry James has set a portion of the scene in which the reading occurred. He and Holmes, with John Gray joining them, had gone to North Conway, New Hampshire, in August and stayed there in the neighborhood of the Temple family. James's recollection of the season called back to his mind "the play of young intelligence and young friendship, the reading of Matthew Arnold and Browning, the discussion of a hundred human and personal things . . . the splendid American summer drawn out to its last generosity." [57]

Before the death of Minny Temple in 1870, when she was but

twenty-five, she evidently deeply touched the affections and hearts of her two cousins and of their friend Gray.[58] Of Holmes's feeling for her there are but scraps of evidence and none of these confirms the suggestion that Holmes "loved" her.[j]

In 1947 one who had been at North Conway as a young child recorded her memories of a day in August 1867 when Holmes, with Henry James, Gray, and a young lady as his companions, was setting out to climb Mount Kearsarge.

> The Captain, catching sight of the child, [Olivia Murray], and perhaps detecting in her face a wistful longing to join the party, said to her mother, "Mrs. Murray, will you let Olivia come with us? I will take care of her." The delighted child was allowed to go; all through the day Holmes stayed by her side, interesting and diverting her with stories. She remembers, in particular, his tale of the "Green-eyed Monster," which she knew to be the story of his devotion to a beautiful young lady of the party and his envy of those he thought more favored.[k]

There is every reason to suppose that the "beautiful young lady" was Minny Temple. The child's perception confirms the judgment

[j] The suggestion is found in Leon Edel, *Henry James: The Untried Years* (Philadelphia, 1953), 235. It is presumably based upon a similar suggestion in Catherine Drinker Bowen, *Yankee from Olympus* (Boston, 1944), 224.

[k] This account of the incident is that of Olivia Murray (Mrs. Bayard Cutting) and was made available to the author by the kindness of Judge Learned Hand. The recollections of Mrs. Cutting, as she recorded them in 1947, continued to later years. "After [Holmes's] holiday was over," she wrote, "he wrote to her occasionally. The girl, of course, adored him; he was her hero and the acme of perfection. She spent many weeks of arduous labor making a bookmark which she sent him, scarcely daring to hope that he would use it.

"Years passed before they saw each other again. Then once, when she was a young married woman, they met at a reception in Washington. When she told him who she was, he exclaimed, 'Why, Olivia Murray, you are my oldest friend; come right over to that sofa with me and we'll start just where we left off.' They spent a delightful hour together but their paths did not cross again until, many years later, when he was an Associate Justice, she went to see him at his home in Washington. They had tea together downstairs; then he said he wanted her to see his study and his books and took her upstairs. As they passed through his secretary's room, he asked the secretary to look on such and such a shelf and bring him a particular book. Out of it he took the bookmark the child had made for him and which he had kept and used for more than sixty years."

of Henry James that Minny Temple was "the heroine of our common scene" and would suggest that Holmes's devotion was similar to that of the Jameses and of Gray. It is worth remembering, however, that neither the child nor Henry James tells us that in other scenes than those of the White Mountains or in other seasons than that of August 1867, Holmes had no other heroines. That was a special place and a special time.[59]

When Holmes returned to the Law School in the fall of 1865 he evidently did so with a renewed zest. Perhaps the appetite for verse and leisure had been surfeited and been replaced by hunger for a tougher fare. In the previous May he had said to Brownell that he thought that his first year of law study satisfied him. Writing to him in October 1865, he spoke with much more vivid confidence of the satisfaction which he found in his professional studies: [60]

> Law, of which I once doubted, is now my enthusiastic pursuit. I am up to my ears in it all the time. One good thing about it is that it makes play of what otherwise would be work, e.g. Metaphysics. Such spongy stuff as Sir William Hamilton, for instance, after a little pile of Contingent Remainders or Pleading goes down like macaroni. You give a little suck, and pwip!! you've swallowed it and never known it.

During the summer and fall months it would seem that the first uncertainties had largely disappeared and were being replaced by the assurance that he could find in the law satisfaction for his deepest tastes and ambitions. It was not for many years that the assurance was to be complete, but a beginning of confidence had come by the fall of 1865. Eleven years later Holmes sent Emerson a copy of one of his first essays in the law. In transmitting it he said:

> It seems to me that I have learned, after a laborious and somewhat painful period of probation, that the law opens a way to philosophy as well as anything else, if pursued far enough, and I hope to prove it before I die. Accept this little piece as written in that faith and as a slight mark of the gratitude and respect I feel for you who more than anyone else first started the philosophical ferment in my mind.[61]

The period of probation, it would seem, began in the opening of Holmes's second year in Law School. From that time on there is no indication that he was ever beguiled by the temptations of verse. Law and philosophy from then on were the commanding interests.

The normal course of study at the Harvard Law School, in Holmes's time, was two years. Had he followed that course he would have continued to attend lectures for the whole of the academic year of 1865–66. In December 1865 he withdrew from the Law School, however, and went to the office of Robert M. Morse, a young member of the Boston bar with whom Holmes's friend, John C. Ropes, had shared an office. The only nearly contemporaneous record of this change is a brief entry in one of the pages in a diary for 1866: [62] "Went to most of the lectures until end of 3rd term when I went into Robert Morse's office towards end of 3rd term. Looked up some cases there." [63]

A number of factors had probably combined to persuade Holmes to withdraw from the Law School and continue his studies under Morse's tutelage. By October 1865, he had decided to go abroad "in the course of a few months." [64] That decision might well seem to make attendance at Law School lectures for only a part of the second term less profitable than the training and experience that could be gained during the intervening months in a law office. Harvard's standards were so lax that a law degree could be awarded, as it was to Holmes in June of 1866, after three terms of unrequired and, therefore, casual attendance at lectures. It must be remembered, furthermore, that it was still a very common practice for law students to get a part if not the whole of their preparation for the bar in a practitioner's office.[65]

When, in October 1870, Holmes and Arthur G. Sedgwick were editors of the *American Law Review,* a brief Note was published in its pages concerning curricular and administrative changes which had just been announced by the Faculty of the Harvard Law School.[66] Professors Parsons and Parker had resigned and President Eliot had invited Christopher Columbus Langdell to join the Faculty as Dean. The first important decision of the new Faculty was that henceforth all candidates for the degree of LL.B.

must take written examinations before they could be graduated. The anonymous Note in the *American Law Review* hailed the announcement with enthusiasm. Although it cannot be established that Holmes wrote the comment it is hardly conceivable that he disagreed with its substance. The youthful editors, in any case, permitted the Note to be published and in doing so gave it their editorial approval. Had its author been satisfied simply to approve the Faculty's decision he and the editors would probably not have incurred the wrath of Professor Parker. As it was, however, the Note included not only commendation of the Faculty's decision but condemnation of the old order which that decision overturned. "For a long time," the Note opened, "the condition of the Harvard Law School has been almost a disgrace to the Commonwealth of Massachusetts." Complete disgrace had been avoided only because "some of its courses of lectures have been good." The School, however, in awarding a degree which signified "nothing except a residence for a certain period in Cambridge or Boston" had been "doing something every year to injure the profession throughout the country, and to discourage real students."

Such a disparaging assault on the institution which he had served for twenty years not unnaturally brought forth a peppery reply from Joel Parker.[67] In a fifty-six-page pamphlet he answered the anonymous critic, and dealt also with complaints which a Committee of the Board of Overseers had recently made concerning the Law School's library. Parker evidently did not know whose pen had actually written the Note in the *American Law Review*, but he held its editors responsible for both the substance and the manner of the attack. Holmes and Sedgwick he described as "two young men . . . who, about four years since, consented to receive the honors of the School in the shape of a degree of Bachelor of Laws, without insisting upon a preliminary examination to show that they deserved them." [68] Parker, after saying that he found it difficult to say "which is most prominent in the article, the conceit which dictated it, or the entire lack of courtesy manifested by it," went on to explain and to defend the practices of the School which had always prevailed, even in the gigantic days of Story, until the

1870 decision. The heart of Parker's defense was his insistence that tradition had approved the ancient ways. Parker's most significant silence was with respect to the concluding criticism of the anonymous critic. The critic had quoted a recent formulation of the proper end which a law school should seek to achieve and which he believed Harvard might achieve under the new dispensation.

> The object of a law department is not precisely and only to educate young men to be practising lawyers, though it will be largely used for that purpose. It is to furnish all students who desire it the same facilities to investigate the science of human law, theoretically, historically, and thoroughly, as they have to investigate mathematics, natural sciences, or any other branch of thought.[69]

Holmes, while a law student, had found that Harvard did not provide those facilities. Perhaps the tone of the *American Law Review*'s criticism was needlessly supercilious, but it is clear that fundamental changes in the objectives and methods of legal education were long overdue, not only at Harvard but at all American law schools, and that the merits of the argument with Judge Parker were with the youthful critics, not with the aging champion of the old order.

From his explorations in the Law School's grab bag of details Holmes had made himself familiar with the shape of law. He had, presumably, developed the capacity to think as lawyers traditionally had thought. He had qualified himself to become a participant in the processes of which his grandfather, Charles Jackson, had been a master. Many young lawyers of Holmes's generation were satisfied to accept the continuities of the profession without question and were happy to feel themselves the heirs of an imposing tradition. In Holmes's temperament, however, there were speculative elements which must be satisfied. Unless he could see his career as related to the deepest tides of destiny, or at least to the significant currents of his times, it would be a lifetime wasted. His teachers of law had been satisfied to accept the self-sufficiency of law and had asked no other significant questions than those which Mr. Justice Jackson had answered. Their view of law had not been appreciably affected by the methods of science which had so shaken the foundations of philosophy. When Holmes left the Law School he had not, perhaps, yet asked himself whether he might seek to apply to law the scientific methods which others had applied to philosophy. It was likely, however, that unless he were to make some such effort he would turn from law to a calling in which he might feel himself engaged in the largest endeavors of the human spirit.

6

Contours of Conviction

To build the structure of Holmes's life around a progression of events—the War, the Harvard training, the journey to Europe—involves the risk of giving a mistaken emphasis and producing a deceptive order. It suggests that Holmes himself saw each event first as an attractive goal and then as a satisfying achievement and that by 1866 he had begun to feel that he was on his way towards a chosen objective. Quite possibly some feeling of that sort was in process of development. Another progression, however, concerned him more deeply, and if one is to understand either what he was or what he was to become it seems essential to pause in the narrative of external events to consider the direction of his curiosity and the shape of his thought during the concluding years of his preparation. The European voyage was not simply the journey of a young Bostonian. It was the pilgrimage of a maturing mind which had already found its tendencies. What England meant to Holmes, what use he was to make of his convictions when he entered his profession, turned to an extraordinary extent upon the intellectual commitments towards which his reading outside the law was leading him. Without an appreciation of the character of the doubts and convictions which an inquiring mind confronted when it surveyed the intellectual scene of Europe and America in the late 1860's, perceptive understanding of the convictions and doubts of Holmes's maturity would be impossible. A brief interlude in the narrative of events, accordingly, seems justified.

The nineteenth-century pastor who told his farming parishioners that it would be useless to pray for rain until the wind had changed was the spokesman of his time.[1] Science had set limits to his faith but had not destroyed it, and he was able to live happily with himself in a mood of temperate confidence. He, like Holmes, might have acknowledged that "the scientific way of looking at the world" had profoundly affected his beliefs,[2] yet the pastor, retaining his faith, had not permitted science to govern the mind with that high authority which Holmes came to allow it. It is easy to accept the truism that all thoughtful persons of the nineteenth century were affected, in one way or another, by the scientific point of view. It is much more difficult to discover in the case of an individual the measure or even the meaning of the influence. In the case of Holmes, however, the effort to achieve precision in our understanding is enormously facilitated by the existence of his reading lists. The titles there given, supplemented by his own statements of belief and doubt, afford an invaluable guide to the evolving structure of his thought.

In 1897 Holmes formulated a principle which he had come, through thirty years and more of thoughtful reading, to accept as fundamental. It was, in large part, the product of the scientific point of view. "The postulate on which we think about the universe," said Holmes, "is that there is a fixed quantitative relation between every phenomenon and its antecedents and consequents. If there is such a thing as a phenomenon without these fixed quantitative relations, it is a miracle." [3] As we have already seen, the germ of this conviction may be found in the passage in Holmes's undergraduate essay in which he praised Plato for anticipating the assurance which modern science has given us that "the law of cause and effect is absolute; if we know the data, the results are inevitable." [4] We know that while a student and a soldier he had begun to look into the literature of positivism [5] and it is likely that in discussions with his father he had pressed the claims of science to a point which his antagonist was unwilling to accept. It was not, however, until his legal studies at Harvard were behind him that his reading lists reveal a predominant interest in works of a positivistic and scientific character. From 1865 through 1867 his non-professional reading was principally directed to those works in which the scientific point of view was utilized for the comprehension of man's largest problems. Whether this reading strengthened an earlier tendency or initiated a new conviction in Holmes is, perhaps, unimportant, for in either case they became an element of critical importance in the molding of his convictions. In following briefly the course of Holmes's reading between 1865 and 1867 our purpose is not to discover or clarify particular beliefs of others which Holmes was ultimately to make his own. It is rather to suggest the quality of that way of thinking which was labeled scientific. If we appreciate that quality we shall, perhaps, better understand the direction, substance, and texture of Holmes's own thought in his later years.

Though Holmes's reading list nowhere indicates that he read any of the works of Auguste Comte, the Comtian analysis of history and the positivistic philosophy which accompanied or produced that analysis absorbed much of his attention in 1865 and 1866. In George Henry Lewes's *Biographical History of Philosophy* and his *Aristotle* the principles of positivism were given telling and relentless application. In the former, Lewes proudly asserted that there was no other "History of Philosophy written by one disbelieving in the possibility of metaphysical certitude." [6] The time had come, he believed, to show that the only legitimate basis of interest in philosophy was historical; the earlier illusion that truth was discoverable by metaphysical speculation was no longer defensible. The modern advance of science had taught mankind that the only proper method by which truth may be discovered is by observation and experiment. Since metaphysics neither deals with observable facts nor utilizes the experimental method, its discoveries may never be described as "true." Its concern is with the logical coördination of unverified facts; science, on the other hand, coördinates facts which have been verified by observation. The positivist is faithful to the traditions of science since his objective is nothing more ambitious than the detection of the exact relations of coexistence and succession which determine the order of the universe. The metaphysicians of the modern world are best represented, if not caricatured, by Hegel who made logic the sole test of truth and thus applied subjective standards to the objective world in the happy assurance that the objects of the world around us are moved as we are. The metaphysicians, though they have abandoned the theological assumptions that phenomena are variable and that the variations are to be explained by a supernatural will, are, like the theologians, satisfied of their capacity to discover an ultimate cause. The confidence that logic is the all-sufficient instrument of discovery persuades them that decisions are final. Their refusal to let experience measure their confidence leads them to repudiate that skepticism which gives the method of science its vitality.

Had positivism done no more than challenge the pretensions of theologians and metaphysicians its significance in nineteenth-century thought would have been relatively slight. Its influence, of course, was far more extensive, for what it demanded was that all problems with which the mind of man is confronted should be considered scientifically. This demand meant not only that the objective method—verification by the tests of sensible experience—should be followed, but that the motives of inquiry should be purified. No longer should man's quest for truth be prompted by the hope that a true theology or a valid metaphysics might provide mankind with reassurance. When comfort is the motive of inquiry its method becomes subjective. Man must so discipline his motives as to exclude the hope of cosmic reassurance as an impulse for inquiry. When speculative exploration is carried on with reassurance as its goal the mind not only forgets the limits of its own capacity but molds the universe to its taste. Herbert Spencer expressed basic principles of positivism when he asserted that it is our duty "to submit ourselves with all humility to the limits of our intelligence; and not perversely to rebel against them." [7] Quoting Sir William Hamilton, he warned us that "the capacity of thought is not to be constituted into the measure of existence" and cautioned us against "recognizing the domain of our knowledge as necessarily co-extensive with the horizon of our faith." [8] Doubtless these phrases which Holmes had read in 1866 had passed from his recollection in the second decade of the twentieth century, yet it is hard to believe that the impression which they had made was fleeting. "I do not venture to assume that my inabilities in the way of thought are inabilities of the universe." [9] "Why should we employ the energy that is furnished to us by the cosmos to defy it and shake our fist at the sky? It seems to me silly." [10] "Now when we come to our attitude toward the universe I do not see any rational ground for demanding the superlative—for being dissatisfied unless we are assured that our truth is cosmic truth, if there is such a thing—that the ultimates of a little creature on this little earth are the last word of the unimaginable whole." [11] If these formulations of doubt sound in our ears like the skepticism of the twentieth century it is well to remember that they echo the positivism of the nineteenth.

If Holmes's reading of Lewes and Spencer made him sympathetically familiar with the philosophical generalities of positivism, he saw in John Stuart Mill's writings what the fruits of its methods and purposes might be when the generalities were applied to ethics and political science. There were many streams of thought which nourished Mill's mind and it would be a gross distortion to label him a disciple of Comte. Though not a Comtian he was, however, a positivist fully dedicated to the scientific point of view. Among the many tasks which he set himself none was more important than that of applying the objective methods of experimental science to human affairs and aspirations. Other positivists like Lewes were satisfied to use the scientific method as an instrument of criticism; Mill's purpose was to establish a system of ethics and a theory of society which should be scientific. No system and no theory could in Mill's judgment satisfy that end unless it were free from the infection of theology and metaphysics. He believed that theories of morality and politics might properly be brought within the Comtian categories. They might, in other words, be classified as theological, metaphysical, or positive.[12] The theological and metaphysical theories of morality and politics reject the thesis that moral rules and political institutions are human creations designed to secure the common good as mankind sees it. Those persons whose cast of mind is theological find that the principles of morality are ordained by God. Being so ordained, their legitimacy is not to be questioned nor is their truth to be tested by the crude instrument of human intelligence. Those whose inclinations are metaphysical substitute a Law of Nature for the Law of God, but like the theologians, invest the rights and duties of human beings with an objective validity not dependent upon merely human standards of utility. The metaphysical, a priori mode of thought, has the same result in morals and jurisprudence that it has in all other areas—it erects "a mere creation of the mind into a test . . . of external truth, and present[s] the abstract expression of the beliefs already entertained, as the reason and evidence which justifies them." [13]

Holmes became familiar with these reflections when he read Mill on *Auguste Comte and Positivism* during the winter before his European trip. Probably he had no specific recollection of them in 1928, yet in that year he showed himself to be a faithful disciple of Mill when he asserted that "for legal purposes a right is only the hypostasis of a prophecy"—"the empty substratum [which we construct] to pretend to account for the fact that the courts will act in a certain way." [14] Though a question might be made as to whether Holmes's theory of law was shaped by positivism, it seems abundantly clear that his theory of morals had its roots in the skepticism of Mill. Fitzjames Stephen asserted that the utilitarians could give no satisfactory answer to the man "who says boldly, 'I am bad and selfish and I mean to be bad and selfish,' [for] the positivists can only reply, 'Our tastes differ.' " [15] The words which Stephen put in the mouth of his antagonist are virtually the same words which Holmes used when he considered the same problem. With the positivists he agreed that there is no final arbiter to select our values for us and that ultimately we make our choice on the basis of our taste. "Do you like sugar in your coffee or don't you? You admit the possibility of difference and yet are categorical in your own way, and even instinctively condemn those who do not agree. So as to truth." [16] "Pleasures," he said, "are ultimates and in cases of difference between oneself and another there is nothing to do except in unimportant matters to think ill of him and in important ones to kill him." [17] Those in the contemporary world who have condemned the positivism of Holmes have often failed to recognize that it was as much the philosophy of a school as the conviction of an individual which he expressed. Bertrand Russell in 1935 formulated a basic doctrine of logical positivism: "Since no way can be even imagined for deciding a difference as to values, the conclusion is forced upon us that the difference is one of tastes, not one as to any objective truth." [18] The common ancestry of Russell's principle and of Holmes's is found in the writing in which Holmes absorbed himself from 1865 to 1867.

Mill's utilitarianism was not derived from but was confirmed by Comte's positivism. From his father and from Bentham—in fact from the whole tradition of British empiricism—Mill inherited both his distrust of a priori certitudes and his conviction that the limits of man's knowledge of external reality are set by the boundaries of experience. A theory of morals which finds its ultimate standards in an inherent Moral Sense, in Mill's eyes, is no better than theories of government which justify Democracy by the Law of Nature or Monarchy by the Divine Right of Kings. The moral sentiments of man are simply the conclusions which he has drawn from experience as to the ways in which the greatest happiness of the greatest number is to be achieved. Their source is not an internal intuition but "an external standard." [19] This is not an appropriate place to consider whether Holmes's later theories of legal liability with their insistence that "the standards of the law are external standards" [20] were influenced by utilitarian theories of ethics. The possibility that a relationship exists is, however, worth suggesting at this point.[21]

The doctrines of utilitarianism were neither created by John Stuart Mill nor given to him by Comte. Had it not been for two fortunate accidents it is not likely that Mill's influence on the intellectual history of the nineteenth century would have been as great as Bentham's or have gone far beyond James Mill's. The first accident was the fortitude of mind and character which made him more than the disciple that his father expected him to be. The second was the fact that the amazing successes of the natural and physical sciences were contemporaneous with Mill's maturity. Those successes seemed dramatically to confirm the thesis that truths with respect to the external world are discoverable by the skeptical processes of experiment and observation. The old insistence of the empiricists that man himself and man's values should be examined by similar processes gained new force in a world which could not deny, however much it might fear, the massive successes of science. Mill made the most of the opportunity which at long last had come to empiricism. With inexhaustible energy he maintained the offensive against those believers who either stubbornly refused to abandon their theological ways of thought or, rolling with the punches, became philosophers and sought refuge in German metaphysics.

The positivists of Mill's generation, with his hearty support, grasped one weapon which Bentham had never taken in hand. They had come to see, as Holmes was later to put it, that "a page of history is worth a volume of logic." [22] It was not a mere coincidence that the same period of time saw the differing problems of philology,[23] religion,[a] philosophy, and law treated historically. Behind each effort to secure a fuller understanding of human institutions and values by the historical method lay the empiricist's conviction that the true source of knowledge is experience. That conviction told the scholar that he who seeks a theory of language, of religion, of knowledge, or of law will succeed only if he makes his first task the painstaking accumulation of facts. History itself must be made over from a dramatic art to a descriptive science. When Blackstone asked why the King is one of the three branches

[a] *Ecce Homo* [by Sir John Robert Seeley] (1866). When Holmes finished the book on Dec. 23, 1866, he made the following entry in his diary: "A noble book not for its theology which seems to us halfway but for its ardor and humanity—'No soul is pure which is not also passionate.'" Lord Shaftesbury spoke of Sir John Seeley's effort to tell the story of the life of Christ in somewhat different terms when he described *Ecce Homo* as "that most pestilential book ever vomitted, I think, from the jaws of hell." See review by Charles Eliot Norton, *North American Review,* CIII, 302 (July 1866).

of the British legislature he gave an answer which satisfied the eighteenth century: "Because it is highly necessary for preserving the balance of the Constitution." [24] The nineteenth century found the answer unsatisfactory; a scientific age is concerned with causes not with justifications. It is not surprising, of course, that this new concern should take command of thought in the age of Darwin, but it is too often forgotten that even before *The Origin of Species* was published the scientific point of view had applied the skeptical methods of history to nearly all fields of inquiry, whether sacred or profane. It was a significant fact that a churchman, William Whewell, in the 1840's should write a *History of the Inductive Sciences;* it was perhaps even more significant that he found it inadvisable to acknowledge that his analysis was derived from the positivism of Auguste Comte.[25]

The association of history and science did more than bring their methods into alliance. To certain philosophical radicals it meant that the story of man was to be considered as a branch of natural history; in the United States John William Draper sought to find the key to biography and to history in physiology,[26] and in England Buckle made a more persuasive and influential effort to show that the nature and destiny of man are determined by the laws of matter and the laws of intellect—to establish, in brief, the science of history. His resolute temperament was not troubled by the necessitarian direction of this effort, and he took satisfaction in the belief that if we were acquainted with all the antecedents of our motives "and with all the laws of their movements, we could with unerring certainty predict the whole of their immediate results." [27] It was, of course, inevitable that in the age of science the famous maxim of Laplace [b] would be applied to human beings and that such conservatives as Francis Bowen of Harvard should consider the application a foul and dangerous heresy.[28] Mill, in

[b] "A mind that in a given instance knew all the forces by which nature is animated and the position of all the bodies of which it is composed, if it were vast enough to include all these data within his analysis, could embrace in one single formula the movements of the largest bodies of the universe and of the smallest atoms; nothing would be uncertain for him; the future and the past would be equally before his eyes." *Essai politique sur les probabilités* (1921 ed.), 3.

his *Logic,* had already committed a similar offense. He had asserted that "the state of the whole universe at any instant, we believe to be the consequence of its state at the previous instant; insomuch that one who knew all the agents which exist at the present moment . . . could predict the whole subsequent history of the universe." [29] Nor had Mill allowed mankind exemption from the principle of uniformity; the person who not only knows his neighbor thoroughly but also understands the inducements prompting him to action could foretell his conduct "with as much certainty as . . . any physical event." [30] In Mill's view, however, this doctrine did not involve a commitment to despairing fatalism, for character is itself a cause of action and the individual's character is molded in part by his desire to give it a certain shape.[31] When Holmes said that "the mode in which the inevitable comes to pass is through effort" [32] he restated a principle accepted in Mill's *Logic* and popularized in Buckle's *History.*

The father of positivism, Auguste Comte, when he promulgated the Religion of Humanity was not troubled by the despotism which would accompany the new faith and was gratified when his disciples addressed him as "Your Reverence" and "First Supreme Pontiff of Humanity." [33] This tendency of the master towards tyranny might suggest that the logic of positivism when applied to problems of politics would endorse authoritarian principles. In fact it is clear that the temperate positivism of Mill and his English allies, which rejected the most exuberant fantasies of Comte, contributed significantly to their preference for a laissez-faire society. Of course there were many elements in the atmosphere of nineteenth-century England which made it natural that men of a progressive bent should ask for a reduction of public authority over the individual, but not least important among those elements was the scientific bias. In his *Autobiography* Mill seems to recognize the relationship when he indicates that the intuitionist school of ethics and psychology, largely indifferent to the experimental methods of science, had erected barriers to practical reform in an age of progress.[34] The political allies of the intuitionists were those who believed that government could discover and should enforce rules of conduct authenticated by an authority higher than that of reason. Positivism translated to political terms insisted, on the other hand, that the utility of conduct is the measure of its morality and must, accordingly, be established by experiment. When government or social authority denies the individual the opportunity to carry on the experiment of life in accordance with his own capacities, it rejects the best method—the scientific means—of discovering truth and solving the greatest problems of society. When Alexander Bain turned from psychology to political theory he also revealed why the political tendency of positivism was towards a laissez-faire society. Bain was not surprised that the intuitionists insisted that a Christian society and a God-fearing government should enforce immutable principles of morality; any decent person who concedes that the principles exist and are discoverable would adopt the same position. But Bain, like Mill, would not make that concession. Believing that the principles are illusions bequeathed to mankind by theologians and metaphysicians, Bain demanded that government should cease its effort to convert illusions to realities by labeling them rules of conduct. The sole justification that a government may legitimately give for any law is that its enactment and enforcement are necessary for the protection of the public security. When that security is not endangered by an individual's conduct the state should remain indifferent and unconcerned.[35]

Whether positivism contributed significantly to Buckle's hostility to government is doubtful. He sought to clothe his conviction in respectable dress, yet feeling constantly bursts the buttons with which he tried scientifically to harness his emotions. The formula of positivism is applied when he asserts that an unbiased observation of history establishes that human progress is the consequence of expanding knowledge and not the result of moral growth. His examination of the history of European civilization convinced him that "no great political improvement, no great reform, either legislative or executive, has ever been originated in any country by its rulers," [36] that the traditional role of government has been to restrict the boundaries of knowledge, and that the best laws which any government has passed "have been those by which some former laws were repealed." [37] The ultimate conviction that "nearly everything which has been done [by government], has been done amiss" [38] purports to be grounded in Buckle's scientific view of history. A later generation, doubting that source of the conviction, may still believe that irresponsible powers of government have often so controlled its functioning that the one progressive force in civilization—knowledge—has often been repressed through state authority. Buckle, studying the scene of English and European history, discovered that a minority of clerics and nobles had made governments their agents of repression. Mill, who was less concerned with history, in his essay *On Liberty* considered the threat which a democratic society presented that a tyrannical majority might establish directly or indirectly similar restrictions on freedom. Each in his way found that the principles of positivism led him to suspicion of government.

Herbert Spencer evidently believed that his hostility to government was a scientist's response to observed data and not the consequence of a political bias. Yet Mill and Bain were surely right in believing that Spencer had never renounced the wholly unscientific principles of the intuitionists and in fact had built his political philosophy on the assumption that man is possessed of natural rights. To treat morality, as Spencer did, as a species of transcendental physiology, compelled him to use scientific language, but to the extent that he was concerned with a priori values he dealt with matters beyond the reach of science and observation. It is true that between the basic libertarian propositions of Mill and Spencer there is little substantive difference. Mill asserted that "the only freedom which deserves the name is that of pursuing our own good in our own way, so long as we do not attempt to deprive others of theirs, or impede their efforts to obtain it." [39] Spencer's major premise asserted that "every man may claim the fullest liberty to exercise his faculties compatible with the like liberty of every other man." [40] The essential difference between the theories of the two men was that Mill valiantly endeavored to remain true to the scientific faith and to find justification for his thesis, not in an idea of abstract right, but in the principle of utility. Spencer, on the other hand, considering that history was "fit only for the attention of 'immature minds,'"[41] was satisfied to accept an a priori conception of individual rights. His theory of liberty, as a consequence, was more like that of Baron Wilhelm von Humboldt's than it was like Mill's. The character of Humboldt's mind is revealed in a suggestion which he made in his essay on *The Sphere and Duties of Government:* "With regard to the whole conduct of the inquiry," he wrote, "I would desire that all considerations of a general nature contained in these pages, be viewed entirely apart from the reality of actual practice."[42] Humboldt and Spencer were not only in almost perfect accord as to the necessity of so restricting the powers of government as virtually to eliminate its authority, but they were in basic agreement that actualities are irrelevant to a consideration of the nature of human liberty. Mill's confidence in observation, his concern with verification, made the a prioristic, almost Kantian, methods of Spencer wholly unacceptable. Yet it is important to remember that each, by his different route, came to a theory of liberty that was not significantly unlike the other's. When Holmes finished reading Humboldt's essay in October 1866, he wrote in his diary that it was "a lofty rhapsody" in which Humboldt's "conclusions show his singular insight and a kind of prophetic genius—his reasonings are sometimes rather nebulous—and such a book must suffer from the want of illustration by copious examples."[43] It is not unlikely that when he closed Spencer's *First Principles* a short time before, some of the same impressions passed through his mind.

Another figure in the tapestry of nineteenth-century thought was brought constantly to Holmes's attention in his readings from 1865 through 1867. His early reading list does not include Malthus and we do not know, therefore, when it was that he became the "devout Malthusian" which he proclaimed himself to be.[44] His readings in Mill, Spencer, and the other positivists, however, brought him in constant touch with Malthusian doctrine. It is clear that the gloomy diagnosis of Malthus contributed substantially to Holmes's conviction that socialist reformers and other "do-gooders" were unwilling to recognize the ugly facts of a cruel nature. He was convinced that Malthus had "ripped the guts out of some humbugs" and was discouraged to find that "they are as alive as ever today." "Humbugs," he observed, "have no guts—and live all the better without them." [45] The confidence of the socialist that man's regeneration may be achieved by "tinkering with the institution of property" was destined to disappointment for it failed to learn the lesson that improvement in man's lot will be made possible "only by taking in hand life and trying to build a race." [46] When Holmes spoke these thoughts in 1915 he followed in the steps of Mill who had urged in his *Political Economy* that "unhappily, sentimentality rather than common sense usually presides over the discussion" of the ways and means by which the condition of the poor may be improved, and protested that the law of population was commonly dismissed "with such terms as 'hard-hearted Malthusianism'; as if it were not a thousand times more hard-hearted to tell human beings that they may, than that they may not, call into existence swarms of creatures who are sure to be miserable, and most likely to be depraved." [47]

It would do less than justice to the scientific point of view to suggest through this survey that Holmes's experience of its influence was merely literary. Among his intellectual companions fidelity to the postulates of positivism involved something more than the ritual of verbal homage. William James turned from an artistic career to medicine at the time when he was under the sway of positivism; John Fiske chose his course in life in devotion to Herbert Spencer; Chauncey Wright became a principal spokesman among philosophers of the scientific spirit; Henry and Brooks Adams, in their turn, came to history seeking science. Some among this number departed later from the faith, but each had made it for a time his deepest commitment. Unlike William James the others chose not to make their careers in science. Perhaps that fact explains, in part, the persistence of their faith that the methods of science were preferable to all other methods. It is well, in this connection, to remember that a friend of Holmes's later years who was a scientist of considerable distinction not only emphasized that

Holmes "knew of science only by hearsay, so to speak," but insisted that his "curiously definite idea about science [was] an utterly erroneous one." The error, according to Thomas Barbour, was derived from Holmes's mistaken belief "that the scientist, given time and painstaking research, could reasonably be expected to solve all problems." He was, in brief, "extraordinarily trusting and uninformed." [48] The confidence, whether it was innocent and ignorant or far-sighted and profound, was built on foundations which other hands had laid.

7

Europe

As Holmes looked forward to his European trip he saw the voyage as a pilgrimage. His father's influence, provincial as it may have been in certain aspects, had made the civilization of Europe, its art, its letters, and its philosophy, vivid realities in the Holmes household. An education for Dr. Holmes's children was not complete until they had observed the European scene. In addition to a cultivated appreciation of the European past Holmes carried across the Atlantic that special interest in its contemporary thought which was reflected in his reading. Like all other travelers Holmes could look at Shakespeare's tomb or wander through the Louvre, but few other young Americans could set forth with the expectation that they might dine with John Stuart Mill, or talk with Herbert Spencer and Alexander Bain. Holmes's pilgrimage, accordingly, was not merely a voyage in the discovery of a significant past but a venture in appreciation of an imposing present. The young man who sailed for England in April 1866 had about him qualities which assured that his reception would be warm—if not in all circles, at least among "the cultivated radicals" of London.[1] These were the handful of men and women of relatively high station whose Northern sympathies during the Civil War had set them apart from their English peers and brought them into close relation with Boston's antislavery leaders. They were the friends and admirers of Charles Sumner, of James Russell Lowell, of Motley—men who if not their brothers, were at least their cousins in cultivation and radicalism. The Civil War was a sufficiently vivid memory in 1866 to mean that a wounded veteran carrying letters of introduction from Sumner, Lowell, and Motley, and bearing the familiar name of Oliver Wendell Holmes, would be a visitor deserving of attention. The English friends of the North might be expected to find the same satisfaction as did Motley in the fact that Boston had sent "so true a representative of [its] 'jeunesse dorée,' not the electroplated article, but the true thing tried in the fiery furnace of a four years' war, [into] places where the ring of the true metal is known." [2] That the young visitor was strikingly handsome, spirited in his interests, and eager to extend his horizons of appreciation made offers of hospitality frequent and whole-hearted.

The record of Holmes's European journey is found in the same small diary in which he charted, by author and title, the course of his intellectual travels. Sparing in comment, the diary nonetheless more fully reports daily events than any other record which he kept for any other period. In its notations of detail it reveals the young man's desire not to permit the happenings to drop into oblivion. Of the crossing on the *Persia* it tells nothing; the English scene opens on the evening of May 7 in Liverpool: "N.B.: black smoke of tugs—green grass ashore—Adelphi Hotel very poor." On Wednesday, May 9, Holmes's first full day in London, he made three calls, each familiar in the routine of travelers. His first stop was at the banking house of Barings, the second was at the American legation, the third was at the tailor's. The scenes of the city "all seemed an old story after the stereoscopes" which had been so popular on Charles Street. That "everybody tries to be a swell" was probably not surprising and the Bostonian's eye was quick to notice that "few of the gentlemen [were] real ones" and that the ladies were "devilish frowsy in the hair." Yet the distance between home and England did not seem great when Holmes heard a Londoner whistling "When Johnny Comes Marching Home." The concluding entry in the diary for May 9 summarized the "first impressions." "Common people like ours. Swells finer. Two types, Saxon and dark. All dressed alike—lavender gloves and sailors ties. Evening, whores stop you everywhere."

These were but flashes of light from the surface of London, and the young visitor, eager to plunge beneath the surface, turned to the family of Charles Francis Adams, the American Minister, for aid and guidance. There he found Mary Adams, the youngest daughter of the Minister, and Henry, serving as secretary to his father, each evidently willing to help the traveler. The American legation was the meeting place of all the visiting Bostonians and if it served to broaden Holmes's horizon as a center for gatherings of cultivated and radical Englishmen, it also was the spot at which he could recapture the mood of Beacon Hill by dining with Higginsons, Crowninshields, Sohiers, or Hoopers. Evidently Mary Adams' presence in the household was something of an attraction to Holmes; on June 3rd his diary reports "a long and very pleasant talk with Miss A."; on the 8th he describes her as "each time prettier and more charming than the last"; and on his final evening in London after dining at the Adamses' he went to "a nasty little American party" for the purpose of "having a talk with Miss A.—which I done it." Another visiting American was William Morris Hunt, then doing a portrait of Charles Francis Adams, and one may surmise that he and Holmes not only spoke of art but of Hunt's Newport pupils, William and Henry James. It was presumably through the Adamses that Holmes found himself on May 12 a visitor at Mount Felix, the house of Russell Sturgis at Walton-on-Thames—a "regular English country place" with nightingales overhead, the Thames at the end of the lawn, and "turf like moss in which the foot sinks deep" and where an evening with Copperhead guests and General Sir Edward Bruce Hamley, literary veteran of the Crimean War, was brought to a pleasant close "with cigars and hot toddy."

It was in London, however, that the chief associations were made. Lord and Lady Belper were not only friends of the North, but, perhaps, more important to Holmes, were friends of Lecky, Grote, Browning, and John Stuart Mill. On May 11 Holmes dined with Henry Adams at Lady Belper's and there met Lady Trevelyan, Macaulay's sister, and "other lords and ladies." Holmes noted of the latter that they "let their eyes wander while they talk to you, very freely [and] wear lower necked dresses than at home," but added the discouraged comment: "No one pretty there." A similar impression is recorded after attending "a regular squash" at Lady Waldegrave's "drum"—"noticed as usual good arms, ears, teeth, and bad looks." On another occasion, a party on Upper Belgrave Street was "signalized by bad looks, bad manners, and bad feed." Possibly the sour mood of Henry Adams, who felt that "no one could possibly admire an English dinner-table," [3] had infected his friend and encouraged him to announce in a gloomy letter to his mother that "I think the English manners not very good and rather repulsive." [4] In his diary, however, appeared a confession which suggests that deficiencies in manners occasionally marked the conduct of the guest. After dining with Colonel and Lady Mary Herbert on June 5, Holmes admitted that "somehow though I drank little, I felt the wine and was too talky and loud."

The meager diary and the single surviving letter to his parents give little more than intimations that London offered Holmes intellectual excitement. Remembering his reading list, however, one may feel some confidence that when he dined, as he often did, with Sir Charles Lyell, the geologist, and his wife ("both agreeable and first rate Americans"), when he talked with Frederic Harrison, "a Comte man who was civil," or with David Masson, the historian of nineteenth-century British philosophy, when he met Froude, Browning, Tom Hughes, Sir John Millais, and Barry Cornwall (who had been a schoolmate of Byron's), he saw his pilgrimage as something more significant than a round of social engagements. We know that he made a fruitless call on Herbert Spencer, who proved to be out of town at the moment, but that the letter which John Lothrop Motley had given him to Mill effectively served its purpose. Mill came from the floor of the House "and was very civil" and made arrangements for Holmes to meet him at the House of Commons on June 1 at 5:30 P.M. in full dress. At the appointed time Mill appeared and "in company with Professor Fawcett took me to [the] Political Economy Club to dine. Discussion afterwards. [Sir Rowland] Hill, Professor [John Elliott]

10. Officers of the Twentieth Regiment, Massachusetts Volunteers, at Reunion in Boston, 1869

Left to right: *Gen. Francis W. Palfrey; Lt. Henry H. Sturgis; Lt. Col. O. W. Holmes, Jr.; Gen. Edward N. Hallowell; Maj. Gen. William F. Bartlett; Gen. Charles L. Peirson; Capt. Edward F. Robins; Col. William Raymond Lee; Gen. George N. Macy; Gen. Charles A. Whittier; Capt. John C. Putnam; Capt. Henry W. T. Mali; Capt. C. Linsee Tilden; Lt. Nathaniel T. Messer; Capt. N. P. Hallowell*

11. Fanny Bowditch Dixwell with her younger sisters and brother

12. Embroidery by Fanny B. Dixwell

Cairnes, Baron Bramwell etc. present." In 1929 Holmes gave a fuller account of the occasion than he did in his contemporary diary. The subject of the evening's discussion was "whether the financial policy of England should be governed by the prospective exhaustion of coal in H years as predicted by Jevons . . . I whispered to my neighbor," Holmes told Harold Laski, "that 90 years was too far ahead to take into account for such purposes—so many things might happen." In the same letter of 1929 Holmes added another touch of reality which was omitted from the diary—that James Fitzjames Stephen at the august meeting of the Political Economy Club "went to sleep at the table." [5] The diary tells us, however, that after the dinner Stephen and Holmes walked the London streets until 11:30 and had "a good talk" while doing so. This was the first occasion on which Holmes's path had crossed that of the elder Stephen brother, though Leslie had seen Holmes in Boston in 1863.[6] That a spark of sympathy was struck between Holmes and the elder brother, Fitzjames, is indicated by the fact that on the day after their first meeting Stephen sent him copies of his *Essays by a Barrister* and his *Defence of Dr. Williams*. When Holms turned to the *Essays,* as his reading list indicates that he did, he found opinions which were strikingly similar to some of his own favorite "chestnuts" of later years. Stephen's reflections on Philanthropy and on Doing Good have an emphasis on the utility of the vigorous pursuit of one's own calling, unmixed with pretensions of altruism, which would have qualified him for charter membership in Holmes's Society of Jobbists.[a] Like Holmes, Stephen put two virtues at the pinnacle of human achievement—wisdom and manliness.

[a] One of Holmes's fullest descriptions of his imaginary Society of Jobbists was in a letter to Lady Ellen Askwith: "This society recognizes that altruism and egotism are only the ways you feel about your work in the half hour's recess, or on the usual Saturday half holiday—but that when you are on your job, if you do it well, you are neither altruist nor egotist, and that the important thing is how you do your job and not how you think or feel about it afterwards. Hence members are to be allowed their idiosyncrasy in recess—if they forget it while they are at their task. It is a club for the abolition of altruism as a requirement of salvation." Autograph letter, March 3, 1915. (Copy at Harvard Law School.)

> The condition of our life is that we stand on a narrow strip of the shore, waiting till the tide, which has washed away hundreds of millions of our fellows, shall wash us also into a country of which there are no charts, and from which there is no return. . . . It is surely wiser and more manly to walk silently by the shore of that silent sea than to boast with puerile exultation over the little sand-castles which we have employed our short leisure in building up.[7]

In the *Defence of Dr. Williams* Stephen published the arguments which he had successfully made a few years before on behalf of a liberal cleric charged with contributing an heretical review to the notorious volume, *Essays and Reviews.* The eloquent plea for liberty showed that the sand-castle built by a jobbist may be a work of art. As Holmes and Fitzjames Stephen walked the streets of London, it is not impossible that the forthright Englishman complained, as he had to others, of the "anti-legal view of human nature in general and crime in particular" [8] which Dr. Holmes had revealed in *Elsie Venner,* and that the son, who was not entirely unsympathetic to his father's thesis, came to the Doctor's defense.[9]

Holmes's final meeting with Mill was on the evening of June 11: "Dined at the Members' Dining Room with Mr. Mill, with whom was Mr. Bain, psychologist—and we talked. I was struck with the absence of imaginative impulse, especially in Mr. Bain—excellent for facts and criticism but not open to the infinite possibilities—Eh? " Again we find in a letter written in the next century a fuller account of this dinner at the Commons. "By way of politeness," Holmes told Baroness Moncheur, Bain and Mill "talked of English reputations that began in America—mentioning, I think, Coleridge and Carlyle. I ventured to add Browning, whom my crowd admired but who hardly had got his later standing in England. The suggestion was coldly received." In the same letter Holmes made a comment on Mill which reveals an important aspect of the young American's impression of the English character. Mill seemed to Holmes to be "the one middle class man who did not show disadvantageously the consciousness of a class above him. He had the democracy of intellect (which also is aristocratic from another point of view)."[10] Again writing to the Baroness in 1928, Holmes touched on the same matters. "The first time that I went to England," he said, "J. S. Mill was the only man of the middle class who seemed to me socially unconscious, but my impression is that that had changed in latter days, but that the upper class are still a good way off from the simple, human basis on which an unspoiled American meets you."[11] The evident success which Holmes had in London suggests that perhaps he had those very traits of character which he missed in most Englishmen. Barry Cornwall's description of him would bear out this suggestion. "We were very much pleased with Colonel Holmes," he wrote to James T. Fields in Boston. "He seems a very intelligent, modest young man; as little military as need be, and, like Coriolanus, not baring his wounds (if he has any) for public gaze."[12]

On the evening of May 26 Holmes accompanied the Adamses to a reception at the Gladstones'—an occasion which Mrs. Adams described as "the greatest squash she'd seen," and one on which the veteran's wounds, apparently, did not go unnoticed. There the young man met Sir Roundell Palmer, the Attorney General, later to become Lord Selborne, and Monckton Milnes (Lord Houghton), known to his contemporaries as "the cool of the evening." In his diary Holmes reported that "I had quite a long talk with the great Panjandrum G[ladstone] himself—whereat people stared. G. in consideration of my wounds made me sit and I was a great gun." On June 7 came another, far more satisfactory, meeting with Gladstone, a breakfast of the elect, including Charles Francis Adams, the Duke and Duchess of Argyll, Lord Houghton, and Lord Lyttleton. Holmes tells us that "Mr. Gladstone seated himself on my right." Further details of the gathering were recorded in Mr. Adams' diary.

We sat at two round tables, thus dividing the company; but Mr. Gladstone took ours, which made all the difference in the world. His characteristic is the most extraordinary facility of conversation on almost any topic, with a great command of literary resources, which at once gives it a high tone. . . . [W]e passed from politics, the House of Commons, and Mr. Mill, to English prose as illustrated from the time of Milton down to this day and contrasted with German, which has little of good, and with French. . . . After an hour thus spent we rose, and on a question proposed by Colonel Holmes respecting a group of figures in china, which stood in a corner, Mr. Gladstone launched forth into a disquisition on that topic, which he delights in, and illustrated his idea of the art by showing us several specimens of different kinds. . . . This is the pleasantest and most profitable form of English society.[13]

If Henry Adams felt that "no one could possibly admire an English dinner-table" his father was evidently satisfied that London's breakfast-tables were, on rare occasions, admirable. He went so far as to say that the morning party at the Gladstones' "reminds me a little of my father's breakfasts [in Washington] when he was Secretary of State and I a boy." From an Adams, that was a significant concession, if not a glowing compliment to British graces. Holmes also found familiar qualities in Gladstone. In 1927, recalling his first meetings with him, he said that "he had a voice like Emerson's and . . . seemed to me the one man who was like an American. He came out to meet you and had gusto." [14]

Adams' account of the Gladstone breakfast contains one passage which throws light, perhaps, on Holmes's habits in reading. Telling of the surprising breadth of Gladstone's cultivation, Adams says that his host asked him if he had read Erckmann-Chatrian's *Conscrit de 1813*.

Luckily for me, who have little acquaintance with the light current literature, I could say "Yes," and could contrast it favorably with the artificial manner of Hugo. It is a cause of wonder to me how a man like Gladstone, so deeply plunged in the current of politics, and in the duties of legislation and official labor, can find time to keep along with the ephemeral literature abroad as well as at home.[15]

Perhaps the conversation of Adams and Gladstone passed unnoticed by Holmes, but the fact that his reading list carries the novel of Erckmann-Chatrian among those which he read on his return from Europe suggests that he was not heedless to the literary conversation of the elder statesmen.[16]

On Sunday, May 27, Holmes dined with Tom Hughes, friend

of James Russell Lowell, author of *Tom Brown's School Days,* and eager supporter of "muscular Christianity." Evidently a warm affection sprang from the meeting and a few surviving letters from Hughes suggest that the young American's willing capacity to charm was felt by others in the Hughes household. Writing to Holmes on New Year's Eve, 1866, Hughes promised to send his young friend a picture of "the young lady of the mature age of 12 whose waiting [on table] you did your best to spoil one Sunday evening last summer. What is the use," asked Hughes, "of one's trying to teach a child simple and useful habits in this corrupt and plethorically rich civilization if impetuous republican colonels will burst in and make eyes at her while she is handling the potatoes?" [17] Holmes's letters to Hughes have not, apparently, survived, a loss which is peculiarly tantalizing in view of what Hughes wrote to him in February 1868. Holmes had evidently made such feeling inquiries about Miss Carrie Hughes as to lead her troubled father to think that his young friend was seriously smitten, and to write a somewhat reproachful letter. Holmes then replied in terms which Hughes owned were "a great relief." In some shame the troubled father acknowledged that his fears, if not groundless, had been foolish, and requested that his earlier letter should be burned. Perhaps it was, for it has not survived. In his February letter Hughes explained why he had been concerned.

> Nothing I should like better than that my girls should marry New Englanders, but that a young Yankee for whom I entertained a strong personal liking should have taken a serious fancy to one of them who tho' old for her age is still a child, having regard to all the chances of their never meeting for no one knows how many years was a gravamen . . . of a hopeless kind. I was an ass to fancy such a thing, but such queer things do happen and you did really come it so strong in one or two of your letters that I was fairly puzzled what to think or say.[18]

Surely a young man who could "come it so strong" in letters to a girl's father did not miss the opportunities which travel offered him of playing, seriously or half-seriously, with other hearts than that of the twelve-year-old girl.

Early in his stay Holmes was taken to Oxford by Henry Adams' friend, Ralph Palmer, a young lawyer who was cousin to the Attorney General and who did Holmes many kindnesses, as when he arranged that Holmes should have a visitor's privileges at the St. James Club in London. At Oxford the two young men stayed at Balliol with "that Eminent Churchman, Edwin Palmer," later Archdeacon of Oxford.[19] On Sunday, May 20, Holmes breakfasted with Goldwin Smith, a leading publicist of the Union cause during the Civil War, whose later career in history took him to Cornell and Toronto. Holmes found him "pleasant and interesting" but observed that he "lays down the law like a school master." Glimpses of cricket and boating, of the proctor, his marshal and bulldogs, dinners, dons, and teas made up what he described to his mother as "a charming visit to Oxford." [20] The interlude came to a suitable conclusion with a breakfast "with Jowett (of *Essays and Reviews*)" whom Holmes described as a "delightful man, fine forehead, but face not commanding." Did this last failing contribute, one wonders, to Holmes's later skepticism which led him to doubt whether "anyone out of England cares for Jowett," [21] and to suspect that he was "no more than a retail dealer in notions, not the originator of large ideas." [22]

It was proper, surely, that the representative of the *jeunesse dorée* of Boston should breakfast with Gladstone and Jowett and dine with Charles Francis Adams and Mill. Holmes, however, stood on the brink of a career in the law and it was fitting that he should have a glimpse of the professional figures and institutions in the capital of the common-law world. His first taste of the law in London seems, however, to have been in the ecclesiastical courts. Under the wing of Edward Lyulph Stanley, later Baron Sheffield, free-thinking uncle of Bertrand Russell, he visited the Court of Arches on May 12 where Dr. Stephen Lushington "was hearing a case and the wife of a parson was telling how another parson solicited her favors." On May 14, with Mrs. Adams as his companion, he left a letter of introduction at Lady Cranworth's, the wife of the Lord Chancellor, an effort which soon was to bear fruit. (It was on the same afternoon that Mrs. Adams left him in charge of the carriage and he "drove through the Horse Guards which only foreign ministers can do—and I felt very swell. She left me at home," he stated in his diary, "her footman knocking loudly to impress my servants with respect.") It was on May 24 that Holmes dined with the Lord Chancellor and "found him and Lady Cranworth delightful." He sat on his hostess' left "and when the ladies moved the Lord Chancellor came and sat in Lady Cranworth's place." On the following morning at 10:30 Holmes appeared at the Chancery Court, Lincoln's Inn. "When the Chancellor saw me he called me up and had me sit beside him which I did until the adjournment. People looked at me and grinned." [23] The smiles might have had a different quality had the spectators realized that the grandfather of the Chancellor's companion had, in his day, similarly joined Lord Stowell on the bench and that the young man himself would later become Chief Justice of Massachusetts, Associate Justice of the Supreme Court of the United States, and finally an Honorary Bencher of Lincoln's Inn.

Holmes's other meetings with dignitaries of the bench and bar were less formal than that with Lord Cranworth. In London he dined with the eighty-four-year-old Lord Wensleydale who, as Baron Parke, had achieved an extraordinary reputation as judge of the Court of Exchequer, and was described by Lord Blackburn as "probably the most acute and accomplished lawyer this country ever saw." [24] Fellow guests of the evening were William Wetmore Story and his daughter, the son and granddaughter of Mr. Justice Story of the Supreme Court of the United States. In late July, after his Alpine trip, Holmes as a visitor in Devonshire also spent an evening with Sir John Coleridge who had been Judge of the Queen's Bench and whose son, Sir John Duke Coleridge, was destined to become Lord Chief Justice of England and to engage in mild journalistic combat with Mr. Justice Holmes of the Supreme Judicial Court of Massachusetts.[25]

The summer's diary contains no intimation of when Holmes first planned his Alpine expedition. We know that on June 7 Holmes dined with Fitzjames and Leslie Stephen. On the 12th he went to a dinner of The Alpine Club, of which Leslie was president, "at a pothouse near Leicester Square," and it is not improbable that Stephen then suggested that since Holmes was about to go to the Continent they should join forces in some Alpine climbing. A letter dated June 28 from Stephen to Holmes, who at that time was in Paris, expressed delight that Holmes could join him in the Alps and suggested that they should meet in Paris on the evening of July 2.[26] It is not improbable that Holmes had made plans to go to Switzerland before the opportunity to put himself directly under the expert charge of Stephen was offered, for among his papers survives a "suggested" Alpine itinerary in Leslie Stephen's handwriting,[27] an outline which would scarcely have been prepared if its author were planning to accompany the traveler. It thus seems likely that when Holmes left England for France on June 14 he looked forward to a solitary Alpine journey after his stay in Paris.

When Holmes arrived on the Continent the waters which cut him off from a familiar world were those of the Channel, not those of the Atlantic. His diary shows him in Paris to have been an isolated traveler, interested to be sure in the galleries, the theaters, and the spectacle of the city, but nonetheless a wandering American whose wounds and whose aspirations meant nothing to the community in which he found himself. Such entries in his diary as the following are sufficient to reveal the contrast between the successes enjoyed in London and the neglect experienced by the young Bostonian in Paris.

Saturday, June 16: . . . Looked up Higginson who took adjoining room to mine. Called on Crowninshields. . . . Afterwards to Jardin Mabilée—3 francs admission. A damned sell . . . But the can-can is very amusing. Talked bad French with one who was ugly but frail.

June 18. . . . Had a delightful call on Cora Crowninshield. Then up to the legation . . . and found John Hay with whom after talking I walked to the Arc de Triomphe.

June 19: . . . After breakfast drove with Higginson round and about and enfin to Notre Dame. . . . Wandered a while forlorn, then at 7 to Meurice's and to dine with Crowninshields. Home at 10 and to bed early.

July 2: . . . Saw Joe Gardner . . . and learned from him the Putnams had been at our house 3 days & we never knew it!

These excerpts from a Bostonian's diary are not wholly fair to the young man, for he had larger interests in Paris than these entries would suggest. Visits to the Louvre were not in his case merely the ritual of travel. On June 22 he made his fourth visit and stayed from 11 to 1 o'clock seeing, for the first time, the two captives of Michelangelo and asking in his diary whether there was not less pathos and more beauty in the famous one than in the copies and suggesting that the figure was a little thickset. On the 29th he completed a circuit begun on the day before and reported that

the John Van Eyck opposite Paul Veronese's Marriage of Cana grows on me more and more—so does Veronese in a certain way. Titian more feminine than I expected. . . . Vandyck is generally a little conscious —Velasquez always a grand unconscious gentleman. The Rembrandt of a carcass illustrates & verifies Bill Hunt's saying that one who could paint a beefsteak could an angel.

On the next day Holmes called on Hunt "and talked much art with him."

In so far as Holmes's associations with the Parisians is concerned there is no indication in his diary that they were more than casual. He made a number of unsuccessful efforts to meet with his father's admired teacher, Dr. Pierre Louis. He evidently followed his father's advice as to notable sights which he must not miss and went, accordingly, to St. Étienne du Mont to see the inscription marking the spot where in the seventeenth century two girls had fallen from the gallery to the pavement and miraculously escaped uninjured.[28] He also visited the Rue M. Le Prince where Dr. Holmes had lived while a medical student. To the record of his visit of filial piety he added the parenthetical memorandum: "Saw lots of suspicious young women there."

All in all, one has the impression that when Holmes left Paris for Basle he was readier to make the journey than he had been two and a half weeks before when he left London bound for Paris.

We know that he met Leslie Stephen at the railway station on the evening of July 2 and it is not impossible that in finding his friend among the other travelers Stephen's description of how he might be identified was helpful. Stephen had told Holmes that he was "to look out for a slight but commanding figure, with a singularly handsome face surmounted by a wideawake—an Alpenstock in one hand & a knapsack in the other, parading the Eastern Railway Station and surveying Frenchmen with a contemptuous smile." [29]

Sometime in 1866, perhaps while he was in Europe, Holmes read Ruskin's *Sesame and Lilies.* To accompany Leslie Stephen on an Alpine journey after reading Ruskin's strictures on British mountaineers was an act of defiant emancipation in a young man who acknowledged that "Emerson and Ruskin were the men that set me on fire." [30] Ruskin saw the Alps as sculptured Revelation. "[T]he feeding of the rivers and the purifying of the winds are the least of the services appointed to the hills. To fill the thirst of the human heart for the beauty of God's working—to startle its lethargy with the deep and pure agitation of astonishment,—are their highest mission." [31] The religious eye sees that the structure of the Alps is infused with "perfect wisdom and kindness" to assure the safety of the Alpine villagers. The mountain peaks, says Ruskin, are set back from the villages so that rocks will not fall in their streets.[32] The gentlemen of the Alpine Club commit an act of sacrilege in treating these mountains "as soaped poles in a bear-garden, which [they] climb, and slide down again, with 'shrieks of delight' . . . and rush home, red with cutaneous eruption of conceit, and voluble with convulsive hiccough of self-satisfaction." [33]

Whether in Holmes's Alpine journey the reverence of Ruskin or the exuberance of the mountaineer had the upper hand we cannot know with certainty. His first view of the mountains from Basle led him to a reflection more suitable to an Alpine sportsman than to an Alpine communicant: "This is not the place for squirts." An occasional entry in the diary shows, however, that the Alps meant far more than a bear-garden to him; after ascending the Balme Horne he recorded an impression which differed from a gymnast's: "When we were nearly up, the finest sight I ever saw burst upon us beyond the precipice—vast rolling masses of cloud and, above and beyond that, a panorama of the greatest Alpine peaks. . . . Stephen said he never'd seen the like." This reverent note, however, is followed by the sportsman's entry: "Mem. Slide down hill sitting. Bully." The contemporary record of the day's climb on July 11 and the later recollection of the venture, in combination reveal the spirit which Holmes brought to his Alpine trip. On the 10th the two companions, with guides, had made a partial ascent of the Mönch and had come to rest for the night in a cave—the Eiger Höhle—whence they watched "a first-class sunset . . . produced for our benefit, . . . the glacier lying below, dark and cold like a slain dragon." On the morning of July 11

> we started at 3½—snow in fine condition. Up steeps of snow and rock we went which were like the side of a house until at about 6½ or 7 we reached the foot of the peak—the Monk—which we were to ascend. Grub, & then to work up a pull of rock, then along interminable ridges of ice covered with snow—a precipice on either side—guides cutting steps—and at 10:10 the top. Saw a wilderness of mountain tops mostly below us—and vast mountains of clouds which we also looked down upon. . . . Left a bottle with a paper in it, and descended. (Mem. found one, part way up, of a party which could not get farther.) Then after grub down the Aletsch Glacier which was covered with snow in the nastiest manner to the very bottom. We didn't leave the snow till 5½ p.m.—14 hours—and got to Eggischorn at 8, burned, stiff, exhausted. There is nothing to say about that most horrible grind—it almost recalled an army march.

This was the contemporary account. Forty-eight years later recollection emphasized another aspect of the day. "I came down from the Mönch to the top of the Aletsch Glacier and felt as if we were committing a shuddery sacrilege, surprising Nature in her privacy before creation was complete. . . ." [34] Though sunburn and exhaustion might push the reverence of Ruskin from the pages of the diary, the lasting memory was not of "that most horrible grind" but of the splendor of nature. In later years Holmes liked to say that "the great emotions" that he had known from natural events "were due to the Swiss mountains, a storm at sea, battle, and a total eclipse of the sun." [35] These, he said, "all stir the mind at the bottom of one's brain." [36]

We need not follow the physical trail of Holmes and Stephen through the Alps. It is enough to know that Holmes valiantly accepted the pace set by the redoubtable and experienced Stephen—"the best of fellows and companions all through, and hasn't he lamed me?"—that stopping overnight at Swiss inns they "made merry,"—the landlord, on occasion, furnishing "punch ad libitum." The story of the companionship as told by Stephen to Tom Hughes and repeated by him to Holmes emphasized the pluck with which the novice followed in Stephen's wake: "limping like the pilgrim who forgot to boil his peas, and swearing quietly to yourself all the profane oaths which you had ever heard in the War, but still getting through your day's march and coming up in time for the next." [37]

Between Stephen and Holmes there were striking similarities and important contrasts. Stephen had come to his maturity before he found or recognized his skepticism. He had taken orders in the Church of England and had settled comfortably into a tutorship and fellowship at Cambridge. Slowly, almost imperceptibly, he discovered that the belief on which his chosen career must be based had been dissolved by doubts. In 1865, at the age of thirty-three, he took his final departure from Cambridge, recording the simple fact that his "faith in anything like religion has been gradually growing dimmer. I can scarcely believe," he wrote, "that two and a half years ago I was still reading prayers as a parson, and that little more than a year ago I was preaching. I now believe in nothing, to put it shortly; but I do not the less believe in morality, etc. I mean to live and die like a gentleman if possible." [38] In this terse passage of self-revelation Stephen says nothing of the intellectual influences which had slowly undermined his faith. Others, however, have made it clear that Comte, Mill, and Darwin were largely responsible.[39] They had upset the belief which Stephen had carried into his maturity. The fall of that belief left scars on the spirit of Stephen which revealed themselves in the bitterness of his agnosticism. With Holmes the skepticism, produced by similar influences, had come earlier and in its coming did not uproot settled convictions. He, like Stephen, could retain belief in morality without a belief in God and accept the standards of gentlemanly conduct as self-justifying principles of taste. His agnosticism was no less real but was far more casual than Stephen's. Never having been in the camp of believers he looked upon them with less bitterness than did the skeptic who had suffered the pain of emancipation.

As the two friends climbed the Alps, talking "comfortably of metaphysics," the similarities and contrasts must have given flavor to their companionship. Some four years later, after Holmes had read Stephen's paper on *The Broad Church,*[40] he wrote a letter to his friend which evidently contained both words of praise and words of reservation. Stephen replied that "your criticism is that you like it on the whole, but do not like it so much when I cease to be sympathetic." [41] Stephen's comment on this criticism reflects his shrewd appreciation of the fact that his agnosticism had a sting which was lacking in Holmes's.

> The criticism is very sound. It is quite true that I generally am too savage or rather have too little sympathy with the orthodox of all kinds. You are in a happier position; but, to make excuses for me, you must remember that I am rather bitter, first, as having wasted a large part of my life in the damnable fetters of the 39 articles and can never quite forgive my slave-drivers; secondly, that in this country we are still compassed around with the most noxious and bumptious orthodox people and are naturally inclined to say "In the Name of the Lord, I will destroy them." My righteous soul is vexed at the sight and sound of the cant and rubbish and lying that is still more or less triumphant and when I get a chance I will smite somebody under the fifth rib. Yes I will do even as Ehud did and pierce their bowels till the dirt comes out—but that is tolerably conspicuous at all times.

On the 18th of July, after a few days of rest at Zermatt, the friends went by the Theodule Pass to Gandegg, and on the 19th separated, Stephen to join a party of English friends, which included Thackeray's daughter who a year later was to become his wife, and Holmes to make his way via Aosta, Courmayeur, Chamonix, and Geneva to Paris. His last few days in the Alps were less strenuous than those which he had shared with Stephen—the one memorable expedition being that from Courmayeur to Chamonix by the Col de Géant, a trip which had begun at 2:30 in the morning. At Chamonix there were Boston friends in whose company Holmes took leisurely climbs in the neighboring mountains, sipping champagne with Eugenia Mifflin on the peak of the Flegères, giving "her an arm down" and finding her "very pleasant."

On Saturday, July 28, Holmes found himself back in England, a two-day stopover in Paris having been marked by no special incidents. In England, Holmes did not return to the stimulating gaieties of London but set his path towards the quieter ways of the country. His first stay was with the family of Sir John Kennaway at Escot House, Ottery St. Mary in Devonshire. Sir John's eldest son, John Henry, was to succeed to the baronetcy in 1873 and had quite possibly seen Holmes in Boston in the course of an American tour which he had made in 1865.[42] The son was to become one of Holmes's most intimate English friends. The family at Escot, reminding Holmes of the world of Roger de Coverley, observed the traditional orthodoxies and Holmes participated with good-natured tolerance in the morning ritual which prescribed that "all the servants [should come] in [to hear] Sir John read and expound the Bible in patriarchal fashion." The young visitor spent some time seeing the local sights in the company of Sir John's daughter. Noting that as they followed their pilgrimage the villagers showed appropriate respect—"men touching their hats and women dropping courtesies [*sic*] "—Holmes felt the pricks of an American conscience: "Everything smacked deliciously of feudalism, to the artist, that is, though hardly to the republican." The life of a country gentleman was brought to its suitable conclusion hunting rabbits: "I killed four—hunky boy!"

Holmes's final weeks were to be spent in Scotland as guest of the Duke of Argyll. His journey from Devonshire took him on August 2 through Stratford-on-Avon. There he went at once to the church and "gazed long at Shakespeare's bust—got up on tomb to see it nearer—eyes hazel—head rising toward crown like Sir W. Scott—mouth feminine and vinous. [T]his and a look about the cheek bone suggested a post mortem mask," an opinion which Holmes was pleased to learn was shared by Sir Francis Chantrey. The glimpse of Stratford was followed on the 3rd by a visit to Kenilworth Castle, and on that night Holmes took the train to Glasgow.

On Sunday, August 5, while stopping at a hotel in Arrochar, Holmes was "compelled by moral pressure to go to church," but in the afternoon and evening "made up for it . . . for after a dine I made some good love to a maiden by name Campbell and then later walked largely into scotch whiskey." On the following day Holmes reached Inverary Castle, the seat of the Duke of Argyll, in time to join the festivities in celebration of the coming-of-age of the Duke's eldest son, Lord Lorne. The occasion was of sufficient moment to justify the presence in the harbor of a man-of-war "gaily decorated with flags" and a series of dinners, sporting events, and dances which continued for a space of some days. At one of these dances Holmes fell in with Miss Jessie Robertson, daughter of the Duke's factor, "to whom I fain would have made love but she threw me over for Sir John Orde." At a dinner on the 8th Holmes talked art and religion with Sir John's daughter, "and shocked her." After dinner he moved on to the county ball at the hotel where evidently he was guilty of some sort of indiscretion. The diary conceals the facts in the tantalizing entry: "I regret to say ______________________________. Campbell of Islay (author of 'Frost and Fire,' devilish good fellow) stood my friend and no one was wiser."

The glimpse which one has of Holmes's visit at Inverary shows the figure of a gay and attractive young man, capable of finding satisfaction in the simplicities (if somewhat expensive) of country life. The young visitor in London had not forgotten the problems of philosophy which had concerned him at home; the lonely tourist in Paris made the most of the opportunity to pursue his interest in art; the Alpine climber had experienced the challenging effort of conquering the obstacles of nature. Against the background of Scotland the silhouette of the Bostonian assumed a somewhat less somber shape than it had in its other European settings. The energies of a companionable young man found satisfaction in the deer hunt, in grouse and duck shooting, in evening flirtations with attractive young women. The veteran, no less sentimental in his youth than in his age,[43] was evidently quite willing to bring to Scottish ears Civil War verses which moved him deeply. In particular, he was easily prevailed upon to give readings of "The Old Sergeant," the poem which his friend Forceythe Willson had written in 1863. Perhaps the pro-Southern inclinations of his hosts at Stonefield led him to seek a conversion by poetry which he could not achieve by argument. In any case, one may assume that neither the reader nor the audience was reluctant to hear again of the death of the old sergeant, wounded at Shiloh:

"Come a little nearer, Doctor,—thank you,—let me take the cup!
Draw your chair up,—draw it closer,—just another little sup!—
May be you think I'm better; but I'm pretty well used up,—
Doctor, you've done all you could do, but I'm just going up!"

The dying sergeant describes a confused dream of Shiloh and Heaven as it unfolds itself before him. The poem comes to its inevitable conclusion at midnight of the old year:

"Doctor—did you hear a footstep? Hark!—God bless you all! Good by!
Doctor, please to give my musket and my knapsack, when I die,
To my Son—my Son that's coming,—he won't get here till I die!

"Tell him his old father blessed him as he never did before,—
And to carry that old musket"—Hark! a knock is at the door!—
"Till the Union—" See! it opens!—"Father! Father! speak once more!"—
"Bless you!"—gasped the old, gray Sergeant, and he lay and said no more!

These last days in Scotland were evidently among the pleasantest which Holmes had experienced in his first glimpse of Europe. The company of "Miss Campbell of Stonefield" he found most satisfying: when he met her at a ball at Inverary on August 6 his diary mentions that he had seen her on June 2 in London.[b] The entry for that earlier day had described her as "the prettiest girl I've seen here." After Holmes had stayed for a few days at Stonefield and had given his readings of "The Old Sergeant," his diary records the fact that at breakfast "Miss C. [was] making eyes like a horned owl." It must have been with considerable regret that on August 29 Holmes left Stonefield for a day's stopover in Edinburgh before turning towards Liverpool and home.

When Holmes boarded the *China* on September 1 he had virtually arrived on Beacon Hill though he had not reached the United States. Jacksons, Perkinses, Gardners, and Lowells were his fellow-passengers and Boston was their destination. To feel at home among such companions did not, for Holmes, mean that he had felt himself a stranger in England. The people with whom he had associated as visitor, both in their traditions and in their aspirations, were strikingly similar to those among whom he had grown up. Though Holmes as soldier had learned that the Bostonian was an American, as traveler he had discovered that he was also, in many respects, an Englishman. Perhaps it did not take travel to teach Holmes that lesson, for his intellectual, artistic, and professional commitments had already thrust him into the stream of British tradition. He had, of course, seen glimpses of a world of London fashion which was very different from the community of Boston's elect, but his intimacies in England and Scotland had been with persons whose outlooks were entirely familiar. They had, almost without exception, been politically sympathetic with the Northern cause. The philosophical inclinations of younger men like Leslie Stephen and of older men like Sir Charles Lyell were parallel to those of Holmes and his American friends. In literary matters the tastes of Boston's intellectuals and of London's were essentially the same. In so far as Holmes had pursued the study of law he had kept within the framework of the English tradition.

[b] It seems likely that Holmes's attentions were given to Elizabeth Campbell, later Mrs. William Thomas Trench. She was the elder of two daughters of Campbell of Stonefield. Possibly she was the same Miss Campbell to whom Holmes had "made some good love" on Aug. 5; see, *supra,* p. 241.

These affiliations of taste are not emphasized in order to suggest that when Holmes returned to the United States he came reluctantly or with scorn for what lay ahead of him. It is only to emphasize that the aspects of American life which concerned him most were more representative of contemporary England than of contemporary America.[c] As time passed Holmes discovered that certain of his achievements received a more discriminating recognition in England than they did in his own country.[44] It disheartened him that this was so, but that it was indicates how deeply he was committed to the English tradition. That commitment set him out of the central stream of American life.

As the *China* sailed westward, beyond the sea's horizon lay not merely the prospect of reassurance that is found in familiar surroundings and familiar faces but the challenge that is offered at the beginning of a career. The education to be found in study, war, and travel lay behind him. The opportunities and mysteries of maturity lay ahead.

c Within the English world the spirit which moved Holmes's friends was progressive, not only at the political level but at the philosophical level as well. Transplanted to the United States the same spirit may not, perhaps, properly receive the same label. Yet it would be mistaken to assume that the opposite label is any more suitable.

8

Apprenticeship

When *Holmes returned* to his father's household he went, almost immediately, into one of the leading Boston firms—Chandler, Shattuck and Thayer—for his final months of preparation for admission to the bar.[1] Unfortunately office records have not survived to tell us with clarity of the character of the firm's practice. The traces of its activity which remain indicate, however, that the office was more concerned with litigation than with counseling. Its practice was general, yet it would seem that the partners were less frequently involved in planning the affairs of their clients to avoid difficulties than making the best of unfavorable circumstances after things had gone wrong. They represented such business organizations as street railways, banks, and mercantile houses and carried on an extensive practice in the Federal Court of Admiralty. The office, one feels, was in tune with ancient professional ways and was not so constituted as to become, like some competing firms, a center of economic planning and business strategy.

The senior partner was Peleg Whitman Chandler, a lawyer of versatile talents whose position of prominence, if not of preëminence, at the trial bar had been jeopardized in the 1850's by almost total deafness. His career thereafter was not in the courtroom but in the office where he maintained his reputation as a lawyer of great competence. In his earlier years he had been an important figure in Boston politics, had edited a legal periodical of more than local importance—*The Law Reporter*—and had published a valuable collection of criminal cases decided in the courts of Massachusetts. An ardent Swedenborgian, he published a theological work, *The Authenticity of the Gospels,* which Holmes dutifully read shortly after going into the Chandler office.[a] Although in these ventures beyond the practice of law Chandler showed himself to be something of a scholar, he "studied the law, not so much as a science as a practical administration of the affairs of men. He loved to trace its great principles not so much in their workings through wheel and shaft and gearing, as at the spindle point where they threw off their perfected thread into the woof and warp of daily life." [2] He considered that "the deliberate opinions of judges [were] more worthy of study, than the mere theories of any legal scholar, however profound the reasoning, or pleasing the style in which they are written." [3] His learning, in other words, was essentially professional and his scholarship was designed more to serve the needs of practitioners than to satisfy the tastes of jurists.

James Bradley Thayer, the junior partner of Chandler and Shattuck, in his talents and interests was a person much more like Holmes than like his senior associates. Ten years older than Holmes, he had come to the bar from the Harvard Law School in 1856. Although he had prompt success as a practitioner he had many interests outside the law and revealed such literary talents in miscellaneous critical writings that President Eliot in 1872 offered him a Professorship in English at Harvard College. Through his wife's relationship with the Emerson family, Thayer had become a close friend of Ralph Waldo Emerson and in 1884 published a charming portrait of Emerson in the form of a journal of a Western trip which he had made with Emerson in 1871. His lifelong friendship with Chauncey Wright, "a recognized master" [4] in that philosophical circle which included Holmes, William James, and Charles S. Peirce, was revealed in Thayer's edition of the *Letters of Chauncey Wright.* Thayer's name survives, however, not for his

[a] Holmes's diary contains the following entry for Jan. 7, 1867: "Cambridge. In the cars I read Panjandrum Chandler's 'Authenticity of the Gospels' an unremarkable tract."

distinction at the Boston bar, nor for his work outside the law, but for his great achievements as teacher and scholar after he became Royall Professor of Law at the Harvard Law School in 1874. His qualities as a scholar were shown in their manifold aspects in his *Preliminary Treatise on Evidence at the Common Law.* It was characteristic of Thayer's erudition that the treatise was a work of imaginative scholarship which extended knowledge of English legal history to depths that others had not probed. It was characteristic of his modesty that he considered the treatise to be merely "preliminary," and a reflection of his painstaking accuracy that the work was not published until 1898.

Thayer's name survives in scholarship not only for his important contributions to the law of evidence but for the influence which he had on American constitutional theory. This influence was effected through his teaching at the Harvard Law School, through his extraordinary collection of *Cases on Constitutional Law,* and, more specifically, through his essays on constitutional history and constitutional law. Of these papers none was more influential than "The Origin and Scope of the American Doctrine of Constitutional Law" which he delivered and published in 1893.[5] He was there concerned with the power of American courts to condemn legislation for its unconstitutionality. Thayer's perceptive use of history supported his thesis that the judges on State and Federal courts had exercised the power with an almost reckless enthusiasm. He did not argue that the power had been unlawfully assumed but only that it had been unduly extended by the failure of the judges to pay sufficient respect to the judgment of legislatures. When Thayer's paper was published Holmes had already, on the Massachusetts bench, committed himself to the same views.[6] Writing to Thayer in acknowledgment of the receipt of a copy of Thayer's paper, Holmes said that "I agree with it heartily and it makes explicit the point of view from which implicitly I have approached the constitutional questions upon which I have differed from some of the other judges." [7] The time was soon to come and was long to continue when Holmes would insist with Thayer, and in the most explicit terms, that American judges were abusing their powers at the expense of the nation. Foreshadowing the conviction of Judge Learned Hand that when liberty dies in the hearts of men "no court can save it," [8] Thayer, with Holmes's full concurrence, asserted that "under no system can the power of courts go far to save a people from ruin." [9] The view of Thayer and Holmes very surely was not that of most lawyers at the close of the nineteenth century. Their older associate, George Otis Shattuck, expressed the more conventional opinion when he told Thayer that his essay on the constitution "ought to convert me, but I must admit that I take satisfaction (wicked I am afraid) whenever the court upsets an act of the legislature." [10]

Although Holmes's interests and convictions were more like Thayer's than like Chandler's or Shattuck's, it is clear that Shattuck was the partner whose influence on Holmes was most important. When Holmes entered his office as a student in 1866 he did not realize that in six years, after Shattuck had withdrawn from his partnership with Chandler and Thayer, he would become a partner in the new firm of Shattuck, Holmes, and Munroe. Holmes's association with Shattuck, from its beginning, evidently meant much to him—probably more than did that with Thayer. There is no reason to question the truth of Holmes's assertion that "I owe to Mr. Shattuck more than I have ever owed to anyone else in the world, outside my immediate family." [11] This expression of indebtedness would be less striking had Holmes spoken words of gratitude with easy generosity. There was little if any of the hero-worshiper in his temperament and for those older men and contemporaries who traveled the same paths that he did his words of praise were always chosen with moderation. He felt affection and respect for many of the persons of notable ability with whom he was associated during his lifetime, but there was always a marked reluctance to give them larger credit than might be their due.[b] There was nothing grudging, however, in Holmes's regard

[b] Of Sir Henry Maine Holmes said that "He seems to have been impatient of investigation himself and I do not think will leave much mark on the actual structure of jurisprudence, although he helped many others to do so." *Holmes-Pollock Letters,* I, 31. Of James Fitzjames Stephen, Holmes observed that his "opinion of him as a law writer does not grow higher. . . . He knows nothing, it seems to me,

for Shattuck. Quite probably the ardor of his admiration was intensified by the fact that his own qualities were essentially different from Shattuck's. When Holmes estimated the talents of men of his own type—persons of a speculative inclination—he was quickly aware of their limitations. When he assessed the capacities of forceful men of affairs who made no pretensions to a scholar's mind or a philosopher's attitude he gave them every benefit of the doubt and tended, perhaps, to give them a larger credit than on balance was their due. He admired "a splendid old Philistine who had fought his way to wealth." [12] He admitted that he had "reverence for men of action" [13] and said that he believed that such a man as James J. Hill, the railroad magnate, represents "one of the greatest forms of human power." [14] To discover something naïve in this uncritical regard for human energy is not to say that "so voluminous a nature" [15] as Shattuck's did not deserve the admiration which Holmes gave it; it is merely to emphasize an element in the responsiveness of Holmes. From Shattuck Holmes did not gain a wider understanding of the universe; he did, however, gain

of the scientific aspects of the history of law, and is to my mind rather a model of a fine old 18th century controversialist than a philosopher." *Id.*, 21. Though Holmes evidently had a high regard for Maitland he warned Harold Laski that he did not "mention [him] with hushed breath," as Laski seemed to. *Holmes-Laski Letters,* I, 803. Speaking of the Stephen brothers and of their cousin, Albert Venn Dicey, Holmes said that while he greatly admired their "manifestations *en bloc*" he thought that "they sometimes miss the most exquisite *apercus*." *Id.*, 175–176. Of John Morley, Holmes said that he "seems to me a razor, not a sting–and the finest edge of his thought a little blunted by respectability." *Id.*, II, 957. This contrast between razors and stings was a favorite of Holmes's. "I divide able lawyers (and the rest of the world) into kitchen knives, that slide between the tissues on lines of least resistance; razors, that cut across; and stings that carry poison with their blade, and not only cut but disintegrate. The sting is rare, but we want it even if it hurts." Autograph letter to Clara Sherwood Stevens, April 28, 1907 (Harvard Law School). Referring to his friend, Lord Bryce, Holmes said that "he has been too industrious. A man can't have a stream going through his person all the time and send it out highly tinctured with his acids and deposits (not elegant but relevant I think)." *Holmes-Laski Letters,* I, 327. After receiving a letter from Felix Frankfurter in which there were warm expressions of admiration for Judge Cardozo, Holmes replied that "all I have read of his writing leads me to agree with you. You feel the edge of his blade cutting and not merely sliding down the lines of least resistance. He certainly is a razor and not a kitchen knife." Autograph letter, April 20, 1921 (Harvard Law School).

an appreciation of those capacities which found their fulfillment in the practice of law.

Holmes not only recognized the force of Shattuck's professional talents and personal qualities but he appreciated the fortunate circumstances in which he came to know them. "Young men in college or at the beginning of their professional life are very apt to encounter some able man a few years older than themselves who is so near to their questions and difficulties and yet so much in advance that he counts for a good deal in the shaping of their views or even of their lives. Mr. Shattuck," said Holmes, "played that part for me." [16] George Otis Shattuck was Holmes's senior by twelve years and had been at the Boston bar since 1855. Shortly after his admission to practice, as Peleg Chandler's partner he had succeeded to much of Chandler's trial practice. It is evident that Holmes's admiration for Shattuck's professional talents was centered on his capacity as an advocate; "I think that Mr. Shattuck in his prime was the ablest advocate I ever knew. . . . He was profound and far-reaching in plan. He was vehement in attack and stubborn in defense. He was fertile in resources and very quick in seeing all the bearing of a fact or a piece of testimony, a matter in which most men of weighty ability are slow." [17] Holmes first felt the influence of Shattuck when the younger man was still unsettled in his ambitions, when the lure of philosophy was strong, when he might, in his own words, "have fostered a faculty at the expense of [his] total life." [18] To have followed that course might have proved him to be his father's son but it would not have satisfied that deeper ambition which pressed him forward. Surely there was a real possibility that a young lawyer, industrious in metaphysics, would not be responsive either to the precepts or to the example of such a man as Shattuck. Yet by some means he taught Holmes that the lawyer's most important talent is that of dealing with the actualities of daily life, the capacity "to think under fire—to think for action upon which great interests depend." [19] There was no question that Holmes's mind in its analytical and logical capacities was suited to the law. There was real question, however, whether his temperament was suited to its traditional successes.

On Holmes's return from Europe in October 1866, and continuously throughout 1867, he continued the habit which he had begun in England of recording in small diaries notes concerning his personal and professional doings. In the opening months at the bar it is hard to separate the interests which were personal from those which were professional. One may be sure that when he spent an evening or afternoon with William James the time was taken from the law and dedicated to philosophy. When, on the other hand, he gave his evenings, as frequently he did, to John C. Gray it is not easy to say whether the companions were concerned with professional matters or with broader or, perhaps, more trivial distractions. Evidently talk with Gray was concerned on occasion with other subjects than the law. In October 1866, after attending one of Charles S. Peirce's lectures at the Lowell Institute,[20] Holmes stopped off at Gray's and had "some discussion of logical points." On an evening in the following February he "went on a bender with Gray (Museum—'The Frozen Deep')." Between these extremes of logic and experience there must have been much talk of the law. Gray, like Holmes, was a Civil War veteran. His legal education, however, had been concluded before his military service began in 1862 and, like Holmes's, had included study at the Harvard Law School and in the office of Chandler, Shattuck, and Thayer. On his return from the Army, Gray had formed a partnership with John C. Ropes, whose younger brother of the Twentieth Regiment had been killed at Gettysburg. Gray, like J. B. Thayer, was destined to achieve his fame as Professor of Law at Harvard where, combining the teacher's career with that of an active practitioner, he served as lecturer and professor from 1869 to 1913. A man of the broadest learning both within and outside the law, he shared many tastes and friendships with Holmes.[21] The glimpse which Henry James gives of Gray's relationship with Minny Temple reveals the community of interests and affection by which the little band of friends—the Jameses, Holmes, and Gray—were bound together in the opening years of their several distinguished careers.[22] Between Holmes and Gray, however, a common professional concern gave a substance to intimacy that was lacking in the relationship of Holmes to William and Henry James. William was soon to discover that "the mystery of the *Total* is a rather empty platform" [23] on which to build a lasting structure of friendship. As James turned to medicine and found "how fat and satisfactory" [24] discussion of professional problems might be, Holmes turned to law. It was his good fortune that at the point of turning Gray walked by his side and remained always his companion.[25] Though Holmes once indicated that during his early years of friendship with Gray he had not suspected that his friend was a philosopher,[26] he never questioned the breadth of Gray's intellectual interests or the extraordinary scope of his cultivation. He evidently noticed one significant difference between his own desire for knowledge and Gray's inclinations towards scholarship. As the years passed Holmes recognized that his appetite for books was induced by a feeling of responsibility. He read as much for the sake of the improvement of his mind, as he put it, as for the simple enjoyment of knowledge. Gray, on the other hand, possessed a natural and easygoing inclination towards scholarship.[27] In 1895 Holmes wrote to Mrs. Gray and spoke of the envy which he had felt for her husband "when he said he had given up reading books for improvement—although he happens to like improving books. I read and hate—and think, 'Oh, could I grind this man into fish bait, one gleam of joy would flash from the very source of war.' " [28] On another occasion Holmes acknowledged that "I don't enjoy [reading] but feel the necessity of sticking in fuel." [29] This notion that knowledge was fuel lay behind his observation that "the people . . . who have more wood in their woodpile than in their furnace—the cultured folks—repel me." [30] Gray's woodpile was large, but his furnace was neither cold nor empty. Holmes said that Gray's knowledge "not only was converted into the organic tissue of wisdom, but flowered with a quiet humor that sometimes emerged in his writing and that gave habitual delightfulness to his talk." [31] Beyond that, he was a man of affairs and as such received from Holmes some of that same respect which he felt for George O. Shattuck.

The entries in Holmes's diary, with all their brevity, make one thing clear—that Fanny Dixwell was his close companion—obviously the closest of her sex. While Holmes was in England she had kept in touch with him through his family and, occasionally, by correspondence. On July 3 Mrs. Holmes had written to her son reporting that she had had "a particularly pleasant visit from Fanny B. D. last Saturday and found that she had not heard from you either, but she said you told her you shouldn't write. . . ." She went on to say that Fanny Dixwell was "living quietly in Cambridge with the exception of visits from Bill James, who appears to go there at any time from 9 o'clock in the morning. I told her to let me know how the flirtation got on. She said he is a person who likes to know his friends very well. I had a little fun with her about him, and told her I should write to you about it." [32] Because, four months earlier, James had described Fanny Dixwell as "about as fine as they make 'em" [33] it is not unlikely that Mrs. Holmes's twitting of her son's friend had some justification. Though Holmes had warned Fanny that he would not write to her from Europe, we know that on July 16 a letter from the traveler, addressed to her in care of the Holmeses, had arrived and that Mrs. Holmes had assured her son that she would forward it and ask Fanny "to come and read as much as she chooses." [34] After Holmes's return to Boston he saw her with persistent regularity. From such brief notations as "Cambridge & walk," or, simply, "Cambridge" one may draw such inferences as one chooses; these entries may just as well have recorded trips to the Jameses or to his Uncle John Holmes, as calls on the Dixwells. Yet the possibility that many of them recorded visits to Fanny is very real. On December 12, 1866, the entry is somewhat more explicit: "Cambridge—F.B.D.'s Birthday," and on New Year's eve after dining at Parker's where he "made merry with wine" the diary indicates that he went to Cambridge and "returned to F.B.D. her [picture of] trumpet flowers" and "brought in picture of morning glories on gilt background." However such entries as these may be interpreted, it is clear that Holmes did not entirely turn his back on the other young ladies of Boston and Cambridge. There are not infrequent references to walks or evenings in the company of Lily

Winsor, Cora Crowninshield, Anna Hallowell, "Nellie" Shaw, and "Pinkie" Pomeroy and of calls on Minny Temple while she was staying with the Jameses in Cambridge. On December 7, 1866, he went to a dinner for a Miss Haggerty, "with whom I divided winged words and walked home with her & sat on door step & talked till Mr. Dorr came after to let her in." [35] For some months a Sunday walk with Clover Hooper, later Mrs. Henry Adams, was customary. An occasional note, suggesting romantic mystery, appears, as in this entry: "Passed —— in the street. Close to her before I saw." [36] The references to Fanny Dixwell, however, are far more frequent than to any other young lady, and in the case of no other friend of her sex are there indications of intimacy equivalent to those which appear when she went for several weeks as a visitor to Hartford. His diary for that period indicates that he wrote to her with some frequency, on one day twice, and that shortly after her return she came to Boston and spent the night with the Holmeses.

In later years Holmes's friendships, whether with men or with women, were primarily intellectual. That is not to say that they were lacking in warmth, but is to indicate that their center of gravity was nearer to his mind than to his heart. Perhaps in his youth this was less true, but one suspects that then as later his bonds of intimacy found their strength in intellectual sympathy. One cannot be sure, of course, that the spirit of his talk was characteristically as impersonal as the spirit of his correspondence. When, in his later-middle years, he called on Mrs. John C. Gray in Boston he may have spoken otherwise than when he visited Lady Scott in England. His letters to the one might, however, almost as well have been written to the other, and if either had by accident received a letter from Holmes to Sir Frederick Pollock, little but the salutation would have suggested that the letter had been misaddressed. To all of his friends he spoke of the same matters and in much the same language. This may partly explain his success with the ladies; they found his willingness to make them his intellectual companions thoroughly flattering, and if they repaid him with gratifying compliments and attention the score of flattery was balanced. Had he dealt with serious subjects ponderously the sparkle of flirtatiousness would have died and with it much of the pleasure of lively communication. As it was, however, Holmes talked and wrote gaily of large themes. His Puritanism kept his attention on serious problems but from his tongue and his pen his friends learned the meaning of his paradox that "it is not necessary to be heavy in order to have weight." [37] One Bostonian reflected a Yankee's distaste for Holmes's sprightliness when he remarked that "the trouble with Wendell is that he likes to play with his mind." [38]

When Holmes was sixty-one he said that he was "inclined to think that our activities are best employed in the affairs of life, using the infinite rather as a magnet than as a business." [39] If at that age he preferred to speak in terms of inclination rather than of conviction one can be confident that at twenty-five the infinite had more than magnetic attraction. The entries in the diaries of 1866 and 1867, sparing though they are in reflective comments, reveal something of the struggle through which the young man was passing in his effort to determine whether the satisfactions which he sought could be found in the law. The inner impulse towards philosophy might have been more promptly tamed, one suspects, had not Holmes been tempted into speculative dissipation by the alluring companionship of William James. From the time of Holmes's return from Europe in the fall of 1866 until James's departure for scientific studies in Germany in April 1867, the stimulating propinquity of James made it dangerously easy for Holmes to drop his professional studies in order to chase the philosophical rabbits which James had started. Such a distraction occurred shortly before James sailed for Europe. On March 27 Holmes had begun his evening by reading Adams on *Equity,* but dropped his studies to call on the Jameses in Cambridge, where he passed the time "with Bill who has been at work on measure of vis viva and imparted the ferment to me." From that evening until April 23 Holmes pursued his quarry: on April 4 he had "talk with Bill, highly satisfactory as to vis viva"; on April 10 he read essays on the same subject in Youmans' *Correlation and Conservation of Forces;*

on April 21 he "fiddled with vis viva" till he thought he would "go crazy"; again on the 22nd he went to the Athenaeum "looking up v.v." and then rushed to Cambridge "to see C. Wright on vis viva—he wasn't in so went to H. James." On the 23rd the chase was over: "End of vis viva I hope for the present. Understand some of my difficulties at least. Evening . . . wrote in my note book as to vis viva."

The temperamental differences which worked, over the years, to produce antagonisms of attitude between Holmes and James had not yet marred the affectionate relationship between the two young men. During the first years of their friendship the intimacy of that relationship was intensified by the fact that each was concerned with the same problem and that each was attempting to apply the same principle in its resolution. Their deepest aptitudes were speculative, yet each was persuaded that his approach to speculation should be by the pathway of pedestrians rather than by the highway of philosophers.[40] This persuasion, in all probability, was the by-product of empiricism—the natural consequence of their acceptance of the axioms of positivism. The logic of their conviction that truth, if discoverable at all, was to be found through science, not through metaphysics, had led each into the somewhat distasteful enterprise of keeping his feet on the ground. James sought first through medicine and then through physiology to approach the citadel of philosophy. "I feel," he said, "as if I had no right to an opinion on any subject . . . until I know some *one* thing as thoroughly as it can be known, no matter how insignificant it may be." [41] It was a similar conviction that led Holmes to say that "if a man chooses a profession he cannot forever content himself in picking out the plums with fastidious dilettantism and give the rest to the poor, but must eat his way manfully through crust and crumb—soft, unpleasant, inner parts which, within one, swell, causing discomfort in the bowels." [42] Holmes sought, through mastery of the law, to qualify himself for the resolution of the larger questions which lie beyond its outer limits. Perhaps his positivism might have found expression more readily in one of the natural or biological sciences, but by paternal authority he had been kicked into the law, and it was there that he found himself. By 1868, and probably earlier, he was satisfied that a lawyer may handle the materials of his craft as the natural scientist handles the data of his speciality. "Law," he told James, "as well as any other series of facts in this world may be approached in the interests of science." [43]

Holmes was not the only member of his circle to believe that the institutions of society, like the facts of the physical world, must be dealt with scientifically. William James said of Chauncey Wright that "never in a human head was contemplation more separated from desire." [44] Wright's persistent effort to separate his beliefs from his hopes led him to demand that the language of the social sciences should be cleansed of all "*good* and *bad* words, which retain the unction of all effective past authority."

> Words have "reputations" as well as other authorities, and there is a tyranny in their reputation even more fatal to freedom of thought. True science deals with nothing but questions of fact. . . . If the facts are determined, and, as far as may be, free from moral biases, then practical science comes in to determine what, in view of the facts, our feelings and rules of conduct ought to be; but practical science has no inherent postulates any more than speculative science. Its ultimate grounds are the particular goods or ends of human life.[45]

There is no direct evidence to show that Wright's relentless positivism contributed to Holmes's philosophy of law,[46] and it may be that they came to similar conclusions because they accepted the same premises. The possibly direct influence of Chauncey Wright on Holmes is, in any case, less significant than that Holmes was led by his commitments to the scientific method to consider the law as a series of facts not unlike those other series with which the natural scientist is concerned. So looking upon law, he came to believe that the series of facts known as law was susceptible to scientific consideration. That meant for him that he must cultivate the capacity to separate contemplation from desire. Though William James rebelled from that talent as he saw it in Wright, Holmes never weakened in his loyalty to the axioms of positivism. They lay at the foundation of his works of scholarship and gave structure to his thought when he filled the office of judge.

With considerable justification it has been suggested that Holmes's training in the law, and particularly his immersion in the traditions of the common law, may have confirmed and strengthened his experimental and pragmatic inclinations. To assert that Holmes was led by his training in the law to look upon the problems of philosophy pragmatically is not to deny that his reading in the literature of positivism led him to apply its principles to law. The influences were reciprocal. It is well to remember, however, that in the mid-nineteenth century there were relatively few lawyers who had recognized the pragmatic elements in the common law. Bentham had awakened some of the profession to the deceptive nature of Blackstone's generalities, but few lawyers on either side of the Atlantic had come to believe that the strength of the common law was derived not from a set of governing principles but from its case-by-case, experimental method of growth. Holmes was among the first American lawyers to accept this belief. It is probable that he was driven to acceptance not by his study of law but by his consideration of contemporary philosophy.

The diaries that record the direction of Holmes's personal and philosophical interests reveal in greater detail his progress in his chosen profession. His teachers and employers were not slow to set him on the path of the law. At nine o'clock on October 18, 1866, the day on which he reported for work at Mr. Shattuck's office, he was settled in the Social Law Library working on a case then pending before the Supreme Judicial Court—*Warner* v. *Bates*.[47] Chandler and Thayer represented clients who were asserting that they had enforceable rights under a clause in their mother's will by which property was left to her second husband "in the full confidence that . . . he will . . . continue to afford my children such . . . support as they . . . may stand in need of." A number of courts and writers had condemned the traditional doctrine of English law by which such words of confidence, and even

13. Oliver Wendell Holmes, Jr., 1866

14. Fanny Bowditch Dixwell, 1868

15. William James, about 1866

16. John C. Ropes, about 1870

17. Leslie Stephen, about 1866

18. Thomas Hughes, about 1866

American and English friends

gentler words of expectation, had been found sufficient to create enforceable trusts. The task of Chandler and Thayer was to persuade the Massachusetts Court that the condemnation was unwarranted and that on the facts before the Court the children could demand the benefits of their mother's confidence. For five hours Holmes worked at the Social Law Library "making abstracts of endless cases on precatory trusts." Presumably these abstracts were turned over to Thayer to assist him in the preparation of his brief and argument in the Supreme Judicial Court. The extent of Holmes's contribution to Thayer's effort we do not, however, know; whatever it may have been, the result of argument was victory for Thayer, for at the November term, 1867, *Warner* v. *Bates* was decided in favor of the needy children.[48] Perhaps it is a distortion of reality to suggest that in this first professional assignment Holmes may have found early justification for his belief that "the law opens a way to philosophy as well as anything else." [49] Yet four days before he was asked to abstract the cases on precatory trusts he had begun to read Mill's *Political Economy*. As he read the cases in the Social Law Library did he perhaps see that the practical effort to which his working day was dedicated was not unrelated to the speculative problems to which his evenings were given? Mill, as political economist, discussed the moral and legal foundations of a child's inheritance. Holmes, as lawyer, found himself concerned in the formulation for Massachusetts of a rule with respect to that inheritance. We do not know whether Holmes as theorist accepted or rejected the radical views of Mill. We do not know whether as lawyer he sought to provide Thayer with a political economist's arguments to sustain his clients' claim. All that we can say with confidence is that there was reciprocating relevance between the day's professional reading and the evening's speculative inquiry.

Needless to say, there were many days in which the matter professionally in hand bore virtually no relationship to the evening's concern. The lawyer's time is committed so largely to the facts of life that the theory or policy of law is but intermittently the object of his attention. When Holmes was sent to the railroad station to learn whether any cars of the New York Central were on hand available for attachment he was engaged in the activities of a lawyer [50]—certainly in those of a law clerk—but he was hardly discovering that from law "the roads are plain to anthropology, to political economy, the theory of legislation, ethics, and thus by several paths to [his] final view of life." [51] It was not only the mundane nature of Holmes's professional duties which kept the day's concern from mingling more than occasionally with the evening's interest during his first months in the law. At that time he was led, perhaps by William James and perhaps by his own temperament, into speculations which were essentially metaphysical. It was one thing to read Mill on *Political Economy* and on *Logic,* to attend Charles Peirce's lectures on logic, to read Humboldt on *Government* and the third book of Locke's *Essay on Human Understanding;* even such hard-headed preceptors as Chandler and Shattuck might consider that these pursuits were related to a lawyer's education. When, however, Holmes turned to Stirling's *Secret of Hegel,* Tyndall on *Radiation,* Kant's *Critique of Pure Reason,* and Schultz's *Eclaircissements sur la Critique,* it might have seemed to the young man's employers that the magnetism of the infinite was leading their student somewhat far afield. After Holmes had been in Mr. Shattuck's office for a little more than a month the young man made a significant entry in his diary. "This week," he wrote, "I haven't felt very well and debauched on Mill accordingly, by way of removing an old incubus before endeavoring to immerse myself in the law completely—which Shattuck says a man must at some period of his career if he would be a first rate lawyer—though of being that I despair." [52]

This resolution in favor of total immersion in law was, for the most part, faithfully carried out during Holmes's months of final preparation for the bar. The diaries show him working his way through Kent's *Commentaries,* Howe's *Practice in Civil Actions and Proceeding at Law in Massachusetts,* and, as examinations came nearer, annotating the general statutes of Massachusetts. In his hours at home he gave much of his attention to the particular problems on which his office was engaged.[c] On Thanksgiving Day of 1866, for instance, he began to look into the questions of law which were presented in an admiralty matter then in Mr. Shattuck's charge. The issues presented in *Richardson* v. *Winsor* involved not only the complexities of admiralty jurisdiction but the subtleties of maritime law concerning the relationships between the owner and the charterer of a vessel. From Parsons on *Maritime Law* and Kent's discussions of admiralty he moved on to the English and American decisions. At length, on the evening of December 20, he sat down and "wrote 4 pp. argument [for] Richardson v. Winsor" which was soon to come before the United States District Court in Boston.[53] On the next day he "pottered over [his] argument etc. of last evening," walked and dined with Shattuck and discussed the case and other questions of law. The same concern with office business led him into many fields of law. What is the appropriate measure of damages when a common carrier fails

c Although the following entry for Wednesday, Jan. 16, 1867, is fuller than most of Holmes's diary entries it will serve to suggest the general character of the record:

"One of the rare days when I feel as if I had done something at the office.
Read as to transfer of stock:
Sargent v. Essex Mar. Railway Corp. 9 Pick 202
Fisher v. Essex Bank, 5 Gray 373
Boyd v. Rockport Steam Cotton Mills, 7 Gray 406
Gen. Stat. Ch. 63, Sec. 11
"That not informing of previous void policy does not avoid subsequent one:
Hardy v. Union Mut. Fire Ins. Co. 4 Allen 217
Abbot v. Shawmut Mut. Fire Ins. Co. 3 All. 214
& case in 7 All. 42 (as to St. 1861 Ch.)
"As to admissibility of ledger when clerk is dead on proof of handwriting:
Union Bank v. Knapp, 3 Pick 96 & through Eng. note to Price v. Torrington in 1 Sm. L.C.
"Walked to Cambridge with Sedgwick.
"Found letter from Tom Hughes awaiting me at home. Also from Jas. Tolman all the sp. laws since 1829.
"Evg. read (though not apropos of the subject I was looking up) Webber v. Tivill, 2 Saund. 121b & notes referred to in Union Bank v. Knapp as to Stat. of Limit. & diversity between accounts current & stated—good note. Then read in 2 Am. L.C. Whiteridge v. Norris & Gaze v. Reilly & part of note (General Average)."

to deliver flour with reasonable speed and the market value of the flour has fallen between the date when delivery should have occurred and the actual date of delivery? [54] Does the holder of "guaranteed" preferred stock have a right to a dividend when the corporation has net earnings without net profits? [55] Does the driver of an unlicensed cart have a right of action for personal injuries suffered as a result of the negligence of another driver licensed to use the highways? [56] "Is allegation in [a] declaration that payment of dividend 'payable on' a certain day was 'duly' demanded, [a] sufficient allegation of demand on that day for interest to run from them? Semble not." [57] May a corporation be indicted for its misfeasance as it may for its nonfeasance? [58] In such problems as these there was, perhaps, little compensation for a philosopher's curiosity but there was the variety of a lawyer's responsibility and the opportunity to test a young man's intellectual aptitude and professional fortitude.

The process of education led Holmes with some frequency into the court room as observer or aide. When the Supreme Judicial Court was hearing a murder case Holmes was there for two days to see his first preceptor, Robert M. Morse, successfully represent the defendant.[59] He accompanied Mr. Shattuck to trials at the Court House and to hearings at the State House, taking notes of his employer's arguments. On one memorable day Sidney Bartlett, one of the giants of the Boston bar, who was about to argue a point of law, put a problem to Holmes: "Can a contract, void because signed on Sunday, be used in evidence as admission? I suggested unstamped commercial instrument as parallel & gave a reference—for which he thanked me & I felt proud." [60] Such glimpses of the law in action as these and such scattered opportunities to look into particular problems as Chandler, Shattuck and Thayer offered him evidently seemed an insufficient preparation for the impending examinations for admission to the bar. Metcalf's essays on contracts, Fearne on *Contingent Remainders,* Adams on *Equity,* Wallace and Hare's *American Leading Cases,* and Smith's *Leading Cases* gave form and structure to a miscellany of decisions and in doing so encouraged the transformation of learning as a process into learning as an end. Yet mere knowledge could not be neglected, and accordingly Holmes sat down to memorize the Statute of Frauds. On the evening of February 1, 1867, after reading Dickens' account of the poisoner Wainwright, he "recited" the Statute of Frauds to his mother.

Towards the latter part of February Holmes saw that the time for submitting himself for examination could not long be postponed. On the 21st, after a long walk and dinner with Shattuck they spoke of Holmes's future: "et concessum est per cur. that I had better stay by after my admission." He had hoped that he might arrange to have the half-brother of his friend John C. Gray, the learned Mr. Justice Horace Gray, later like Holmes to become Chief Justice of the Supreme Judicial Court and Associate Justice of the Supreme Court of the United States, examine him personally for admission. On Saturday, February 23, however, the diary reports that "as Judge Gray couldn't examine me for some time got Lord, J. to appoint examiners—as I am nervous and don't want to wait." [d] On the following Monday morning Holmes tried to find one of the two examiners whom Judge Lord had designated—Asaph Churchill—"but couldn't catch him and wandered restless all day." On Tuesday, however, he was "examined by Churchill for admission—result satisfactory." Of the examination no contemporary record survives. The only picture of the occasion that we have was sketched by Holmes in an undelivered paper which he prepared as a response to resolutions of the bar of Norfolk County at the time of Churchill's death in 1898.

> It is my misfortune never to have met your dead leader in any extended conversation but once and long ago. But that once left in me the feeling of an impalpable relationship between us. He was, so to speak, my legal godfather. When I applied for admission to the bar . . . Judge Lord, then of the Superior Court, appointed two gentle-

[d] Judge Otis P. Lord, of the Superior Court, some eight years later became an Associate Justice of the Supreme Judicial Court. It was to the seat vacated by his resignation in 1882 that Holmes succeeded. Lord's name is more familiar to literary historians than it is to lawyers; he was the second man to be loved by Emily Dickinson.

men to examine me. One of these was Mr. Asaph Churchill. I carried away from his office the belief that he was a wise and good man, and a sense of quasi-filial deference and respect such as one naturally feels for his sponsor in grave affairs.[61]

On Saturday, March 2, Holmes met with his second examiner, Mr. Charles W. Huntington, at 2 o'clock, "and made a devilish poor show, I thought." On the following Monday "at 2 p.m. Mr. Chandler moved before Morton, J., Superior Court, 2nd Session, that I be admitted. Paid $5 for certificate." [62] On the following day, Tuesday the 5th, his life as a full-fledged lawyer began: "Read 10 Allen. Bought a chair of Smith—$9.50. (Pd. 6th). The rush of clients postponed on account of weather."

During the months which preceded Holmes's admission to the bar he found himself increasingly concerned in the publishing enterprise which his friends Ropes and Gray had recently inaugurated—the *American Law Review*. Under their editorship the magazine was in process of making itself an important—probably the most important—American legal periodical of its day. Although its aims were evidently higher than those of most of its competitors, in that it was hospitable to theoretical essays and was as much concerned with the developments in the law of England as with the current American scene, it was a journal for American practitioners. It was, perhaps, unmistakably Bostonian, both under the editorship of Ropes and Gray and under that of Holmes and Arthur G. Segdwick when they took over the editorial responsibilities in 1870.[63] Who but a Brahmin would have written this paragraph in 1867: "We cannot pass without notice the insufferable practice of spelling 'counsellor' 'counselor.' It ill becomes a profession styling itself learned, to countenance these new-fangled abominations, begotten on the ignorance of the laity by the perverse eccentricities of a man of talent." [64] A few years later, after Holmes and Sedgwick had become editors of the *Review*, the *United States Jurist* protested that "the new editors of [the *American Law Review*] were inclined to play the fop in legal matters." [65] The foppishness in question was found in a scathing book review which had concluded with the comment that "the work will probably be purchased in great numbers by the rural bench and bar." [66]

If the young reviewers were somewhat arrogant in their phrasing of criticism and did not show what some might consider appropriate respect for the learning and dignity of their seniors in the law, they did bring to the critical consideration of books on law a high standard of scholarship and cultivation. Most of the reviews in the volumes published under the editorship first of Ropes and Gray and then of Holmes and Sedgwick were written by young men. Their standards of criticism were not merely those of the practitioner, interested in the utility of new texts and digests, but of the jurist, concerned to discover new insights into the history and theory of law. The achievements of Gray as reviewer are particularly impressive, not only in their number but in their vigorous good sense and abundant learning. The standards which he set as editor must significantly have contributed to those which Holmes was in the process of forming when he first came to the Boston bar.

On a November evening in 1866 Holmes returned to Charles Street carrying under his arm a copy of the sixth American edition of Roscoe's *Digest of the Law of Evidence in Criminal Cases.* The volume had been turned over to him by Ropes and Gray on the understanding that it was to be his "plunder" if he wrote a notice of the book for the *Review.* Exciting as the chance to put some critical thought in print and to become involved even in a minor role in the affairs of the *American Law Review* must have been, Holmes did not immediately drop other matters for the sake of his new opportunity. On the evening when he brought Roscoe home he "knocked off 137 pp of II Mill's Logic" and the next day gave his time in the office "so far as possible" to the same book. Only when he finished Mill, on Saturday, November 24, did he shift his attention to Roscoe. The anonymous notice which was published in the *American Law Review* for January 1867 said of the book all that a practicing lawyer was likely to want to know. Beyond that, however, it revealed those lines of interest which Holmes's reading outside the law had followed in recent months.

The respect in which he held the scientific method is suggested when he summarized the arrangement which Roscoe had chosen for his *Digest*. Holmes described the structure of the book as

> not unlike that which is pursued in treatises on Natural History, and which has been followed with advantage in some psychological works. . . . The subject is divided into two parts. The first states general properties, or, in this case, general principles, and sets forth a system of classification. These principles are in turn discussed, and instances are given of their various modes of operation. The second part treats of the different species in detail; in this case, the species being the various crimes known to the law.[67]

This analysis of the structure of the *Digest* was not surprising from one who had made the contemporary literature of science and psychology his especial concern. Holmes was, however, sufficiently aware of the practical uses of a treatise on the law to be grateful to Roscoe for not endeavoring to adopt a classification in order to exemplify a theory and for his effort to present the law of evidence in criminal cases "with a view to convenience which is here the only thing to be considered."[68]

Just as it is possible, without distortion, to see in this review the reflection of Holmes's contemporaneous concern with the methods and attitudes of science, so it is possible to discover in the notice a point of view which was to characterize his matured philosophy of law. Going far beyond the limits of Roscoe's endeavor Holmes considered the contrast between the expectations on which the law of evidence in criminal cases is founded on the Continent and those on which it has been built in England and the United States. In France, the law of evidence is designed to facilitate the prosecutor's task of offering the Court an acceptable theory concerning the true facts under consideration. In French tribunals, therefore, "any evidence is admitted which will enable trained experts to form a theory. . . . In the English and American courts, the object is very different. It is, in a word, to enable ordinary men to arrive at a working belief,—to come to a conclusion such as they would feel justified in acting on in a business matter of their own. . . . [T]he object to be attained is not hypothesis but belief. . . ." [69]

Without question, one is justified in finding in this earliest of Holmes's published comments on law the seeds of doctrine which were basic to his legal philosophy. Certainly the preference for "working beliefs" to logical hypotheses was to characterize his later thought as was the skepticism—or, perhaps, pragmatism—implicit in that preference. Although it is quite appropriate to emphasize the germinal aspect of Holmes's review, it is important to remember that the ideas which it embodied were not original. His diary tells us that by way of preparation for his review of Roscoe he had turned to Chapter Seven of James Fitzjames Stephen's *General View of the Criminal Law of England.* Stephen's penetrating analysis of the principles of the law of evidence provided a most suitable bridge by which to cross from Mill's theory of logic to Roscoe's digest of evidence.[70] In earlier portions of the *General View* Stephen had contrasted the Continental and the English processes of adjudication in criminal cases. In his description of French criminal procedure he had characterized the result of the inquisitorial process in France as "the gradual elaboration of a theory on the subject of the crime, supported by a mass of evidence which has been collected and arranged by a set of public functionaries . . . bound by all the ties of official *esprit de corps* and personal vanity to maintain the accuracy of the conclusion at which they have arrived." [71] When Holmes, in reviewing Roscoe, stated that in French criminal trials "any evidence is admitted which will enable trained experts to form a theory" he was rephrasing the thesis of Stephen. Similarly he built upon Stephen's foundations when he came to emphasize the pragmatic nature of the Anglo-American law of evidence. In his seventh chapter Stephen endeavored to uncover the psychological foundations of that law and suggested how limited a role principles of logic have played in the administration of the law of evidence in English courts. He examined the "tacit major propositions" [72]—what Holmes might later have called the "inarticulate major premises" —on which the law of evidence was built, discussed the differences between chance and probability, and examined what he called "the natural history of belief." [73] In this examination he considered the relationship between truth and belief and developed the pragmatic thesis that "the ultimate reason for believing is, that without belief men cannot act" and that "the reason for believing what is true is, that without true belief [men] cannot act successfully." [74] It was from this rationale of belief that Stephen's analysis of the English law of evidence was derived. Fairly to estimate the merits of a particular rule of evidence calls not for a determination

> whether an impartial, unfettered inquirer into historical or scientific truth would be bound by them in all cases, but by considering whether they are well fitted to confine eager disputants within such limits as will enable a jury to deal with the subjects before them; . . . above all things, whether they provide a security that no one shall be punished till his guilt is proved by plain solid reasons, such as experienced men act upon in important affairs of their own.[75]

To find in Holmes's first review little but an echo of Stephen's voice is not to tarnish his accomplishment. It is merely to emphasize the extent to which his early thought was affected by the contemporary doctrine of the "radicals." Stephen's analysis of belief was based upon that which Alexander Bain had offered in his work on *The Emotions and the Will,* a book which Holmes had read after his return from England and which applied utilitarian doctrine to the problems of psychology. When Stephen, in his turn, applied Bain's psychology to the law of evidence the application was naturally accepted and taken for granted by Holmes. Another reviewer might, of course, have neglected the philosophic problems and concerned himself entirely with the professional utility of Roscoe's work. That, however, was not Holmes's way. Since his temperament was philosophic the choice for him was to align himself with those who dealt with law "scientifically" or with those who dealt with it "metaphysically." The alignment which he chose to reveal in his first book review was, of course, to be expected.

It is generally agreed among the historians of ideas that the principles of pragmatism began to take recognizable shape in discussions among the members of the so-called Metaphysical Club when they met in Cambridge for philosophical conversation during the period from 1870 to 1872.[76] In those gatherings of lawyers and philosophers Holmes and Nicholas St. John Green brought a common attitude towards law to bear on the problems of philosophy. They exposed their philosopher friends to the common-law lawyer's distrust of general principles and by the vigor of their challenge drove the philosophers towards pragmatism. Within the group, however, there were other strong minds that moved quite naturally in the same direction. Chauncey Wright applied the acid skepticism of science to the aspiring speculations of his friends, and Charles S. Peirce brought the skill of a systematic logician to metaphysical inquiry. In his later years Peirce emphasized the extent to which Green's insistence that the disputants should accept Bain's definition of belief—"that upon which a man is prepared to act"—affected the philosophy of all who participated in the discussions. Peirce, claiming that he was the father of pragmatism, said that Green was its grandfather.[77] The lineage of ideas is always difficult to trace. When Peirce recognized that Bain's conception of belief was pragmatic he tacitly acknowledged that the remote ancestry of pragmatism might be discovered outside of Cambridge. It is not improbable that for Holmes and Green the value of the pragmatic attitude was established more by what Stephen had done in applying Bain's theory of belief to the law than by Bain's own formulation of the theory. It is important, in any case, to remember that neither Holmes nor Green was the first lawyer to see that the utilitarianism of Bentham, the logic of Mill, and the psychology of Bain might fruitfully be applied to law. Having discovered the fruitfulness of that application in the work of Stephen they followed the path of the law in his pragmatic footsteps, suggesting to their friends that they should do likewise on the highways of philosophy. Stephen was a wholehearted Benthamite who remained stubbornly loyal to "the proper principles of rigidity and ferocity" [e] which lie at the foundation

[e] The phrase was Fitzjames Stephen's; see, Leslie Stephen, *The Life of Sir James Fitzjames Stephen* (London, 1895), 308.

of utilitarianism. We do not know with certainty whether his pragmatic analysis of belief was taken from Bain, as it would appear to have been, or whether it was Stephen's own interpretation of Bentham's analysis.[78] It is enough to know that when Holmes referred to the working beliefs of ordinary men as the stuff of law he was not only using words but expressing thoughts which had their roots in British empiricism.

In Volume One of the *American Law Review* two other anonymous reviews by Holmes were published. Neither was as philosophic in its tone as was the notice of Roscoe, yet each gave some indication that the reviewer had interests beyond those of the mere practitioner. In noticing the sixth American edition of Dr. Alfred Swaine Taylor's *Manual of Medical Jurisprudence* Holmes made some reflections on the relationship between medicine and law which may well have passed under the eye of Dr. Holmes before they were turned over to Ropes and Gray. Conceding that the legitimacy of mixing law and medicine and labeling the mixture "medical jurisprudence" should turn upon utility, he doubted the possibility of serving either the ends of science or those of law by such a combination. Admitting that he might not be qualified to speak for the doctors, Holmes expressed the doubt whether you can "make a physician look at a question in a legal way by such a short hand process" as that which Dr. Taylor had chosen and he warned the doctors that if they took the witness stand "with a theory about the law as well as the facts [they would be] in danger of usurping the place of the judge. . . ." When Holmes considered the utility of the volume for lawyers he spoke with more confidence. If a lawyer who represents a criminal defendant wants "to know under what circumstances the courts have admitted [the defense of insanity] in criminal action" a reference to Taylor's *Medical Jurisprudence* will scarcely meet his needs. The note to *Commonwealth* v. *Rogers* in Bennett and Heard's *Leading Criminal Cases* will serve him better; there "he gets the law, the whole law, and nothing but the law, concisely stated in a legal way." [79]

A generation which has come to believe that the maintenance

of fixed boundaries between the law and other areas of human concern has bred an unfortunate provincialism in the professions and which has commended Holmes's efforts to destroy the barriers may find it hard to reconcile his early suspicion of such an effort as Dr. Taylor's with his later insistence that the lawyer's horizon must be broadened.[80] If a lawyer who seeks to defend a client on the ground of insanity is concerned with "nothing but the law" should he not disregard the speculations of criminologists concerning the character of criminals? It would seem that he should. Yet if he does he finds himself condemned by the later Holmes who urged that the questions, if not the answers which criminologists have contributed to law, must be of concern to lawyers.[81] Undoubtedly there were changes in the point of view of Holmes between 1867 and 1897, and the mere acknowledgment of those changes may be a sufficient commentary on his review of Taylor. It is probable, however, that thirty years after the review was published Holmes would have said the same thing of Taylor's volume that he had said in 1867. Dr. Taylor had not attempted to subject the principles of law to the tests of science. He had accepted law and medicine as he found them and had set himself a no more ambitious task than that of providing a grammar of law for the doctor and a primer of medicine for the lawyer. Whether Holmes were to apply the standards of 1867 or those of 1897 to such an effort his final judgment was sure to be less than enthusiastic.

One other phrase in the review of Taylor deserves emphasis. When Holmes spoke of the practitioner who is seeking to discover what the law considers to be insanity in a defendant he said that the "lawyer wants to know under what circumstances the courts have admitted the defence in a criminal action." [82] Although Holmes was not attempting in this passage to define the law its phrasing foreshadows his familiar definition of later years: "Law is a statement of the circumstances in which the public force will be brought to bear upon men through the courts." [83] One who looks upon the formulation of a defensive rule of law as the statement of the circumstances in which courts have allowed a defense to defeat a charge does not significantly alter his perspective when he comes to frame his definition of law in predictive terms. One may, accordingly, see in Holmes's second published review the shape of things to come.

When Holmes was asked to review Roscoe's *Digest* he had turned at once to Stephen's *General View* in order that he might see the work in a philosophic frame of reference. When he was asked a few months later to do a notice of Judge Redfield's edition of Story's *Commentaries on Equity Jurisprudence* Holmes's diary indicates that he went back to Maine's *Ancient Law* to reread the chapter on the Law of Nature and Equity. Again he was seeking to bring to his consideration of a practitioner's text the generalities which contemporary scholarship had added to learning. Although most of Holmes's brief review is concerned with the details of Judge Redfield's editing of Story, the concluding paragraph of the notice reflects the light which Maine had cast on legal history. The terms in which Holmes speaks of the history of equity are not all taken from Maine, but the concluding generalization in the review is clearly derived from Maine's interpretation of legal history.

> The ecclesiastical conception of a right supplementary to the law, and at times transcending it, was an embryo of vague and doubtful figure. By an organic necessity, however, it has slowly developed into a stable body of principles. Centuries have firmly knit its tissues, and have shaped its exact contours. Many portions of its structure have even ossified so far as to have united with the rigid skeleton of legal doctrines. The rest may do so in time. Meanwhile, legislation, gaining in flexibility as the courts lose it, supplies many of the aids for which, four centuries ago, the suitor must have looked to the churchman who administered the conscience of the king.[84]

In this paragraph Holmes made the generalizations of Maine the foundation of his analysis. He does not, to be sure, say anything of the first of the instrumentalities of progress in law—Legal Fictions—to which Maine had given much of his attention. He does, however, accept as valid the thesis that in modern times the agencies of progress have been Equity and Legislation, and that of these two the latter has become the primary instrument of reform. What Holmes asks of the readers of Story's *Equity* is that they see its professional utility in the perspective of a scientific conception of legal history.

In one other paragraph Holmes revealed the philosophic inclination of his mind. Not only did he protest against Judge Redfield's "habit of moralizing," but he observed that the habit "is notably out of place among the rules and precedents of courts." [85] Here one may find the intimation of doctrine that Holmes was later to develop more fully—the thesis that the lawyer should strive to keep morality and law in separate compartments within his mind. Yet to read the protest prophetically is perhaps to disregard the provocation which inspired it. Judge Redfield had brought Story's two volumes to a close with his own criticism of a decision of Sir John Romilly, Master of the Rolls.[86] Judge Redfield had observed that such a decision would "tend to bring the administration of justice into discredit with those whose instincts are in favor of the firm adherence to principle, and trusting consequences to Him with whom are all the issues of life." To this eloquence Holmes made the astringent response: "When the learned editor calls in the authority of religion to make weight against the Master of the Rolls, by doing so he only renders the want of legal authority more conspicuous." [87]

If one were to designate the year in which Holmes's period of preparation and apprenticeship came to its close, 1869 would seem to be that year. The events of 1870 gave clear proof that the days of professional maturity had come. He opened his own office with no associate but his younger brother; he assumed the coeditorship of the *American Law Review* in place of its founders, Ropes and Gray; he was named University Lecturer on Constitutional Law in Harvard College; he began his work as editor of the twelfth edition of Kent's *Commentaries*.[88] In January 1870, Arthur G. Sedgwick, writing to Henry James, spoke of some of these marks of recognition which had come to Holmes and asserted that "he knows more law than anyone in Boston of our time, and works harder at it than anyone." [89] A more mature judge, John C. Ropes, in the previous year, had told William James that "he had never known of anyone in the law who studied anything as hard as Wendell," a comment which led James to suggest that such devoted energy "must lead to Chief Justice, U. S. Supreme Court." [90] It is evident that the period of Holmes's apprenticeship was not a period of leisurely waiting for advancement but a season of relentless effort. It is noticeable that in a city where "good works" were a traditional obligation of the elect, Holmes gave, so far as one can discover, no time or interest to civic or charitable activities. He once skipped a lecture of Peirce on logic in order that he might attend a Ward meeting to oppose the efforts of others to secure bonuses for Civil War veterans, but otherwise there is no indication that he concerned himself with political affairs. On one Sunday afternoon in 1867 its appears that he took his sister's place as teacher at James Freeman Clarke's Sunday School. The entry in his diary indicates that he carried his religious liberalism into the classroom, and suggests that the pupils may have had a pleasant taste of where Unitarian emancipation may lead an instructor: "Showed Doré's Munchausen and read 'Ugly Duck' to A. H.'s class at J. F. Clarke's Sunday School."

There were a few times when Holmes dropped his labors and sought relaxation away from Boston and Cambridge. In May of 1867 he went for two weeks on a fishing trip in Maine seeking land-locked salmon, and in August of the same summer he spent some ten days in New Hampshire in the company, as we have seen, of John Gray, Henry James, and Minny Temple.[91] In the following summer he went with a Harvard undergraduate—Henry Cabot Lodge—on a week's expedition to Illinois shooting prairie chickens.[f] In the summer of 1869 Holmes took a hurried trip to

[f] At a dinner of the Chicago Bar Association in Oct. 1902, misdating by one year his first trip to Chicago, Holmes recalled his shooting trip with Lodge: "Only twice before in my life have I had a glimpse of your wonderful city. Once in 1867, with Mr. Cabot Lodge, not then a Senator of the United States, on our way to try to shoot prairie chickens. We had met a perfidious friend who hoped we had thick boots, on account of the rattlesnakes. So we rose early, before even Chicago was awake, in the hope of buying some, and jumped a yard on the prairie every time a cricket stirred in the grass. But we were temperate and saw no snakes." *Chicago Legal News,* XXXV, 83 (Oct. 25, 1902). The more accurate dating of the trip would

Connecticut with Gray where they saw the Jameses at Pomfret; Mrs. James, noting that Holmes looked "as if he needed recreation," nonetheless was able to add "how charmingly fresh and boyish he is, and with such a power of work too." [92]

The first occasion on which Holmes argued a case in the Supreme Judicial Court occurred in November 1867, eight months after his admission to the bar. The case was *Richardson* v. *New York Central,* the litigation which had commenced when Holmes, at the very beginning of his apprenticeship with Shattuck, had been sent to the depot to discover whether any cars of the New York Central were on hand available for attachment.[93] The substantive issue between the parties concerned the difficult question in the conflict of laws whether Shattuck's client, a Massachusetts administratrix, could recover in the courts of Massachusetts on a claim for wrongful death arising in New York, under a statute of that state. When the case first came to the Shattuck office Holmes had concerned himself not only with the problem of process but had looked into the questions of law upon which the defendant's liability would turn. When Mr. Shattuck had put the problem to him on Saturday, November 17, 1866, Holmes had spent the evening in the first volume of Smith's *Leading Cases* reading *Mostyn* v. *Fabrigas* and the annotations to the case by the American editors, and had "made out" his argument in support of the action. A short time later the action had been commenced, the defendant had filed a demurrer to the plaintiff's declaration, and the question thus presented had been reserved for argument before the Supreme Judicial Court. On November 14, 1867, Judge Ebenezer Rockwood Hoar, Associate Justice of the Supreme Judicial Court, wrote to Dr. Holmes of the argument.

[I] have just had the pleasure of hearing your son make his first argument before our court—and found it very curious to notice the general Jackson style and manner (I don't mean Gen. Jackson, by the by . . .) with your expression now and then coming over it or

seem to be that appearing in the back pages of his diary for 1867; see Little, "The Early Readings of Holmes," *Harvard Library Bulletin,* VIII, 163, 177 (Spring, 1954).

out of it. He made a very creditable appearance—had a case a little savoring of experimental philosophy, but none the worse as a test of capacity on that account; and I rather think will in the long run shew that the materials of a good lawyer which Judge Jackson's grandson inherits have not been crowded out of his composition by your poetry and anatomy—whether of mirth or melancholy.[94]

If Holmes saw this letter, as very surely he did, it is not unlikely that, despite the compliments, his heart sank. The Judge's suggestion that the plaintiff's argument savored a little of experimental philosophy would justify the prediction that the Court would find for the defendant, as in fact it did in an opinion by Mr. Justice Hoar.[95] The public compliment paid in that opinion to the "ingenious and impressive argument" of counsel for the plaintiff was, perhaps, some consolation for defeat, but there were greater satisfactions, perhaps, in Holmes's later participation as Judge in the process of so qualifying the decision in the Richardson case [96] that ultimately it was overruled.[97]

Other traces of Holmes's first years at the bar are dim and impersonal. The diaries show him to have been an active junior to Mr. Shattuck in the preparation of cases. Shortly after his admission to the bar Holmes seems to have taken full charge of voluntary insolvency proceedings which clients of the firm initiated in the Probate Court for Middlesex County.[98] The schedules of creditors, and of the property owned by the debtors, the accounts of the assignees, like other dreary documents in the proceedings, were written in Holmes's hand and show him capable of handling affairs that did not savor of experimental philosophy. The trivialities of practice were not infrequent and were hardly justified by the financial return: "Wrote to Bob Forbes to pay $6 to one Mulvey which he called next day and refused to do. Whereupon Waldo Higginson paid me a dollar." In March 1867, he drafted wills for his father and mother and drew up an agreement by which his cousin Ellen Jackson was to take charge of the upbringing of a child until it should reach eighteen years of age, following the form which he discovered in the Massachusetts Reports. On the afternoon of May 9 he "started with Putnam and Smith to take a deposition in Roxbury but found the man was dead." On June 14 a livelier controversy demanded his attention: "Defended in Municipal Court criminal session Mrs. Gallagher from charge of assault and battery on Mrs. Allen by spitting in her face. For my efficient aid she had to pay $2 and costs, and I magnanimously did not charge her anything for my private pocket."

It is scarcely surprising that Holmes's hunger for ultimates was not satisfied by such crumbs as these. The steady increase in his contributions to the *American Law Review* shows that he was still willing to give his energies to the law, but that he was persuaded that his best chance of making himself a figure in the profession was through industrious and critical scholarship. During the years 1868 and 1869 nine book notices by Holmes appeared in the pages of the *American Law Review*.[99] Few of them sought to do more than give a descriptive account of the books under consideration, and since seven of the nine volumes noticed by Holmes were law reports the opportunities for the expression of philosophical or critical attitudes were limited. In the case of one review there were intimations of Holmes's concern with a problem of the form of the law which was later to receive his fuller attention. In reviewing Judah P. Benjamin's treatise on the Law of Scales, Holmes suggests that an effort to arrange the law philosophically, to adopt, in other words, a scientific classification of its subject matter and its principles, might have fruitful consequences. He was troubled by the fact that as the common law had developed it was necessary for each scholar who examines a particular subject in the law to deal with principles which have a far broader revelance than that which is manifested in their specialty. Thus each author is compelled to reformulate principles that others have already adequately presented. Until the law is philosophically arranged,

> a book of reference on any subdivision of the law . . . must set forth at length, not only those principles constituting the specific difference of the subject matter, but also those common to it and to many other classes of the same genus. Thus, it may be doubted, whether in a com-

prehensive summary of our law, *fraud* would not more properly be treated under the general title *contract,* or possibly under some still wider head, rather than repeated in every text-book dealing with every one of the different sorts of contract known to modern commerce.[100]

The suggestions thus outlined, by which Holmes again indicated his faith that the materials of law might be organized in much the same way as are those of science, he was to develop more fully in three of his earliest essays in the *American Law Review.*[101]

In his review of the twenty-third volume of the Iowa Reports Holmes went beyond details to generalities and once more gave intimations of doctrine which he developed more fully in his later writing.[102] Expressing some personal liking for "that flavor of legal learning which is so pleasant in the decisions of some longer established [American] courts" and some sympathy for the tendency of conservative New Jersey to furnish "a quiet Southern exposure for the ripening of lawyers of the Old School," he spoke out in vigorous defense of the judges of the busy West who were "more intent on adapting the law to modern requirements than on standing in the ancient ways." Communities of abundant scholarship may suffer from their learning. Though they may be able "to extract philosophy from the history of law," one may not expect of them that "business-like common sense" which is found in the law of the Western states.

No branch of knowledge affords more instances than the law, of what a blessing to mankind it is that men begin life ignorant. Every one knows that it often happens, that, from historical causes, analogous cases are governed by dissimiliar rules, and that forms which have lost their significance by lapse of time remain as technicalities. One who is familiar with these nice distinctions has no interest in their reform, even if he does not become prejudiced in their favor.[g]

Holmes then indicated something of the spirit which colored his first years at the bar. "[W]hen, after barely three years' study, a young man finds himself at once in active practice, to simplify

[g] Cf. Holmes's statement in *The Common Law* (1881), 78: "Ignorance is the best of law reformers. People are glad to discuss a question on general principles, when they have forgotten the special knowledge necessary for technical reasoning."

rules, to destroy anomalies, to make partial analogies complete, is his only safeguard."

That Holmes, at the beginning of his career, saw law reform as a challenging responsibility might suggest that he was eager to participate in the efforts of progressive lawyers to effect reform through legislative processes. There were some among his friends and contemporaries at the bar who made their contributions to reform in that way. It is clear, however, that it was not by those means that Holmes intended to participate in the process of reform. His review of Benjamin on Sales confirmed what was implicit in his philosophical commitment—the persuasion that a scientific ordering of legal principles was the first necessity. Much as he might respect the "business-like common sense" of practical lawyers, and fully as he might recognize the value which their "ignorance" had in encouraging a reformation in the law, he knew his own capacities sufficiently well to realize that his contributions must be of another sort. Judge Walker in his treatise on American Law had shown the importance of hard-headed practicality as an instrument of reform. "While one would not expect from the West a second Maine, to extract philosophy from the history of law," might not one hope that such a talent might be nurtured in the East and come to fruition in Boston? The question was not, of course, asked explicitly, yet it was implied in Holmes's earliest book reviews and was answered in his later writing.

In the issue of the *American Law Review* for April 1868, there was printed a long descriptive account of the impeachment proceedings against President Andrew Johnson.[103] It was written by Holmes. The summary has the neutrality of a report rather than the conviction of an editorial and it is, therefore, difficult to find in it any suggestion of its author's approval or disapproval of the proceedings. It is clear that Holmes believed that the President had a technical defense to the charge that he had violated the Tenure of Office Act.[104] The one large issue in the case on which Holmes expressed a decided opinion concerned the question whether a President could be impeached for his refusal to observe the provisions of a statute which the Supreme Court had determined to be unconstitutional. Mr. Chief Justice Chase had indicated that the Congress was not bound to accept as conclusive an adjudication of the Court that a Congressional enactment was void. Holmes, quoting the Chief Justice, asserted that "it certainly would have seemed, but for this language, that, when the Supreme Court of the United States had declared an act unconstitutional, every department of government was bound to respect their decision." [105] In this assertion Holmes revealed what is surely not surprising in him—a willing acceptance of the principle of judicial supremacy.

In all probability the special quality of Holmes's ambition did not reveal itself until he saw that his choice of law as his profession was final. He was always possessed by an impelling sense of time's urgency,—a Puritan's feeling of responsibility that no moment should be wasted.[h] In June of 1866 his mother warned him that he should not feel while a traveler in England "as you did at home that you must accomplish just so much each 24 hours." [106] This feeling of responsibility did not mean for Holmes that pleasures were sinful. It did mean, however, that they were serious and should be pursued artistically. Conversation with a pretty woman was always a pleasure but it was doubly pleasing if her responsive intelligence stimulated him to test a paradox or challenge a prevailing piety. When he observed that "there is nothing like a paradox to take the scum off your mind" [107] he expressed his hope that through lively talk intelligence might be refreshed. Time was not wasted in pleasure if its by-product was a new insight or a sharpened perception. Yet in his early years he rationed his hours of relaxation with some rigor in order that he might put his capacities to the test of achievement.

In his later years Holmes frequently insisted that he could not understand how men could make the holding of a particular position an objective in life. Writing to Judge Learned Hand in 1922 he said: "I assume that your ambition, like mine, cannot be satis-

[h] In 1930 he asked, "Why not be content with pleasure? I can't answer, except that by my experiences in life and more by the temperament I get from my mother, without some feeling of accomplishment I feel as if it were time for me to die." *Holmes-Laski Letters,* II, 1278.

fied by office or anything resting in the will of others but only by the trembling hope that you have hit the *ut de poitrine*." [108] This frequent insistence that he was not concerned with attaining particular posts of honor and responsibility may seem to be belied by the testimony of one who knew Holmes at the bar. George B. Upham, a distant cousin through marriage, found himself in 1879 working for many evenings in the Social Law Library at the Suffolk County Court House. Another lawyer was regularly a neighbor at a nearby desk and ultimately identified himself as Holmes. The two men picked up the habit of taking a walk together through the Boston Common after the closing of the Library and Mr. Upham in 1936 summarized his recollection of their meetings.[109]

> In our conversations he told me he had a theory that anyone could accomplish anything he wished, if he only wished it hard enough, continuously, morning, noon, and night, and perhaps subconsciously while sleeping. Expressing my interest in this theory, I asked what he wished most to do. He replied that he was trying to write a book on the common law which he hoped would supplant Blackstone and Kent's Commentaries. . . . Pressing him to tell me of further ambitions he said he wished to become Chief Justice of the Supreme Court of Massachusetts, and eventually, impossible as it might seem, a Justice of the Supreme Court of the United States.

This anecdote recorded fifty-seven years after the event may seem so dramatically fitting as to be questionable in its accuracy, particularly in the light of Holmes's frequent assertions that he did not "understand ambition for an office." [110] It is significant, however, that Holmes, so far as we know, never denied that he had ambition to be given the opportunity which comes with office. Such a questing temperament as his could not find satisfaction in high station as such. But such a man as Holmes might feel that if he secured a certain post from that position he might prove his greatness. The post became an ambition not as an end but as a means of testing his capacity. In 1930, Holmes said that he had "got beyond the time when anything that anybody can give me will satisfy or even gratify my ambition. The only thing that could be given at an earlier stage was opportunity, and that I have had." [i] In this assertion is implicit the admission that there had been a time when he was eager to secure what others might give him—a seat on the Massachusetts bench, a seat on the Supreme Court of the United States. This admitted eagerness bespoke a deeper hunger than for office. It expressed a relentless desire for another challenge to his capacity, another opportunity to prove his strength.

There were those among Holmes's early friends who came to believe that his self-centered ambition was unpleasant and excessive. William James, in particular, believed that Holmes allowed his passion for achievement to blunt his human nature. "The more I live in the world," James wrote to his brother Henry in 1869, "the more the cold-blooded, conscious egotism and conceit of people afflict me. . . . All the noble qualities of Wendell Holmes, for instance, are poisoned by them. . . ." [111] Seven years later James found himself still offended by Holmes's self-seeking qualities: "He is a powerful battery, formed like a planing machine to gouge a deep self-beneficial groove through life. . . ." [112] James Bradley Thayer, after Holmes had hastily resigned his Law School professorship to accept appointment to the Supreme Judicial Court, acknowledged Holmes's "attractive qualities and solid merits" but went on to say that he was "wanting sadly in the noblest region of human character,—selfish, vain, thoughtless of others." [113] That some persons of retiring sensitivity found Holmes's ambitions excessive is not surprising and it is probably true that he longed so eagerly for new challenges to his capacities that he seemed ruthless in his aspirations. On at least one occasion he expressed some awareness that his ambition lacked the purity which he found in that of others.[114]

[i] *Holmes-Laski Letters,* II, 1224–1225. Similar attitudes were expressed when he was nominated to the Supreme Court of the United States in 1902: "As to this making me happy, I never have set my happiness on anything that was in the power of anyone else, so far as personal achievement is concerned. The only question is whether one does his work successfully after he gets a chance to do it." Autograph letter Aug. 15, 1902 to Miss Sally Fairchild. (Copy, Harvard Law School.)

It stings me with self-criticism [he wrote in 1906], when I see some of those Englishmen who have done noble work, never making themselves the centre—thinking of what they do only as humble work for the Empire or their fellow-men and treating it as much on a level with cricket. I feel genuine cosmic modesty—modesty for my race, which I surmise not to be the repository of God's final secrets. But when it comes to the purely human basis I can't help feeling in a personal way and wanting to beat the whole crowd—thinking about my work as *my* work and not simply as work which I hope may be useful. I fail too in regarding my work as simply part of my life—on a par with the rest of what one does. That seems to me a big way of taking it. I suppose that one should put one's heart into producing and be indifferent to the product.[114]

A less self-confident person than Holmes would have considered that the question whether or not he had beaten "the whole crowd" would be settled by the dignity of the offices which he attained. It is clear that Holmes sought the verdict of the elect, that he was never satisfied until his achievement was recognized as distinguished by the few who, in his judgment, were qualified by learning and imagination to estimate his accomplishment. "The only thing an internal man cares for is to believe that he is taking the right track for intellectual mastery. Only a few men in this world . . . can do anything to assure one's ever-doubting soul about that." [115] Praise by the undiscriminating might please Holmes's vanity but it could not satisfy his ambition. In 1902 his nomination to the Supreme Court received general acclamation in the press, yet he was hurt and injured that the praise seemed [116]

hopelessly devoid of personal discrimination or courage. . . . It makes one sick when he has broken his heart in trying to make every word living and real to see a lot of duffers, generally I think not even lawyers, talking with the sanctity of print in a way that at once discloses to the knowing eye that literally they don't know anything about it. . . . If I haven't done my share in the way of putting in new and remodeling old thought for the last 20 years then I delude myself. Occasionally some one has a glimpse—but in the main damn the lot of them.

To another friend he expressed in the same season of recognition

the depth of gloom in which [he] was plunged for a time in what so far has been a triumph because the incompetents . . . more frequently pronounced my style good than me a great judge. . . . Of course, my own judgment of myself does not vary so much—but the *feeling* of success or failure does depend a good deal on what is said—and a little adverse or cold comment will pull down more than reams of praise will build up, except when once in a while you get a word from the masters.[117]

When Holmes became Chief Justice of the Supreme Judicial Court, Mrs. John Chipman Gray, one of his closest friends, wrote him a note of congratulation. In her letter she spoke in sympathetic friendliness of a mood which she had noticed in him from time to time. "Once in a while," she said, "in some tired moment, I know you have had just a little the feeling that every man's hand was against you. . . ." [118] What she referred to was evidently a recurrent bitterness in Holmes that his work was not sufficiently appreciated. Seven years after his appointment to the Supreme Court of the United States he protested that he had not had "as much recognition" as he would have liked, and in 1910 said, half humorously perhaps, that "I want more and louder [praise] to be satisfied." [119] Ultimately, he came to feel that he had received due credit. In 1914 he was able to admit that "in these days" he seemed to get "a great many kind and appreciative notices of one sort and another" and, paraphrasing Goldsmith, observed that "Fame accumulates as man decays." [120] With the accumulation came a deeper satisfaction than any which Holmes had earlier enjoyed. There was added pleasure in the fact that his greatest admirers through his later years were the young. In their devotion and respect he found final reassurance that the work and the ambition had not been in vain. When that reassurance had come the quality of selfish aspiration which had offended some of his earlier friends had dissolved.

When Holmes's apprenticeship came to its close in 1869 the figure of his mind and the shape of his temperament were formed. They had been molded by many elements; some of them hung in the air of New England as the tradition of Puritanism, a tradition no longer dependent on the sanctions of religion for its authority but still impelling those who felt its influence to treat the favorable opportunities of life as solemn responsibilities. Another element had been more personal. The mind and temperament of Dr. Holmes had both stimulated and irritated his son, leading him to make his father's larger qualities a standard to be followed and his smaller failings an example to be rejected. The lasting traditions of Puritanism and the special attitudes of the household provided the soil in which fell the seeds of contemporary thought and speculation. Philosophy offered, of course, other answers than those of the empiricist, but one who was brought to his maturity under the guidance of Dr. Holmes, who found the charm of William James irresistible, and the swift intelligence of Leslie Stephen and of Chauncey Wright wholly admirable, quite naturally made their premises his own. That those presuppositions dominated English philosophy and seemed to have made possible the impressive strides of science gave them a vastly persuasive authority. To these intellectual influences which had gone to mold Holmes's mind there should be added, of course, his experience of war. From that experience Holmes had learned a special lesson. He had seen a number of his own convictions crumble when they felt the impact of reality. He had seen opposing convictions withstand the strain of war. It would always be hard for one who had been sensitive to this experience to consider that his own principles of morality were sanctioned by a cosmic or universal authority. Quite probably the skepticism of Holmes's temperament would have led him ultimately to this negative position had he never gone to war. It is doubtful, however, whether without that experience the affirmative corollary would have accompanied his doubts. From war he had learned not only to distrust his own absolutes. He had also learned to respect the convictions of others. As a logical matter there is difficulty, perhaps, in combining skepticism with enthusiasm. Certainly Holmes never reconciled, or attempted to reconcile his faith in the value of heroic action with his doubts of the cosmic significance of man. "Our business is to commit ourselves to life, to accept at once our functions and our ignorance, and to offer our heart to fate." [121] The forces that had made him were stronger than logic, and the merging of tradition and experience has not always been an easy process. In Holmes the struggle to find himself, to make the final choice of a career in which ambition could be satisfied, had not been easy. When 1869 came to its close, however, the choice had been made, and the testing of capacity had been concluded. The prologue was over and the performance was about to begin.

NOTES

Abbreviations

A.l.	Autograph letter
CLP	Holmes, *Collected Legal Papers* (New York, 1920)
HL	*Holmes-Laski Letters* (2 vols., Cambridge, 1953)
HLS	Harvard Law School
HP	*Holmes-Pollock Letters* (2 vols., Cambridge, 1941)
HUA	Harvard University Archives
HUh	Houghton Library, Harvard University
TWF	*Touched With Fire: Civil War Letters and Diary of Oliver Wendell Holmes, Jr.* (Cambridge, 1946)

1. *Childhood and Inheritance*

1. A.l. (HLS).
2. J. T. Morse, Jr., *Life and Letters of Oliver Wendell Holmes* (Boston, 1896), I, 322.
3. Letter to Phineas Barnes, Dec. 4, 1842; *id.*, 194.
4. This memorandum preserved by OWH in a scrapbook, now at the Houghton Library, is ascribed to Dr. Holmes by Miss Tilton; Eleanor M. Tilton, *Amiable Autocrat: A Biography of Dr. Oliver Wendell Holmes* (N.Y., 1947), 162. It is my impression, however, that the handwriting is that of Mrs. Holmes.
5. This report is in the copybook which Holmes kept while he attended Mr. Sullivan's school.
6. HLS.
7. A.l. (HLS).
8. *Mass. Hist. Soc. Proc.*, 2nd Ser., XVII, 517.
9. Charles Francis Adams, *Autobiography* (Boston, 1916), 22, 23.
10. Charles William Eliot, *A Late Harvest* (Boston, 1924), 18.
11. Henry Cabot Lodge, *Early Memories* (N.Y., 1913), 81.
12. A.l., Dec. 10, 1882 (HLS).
13. *Mass. Hist. Soc. Proc.*, LXV, 214.
14. *The "Original Poems" and others by Ann and Jane Taylor and Adelaide O'Keeffe* (Lucas, ed., London, 1903), xvii.
15. Francis Biddle, *Mr. Justice Holmes* (N.Y., 1942), 30.
16. A.l., Feb. 13, 1932 (HLS).
17. OWH conversation with author.
18. A.l., Morse to Henry Cabot Lodge, Oct. 5, 1914 (Lodge Papers, Mass. Hist. Soc.).
19. A.l., March 5, 1931 (HLS).
20. A.l., July 29, 1899 (HLS).
21. Morse to T. S. Perry, Sept. 13, 1918 (copy, HLS).
22. A.l., March 9, 1821 (HLS).
23. A.l., Nov. 24, 1922 (HLS).
24. A.l., Feb. 13, 1932 (HLS).
25. F. C. Fiechter, Jr., "The Preparation of an American Aristocrat," *New England Quarterly*, VI, 1, 7–8 (March 1933). The same incident was recounted by OWH to the author.
26. A.l. to Baroness Moncheur, Aug. 28, 1911 (HLS).
27. Holmes to Pollock, Oct. 27, 1901; HP, I, 99.
28. Holmes to Pollock, June 23, 1906; *id.*, 127.
29. HP, I, 64.
30. A.l. to Mrs. Clara Sherwood Stevens, Aug. 4, 1914 (HLS).
31. *Alice James: Her Brothers, Her Journal* (Anna Robeson Burr, ed., N.Y., 1934), 102.

32. *Supra,* note 31.
33. Morse, *Life and Letters,* I, 210.
34. Henry James, *Notes of a Son and Brother* (N.Y., 1914), 350.
35. *Id.,* 351–352.
36. HP, II, 41; HL, I, 485.
37. Undated letter to Harriet Beecher Stowe, Morse, *Life and Letters,* II, 245, 246.
38. To Harriet Beecher Stowe, May 29, 1859; *id.,* 226.
39. A.l. to Baroness Moncheur, Aug. 29, 1908 (HLS).
40. *Mechanism in Thought and Morals, Works,* VIII, 260, 312.
41. To Harriet Beecher Stowe, Morse, *Life and Letters,* II, 230.
42. "Jonathan Edwards," *Works,* VIII, 361.
43. To Harriet Beecher Stowe, *supra,* note 41.
44. *Over the Teacups, Works,* IV, 105.
45. Writing to Harold Laski, Nov. 23, 1928; HL, II, 1113.
46. A.l. to Harold Laski, June 26, 1919 (HLS).
47. HL, I, 470. The book in question was May Sinclair's *Anne Severn and the Fieldings* (N.Y., 1922).
48. *Supra,* note 44.
49. A.l. to Ellen Askwith, March 3, 1915 (copy, HLS).
50. Tilton, *Amiable Autocrat,* 99, 100.
51. *Journal of the History of Ideas,* IX, 14, 15 (1948).
52. "Professor at the Breakfast Table," *Works,* II, 295.
53. A.l., Henry James to Henry James, Sr., March 18, 1873 (HUh).
54. A.l., Oct. 5, 1914 (Lodge Papers, Mass. Hist. Soc.).
55. A.l, June 11, 1866 (HLS).
56. HL, II, 1278.
57. Morse, *Life and Letters,* I, 247.
58. A.l. to Mrs. John C. Gray, Dec. 23, 1926 (HLS).
59. Morse, *Life and Letters,* I, 248.
60. *Id.,* 247.
61. *Id.,* 246.
62. See Harold J. Laski, in *Mr. Justice Holmes* (Frankfurter, ed., N.Y., 1931), 157.
63. Morse, *Life and Letters,* I, 264.
64. *Speeches,* 24.
65. *Speeches,* 85.
66. *Works,* II, 38.
67. In *Towne* v. *Eisner,* 245 U.S. 418, 425 (1918).
68. *Works,* II, 6–7.
69. "Law in Science–Science in Law," CLP, 210, 238.
70. "Natural Law," CLP, 313.
71. "The Professor at the Breakfast Table," *Works,* II, 117.
72. A.l. to Clara Stevens, Nov. 24, 1909; to Dean Wigmore, May 14, 1930 (HLS).
73. "The Path of the Law," CLP, 188–189.
74. To James Freeman Clarke, Oct. 24, 1862; Morse, *Life and Letters,* I,

306. In wartime, however, the Doctor spoke eloquent words in defense of the reformer; see "The Inevitable Trial," *Works,* VIII, 78, 90–91.

75. Morse, *Life and Letters,* I, 298.

76. HL, II, 948.

77. A.l. to Dean Wigmore, Dec. 4, 1910 (HLS).

78. A.l., Nov. 19, 1915 (HLS).

79. A.l. to Lady Ellen Askwith, March 3, 1915 (copy, HLS).

80. "Mechanism in Thought and Morals," *Works,* VIII, 260, 307.

81. *Id.,* 301.

82. "The Soldier's Faith," *Speeches,* 57

83. Morse, *Life and Letters,* I, 270.

84. "The Soldier's Faith," *Speeches,* 63.

85. A.l. to Felix Frankfurter, May 21, 1926 (HLS).

86. A.l., Nov. 12, 1875 (HLS).

87. Morse, *Life and Letters,* I, 171.

88. A.l., July 22, 1866 (HLS).

89. *Id.*

90. The phrases appeared in Holmes's letter of Sept. 23, 1861, addressed to his mother; TWF, 8, 12.

91. See in general Kenneth Wiggins Porter, *The Jacksons and the Lees* (2 vols., Cambridge, 1937).

92. HL, I, 165.

93. The best recent account of the controversy between Abiel Holmes and his parishioners is in Eleanor M. Tilton's *Amiable Autocrat,* 43–49.

94. *Baker* v. *Fales,* 16 Mass. 488 (1820).

95. A.l. to Mrs. John C. Gray, July 21, 1891 (HLS).

96. A letter from Mrs. Holmes to Miss Emily Hallowell of Aug. 5, 1863 (HLS), when Holmes was in Boston recuperating from his wounds at Antietam, reported that "Wendell . . . has begun to take lessons on horseback."

97. Tilton, *Amiable Autocrat,* 219.

98. "Natural Law," CLP, 310, 311.

99. A.l. to Baroness Moncheur, Aug. 31, 1910 (HLS).

100. A.l. to same, Aug. 29, 1908 (HLS).

101. A.l. to same, Jan. 9, 1915 (HLS).

102. *Id.*

103. A.l. to Lady Leslie Scott, May 21, 1923 (HLS).

104. Speech at the Tavern Club, Nov. 14, 1902 (MS, HLS).

105. HL, I, 712–713.

106. *Supra,* note 104.

107. Writing to Harold Laski on Feb. 25, 1925, he spoke of this work as "the delight of my boyhood"; HL, I, 709.

108. HL, I, 564–565.

109. HL, II, 207.

110. Letter to Learned Hand, May 6, 1924 (copy, HLS).

2. *Harvard College*

1. Unpublished letter of Jan. 27, 1860, quoted in Allan Nevins, *Ordeal of the Union* (N.Y., 1947), I, 78. Bowen's review of *The Origin of Species* appeared in the April issue: *North American Review*, XC, 474 (1860).

2. Francis Bowen, *Principles of Metaphysical and Ethical Science Applied to the Evidences of Religion* (Boston, 1855), vii.

3. Henry M. Rogers, *Memories of Ninety Years* (Privately Printed, 1932), 55–56, quoting from an unnamed member of the class of 1862.

4. *The Education of Henry Adams* (Boston, 1918), 55. There is no better description of Harvard in the late fifties than in Herbert Samuels, *The Young Henry Adams* (Cambridge, 1948), chap. i.

5. *Charles Francis Adams, 1835–1915; An Autobiography* (Boston, 1916), 35.

6. *The Letters of John Fiske* (Fisk, ed., N.Y., 1940), 58.

7. These votes are recorded in minutes of the Faculty meetings between the fall of 1857 and June 1861 (HUA).

8. *Id.*

9. President's correspondence, 1857–1861 (HUA).

10. *War Diary and Letters of Stephen Minot Weld, 1861–1865* (Privately Printed, 1912), 14.

11. Samuel E. Morison, *The Development of Harvard University, 1869–1929* (Cambridge, 1930), lxviii.

12. Other roomers at Danforth's during Holmes's college years were Josiah Bradlee, John Homans, Henry Ropes, Francis Lee Higginson, Charles Jackson, Robert Shaw Perkins, and Francis Lowell Gardner.

13. By action of the Faculty these bloody conflicts were terminated during Holmes's senior year. The exercises in which a football was buried, an obituary sermon delivered, and a funeral dirge sung were described by John Fiske, *Letters*, 48–50.

14. *The Early Years of The Saturday Club* (Emerson, ed., 1918), 164.

15. Hubert Weir Smyth in Morison, *Development of Harvard*, 38.

16. HL, I, 727.

17. See, e.g., HP, I, 258.

18. *Harvard Magazine*, IV, 408.

19. In fairness to Professor Cooke it is worth remembering that Holmes in 1867 gratefully recalled his exceptional talent as lecturer in translating mathematics into English. See Ralph Barton Perry, *The Thought and Character of William James* (Boston, 1935), I, 505, 507. The words which Perry there reads "on terms" should be *"ore tenus."*

20. The records of both organizations are preserved in the Harvard Archives.

21. The records of the Hasty Pudding show that Holmes held the offices of Secretary and Poet in his senior year (HUA).

22. A corrected copy of Holmes's remarks on the occasion is preserved among his papers.

23. *Harvard Magazine,* VII, 26. The contribution is identified as Holmes's in an index of the magazine made by Holmes's classmate F. W. Hackett (HUA).

24. Letter to Arthur Garfield Hays, April 20, 1928 (copy, HLS).

25. HL, I, 772.

26. The obituary appears in the records of the Porcellian Club and was made available to me by the kindness of Mr. Benjamin Joy. Gardner, who roomed at Mr. Danforth's house on Linden St., had died while on a shooting trip at Cotuit, on Cape Cod. From the unpublished diary of Francis William Bartlett shown to me by his daughter, Miss Edith Bartlett of Pittsfield, it appears that Holmes was among Gardner's companions on the trip.

27. Samuel E. Morison, *Three Centuries of Harvard* (Cambridge, 1936), 308.

28. Edwin H. Hall in Morison, *supra,* note 11, 278.

29. Letter to John T. Morse, Jr., Nov. 8, 1926 (copy, HLS). See Dr. Holmes's *Ralph Waldo Emerson, Works,* XI, 58.

30. Letter to Learned Hand, May 8, 1924 (copy, HLS).

31. The account of these conversations given by Elizabeth Shepley Sergeant in her essay "Justice Touched with Fire," reprinted in her *Fire under the Andes* (N.Y., 1927) in *Mr. Justice Holmes* (Frankfurter, ed., N.Y., 1931), 183, 192–193, is based upon Holmes's own statement of the incident in a letter to Miss Sergeant of Dec. 7, 1926 (copy, HLS). See also Dr. Holmes's, *Ralph Waldo Emerson, Works,* XI, 56.

32. *University Quarterly,* II, 217.

33. *Id.,* 216.

34. *Id.,* 215.

35. *Id.,* 216.

36. *Id.,* 210.

37. *Id.,* 207.

38. *Id.,* 217.

39. *Id.*

40. *Id.,* 214–215.

41. *Harvard Magazine,* VII, 41 (Oct. 1860). A penciled note at the head of Holmes's copy of the essay states that it was written during the summer vacation in 1860.

42. Wolfgang Stechow, "Justice Holmes' Notes on Albert Dürer," *The Journal of Aesthetics and Art Criticism,* VIII, 119, 120 (Dec. 1949).

43. *Harvard Magazine,* VII, 43–44.

44. *Id.,* 143. Holbrook is identified as the author in the Hackett index, *supra,* note 23.

45. Holmes's associates as senior editors, who were elected by their classmates, were Wendell Phillips Garrison and Albert Stetson.

46. Letter of Jan. 17, 1861 (HUA).

47. Garrison is identified as the author in the Hackett index, *supra,* note 23.

48. *University Quarterly,* I, 21 (Jan. 1860).

49. *Harvard Magazine,* VII, 345 (June 1861).

50. *Id.*

51. In the issue for Nov. 1860 (VII, 111) a notice of new editions of Macaulay's *History of England, The Works of Charles Lamb,* and Izaak Walton's *Lives* is identified as Holmes's in the Hackett index, *supra,* note 23.

52. *Harvard Magazine,* VII, 235.

53. Preface, iii–iv.

54. *Id.,* 31.

55. *Id.,* 47.

56. Bowen, *The Principles of Political Economy* (2nd ed., Boston, 1859), 22–23.

57. See, e.g., at 271: "The intention of Providence seems to be, that the time and labor economized through the use of machinery and improved modes of production, in the production of necessaries, should be devoted to the creation of luxuries for very general use. . . ."

58. The American phenomenon of high wages was explained as follows: "I attribute the result, therefore, to moral rather than to physical causes,—to American institutions, more than to the fact that America is still a new country, and is rich in fertile and yet unoccupied land." *Id.,* 203.

59. *Id.,* 141.

60. HL, I, 658.

61. Bowen, review of *The Origin of Species, North American Review,* XC, 474 (April 1860).

62. HL, II, 893.

63. See undated pamphlet, *Richard P. Hallowell* [1835–1904]: *"A Soldier in the Army of the Lord."*

64. *The Liberator,* XXXI, 15, col. 1 (Jan. 25, 1861).

65. The fullest accounts of the bodyguards and of the events of Jan. 1861 are in George W. Smalley, *Anglo-American Memories* (London, 1911), chaps. 9–11, and Thomas Wentworth Higginson, *Cheerful Yesterdays* (Boston, 1891), 240–241.

66. Original at HLS.

67. Boston *Herald,* Jan. 24, 861, 2, col. 3.

68. *The Liberator,* XXXI, 28, col. 6 (Feb. 15, 1861).

69. See Smalley, *Memories,* 87–88.

70. *The Liberator,* XXXI, 19, col. 4 (Feb. 1, 1861).

71. The precise date of Holmes's enlistment is not known. Facts concerning the 4th Battalion are to be found in *Record of the Service of the Forty-Fourth Massachusetts Volunteer Militia in North Carolina* (Privately Printed, 1887), chap. i, and Roe, *The Twenty-Fourth Regiment, Massachusetts Volunteers* (Worcester: Privately Printed, 1907).

72. College Letters, V, 144 (HUA).

73. Letter of July 24, 1861, printed in M. A. DeW. Howe, *Holmes of the Breakfast Table* (New York, 1939), 102, 103.

74. Letter of July 26, 1861; College Letters, V, 210 (HUA).

75. Letter of July 6, 1926 (copy, HLS).

76. Letter of Feb. 8, 1927 (copy, HLS).

77. Letter of Nov. 17, 1926 (copy, HLS).

78. TWF, 122, note 1.

79. "Plato," *Harvard Magazine,* II, 205, 217.

80. "Notes on Albert Dürer," *Harvard Magazine,* VII, 41, 43.

81. This unpublished diary is in the possession of General Bartlett's daughter, Miss Edith Bartlett of Pittsfield, and is quoted with her generous permission. The account of life at Fort Independence is based principally on that diary.

82. "The Soldier's Faith," *Speeches* (1913), 56, 64, 63.

83. Bartlett diary, entry of June 2.

84. Roe, *The Twenty-Fourth Regiment, Massachusetts Volunteers* (Worcester, 1907), 12.

85. In his Autobiographical Sketch in the Class Album, Holmes, writing on July 2, 1861, said, "When the war broke out I joined the '4th Battalion of Infantry' and went down to Fort Independence expecting when drilled to go south (as a private)." Reprinted in Max Lerner, *The Mind and Faith of Justice Holmes* (Boston, 1943), 6, 7.

86. *Charles Francis Adams, 1836–1915: An Autobiography* (Boston, 1916), 117.

87. A.l., Colonel Lee to Holmes, June 10, 1884 (HLS).

88. M. A. DeW. Howe, *Holmes of the Breakfast Table,* 101.

89. The statement of Howe in *Holmes of the Breakfast Table* and of Miss Tilton in *Amiable Autocrat,* 264, that Holmes did not take his June examinations appears to be inaccurate. Not only was he awarded his degree, which would seem to indicate compliance with the Faculty's vote of June 10, but writing to Dr. Holmes on June 20, 1861, President Felton stated that the son had credit for the examinations at the close of the term; College Letters, V, 201 (HUA).

90. *The Education of Henry Adams* (Boston, 1918), 68.

91. Cambridge *Chronicle,* Sat., June 22, 1861. Other reports of the Class Day exercises were published in the New York *Tribune* for July 8, 1861, the Boston *Evening Transcript* for June 21, 1861, and the Boston *Daily Advertiser* for June 22, 1861.

92. Boston *Evening Transcript, supra.*

93. Lerner, *supra,* note 85, 6, 8.

94. A.l. to Felix Frankfurter, Nov. 2, 1916 (HLS).

95. College Letters, V, 201 (HUA).

96. Howe, *Holmes of the Breakfast Table,* 102–104. General Winfield Scott had been given an honorary degree at the Commencement exercises.

97. Lerner, *supra,* 7.

98. *Harvard Memorial Biographies* (Boston, 1867), I, iii, quoting Plato's Menexenus, Sec. 9.

3. *Civil War: 1861–1862*

1. The official records give the date of Holmes's first commission as July 10, 1861. It is clear, however, that that date was selected retroactively. Though John Lothrop Motley on July 7 wrote to his wife saying that "young Wendell

Holmes . . . has a lieutenant's commission in Lee's regiment," four days later he spoke as if no commission had yet been issued and indicated that on July 12 Dr. Holmes was going to appeal personally to Colonel Lee on his son's behalf: *Correspondence of John Lothrop Motley* (Curtis, ed., N.Y., 1889), II, 8, 11. A letter from Holmes to Lieutenant Colonel Henry Lee indicates that on the 23rd the two had spoken of problems concerning the Twentieth Regiment: Executive Department Letters, XXIII, #15 (State House Archives). Holmes's Captain in the Fourth Battalion on July 9 had written to Governor Andrew on Holmes's behalf stating that Holmes had, for the last three months, been under his command and "to judge from the faithful manner in which he has always performed his duties as a private, and the progress he has made, I think he will prove himself a capable and efficient officer." Executive Department Letters, XXIII, #10.

2. William Raymond Lee, "Paul Joseph Revere," *Harvard Memorial Biographies* (Cambridge, 1867), I, 204, 206. See also F. J. Child, "James Jackson Lowell," *id.*, 395, 398.

3. George A. Bruce, *The Twentieth Regiment of Massachusetts Volunteer Infantry, 1861–1865* (Boston, 1906), 5–6.

4. Unpublished Reminiscences of Joseph F. Murphy of Company I (Twentieth Regiment Papers, Boston Public Library).

5. Letter of Jan. 20, 1863 to Lieutenant LeBarnes, Executive Department Letters, XXIII, #43 (State House Archives).

6. A.l., Henry L. Abbott to his father, Josiah G. Abbott, Sept. 14, 1863: "Thank God, however, that in the regiment they are all unanimous on the right side. The few abolitionists in the army call this the copperhead regiment." Again, writing to his mother on Dec. 6, 1863, Abbott spoke of "this army of noble copperheads." See also his letter to his father of July 27, 1863. (Originals in HUh.)

7. A.l. to Holmes, Nov. 10, 1863 (Civil War Scrap-Book, #1, HLS).

8. In the spring of 1862, while Lieutenant Colonel Palfrey was commanding the Regiment, he ordered that all Negroes who had come as fugitives from slavery within the Regimental lines and had been employed by officers as personal servants, should be turned out of camp. Lieutenant John W. LeBarnes refused to carry out the order, and was arrested. Tendering his resignation from the Regiment to Governor Andrew, he protested vigorously not only against the inhumanity of Palfrey's order by which Negroes were sent back into slavery, but against the "particular proteges" of Palfrey who had inspired it. LeBarnes's account of the incident is in Executive Department Letters [State Archives], XLVI, #135. Another similar incident had already brought Palfrey and Governor Andrew into conflict; see Albert Gallatin Browne, *Sketch of the Official Life of John A. Andrew* (N.Y., 1868), 84 *et seq.*, *Works of Charles Sumner* (Boston, 1874–1883), VI, 146. See also Bruce Catton, *Mr. Lincoln's Army* (N.Y., 1954), 72 *et seq.*

9. *Massachusetts in the Army and Navy During the War of 1861–65* (Higginson, ed., Boston, 1896), 39. Cf., *id.*, 135.

10. Executive Department Letters [State Archives], XLVI, #158. Cf. *id.* XXIII, #56.

11. Bruce, *The Twentieth Regiment of Massachusetts Volunteer Infantry, 1861–1865.*

12. The *Boston Post,* for Dec. 24, 1889, published a resolution from the surviving members of the Twentieth Regiment to Colonel Palfrey's widow which was written by Holmes. The resolution included the following passage: "At last the shot which struck him upon the field of Antietam has done its work and he suffers no more. His name is added to the glorious list of those whom he loved and who loved him—Revere, Bartlett, Abbott, Lowell, Ropes, Putnam and so many more—who like him and no more than he fell in battle, although the end was less delayed."

13. Boston *Evening Transcript,* Sept. 20, 1910, p. 10, col. 6.

14. A.l. to Felix Frankfurter, Nov. 2, 1916 (HLS), quoted *supra,* p. 77. See also Carolyn Kellogg Cushing, "The Gallant Captain and the Little Girl," *Atlantic Monthly,* CLV, 545 (May, 1935). It would seem that Mrs. Cushing's recollections misled her when she brought Holmes to Pittsfield in the late summer of 1861.

15. Bruce, *Twentieth Regiment,* 6.

16. *Id.,* 7–9.

17. "A Short History of the Service of Daniel McAdams in Company I 20 Regiment Mass. Vol. 30 Years after the War Wrote from Memory" (Loyal Legion Papers, HUh).

18. "Journal of Brevet Brigadier General Caspar Crowninshield" (Boston Public Library, Twentieth Regiment Collection).

19. Norwood P. Hallowell, *Reminiscences Written for my Children at the Request of their Mother* (Privately Printed, 1897), 20–23.

20. Bruce, *Twentieth Regiment,* 12.

21. *Boston Journal,* Sept. 7, 1861.

22. Crowninshield, "Journal." See also TWF, 4.

23. Hallowell, *Reminiscences,* 23.

24. Crowninshield, "Journal."

25. Bruce, *Twentieth Regiment,* 12.

26. A.l., Henry L. Abbott to his mother, Sept. 7, 1861 (HUh).

27. TWF, 4–6.

28. *Id.,* 6–8.

29. Brigadier General Frederick W. Lander was commanding a Brigade in General Charles P. Stone's Corps of Observation.

30. Francis W. Palfrey, *Memoir of William Francis Bartlett* (Boston, 1881), 7–8.

31. C. A. Whittier, "Egotistic Memoirs" (Unpublished MS, Boston Public Library, Twentieth Regiment Collection), 1.

32. Palfrey, *Bartlett,* p. 8.

33. A.l., Edward G. Abbott to his father Josiah G. Abbott, Sept. 17, 1861 (HUh).

34. Crowninshield, "Journal," 36.

35. Andrew E. Ford, *The Story of the Fifteenth Regiment Massachusetts Volunteer Infantry* (Clinton, Mass., 1898), 56.

36. TWF, 8–12.

37. Charles A. Whittier, later to be Holmes's companion on the staff of the Sixth Corps, was 2nd Lieutenant in Holmes's company—Company A.

38. Captain Caspar Crowninshield commanded Company D and Captain Edmund A. Walleston, Company F.

39. On Sept. 10 General Stone had issued the following "order": "The General commanding, desires to caution all under his command against the unmilitary and treasonable practice, too much followed in some corps of the army, of writing private reports of military movements and operations which may find their way into the newspapers and thence to the enemies of the country." Ford, *Fifteenth Regiment,* 58.

40. See HP, II, 36.

41. Bruce, *Twentieth Regiment,* 18–22.

42. A.l., Colonel Lee to Dr. Holmes, Oct. 9, 1861 (HLS).

43. Bruce, *Twentieth Regiment,* 20.

44. It was so described by Thomas Wentworth Higginson, *Massachusetts in the War,* 34.

45. Crowninshield, "Journal," entry for Oct. 21, 1861.

46. A.l., C. A. Whittier to Dr. Holmes, Oct. 22, 1861 (HLS).

47. Palfrey, *William Francis Bartlett,* 23–25.

48. A.l., Holmes to Sir Alfred Zimmern, Jan. 22, 1918 (copy, HLS).

49. Whittier to Dr. Holmes, *supra,* note 46.

50. A.l., Nov. 24, 1861 (Reports, Letters, and Papers Appertaining to the Twentieth Massachusetts Volunteer Infantry, I (Boston Public Library).

51. TWF, 14–17. The reading of the original letter there suggested has been slightly revised.

52. Colonel Lee, Major Paul Revere, Adjutant Charles L. Peirson, and Lieutenant George B. Perry were all captured. Captain Babo and Lieutenant Wesselhoeft, of the German companies, were shot or drowned while attempting to swim from the Virginia shore to Harrison's Island.

53. The memorandum has not been preserved.

54. *Supra,* note 46.

55. A.l., Oct. 25, 1861 (HLS).

56. A.l., Oct. 26, 1861 (HLS). The portrait was presumably of Holmes's friend Miss Ida Agassiz, later Mrs. Henry Lee Higginson.

57. *Harper's Weekly,* V, 706 (Nov. 9, 1861).

58. A telegram from Anna Hallowell to Dr. Holmes, dated Nov. 1, announced that "Wendell arrived here last evening and is doing very well." (Original, HLS.)

59. A.l., Nov. 3, 1861 (HLS).

60. A.l., Nov. 8, 1861 (HLS).

61. Writing to Motley on Nov. 29, Dr. Holmes said that "a fortnight ago yesterday I brought him [Wendell] to Boston on a bed in the cars." Morse, *Life and Letters,* II, 157, 158. Dr. Holmes evidently made an inaccurate count of time in dating his son's return, for Holmes arrived in Boston on Nov. 9.

62. CLP, 300.

63. *Id.* Cf, his statement to Harold Laski: "I care a damn sight more for

ideas than for facts." HL, I, 128. Writing to Baroness Moncheur he said that he contrasted the internal and external men by calling them "ideasts and thingsters." A.l., April 4, 1919 (HLS).

64. The diary which Holmes kept in 1864 when he was a Staff Officer with the Sixth Corps is principally concerned with external events. The loose sheets enclosed in that small notebook, and in which the account of Ball's Bluff is contained, were evidently torn from another memorandum book which has not survived. References in the account itself indicate that it was written either toward the very close of Holmes's military service or a short time after the Civil War.

65. TWF, 23–33.

66. "Wilder Dwight," *Harvard Memorial Biographies* (Cambridge, 1867), I, 252, 268, 271.

67. The list purports to include visitors during November only.

68. See Dr. Holmes's letter to Dr. Hunt, Nov. 12, 1861: Howe, *Holmes of the Breakfast Table,* 105–106.

69. *Works of Charles Sumner,* VI, 130.

70. HL, I, 164.

71. *Works of Charles Sumner,* VI, 145.

72. Morse, *Life and Letters,* II, 157, 158.

73. *Id.*

74. M. A. DeW. Howe, *Memories of a Hostess* (Boston, 1922), 21.

75. On Feb. 3, 1862, Dr. Holmes wrote to Motley that "my boy is here—still detailed on recruiting duty—quite well." Morse, *supra,* note 72, 159, 163. See also, Bruce, *Twentieth Regiment,* 71–72. That Holmes was recruiting in Pittsfield is indicated in Morse as well as in Carolyn Kellogg Cushing, "The Gallant Captain and the Little Girl," *Atlantic Monthly,* CLV, 545 (May 1935).

76. A.l. to Baroness Moncheur, Jan. 23, 1918 (HLS).

77. HP, I, 258.

78. *Supra,* p. 89.

79. TWF, 37, 38.

80. *Id.*

81. Letter of Feb. 16, 1862, to John C. Ropes (Twentieth Regiment Collection, Boston Public Library). Lieutenant Ropes was killed at Gettysburg. His view of Lowell's military prowess was not shared by others: see *Harvard Memorial Biographies,* I, 395.

82. Letter to Baroness Moncheur, Jan. 9, 1915 (HLS).

83. Letter of Nov. 22, 1862, to John C. Ropes (Boston Public Library).

84. A.l. to his father, Josiah G. Abbott, May 19, 1862 (HUh).

85. *Id.,* Sept. 18, 1863.

86. TWF, 38.

87. *Id.,* 44, 45.

88. *Id.,* 42.

89. *Id.*

90. Letter to parents, April 23, 1862; *id.,* 45–46. Holmes's commission as

Captain did not reach him until May 4, according to a penciled note of that date in his Civil War Scrap-Book, #1, 1.

91. A.l. to Josiah G. Abbott, March 17, 1862 (HUh).

92. *Id.,* Sept. 18, 1863.

93. The loss of a leg did not prevent Bartlett's return to duty later in the War as Colonel of the Forty-Ninth Regiment.

94. William Swinton, *Campaigns of the Army of the Potomac* (N.Y., 1866), 140.

95. *Id.,* 137.

96. TWF, 49–50. Another account of Fair Oaks and the engagements which followed it is an A.l. from Holmes to Miss Eugenia Mifflin, dated June 7, 1862 (HLS).

97. *Id.,* 50.

98. *Id.,* 51.

99. *Id.,* 53.

100. *Id.,* 52.

101. *Id.*

102. *Id.,* 52–54.

103. HL, I, 781.

104. TWF, 56.

105. Lieutenant James Jackson Lowell, nephew of James Russell Lowell, after the battle died in the hands of the Confederates; see Child, *supra,* note 2.

106. Lieutenant Henry Lyman Patten later became Major of the Regiment and died of wounds received on Sept. 13, 1864, at Bailey's Creek; see George E. Pond, "Henry Lyman Patten," *Harvard Memorial Biographies* (Cambridge, 1867), I, 415.

107. Lieutenant August Muller of Company E was wounded and taken prisoner.

108. TWF, 58.

109. Miss Ellen Hooper later became the wife of Professor Ephraim W. Gurney.

110. A.l. to John C. Ropes (Twentieth Regiment Collection, Boston Public Library).

111. Channing, *History of the United States* (N.Y., 1925), VI, 472.

112. TWF, 62.

113. "My Hunt after 'The Captain,'" *Works,* VIII, 16. A notation on the original telegram (at HLS) indicates that it was received in the Boston office of the American Telegraph Company at 11:45 P.M., on Sept. 17.

114. HP, II, 270.

115. The MS copy of the speech, which was delivered on Dec. 11, 1897, is among Holmes's papers at the HLS.

116. HP, II, 270. See *supra,* note 57.

117. TWF, 64.

118. Hallowell, *supra,* note 19, 16–18.

119. Original at HLS.

120. Alice Sumner LeDuc, "The Man who Rescued 'The Captain,'" *Atlantic Monthly,* CLXXX, 80 (Aug. 1947). See also TWF, footnote, 65–66.

121. For LeDuc's later account of Mrs. Kitzmuller, see TWF, footnote, 65–66.

122. Anna Howard Kennedy Findlay, "Where the Captain Was Found," *Maryland Historical Magazine,* XXXIII, 109 (June 1938).

123. TWF, 67.

124. *Works,* VIII, 67.

125. *Id.,* 70.

126. *Id.,* 77.

127. TWF, 57, note 1.

4. *Civil War: The Later Years*

1. Henry Greenleaf Pearson, *The Life of John A. Andrew* (Boston, 1904), II, 55.

2. James Schouler, *History of Massachusetts in the Civil War* (Boston, 1868), I, 374.

3. Scrap-Book, #1 (HUh).

4. TWF, 63.

5. *Id.,* 80.

6. A.l. to Clara Sherwood Stevens, March 6, 1909 (HLS).

7. Letter to Albert J. Beveridge, Nov. 17, 1926 (copy, HLS).

8. TWF, 73.

9. *Id.,* 79–80.

10. A letter from Dr. Holmes to an unidentified correspondent, dated Nov. 13, 1862, said that his son was compelled by a recent order to hurry back to his Regiment on the preceding day (A.l., Boston Public Library).

11. TWF, 70.

12. Id., 71. The quoted passage suggests the *mot* of Dr. Holmes in the *Professor:* "I go politically for *e*quality and socially for *the* quality." *Works,* II, 133.

13. TWF, 72.

14. Holmes evidently had been suffering from dysentery since early in December; see Morse, *Life and Letters,* II, 172.

15. TWF, 74–78.

16. Francis A. Walker, *History of the Second Army Corps* (N.Y., 1886), 145.

17. TWF, 90. Cf. Holmes's "Memorial Day," *Speeches,* 1, 8.

18. *War of the Rebellion,* Series I, XXI, 283.

19. A.l., Henry L. Abbott to Josiah G. Abbott, July 27, 1863 (HUh).

20. A.l., Henry L. Abbott to an unidentified correspondent, Aug. 17, 1863 (HUh).

21. "The Inevitable Trial," *Works,* VIII, 78, 109.

22. "The Soldier's Faith," *Speeches,* 56, 59.

23. A.l., Henry L. Abbott to George Perry, Dec. 17, 1862 (HUh). In a

letter to his father dated Dec. 21, Abbott said that Holmes "still has dysentery badly." (*Id.*)

24. A copy of the address is in Reports, Letters and Papers Appertaining to the 20th Massachusetts Volunteer Infantry, II, 50 (Boston Public Library). Holmes is identified as the author in an A.l. of Henry L. Abbott to George Perry of Dec. 21, 1862 (HUh), and in a letter from Henry Ropes to his mother, Jan. 12, 1863 (Boston Public Library).

25. Writing to his daughter on Jan. 8, 1863, Emerson described events of the last few days: "I found Dr. and Mrs. Holmes in the cars at Boston (bound for Philadelphia to find the Captain again who is sick there). . . ." *Letters of Ralph Waldo Emerson* (Rusk, ed., N.Y., 1939), V, 305. A letter to Holmes from Captain Whittier, dated Jan. 3, 1863, was addressed to him in Philadelphia (Civil War Scrap-Book, #1, HLS).

26. Holmes's Civil War Scrap-Book, #1 (HLS) contains a communication, dated Jan. 3, 1863, endorsed by George H. Boker, giving Holmes temporary privileges in a Philadelphia club. "The Crossing at Fredericksburg" is in George H. Boker, *Poems of the War* (Boston, 1864), 82.

27. A.l. to John C. Ropes, Jan. 17, 1863 (Boston Public Library).

28. A.l. to Josiah G. Abbott, Jan. 19, 1863 (HUh).

29. A.l. to John C. Ropes, Jan. 21, 1863 (Boston Public Library).

30. A.l. to Baroness Moncheur, Oct. 23, 1916 (HLS).

31. A.l. to John C. Ropes, April 17, 1863 (Boston Public Library).

32. *Id.,* April 25, 1863.

33. TWF, 85, 86.

34. The sketches referred to are reproduced in *id.,* 87–89.

35. Later Hallowell was made Colonel of another colored Regiment, the Fifty-fifth, and his brother, Edward, who had first been Major in Colonel Shaw's Regiment, was promoted to Lieutenant Colonel of the Fifty-fourth.

36. A.l. in Holmes's Civil War Scrap-Book, #1 (HLS).

37. The majority was filled by Edward N. Hallowell of the Twentieth, brother of N. P. Hallowell.

38. Luis F. Emilio, *History of the Fifty-Fourth Regiment, Massachusetts Volunteer Infantry* (2nd ed., Boston, 1894), 3.

39. A.l. to John C. Ropes, April 25, 1863 (Boston Public Library).

40. TWF, 92, 93.

41. Sumner Paine was the son of Mrs. Holmes's sister. When Holmes was wounded he took command of his cousin's company. Paine was killed at Gettysburg. See Mrs. Fanny C. Paine, "Summer Paine," *Harvard Memorial Biographies,* II, 453.

42. A.l. to Holmes, May 15, 1863 (Civil War Scrap-Book, #1, HLS).

43. Conversation with the author, Jan. 30, 1934.

44. J. T. Morse, Jr., *Life and Letters of Oliver Wendell Holmes,* II, 24–25.

45. A.l. to Baroness Moncheur, May 7, 1907 (HLS).

46. A.l. to Clara Sherwood Stevens, April 28, 1907 (HLS).

47. HP, I, 58. Cf. HL, I, 21–22.

48. A.l. in Holmes's Civil War Scrap-Book, #1 (HLS).

49. Henry M. Rogers, "Henry Ropes," *Harvard Memorial Biographies,* II, 304, 311.

50. A.l. in Holmes's Civil War Scrap-Book, #1 (HLS).

51. Abbott, writing to his mother on May 17, 1863, said that "Holmes spoke to me openly about the question whether he should waive his claim to promotion for me, and I advised him not to do it by any means." (A.l. HUh.)

52. Writing to his father on Aug. 7, 1863, Abbott said: "I should a thousand times rather see [Holmes] in the place his rank entitles him to have than to have him offer it me, for of course I should only return it to him." (A.l. HUh.) See also A.l. Henry L. Abbott to Governor Andrew, Aug. 6, 1863, Executive Department Letters, XXIII, #106. (State House Archives.)

53. A.l. to Lieutenant Colonel Ritchie (undated), *id.,* #104: "I see that my name is on the roster of the 20th as Lt. Col. I only write to say (to prevent any misapprehension) that I have decided to take the promotion and have given up the idea I mentioned to you the other evening of waiving my seniority in favor of Abbott."

54. A.l., Henry L. Abbott to Holmes, Sept. 22, 1863 (HUh).

55. A.l. to Holmes, Oct. 8, 1863 (HUh).

56. In August Edward Hallowell asked Holmes if he would suggest someone in Boston who might fill a field officer's post in the Fifty-fourth. A.l. E. N. Hallowell to Holmes, Aug. 12, 1863 (Civil War Scrap-Book, #1, HLS).

57. A.l., Charles A. Whittier to Holmes, Aug. 10, 1863 (Civil War Scrap-Book, #1 (HLS).

58. *Id.,* see also, A.l., Whittier to Holmes, July 10, 1863 (Civil War Scrap-Book, #1, HLS).

59. A.l., Dr. Holmes to Charles Sumner, Jan. 4, 1864; Sumner Papers, LXVII, #4 (HUh).

60. Holmes's Civil War Scrap-Book, #2 (HUh).

61. A.l. of March 27, 1864 (HUh).

62. Thomas W. Hyde, *Following the Greek Cross, or Memories of the Sixth Army Corps* (Boston, 1894), 138–139.

63. See Randall and Current, *Lincoln the President: Last Full Measure* (N.Y., 1955), 144.

64. TWF, 106–108, 109–110.

65. "Memorial Day," *Speeches,* 1, 7–8.

66. Boston *Evening Transcript,* Oct. 17, 1864, p. 2, col. 2.

67. TWF, 117.

68. *Id.,* 133–134. The same incident was described in a letter written to his parents on May 30, 1864; *id.,* 136–137.

69. *Id.,* 141, 142.

70. John Henry Cramer, *Lincoln Under Fire* (Baton Rouge, 1948), 13.

71. *Lincoln and the Civil War: In the Diaries and Letters of John Hay* (Dennett, ed., N.Y., 1939), 208.

72. *Diaries of John Hay,* 208.

73. See Cramer, *Lincoln Under Fire,* 63–64.

74. This detail is found in the letter of an eyewitness, Daniel T. Bull; see Cramer, *id.,* 27.

75. George Thomas Stevens, *Three Years in the Sixth Corps* (N.Y., 1870), 382, footnote.

76. Harold Laski's imaginative reporting of Holmes's description of the affair is found in *The Listener* for March 13, 1941, 359. Alexander Woollcott's sentimental embroidery of Laski's imagination is in his essay "Get Down You Fool," in *Long, Long Ago* (N.Y., 1943), 3.

77. The fullest consideration of the evidence of the encounter of Holmes and Lincoln is in Cramer, *Lincoln Under Fire.* See also, Hicks, "Lincoln, Wright and Holmes," *Journal of Illinois Historical Society* (Sept. 1946), 323.

78. This was Felix Frankfurter's description of the incident as he heard it from Holmes. It is quoted in Cramer, *Lincoln Under Fire,* 116, 117.

79. *North American Review,* XCVIII, 419 (April 1864).

80. TWF, 122, footnote 1.

81. *Id.,* 122.

82. *Id.,* 135.

83. *Id.*

84. *Id.,* 141, 142–143.

85. Letter from Holmes to Agnes Pomeroy, dated June 21, 1864, quoted TWF, 143, footnote 2.

86. *Id.*

87. *Id.,* 151.

88. A.l. to Felix Frankfurter, March 5, 1917 (HLS). Arthur D. Hall reported to the author that Holmes in conversation had expressed the same doubt about his decision of 1864.

89. The original is in Holmes's Civil War Scrap-Book, #1 (HUh).

90. The verses appear in the First Triennial Report of the Class of '61 and are reprinted in Lerner, *Justice Holmes,* 8.

5. *Harvard Law School*

1. Max Lerner, *The Mind and Faith of Justice Holmes* (Boston, 1943), 6, 8.

2. *Macmillan's Magazine,* XIII, 195, 200 (Jan. 1866).

3. Felix Frankfurter's memorandum of conversation between himself, Judge Hitz, and Holmes on Sept. 28, 1932 (copy, HLS).

4. A.l. to Mrs. John C. Gray, April 30, 1905 (HLS). See also his statements in 1919 that he was "shoved into the law"; HL, I, 205.

5. Thomas Wentworth Higginson, "John Holmes," *Contemporaries* (Boston, 1900), 168. See also *Letters of John Holmes to James Russell Lowell and Others* (Thayer, ed., Boston, 1917).

6. *Law Reporter,* XVIII, 607 (1856).

7. *American Jurist,* II, 77 (July 1829).

8. *Id.,* 78, 79.

9. *Report of the Commission to Revise the General Statutes of the Commonwealth* (Boston, 1834), Part III, 154.

10. The label was a favorite of Nathaniel Ames's, brother of the redoubt-

able Federalist ally of Jonathan Jackson, Fisher Ames. Charles Warren, *The Essex Junto* (Cambridge, 1931), 7.

11. The defense of the Federalists, signed by Jackson and twelve others, is in Henry Adams, *Documents Relating to New England Federalism* (Boston, 1877), 43–45.

12. Opinion of the Justices, 8 Mass. 548 (1812).

13. Theophilus Parsons, *Memoir of Theophilus Parsons* (Boston, 1859), 228.

14. Edward Stanley Roscoe, *Lord Stowell* (London, 1916), 51.

15. *Ryan v. Baldrick,* 3 McCord 498, 500 (1826).

16. Perhaps the clearest formulation of those principles by an American judge was that of Kent; see, e.g., James Kent, *Commentaries on American Law* (Holmes, ed., Boston, 1873), I, *3. The Massachusetts conception that it was the state's responsibility to enforce rules of morality through the churches rather than through the law was emphasized by Chief Justice Parsons; see Parsons, *Memoir,* 201–203.

17. John Chipman Gray, *The Nature and Sources of the Law* (2nd. ed., N.Y., 1931), 253.

18. Henry James, *Notes of a Son and Brother* (N.Y., 1914), 347.

19. *Id.,* 348.

20. "The Use of Law Schools," *Speeches* (1913), 28, 35.

21. George W. Smalley, *Anglo-American Memories* (London, 1911), 23.

22. His views on constitutional questions arising in the Civil War were expressed in a series of pamphlets; e.g., "The Right of Secession" (Cambridge, 1862); "The War Powers of Congress, and of the President" (Cambridge, 1863). See, *supra,* p. 135.

23. "Constitutional Law and Unconstitutional Divinity," Letters to Rev. Henry M. Dexter and to Rev. Leonard Bacon, D.D. (Cambridge, 1863), 6.

24. "Revolution and Reconstruction," a lecture delivered at the Law School of Harvard College, Jan. 1865.

25. See *The Centennial History of the Harvard Law School, 1817–1917* (Cambridge, 1918), 251.

26. James, *supra,* note 18, 347, 350.

27. *The Letters of John Fiske* (Fisk, ed., N.Y., 1940), 116.

28. *Centennial History, supra,* note 25, 284.

29. James, *supra,* note 18, 348.

30. "The Use of Law Schools," *supra,* note 20, 28, 35.

31. Reviewing the 2nd edition of Washburn's *Easements and Servitudes* (Boston, 1867), *Am. L. Rev.,* II, 159 (Oct. 1867).

32. HL, I, 363.

33. The original record, in the handwriting of Holmes, is in Moot Court Records (HLS).

34. HL, I, 112.

35. *Speeches,* 82.

36. Eleanor N. Little, "The Early Reading of Justice Oliver Wendell Holmes," *Harvard Library Bulletin,* VIII, 163 (Spring, 1954).

37. "Joel Parker," *Am. L. Rev.,* X, 235, 262 (June 1876).

38. "Why the History of English Law Is Not Written," *Collected Papers,* I, 480, 487.

39. HL, I, 692–693.

40. "Introduction to the General Survey," CLP, 298, 301–302. Writing to George R. Nutter in 1930 Holmes observed that when he had been a law student the resources for "a rational and philosophic education in the law were out of reach or did not exist." A.l., Aug. 21, 1930 (HLS).

41. *Letters, supra,* note 27, 118–119.

42. HP, I, 31.

43. In 1875 Henry Adams told Maine that Holmes "has long been one of your warmest admirers here." Harold Dean Cater, *Henry Adams and His Friends* (Boston, 1947), 64.

44. *Ancient Law* (Dwight, ed., N.Y., 1864), ix–x.

45. A.l., Oct. 31, 1865 (copy, HLS).

46. A.l., April 21, 1865 (in Civil War Scrap-Book, #2, HUh).

47. A.l., May 9, 1865 (copy, HLS).

48. *War Letters, 1862–1865, of John Chipman Gray and John Codman Ropes* (Boston, 1927), 450–451.

49. For a detailed account of the event see Hamilton Vaughan Bail, "Harvard's Commemoration Day, July 21, 1865," *New England Quarterly,* XV, 256 (June 1942).

50. "For the Commemoration Services," *The Complete Poetical Works of Oliver Wendell Holmes* (Boston, 1895), Cambridge edition, 208.

51. Ralph Barton Perry, *The Thought and Character of William James* (Boston, 1935), I, 228.

52. *Id.* On March 27, 1866, James told his friend Thomas W. Ward that "I made the acquaintance the other day of Miss Fanny Dixwell of Cambridge (the eldest), do you know her? She is decidedly A-1, and (so far) the best girl I have known." *The Letters of William James* (H. James, ed., Boston, 1920), I, 76.

53. A.l., OWH to William James, Dec. 15, 1867 (HUh). Other portions of the letter are published in Perry, *William James,* I, 505. On April 19, 1868, Holmes told James that "Fanny Dixwell's eyes have given her but little pain since I last wrote though she has to be careful in their use." (A.l., HUh.) The bulk of the letter is printed in Perry, *id.,* 509.

54. See James's letter of July 23, 1865; Perry, *William James,* I, 221–222.

55. Letter of March 27, 1866, to Thomas W. Ward; *Letters of William James* (James, ed., Boston, 1920), I, 73, 75–76.

56. *Harvard Library Bulletin,* VIII, 171.

57. James, *Notes of a Son and Brother,* 458.

58. The letters from Minny Temple to Gray, excerpts from which were published by James in *Notes of a Son and Brother,* reveal the deep affection between the two.

59. See Leon Edel, *Henry James: The Untried Years* (Philadelphia, 1953), 226 *et seq.* See also "The Letters of Henry James to Mr. Justice Holmes," *Yale Review,* XXXVIII, 410–413. The letters on p. 414 are misdated by the editor as 1865. They should have been dated 1868; see Edel, *id.*

60. A.l., Oct. 31, 1865 (copy, HLS).

61. A.l., April 16, 1876, transmitting his "Primitive Notions in Modern Law" (HUh).

62. Entry on page for Sept. 27, 1866 (HLS).

63. Above this succinct entry is a more detailed summary of the nature of his legal studies during the winter in question. The summary was as follows:

"Cases argued or elucidated in Law Sch. besides others looked up in R. Morse's office—

1. Quantum Meruit (See Cutter v. Powell, 2 Sm. L.C.)
2. On Mass. Stat. of Divorce for fault of party
3. Fraudulent concealment of cause of action—Stat. of limitations—Subs. confession of tort.
4. Interpretation of wills. S.C. 9 Allen 109.
5. Rule of interest on overdue note.
6. Contr. in Restraint of Trade. See Mitchell v. Reynolds, Sm. L.C.
7. Discharge of surety. (Read cases & note in 2 Am. Lead. Cas.)
8. Notice of Diss^n of Partnership.
9. What excuses and what is condition.
10. Right of support from neighboring land & nuisance (Moot Court) Read parts of Washburn & G. & W. on Easements & nearly all the cases.
11. Does participation in profits make partnership?"

64. Dr. Holmes to Motley; Morse, *Life and Letters of Oliver Wendell Holmes*, II, 173, 177.

65. In 1871, reviewing Bryce's *The Academical Study of the Civil Law* (N.Y., 1871), Holmes said that "The common law begins and ends with the solution of a particular case. To effect that result we believe the best training is found in our moot courts and the offices of older lawyers." *Am. L. Rev.*, V, 715, 716 (July 1871).

66. *Am. L. Rev.*, V, 177.

67. Joel Parker, *The Law School of Harvard College* (N.Y., 1871).

68. *Id.*, 5.

69. *Am. L. Rev.*, V, 177.

6. *Contours of Conviction*

1. George Henry Lewes, *Aristotle: A Chapter from the History of Science* (London, 1864), 29.

2. Letter of Holmes to Morris Cohen, Feb. 5, 1919; "The Holmes-Cohen Correspondence," Felix S. Cohen, ed., *Journal of the History of Ideas*, IX, 3, 14, quoted more fully, *supra*, pp. 17–18.

3. "The Path of the Law," CLP, 167, 180. Cf. *id.* at 305.

4. *University Quarterly*, II, 215; quoted *supra*, p. 55.

5. See, *supra*, pp. 53, 156.

6. George Henry Lewes, *Biographical History of Philosophy* (Library ed., N.Y., 1859), xxxi.

7. Herbert Spencer, *First Principles* (London, 1862), 108.

8. *Id.,* 76.
9. "Ideals and Doubts," CLP, 303, 304.
10. "Natural Law," *id.,* 310, 315.
11. *Id.,* 314–315.
12. John Stuart Mill, *The Positive Philosophy of Auguste Comte* (Boston, 1866), 64–65.
13. *Id.,* 67.
14. HP, II, 212.
15. Leslie Stephen, *The Life of Sir James Fitzjames Stephen* (London, 1895), 336.
16. HP, I, 105.
17. HL, II, 862.
18. *Religion and Science* (London, 1935), 250; quoted by Baumgardt, *Bentham and the Ethics of Today* (Princeton, 1952), 137.
19. John Stuart Mill, *Dissertations and Discussions,* III, 132, 136.
20. *The Common Law,* 110.
21. See Melville M. Bigelow, *A False Equation* (Boston, 1911), 77–79.
22. *New York Trust Co.* v. *Eisner,* 256 U.S. 345, 349 (1921).
23. Frederic W. Farrar, *An Essay on the Origin of Language* (London, 1860).
24. See James Fitzjames Stephen, *Essays by a Barrister* (1862), 23.
25. See Richmond Laurin Hawkins, *Positivism in the United States* (Cambridge, 1938), 29–30.
26. *History of the Intellectual Development of Europe* (N.Y., 1863).
27. Henry Thomas Buckle, *History of Civilization in England* (2nd ed., N.Y., 1858), 1, 13.
28. See his review of Buckle, *North American Review,* XCIII, 519 (Oct. 1861).
29. John Stuart Mill, *A System of Logic* (9th ed., London, 1875), I, 400.
30. *Id.,* II, 422.
31. *Id.,* 426–427.
32. CLP, 305.
33. See Hawkins, *Positivism in the United States,* 171.
34. *Autobiography of John Stuart Mill* (Coss, ed., N.Y., 1924), 191–192.
35. Alexander Bain, *The Emotions and the Will* (London, 1859), 254 *et seq.*
36. Buckle, *History of Civilization,* I, 198.
37. *Id.,* II, 200.
38. *Id.,* 201.
39. *On Liberty* (McCallum, ed., Oxford, 1946), 11.
40. *Social Statics* (N.Y., 1872), 94.
41. See Hearnshaw, *The Social and Political Ideas of Some Representative Thinkers of the Victorian Age* (London, 1933), 53.
42. *The Sphere and Duties of Government* (Coulthard tr., London, 1854), 42.
43. Entry for Oct. 12, 1866 (HLS).
44. HL, I, 658.

45. *Id.*, 122.
46. "Ideals and Doubts," CLP, 303, 306.
47. *Principles of Political Economy* (5th ed., 1864, N.Y.), I, 438.
48. Thomas Barbour, *Naturalist at Large* (Boston, 1953), 150–151.

7. Europe

1. *Letters of Henry Adams (1858–1891)* (Ford, ed., Boston, 1930), 97.
2. *Correspondence of John Lothrop Motley* (Curtis, ed., N.Y., 1889), II, 255.
3. *Education of Henry Adams* (Modern Library ed.), 200.
4. A.l., May 26, 1866 (HLS).
5. HL, II, 1207–1208.
6. Maitland, *Life and Letters of Leslie Stephen* (London, 1906), 116.
7. "Christian Optimism" in *Essays by a Barrister* (London, 1862), 114, 120–121.
8. See Charles L. Graves, *Life and Letters of Alexander MacMillan* (London, 1910), 177.
9. See, *supra*, p. 24.
10. A.l., Oct. 30, 1924 (HLS).
11. A.l., Jan. 27, 1928 (HLS).
12. James T. Fields, *Barry Cornwall and Some of His Friends* (Boston, 1876), 118.
13. Charles Francis Adams, *Charles Francis Adams* (Boston, 1900), 368–370.
14. HL, II, 918. Holmes was not the only person to notice a similarity in the voices of Emerson and Gladstone; see *The Amberley Papers* (Russell, ed., London, 1937), II, 65, 67.
15. Adams, *supra*, note 13, at 369.
16. The entry for Nov. 4, 1866 recorded Holmes's impression of the book: "Wonderfully good military tale—a little too much bayonet but generally exceedingly truthful."
17. A.l., Hughes to Holmes, Dec. 31, 1866 (HLS).
18. *Id.*, Feb. 26, 1868 (HLS).
19. HP, I, 75.
20. A.l., May 26, 1866 (HLS).
21. HL, I, 410.
22. HP, I, 74.
23. Writing to a friend in 1930 Holmes described the occasion with a little more detail. "I was but a law student, to be sure, and saw the bigwigs of the bar ask who the —— is that? and drop their monocles with a smile, but I sat there, interested and unintelligent." Letter to George R. Nutter, Aug. 30, 1930 (copy, HLS).
24. In *Brinsmead* v. *Harrison*, 7 C.P. 547, 554 (1872).
25. CLP, 160, 163. See HP, I, 65–66.
26. A.l. (HLS).
27. The original is among the Stephen letters at HLS.

28. Dr. Holmes describes the spot in the Autocrat, *Works,* I, 280.
29. A.l., June 2, 1866 (HLS).
30. Holmes writing to Morris Cohen, Feb. 5, 1919; "The Holmes-Cohen Correspondence," *Journal of the History of Ideas,* IX, 3, 15 (Jan. 1948).
31. *Modern Painters,* IV, 118 (*Works of John Ruskin,* Library Ed., London, 1904, Vol. VI).
32. *Id.,* at 208.
33. *Sesame and Lilies, Works,* XVIII, 89–90.
34. A.l. to Baroness Moncheur, Sept. 5, 1915 (HLS).
35. *Id.,* Jan. 9, 1915 (HLS).
36. HL, I, 541.
37. A.l., Thomas Hughes to Holmes, Dec. 31, 1866 (HLS).
38. Frederic W. Maitland, *The Life and Letters of Leslie Stephen* (London, 1906), 144.
39. Noel Gilroy Annan, *Leslie Stephen* (Cambridge, 1952), chap. v.
40. The essay, first published in *Fraser's Magazine,* was reprinted with additions in Stephen's *Essays on Freethinking and Plainspeaking* (London, 1873), 1.
41. A.l., Stephen to Holmes, July 4, 1870 (HLS). The letter is published in part in Maitland, *Leslie Stephen,* 217–218.
42. The story of his visit to the United States is told in his *On Sherman's Track* (London, 1867).
43. Holmes's close friend Thomas Barbour has said of Holmes that "he was extraordinarily sentimental. I have seen him break down and cry so that he would have to discontinue reading some of the poems about the war. . . ." *Naturalist at Large* (Boston, 1943), 153.
44. See, e.g., his letter to Pollock of Sept. 23, 1902: HP, I, 106.

8. *Apprenticeship*

1. Holmes's diary indicates that on Tuesday, Oct. 11, he had returned to Mr. Morse's office "till Chandler & Shattuck should have a place." A week later, on the 18th, he "began with Chandler, Shattuck & Thayer."
2. C. T. Russell in *Meeting of the Suffolk Bar Held at Boston, June 7, 1889, in Memory of Peleg Whitman Chapman* (Boston, 1889), 14.
3. *The Law Reporter,* I, iv (1839).
4. Perry, *Thought and Character of William James,* I, 520.
5. Originally published as a pamphlet it was reprinted in *Harv. L. Rev.,* VII, 129 (Oct. 1893) and in J. B. Thayer's *Legal Essays* (Boston, 1908), I.
6. See, e.g., his dissenting opinion in *Commonwealth* v. *Perry,* 155 Mass. 117, 123 (1891).
7. A.l., Holmes to Thayer, Nov. 2, 1893 (HLS).
8. *The Spirit of Liberty* (N.Y., 1952), 190.
9. Thayer, *Legal Essays,* at 39.
10. A.l., George Otis Shattuck to J. B. Thayer, Nov. 21, 1893 (HLS).
11. *Speeches,* 70.
12. HL, II, 930.

13. *Id.*, I, 373.
14. HP, I, 167.
15. Holmes in *Proc. Mass. Hist. Soc.*, 2nd Ser., XIV, 361, 368 (1900).
16. *Id.*, 367.
17. *Id.*
18. *Speeches*, 73.
19. *Id.*
20. The unpublished Peirce lectures were entitled "The Logic of Science and Induction"; see Wiener, *Evolution and the Founders of Pragmatism* (Cambridge, 1949), 75.
21. Holmes's tribute to Gray is in *Proc. Mass. Hist. Soc.*, 2nd Ser., XLVIII, 323 (1915).
22. *Notes of a Son and Brother*, chaps. 12 and 13. See Leon Edel, *Henry James: The Untried Years* (Philadelphia, 1953), 231–233, 316–319.
23. William James to Thomas Ward, Dec. 16, 1868; Perry, *William James*, I, 289, 290.
24. *Id.*
25. When Gray was in his last illness Holmes wrote to him as his "dear and oldest friend." (A.l., Feb. 21, 1915, HLS.) Correspondence between the two men was relatively infrequent, but a large collection of letters which Holmes wrote to Mrs. Gray from the early eighties until her death, in 1932, survives not only to reveal his friendship with her but to indicate the intimacy between Holmes and J. C. Gray. The letters are in the custody of the Harvard Law School.
26. HL, I, 693.
27. "I almost wish I could attain John Gray's and H. James's lofty position of no longer reading to improve my mind—but I am a miser as to time and clothes." Holmes to Laski, Oct. 28, 1918; HL, I, 167. Cf. his statement to Sir Frederick Pollock: "I hate to give up the chance to read this and that, that a gentleman should have read before he dies. I don't remember that I ever read Machiavelli's *Prince*—and I think of the Day of Judgement." HP, II, 14. Concerning Gray's light-hearted love of learning, see *Ropes-Gray: 1865–1940* (Privately Printed, Boston, 1942), 148.
28. A.l. to Mrs. John C. Gray, Aug. 7, 1895 (HLS). The book which Holmes was reading at the time was Pollock and Maitland, *History of English Law* (Cambridge, 1895).
29. A.l. to Lady Scott, Jan. 10, 1909 (HLS).
30. A.l. to Mrs. John C. Gray, July 28, 1915 (HLS).
31. *Proc. Mass. Hist. Soc.*, 3rd Ser., XLVIII, 323, 324.
32. A.l., Amelia Jackson Holmes to OWH, July 3, 1866 (HLS).
33. Perry, *William James*, I, 228. See, *supra*, p. 199.
34. A.l., Amelia Jackson Holmes to OWH, July 16, 1866 (HLS).
35. The girl referred to was presumably Miss Clemence Haggerty of New York who in 1867 married James Mason Crafts, the future President of the Massachusetts Institute of Technology.
36. Entry of Oct. 18, 1866. An entry for Feb. 19, 1867, is similarly tantalizing: "Walked with Billy Perk. Saw   ."

37. Remarks before Chicago Bar Association, Oct. 21, 1902; *Chicago Legal News,* XXXV, 83 (Oct. 25, 1902).

38. Quoted by Arthur D. Hill in conversation with the author.

39. A.l. to Clara Sherwood Stevens, July 19, 1902 (HLS).

40. "The year 1867 saw James in Berlin struggling with the decision as to whether to make a physiologist or a philosopher of himself. He finally chose physiology—because he preferred philosophy." Stow Persons in "The Influence of Evolutionary Theory upon American Psychological Thought" in *Evolutionary Thought in America* (New Haven, 1950), 270–271. A similarly paradoxical explanation of Holmes's commitment to law might well be justified.

41. Perry, *William James,* I, 230.

42. Letter to William James, April 19, 1868; *id.,* 509.

43. *Id.,* 510.

44. *Id.,* 522.

45. Chauncey Wright to F. E. Abbot, Aug. 13, 1867; *Letters of Chauncey Wright* (J. B. Thayer, ed., Cambridge, 1878), 108.

46. In a number of letters Holmes gave Chauncey Wright credit for having taught him "that you couldn't affirm necessity of the Universe." HL, I, 565. See also *id.,* 634. Writing to Felix Frankfurter on July 29, 1927, Holmes described his impressions of Spinoza's *Ethics:* "His theological machinery and arguments, of course, leave me unmoved and even bored, but behind that is a conception of the Universe that I share, except that I dare not assume that our logic is binding on the Cosmos—even if it wears a beard, and [I remember] that Chauncey Wright taught me half of a century or more ago that I could not predicate necessity of it." (A.l., HLS.) See also Holmes's letter of Sept. 26, 1929 to Prof. Max Otto; *Journal of Philosophy,* XXXVIII, 389 (July 1941).

47. 98 Mass. 274 (1867).

48. The author of the anonymous article, "Notes on Precatory Trusts in Wills" in *Am. L. Rev.,* IV, 617 (July 1870), is identified as J. B. Thayer in John C. Gray's copy of the *Review* at the Harvard Law School.

49. A.l. to Ralph Waldo Emerson, April 6, 1876 (HUh).

50. The mission was twice performed—on Dec. 8 and Dec. 11. By this attachment the action of *Richardson* v. *New York Central RR.,* 98 Mass. 85 (1867), was begun. For Holmes's later concern with the case see *infra* pp. 275–276.

51. "The Profession of the Law," *Speeches,* 22, 23.

52. Diary entry of Nov. 24, 1866.

53. Preliminary matters were argued in the U. S. District Court by Shattuck for the respondents on Jan. 1, 1867. In 1871 the decision for the respondents was affirmed in the Circuit Court; *Richardson* v. *Winsor,* Fed. Cas. #11795 (1871).

54. On Oct. 19, 1866, Holmes wrote in his diary that "Shattuck gave me an important brief" on this subject and "told me to think it over and make suggestions—did so." The case was *Cutting* v. *Grand Trunk Railway Co.,* 13 Allen 381 (1866).

55. *Williston* v. *Michigan Southern & Northern Indiana Rd. Co.,* 13 Allen 400 (1866).

56. Diary entries of Nov. 2 and 7, 1866.
57. Nov. 13, 1866.
58. Oct. 27 and Nov. 30, 1866.
59. Dec. 12 and 13, 1866. The case was probably *Commonwealth* v. *Snell* and ended somewhat dramatically when the District Attorney requested the jury to return a verdict for the defendant. See Boston *Daily Advertiser,* Dec. 14, 1866.
60. Dec. 20, 1866. For Holmes's recollections of Bartlett, see *Speeches,* 41.
61. The MS is at the HLS.
62. Marcus Morton (1819–1891) was advanced to the Supreme Judicial Court in 1869 and was Chief Justice of that Court when Holmes became Associate Justice in 1882. He resigned in 1890.
63. Arthur G. Sedgwick (1844–1915) was a talented and thoughtful member of the Cambridge circle; see Perry, *William James,* I, 290. Like Holmes he studied law in the office of Chandler, Shattuck and Thayer. He practiced law in Boston until 1872 when he moved to New York to join, successively, the editorial staffs of the New York *Evening Post* and *The Nation.* He returned to the bar in 1877 and engaged in an active practice in New York City for the rest of his days.
64. *Am. L. Rev.,* I, 371 (Jan. 1867). In John C. Gray's copy of the *Review,* in which he identified anonymous contributors to the first four volumes, and which is now in the Harvard Law School Library, he appears to have added this word of protest to a review which John C. Ropes had written of Tyler's *American Ecclesiastical Law* (1866).
65. See *Am. L. Rev.,* V, 740 (July, 1871).
66. *Id.,* 541 (April 1871).
67. *Am. L. Rev.,* I, 375.
68. *Id.*
69. *Id.,* 376.
70. To the extent that Stephen made the principles of logic a foundation of the law of evidence he built upon the structure which Mill had designed in his *System of Logic.* See the Introduction to Stephen's *Digest of the Law of Evidence* (1st ed., 1876), and comment thereon in the appendix to the twelfth revised edition of 1948.
71. Stephen, *A General View of the Criminal Law of England* (London, 1863), 166.
72. *Id.,* 248, 237.
73. *Id.,* 240.
74. *Id.,* 241. Ralph Barton Perry has pointed out that Fitzjames Stephen was "a favorite author" of William James's; Perry, *William James,* I, 210. Concerning the relationship of Bain's analysis of belief to James's pragmatism, see *id.,* II, 407.
75. *Id.,* 264.
76. See Wiener, *Evolution and the Founders of Pragmatism* (Cambridge, 1949), *passim.* Fisch, "Justice Holmes and the Prediction Theory of Law, and Pragmatism," *Journal of Philosophy,* XXXIX, 85 (1942); "Alexander Bain and the Genealogy of Pragmatism," *Journal of the History of Ideas,* XV,

413 (1954); Frank, "A Conflict with Oblivion: Some Observations on the Founders of Legal Positivism," *Rutgers Law Review*, IX, 425 (1954); Perry, *William James*, II, 407.

77. Professor Fisch in his article on Bain (*supra*, note 76) has conclusively demonstrated that Peirce considered Green, not Bain, the grandfather of pragmatism.

78. Bentham's theory of belief was not, perhaps, very different from that which Bain later formulated. Bentham had said that "in general the giving way to [the propensity to believe in evidence] is right, being found to be attended with consequences advantageous on the whole." *Rationale of Judicial Evidence* (London, 1827), I, 112. Though it is possible that Stephen developed his pragmatic definition of belief on Benthamite principles without Bain's assistance it seems more than probable that when Stephen published his *General View* in 1863 he had become familiar with the doctrines of Bain which had been published four years before. Bain had not considered, as Stephen later did, what was the proper test of truth in matters of belief, stating that the distinction between assurance well-founded and ill-founded "belongs more to the theory of evidence than to the theory of belief." *The Emotions and the Will* (2nd ed., London, 1865), 543. He did, however, assert the basic proposition accepted by Stephen that "belief has no meaning, except in reference to our action; the essence or import of it is such as to place it under the region of the will." *Id.*, 524.

79. *Am. L. Rev.*, I, 377 (Jan. 1867). It is interesting that while Holmes was reading Taylor's volume for purposes of review he noted his supplementary excursions in Bennett and Heard's case-book where he found *Commonwealth* v. *Rogers*, 7 Metcalf 500, and an elaborate note on other decisions relating to insanity. Bennett and Heard, *Leading Criminal Cases* (Boston, 1856), I, 87.

80. See, e.g., "The Path of the Law," CLP, 167, 187: "For the rational study of the law the black-letter man may be the man of the present, but the man of the future is the man of statistics and the master of economics."

81. *Id.*, 188–189: "[T]he inquiries which have been started look toward an answer . . . based on science for the first time."

82. *Am. L. Rev.*, I, 377.

83. *American Banana Company* v. *United Fruit Company*, 213 U.S. 347, 366 (1909). Holmes had suggested his predictive theory of law as early as 1872; see his book notice, *Am. L. Rev.*, VI, 723, 724.

84. *Am. L. Rev.* I, 554, 555 (April 1867).

85. *Id.*, 554.

86. *Riemers* v. *Druce*, 23 Beavan 145 (1856).

87. *Am. L. Rev.*, I, 554.

88. The arrangements for the new edition of Kent were evidently concluded in the later months of 1869. On Dec. 5 of that year William James wrote to his brother, Henry, reporting that "O.W.H. Jr. whom I have not seen for three weeks has accepted the $2000 (but two years of hard work) job of annotating Kent's Commentaries."

89. A.l., Arthur G. Sedgwick to Henry James, Jr., Jan. 30, 1870 (HUh).

90. Perry, *William James,* I, 297.

91. See, *supra,* p. 202.

92. A.l., Mrs. Henry James, senior, to Henry James, Jr., Aug. 8, 1869 (HUh). William James wrote of the same visit a few days later. "Wendell Holmes and John Gray . . . seemed in very jolly spirits at being turned out to pasture from their Boston pen. I should think Wendell worked too hard. Gray is going to Lenox for a fortnight, but W. is to take no vacation." A.l., William James to Henry P. Bowditch, Aug. 12, 1869 (HUh).

93. See, *supra,* pp. 259–260.

94. A.l., Judge E. R. Hoar to Dr. Holmes, Nov. 14, 1867 (HUh).

95. *Richardson* v. *New York Central Railroad,* 98 Mass. 85 (1867).

96. See *Higgins* v. *Central New England Railroad,* 155 Mass. 176 (1892) and *Mulhall* v. *Fallon,* 176 Mass. 266 (1900). In the latter case Holmes seems to have taken some pleasure in citing a decision of the Supreme Court of the United States which had rejected the reasoning of Judge Hoar in the Richardson case. *Dennick* v. *Central Railroad,* 103 U.S. 11 (1880). Holmes said of the Dennick case that "the arguments which prevailed in this case did not prevail" in *Richardson* v. *New York Central,* 176 Mass. at 268.

97. *Hanlon* v. *Leyland & Co.,* 223 Mass. 438 (1916).

98. Matter of Mellen, Ward; Middlesex Probate Court (Insolvency), Case #1039. Holmes's diary entries indicate that the debtors later went through bankruptcy in the Federal court.

99. In John C. Gray's copy of volumes 2, 3, and 4 of the *American Law Review* which covered the two calendar years of 1868 and 1869, the following book reviews are identified as of Holmes's authorship:

Byles, A Treatise on Bills of Exchange, *Am. L. Rev.,* II, 328 (Jan. 1868)
Vol. 16, Michigan Reports, *id.,* III, 141 (Oct. 1868)
Vol. 21, Wisconsin Reports, *id.,* 147.
Vol. 3, Nevada Reports, *id.,* 148.
Vol. 3, Ellis & Ellis, Queen's Bench Reports, *id.,* 150.
Vol. 13, Iowa Reports, *id.,* 357 (Jan. 1869)
Benjamin, Treatise on Sales, *id.,* 541 (April 1869).
Vol. 41, Illinois Reports, *id.,* 556.
Vol. 17, Michigan Reports, *id.,* 757 (July 1869).

His single longest contribution to the *Review* during that period was a Report on the Impeachment of President Johnson; *id.,* II, 547 (April 1868), 747 (July 1868). He also prepared the Selected Digests of State Reports in all issues between April 1868 and Oct. 1869, the Digests of the English Law Reports which appeared in the Oct. issues in 1868 and 1869, and the Digest of the Decisions of the Supreme Court of the United States in the issue for Jan. 1869 (*id.,* III, 284).

100. *Am. L. Rev.,* III, 541–542 (April 1869).

101. "Codes and the Arrangement of the Law," *id.,* V, 1 (Oct. 1870); "The Arrangement of the Law: Privity," *id.,* VII, 46 (Oct. 1872); "The Theory of Torts," *id.,* 652 (July 1873). These essays are reprinted in *Harv. L. Rev.,* XLIV, 725, 738, 773 (March 1931).

102. *Am. L. Rev.,* III, 357 (Jan. 1869).

103. *Am. L. Rev.,* II, 547 (April 1868). Holmes also recounted later steps in the proceedings; *id.,* 747 (July 1868).

104. The defense turned upon the fact that Stanton, whom Johnson had removed without observing the Tenure Act, had not been recommissioned as Secretary of War at the beginning of Lincoln's second term. See *Am. L. Rev.,* II, 563.

105. *Id.,* 565.

106. A.l., Mrs. Holmes to OWH, June 11, 1866 (HLS).

107. HL, I, 389.

108. Letter to Learned Hand, March 18, 1922 (copy, HLS).

109. A written memorandum of this anecdote was prepared by Mr. Upham in Jan. 1936, after he had told the story at a meeting of the Tavern Club in Boston. The original is at HLS.

110. HP, II, 72.

111. Letter of William James to Henry James, Oct. 2, 1869; Perry, *William James,* I, 307.

112. Letter to Henry James, July 5, 1876; *id.,* 371.

113. This observation concludes Thayer's contemporaneous memorandum concerning the circumstances of Holmes's appointment to and resignation from the Weld Professorship at the Harvard Law School and is found in his Memorandum Book "D" now in private hands. A copy is at HLS.

114. A.l. to Clara Sherwood Stevens, Nov. 18, 1906 (HLS).

115. A.l. to Dean Wigmore, Dec. 4, 1910 (HLS).

116. HP, I, 106.

117. A.l. to Clara Sherwood Stevens, Sept. 8, 1902.

118. A.l., Mrs. John C. Gray to Holmes, July 28, 1899 (HLS).

119. A.l. to Baroness Moncheur, Nov. 5, 1910 (HLS).

120. A.l. to Clara Sherwood Stevens, Feb. 11, 1914.

121. Unpublished address, A.D. Club, Sept. 27, 1912 (HLS).

Index

Index

Index

Index

Index

Index

Index

Index

Index